NEW ORLEANS

NORA McGUNNIGLE

CONTENTS

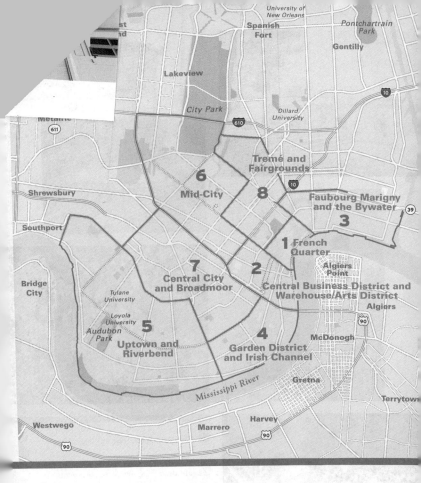

MAPS

1 biking along the river at Woldenberg Park

2 Old Ursuline Convent and Museum

3 array of hot sauces

4 St. Augustine marching band

5 traditional Creole and Cajun dishes

6 a Mardi Gras float

DISCOVER
NEW ORLEANS

In New Orleans, we want visitors to understand what really makes it special here: It's not cheap beads and giant drinks on Bourbon Street, but the smell of jasmine, the sound of music floating on the humid air, the flavors of a city that loves food beyond most anything else. This is a tremendously sensory place, where you may suddenly smell the spicy scent of crawfish boiling in someone's backyard, hear a school marching band practicing for next year's parades, or feel the refreshing condensation clinging to a can of cold soda or beer.

6

Feel the history flowing through the city—through its music, food, celebrations, and most importantly, its people. Sure, if you come to party, you'll find that here. But if you stop and listen to what the city whispers to you as you wander its streets, you'll understand New Orleans on a whole different level.

This is not an orderly or easily digested place. It's got jagged edges, grime, and sweat. Underneath all that, there's a raw beauty that, if you're lucky, you'll get a glimpse of. This city and its people are full of surprises—some glorious, some heartbreaking—but you need to seek them out and find them for yourself. No book can guide you to the "perfect" New Orleans experience. That's for you to discover.

1. biking along the river at Woldenberg Park

2. Old Ursuline Convent and Museum

3. array of hot sauces

4. St. Augustine marching band

5. traditional Creole and Cajun dishes

6. a Mardi Gras float

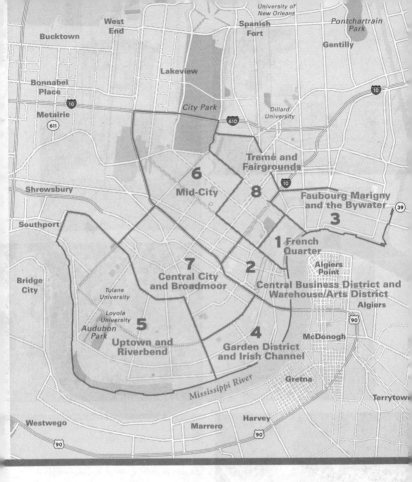

MAPS

1 **Celebrate Everything!** From Mardi Gras (page 274) and Jazz Fest (page 279) to Southern Decadence (page 290) and Essence Fest (page 288), there's always something to celebrate in the Crescent City.

2 Ride the St. Charles Streetcar: This is this oldest continually operating streetcar in the world; its route is a great way to take in the sights and sounds of St. Charles Avenue (page 163).

3 Listen to Live Music on Frenchmen Street: Stand outside and let the music wash over you. These four blocks of venues with nightly live performances let you choose what you're in the mood for... and then move on when you're ready for something else (page 111).

>>>

4 **Wander City Park:** You never know what you'll come across—the New Orleans Museum of Art's outdoor sculpture garden, swamps with egrets and pelicans, or a weekend festival or two (page 194).

5 **Sip a Cocktail:** New Orleans is where the Sazerac and the Brandy Crusta were born. There's no better town to enjoy a fancy cocktail than the "cradle of civilized drinking" (page 20).

6 **Shop on Magazine Street:** This six-mile stretch of shopping, eating, and drinking begins in the Warehouse District and ends at Audubon Park. The Uptown portion offers the densest array of indie boutiques, galleries, and vintage clothing shops (page 184).

7 **Get Artsy on Julia Street:** This four-block stretch, also known as the Arts District, is home to the studios and galleries of internationally acclaimed artists. Buy some local art or handicrafts, or just browse to your heart's content (page 85).

8 **Feast for Days:** From classic French-Creole restaurants and hidden po'boy shops to funky Vietnamese eateries, the culinary scene has endless options for foodies (page 25).

9 **Experience the Louisiana Bayou:** Go on a swamp tour just outside the city and see how many gators you can spot (page 323).

10 Take a Cemetery Tour: Because New Orleans is at such a low elevation, all bodies are interred aboveground. Take a guided tour of **Lafayette Cemetery No. 1** (page 134) or **St. Louis Cemetery No. 1** (page 242) to see countless beautiful and haunting tombs.

EXPLORE
NEW ORLEANS

THE BEST OF NEW ORLEANS

This itinerary has been designed to be easygoing, with the option to explore more if the spirit moves you. There's so much to do in New Orleans, it's hard to fit it all in on one trip. Plus, the languid Southern atmosphere precludes hurrying anywhere. This itinerary assumes you're landing in New Orleans in late morning or early afternoon on the first day.

I recommend finding a hotel that's away from the hustle and bustle, but still close to the action. Staying in the Faubourg Marigny at **Auld Sweet Olive Bed & Breakfast** or the **Hotel Peter and Paul** makes for easy access to both the French Quarter and the Marigny via bus. Staying at an inn on Esplanade Avenue, like **La Belle Esplanade,** allows easier access to City Park and the Tremé by bus or by bike. Staying on or near St. Charles Avenue, at the **Pontchartrain Hotel,** the **Henry Howard Hotel,** or **The Columns Hotel,** means you have streetcar transportation right outside your door.

>DAY 1
AFTERNOON: FRENCH QUARTER

Once your flight lands, check into your hotel. Spend some time at the **New Orleans Jazz Museum at the Old U.S. Mint** for a musical introduction to the city. Walk up to Royal Street and head west, stopping at shops and galleries including **No Rules Fashion** and **M.S. Rau Antiques.**

At this point you'll likely be thirsty, hot, and ready for a snack. At **SoBou** you can grab a traditional Pimms cup, Sazerac, or a creative cocktail from the bar's talented staff. Try the Louisiana sweet potato beignets or the crawfish-boil fried chicken on a stick.

Check out the **Pharmacy Museum** for some odd medical history. On the ground floor is a display of questionable medical practices, including voodoo gris-gris and potions. On the second floor, you'll find exhibits on mid-wifery, optometry, and the role of the doctor in the 19th century.

EVENING: CENTRAL BUSINESS DISTRICT (CBD)

Next, cross Canal to leave the French Quarter and enter the Central Business District, and hit the **Sazerac House** to learn about the history of the Sazerac and general New Orleans cocktail history, watch the distilling process, tour the facility, and have some samples. To continue with this theme, the **Sazerac Bar** at the **Roosevelt Hotel** is only a few blocks away.

When you feel refreshed, head to the new South Market District near the Superdome. There are a variety of restaurants to choose from depending on your mood, from casual sandwiches at **Aglio** to beautiful Louisiana-Southeast Asian food and cocktails at **Maypop.**

NIGHT: FAUBOURG MARIGNY

After dinner, take a cab or ride share or the Loyola/North Rampart streetcar line to **Frenchmen Street** and see what grabs your interest—there are tons of different bands playing, some with cover charges, some not, and it's easy to club hop from spot to spot listening to New Orleans music.

>DAY 2: MID-CITY

MORNING/AFTERNOON

Yesterday was a big day, so today is more relaxed (but still fun-filled). Make your way to the Canal streetcar line and take the Cemeteries or City Park line. Depending on when you get moving, check out **Biscuits & Buns on Banks** for breakfast or **Neyow's Creole Cafe** or **Piece of Meat** for lunch.

Take the streetcar on Carrollton going toward City Park. Get off at the end and check out the **New Orleans Museum of Art,** then go to the **Sydney and Walda Besthoff Sculpture Garden** in back, and make your way to the **New Orleans Botanical Garden.** After enjoying all that beauty, head to **Wheel Fun Rentals** to explore the other parts of **City Park** and **Bayou St. John** by bike, kayak, canoe, or pedal boat.

EVENING

After you've worked up an appetite, get some Cajun food at the nearby **Toups Meatery** and take the streetcar heading downtown.

a brass band in the French Quarter

New Orleans Botanical Garden

Get off at **Chickie Wah Wah** for some low-key live music. Once the show's over, if you're up for it, head back up on the streetcar to **Twelve Mile Limit** or **Revel Cafe & Bar** for a nightcap.

>DAY 3: UPTOWN
MORNING/AFTERNOON

Go to **Commander's Palace** for weekday lunch or weekend brunch. The restaurant is accessible via the St. Charles streetcar.

Now it's time to do some serious walking, shopping, snacking, and thirst-quenching with a stroll up Magazine Street starting at Washington Street, and going up to Napoleon Avenue. Grab a cold beer to go from **Craft Beer Cellar** for your walk. There are countless shops, cafés, and even a few galleries that you'll want to stop and

check out. A few of my personal faves are **Zèle NOLA,** the **Magazine Antique Mall,** and **Levee Baking Co.** Just past Napoleon is the fantastic **Ashley Longshore Studio Gallery.**

EVENING

Make your way to **Freret Street** for a pre-dinner beer at gastropub **Freret Beer Room** or a cocktail at **High Hat Cafe,** which doubles as a diner. Have a nice Italian dinner at **Ancora.**

For post-dinner entertainment, head down Freret Street to **Cure,** one of the best cocktail bars in the city. Afterward, take a cab or ride share to catch some live music at **Tipitina's** on Tchoupitoulas, **Le Bon Temps Roule** on Magazine Street, or the **Maple Leaf Bar** on Oak Street.

DAY 4: TREMÉ

Start with a Vietnamese-style iced coffee and sweet potato pie at Backatown Coffee Parlour for breakfast, then tour Louis Armstrong Park and Congo Square.

The Backstreet Cultural Museum is only a couple blocks from the park, and St. Augustine Catholic Church and the Tomb of the Unknown Slave are just another block past that.

Go to Lil' Dizzy's Cafe for a buffet lunch, then check out Treme's Petit Jazz Museum.

Catch an early show at Kermit's Tremé Mother-in-Law Lounge. There will probably be some food cooking up in the courtyard, and sometimes it's free!

DAY 5: BYWATER

Get breakfast at the Bywater Bakery or Frady's One Stop Food Store. Afterward, check out corner stores like Anchor & Arrow Dry Goods Co., the Bargain Center, and Euclid Records.

Grab a slice of pizza or two at Pizza Delicious and climb the Rusty Rainbow Bridge to see Crescent Park and get a serene view of the Mississippi River.

Next, you have a choice: Check out local art at Dr. Bob's Folk Art and Studio Be, or go on a bar crawl, stopping at Markey's Bar, J&J's Sports Lounge, and Vaughan's Lounge. To round it out, have a glass of wine at Bacchanal Fine Wine & Spirits or a freshly brewed beer at Parleaux Beer Lab.

There are plenty of options for dinner at N7, Red's Chinese, or Bywater American Bistro, but Jack Dempsey's Restaurant and The Country Club are the closest.

the well-stocked bar at Cure

THE ARCHITECTURE OF NEW ORLEANS

The French Quarter, Central Business District, and Warehouse District are the earliest settlements of New Orleans. These areas were where people lived in **Creole cottages** and worked on the docks, in banks, or at the market. Because the French Quarter burned down a couple of times, most of the buildings aren't as old as the city itself. But just walk down any block in the Quarter to find amazing examples of restored Creole cottages and townhouses with **wrought iron balconies.** The CBD and the Warehouse District, the city's two centers of commerce, have very different building styles, including **art deco** and **beaux arts.**

›MORNING

Start your day with a coffee and pastry at **Croissant d'Or Patisserie** on Ursulines Avenue, a historic building with a cool courtyard. It's the former location of Angelo Brocato's gelateria (now in Mid-City), which occupied the space in the early 20th century. You can see the tile work for the "Ladies' Entrance," which separated men from women for purposes of decorum. The marble-topped tables and the rest of the interior and enclosed courtyard give off an old-world European feel.

Just around the corner, the **Old Ursuline Convent and Museum** is one of the very few buildings that didn't burn down in either of the fires that engulfed New Orleans in 1788 and 1794. Go in and check out

Many buildings in the French Quarter feature wrought iron balconies.

the historic structure, which was built in 1745.

Heading toward Jackson Square on a side street called Pirate's Alley is **Faulkner House Books,** located in the building where William Faulkner lived in 1925. Note the interior and exterior glass fan-window transoms, antique shelving and cabinets, and worn brick floors.

>AFTERNOON

Across Canal Street from the French Quarter, the 1907-opened **Roosevelt Hotel** has an intriguing past entwined with former Louisiana governor Huey P. Long. The governor had his own room here, and it was said that he built Airline Highway just so he could get to the hotel's **Sazerac Bar** from Baton Rouge more quickly. The palatial lobby, with soaring vaulted ceilings, mosaic tile flooring, plaster work, art deco murals, and brass accents, is one of the most breathtaking spaces in town.

Across the street from the main entrance of the Roosevelt is the pristinely restored **The Orpheum,** a beaux-arts palace and former vaudeville hall built in 1918. See if you can step in to take a look at the lobby.

Several of the city's hotels have been creatively repurposed from commercial structures. A few blocks south of the Orpheum and the Roosevelt is **The NOPSI Hotel,** where the city's power and transportation company once stood. The structure was originally built in the 1920s in the art deco style. About four blocks east, **The Eliza Jane** was built to honor the first woman publisher in the United States. She worked in the old *Daily Picayune* offices, one of the seven warehouses that have been pulled together to form today's hotel. The Peychaud Bitters factory was once in one of these warehouses as well.

The **International House Hotel,** just northwest of The Eliza Jane, is a beaux-arts-style building that was built in 1906, originally as a bank. Here, owner Sean Cummings has a Banksy piece on display, called *Looters,* which he had restored and preserved after it was vandalized and painted over.

>EVENING

Grab dinner and drinks at **Jewel of the South,** which is set in a meticulously restored 1830s Creole cottage. The dark-wood interior feels authentic to the building's age, and the reintroduction of a once-lost cocktail classic, the Brandy Crusta, adds to the sensation of stepping back in time.

BEST COCKTAILS

New Orleans has been a cocktail town since its inception. It's sometimes called the "cradle of civilized drinking" and is home to many historically significant cocktail bars.

SAZERAC

- Best Place to Get It: Sazerac Bar (page 83)

The Sazerac is the official cocktail of New Orleans. There's even an official seal for bars and restaurants who properly make them. This whiskey drink includes two locally created ingredients: Peychaud's bitters and Herbsaint (an absinthe substitute).

HEMINGWAY DAQUIRI

- Best Place to Get It: Manolito (page 49)

Brandy Crusta

Although the Hemingway daquiri was technically created in Cuba and Miami, the famous writer spent enough time in New Orleans that it counts as an honorary New Orleans cocktail. The classic rum cocktail is made with grapefruit juice and maraschino liqueur. At Manolito, the drink is known as the Papa Doble.

RAMOS GIN FIZZ

- Best Place to Get It: Bourbon O Bar (page 52)

This classic cocktail was first developed in New Orleans by Henry Ramos. The drink got its iconic egg-white froth from 12 minutes of vigorous shaking. These days, no one shakes it for that long—a few minutes at the most. To stay on your bartender's good side, only order a Ramos from someplace that specializes in them.

TWELVE MILE LIMIT

- Best Place to Get It: Twelve Mile Limit (page 207)

This Prohibition-era cocktail is named for the distance from the U.S. coast to international waters, where drinking was legal at the time. Since folks needed to put in the extra effort to imbibe, they wanted a drink worth all the bother; this smooth-drinking cocktail made with rum, whiskey, and brandy delivers.

BRANDY CRUSTA

- Best Place to Get It: Jewel of the South (page 47)

This formerly obscure cocktail was created in New Orleans by Joseph Santini in the 1850s. Bartender Chris Hannah has become its biggest champion, so you can expect it to be the next big thing in trendy cocktails. Made with cognac, lemon juice, Curaçao, maraschino liqueur, and Angostura bitters, and served in a sugar-rimmed glass, it's the house cocktail at Jewel of the South.

A DAY FOR MUSIC LOVERS

Music is everywhere here, so it's easy to head to the nearest event or the closest show. Even just making your way up and down Frenchmen Street will expose you to more music than you know what to do with. Another option is to take a music history-themed walking tour of the city. For up-to-date events information, check out WWOZ (on the radio or online) or *Offbeat Magazine* (in print or online). If you need a place to start, here are a few ideas.

>MORNING

If you're around for the weekend, plan on starting your day with a jazz brunch. There are a few options to choose from. Check out **Atchafalaya** or **Commander's Palace** in the Garden District, or **Buffa's,** a bar on Esplanade that also serves food.

If it's Sunday, you may want to head over to the Tremé for the 10am jazz/gospel Mass at **St. Augustine Catholic Church,** an experience like no other.

>AFTERNOON

Take the North Rampart streetcar or just walk to **Louis Armstrong Park,** where the roots of New Orleans music began with 18th century enslaved Africans congregating in **Congo Square** on Sundays. There are fantastic statues of jazz musicians—obviously Satchmo, but also great pieces celebrating jazz pioneer Buddy Bolden and gospel queen Mahalia Jackson, and a statue commemorating the

entrance to Louis Armstrong Park

Mardi Gras Indians, a historically African American group that puts on dance performances wearing intricate handmade costumes.

Afterward, check out the **New Orleans Jazz Museum at the Old U.S. Mint.** Not only are the exhibits well-curated and fascinating, but they also offer free live performances during the week (most Tues.-Thurs.) at 2pm. In addition to the curated exhibits, you can arrange to take a tour of the museum's collection of artifacts, including sheet music, instruments (Louis Armstrong's first coronet!), photos, original recordings (like the first ever jazz recording in 1917), and more.

Head across the street to the **Louisiana Music Factory** to peruse all sorts of local artists and music styles that were born or simply flourish here. Then take the #5 bus to Piety Street and browse **Euclid Records** to immerse yourself in new and used recordings, with a serious local music selection across all genres. The staff will be more than happy to geek out with you about music. Hop back on the #5 bus to have a pre-dinner drink and listen to live music al fresco at **Bacchanal Fine Wine & Spirits.**

>EVENING

After you've had dinner, it's time to catch a show or two. Start out with the early show at **Preservation Hall,** which has been one of the city's top places to hear true New Orleans jazz since the '60s. If you splurge for the Big Shot tickets, you'll get a reserved seat; otherwise, prepare to wait in line. The shows are just an hour

BEST VIEWS

WOLDENBERG PARK
Take a seat on a bench near one of the statues in this French Quarter riverside park and look out at the Mississippi River as it flows by (page 59).

ST. CHARLES STREETCAR
This is a slow moving, constantly changing view. Watch the urban landscape change from the Central Business District to the Warehouse District to the Garden District to Uptown to Carrollton (page 163).

ALGIERS POINT HISTORIC DISTRICT
As you get off the ferry in Algiers Point, the historic neighborhood across the river, turn around to see the entirety of the French Quarter (page 259).

ABOVE THE GRID AT THE NOPSI HOTEL
This outdoor, wide-open rooftop spot showcases 360 degrees of views. On a clear day, you can see to Lake Pontchartrain (page 304).

HOT TIN AT THE PONTCHARTRAIN HOTEL
The fact that this top-floor bar is in the Garden District means that the entirety of the downtown skyline and the twin spans of the Crescent City Connection are easily seen from its balcony and floor-to-ceiling windows (page 312).

long, so you've got plenty of time for more if you're up for it.

For something more modern and rougher around the edges, head to North Rampart Street where it turns into St. Claude Avenue. That's where all the funkiest music clubs are. Catch a show at the **Hi-Ho Lounge** or **Saturn Bar.** Saturn is across the tracks in the Bywater, so plan on grabbing a ride rather than walking.

THE TOP SIGHTS IN NEW ORLEANS

NEW ORLEANS JAZZ MUSEUM AT THE OLD U.S. MINT

It's a decommissioned mint building! It's a museum dedicated to jazz! It's an academic treasure trove of colonial-era documents and maps! Basically, the **New Orleans Jazz Museum at the Old U.S. Mint** (page 43) is a one-stop shop for New Orleans history through several different lenses.

THE NATIONAL WWII MUSEUM

For any U.S. history or WWII buff, **The National WWII Museum** (page 73) has it all, including a fully immersive experience that lets you follow the path of one of the hundreds of personal stories that the museum has gathered. There is so much information to absorb and so many things to do that you'll need a strategic plan and a good dose of caffeine for a visit here.

The National WWII Museum

BLAINE KERN'S MARDI GRAS WORLD

This is the best place to experience Mardi Gras at any time of the year. A must-see for anyone not in town during Mardi Gras parades, **Blaine Kern's Mardi Gras World** (page 133) encapsulates the true joy and history of Mardi Gras floats and krewes in New Orleans.

ST. ALPHONSUS CHURCH ART AND CULTURE CENTER

This deconsecrated church harkens back to a time when it was one of three on the block known as Ecclesiastical Square. **St. Alphonsus Church Art and Culture Center** (page 133) now stands as a living memory to New Orleans's founding religion of Catholicism, as well as a community space.

AUDUBON ZOO

The **Audubon Zoo** (page 165), set within sprawling Audubon Park, is a magnificent space that allows visitors to learn about a diverse array of animals and their natural habitats.

City Park

CITY PARK

The huge **City Park** (page 194) is the pride of New Orleans. It hosts everything including kid's activities and festivals, and is home to classic Roman architecture, several waterways, and actual swamp life.

ORETHA CASTLE HALEY BOULEVARD

Named after a key Civil Rights-era activist, **Oretha Castle Haley Boulevard** (page 218) was the hotspot for much of the important Civil Rights work done by African Americans in New Orleans in the 1960s. Today, it's one of the best spots in the city to connect with and support the community.

ST. AUGUSTINE CATHOLIC CHURCH AND THE TOMB OF THE UNKNOWN SLAVE

St. Augustine Catholic Church (page 242) is the oldest Black Catholic church in the country. Outside you can see the **Tomb of the Unknown Slave,** an important and grim reminder of the slave trade that thrived in New Orleans. The church's 10am Sunday service features uplifting and energetic gospel and jazz music, and welcomes all.

LONGUE VUE HOUSE AND GARDENS

With 14 or so different gardens and 22 ponds and fountains,

BEST PEOPLE-WATCHING

ERIN ROSE

Sit at the front window overlooking Conti Street or at the bar and you'll come across all kinds: lots of locals, visitors drawn by the frozen Irish coffee and stellar jukebox, and folks stumbling in from nearby Bourbon Street (page 53).

THE COUNTRY CLUB

Between the drag brunch on Saturday and the laid-back, playful, LGBT-friendly poolside area, there's never a dull moment at this Bywater restaurant and bar (page 103).

FRENCHMEN STREET

Wandering Frenchmen Street at night will bring all sorts of types into play—visitors, locals, musicians, street-food vendors, music lovers, drunken lovers, and gutter punk. It's a mishmash of all that is New Orleans (page 111).

COURTYARD BREWERY

This microbrewery in the Lower Garden District attracts beer nerds from all over. Sitting in the courtyard will bring you close to all sorts of people, usually with the right blend of spirited fun and taking it easy (page 146).

THE DRIFTER HOTEL

The clothing-optional pool at this hotel is host to some crazy parties, with live bands, DJs, and lots of people having fun with each other. It's not for the faint of heart (page 311).

Longue Vue House and Gardens (page 258) fills eight acres with the most gorgeous plants, trees, and flowers imaginable.

THE BEST FOOD IN THE CRESCENT CITY

New Orleans has the country's most specialized and unique food culture, with over 1,500 restaurants calling the city home—and more hot spots opening every day.

>CAJUN AND CREOLE

BRIGTSEN'S

When everyone does Creole fusion or modern twists, it's easy to get lost in what these flavors actually are and what they mean. A dinner at **Brigtsen's** (page 168) will put it all back in beautiful perspective.

COMMANDER'S PALACE

Commander's Palace (page 137) is one of the grand dames of high-living Creole food. The traditional turtle soup, pecan-crusted fish topped with crab, and bread pudding soufflé share the menu with chef-created classics like oyster and absinthe stew and green tomato barbecue lamb ribs. It's a splurge, but it's worth it to see decades of ever-evolving Creole fine-dining in action.

GABRIELLE RESTAURANT

Gabrielle Restaurant (page 243), which took 12 years to reopen after Hurricane Katrina, is a much-loved culinary institution. The menu shines with elevated takes on classic New Orleans dinner dishes, like smoked quail gumbo, barbecue shrimp pie, and slow-roasted duck.

HEARD DAT KITCHEN

Heard Dat Kitchen (page 220) serves Creole comfort food in a convenience-store space, but it defies expectations many times over once you dig in.

JEWEL OF THE SOUTH

The **Jewel of the South** (page 47) is a glorious homage to cocktail master Joseph Santini. He had a saloon with the same name (not the same location), which was the first place to sell gumbo and he also invented the Brandy Crusta, a New Orleans cocktail on the cusp of fading away until this place opened up to celebrate his culinary legacy.

>PO'BOYS

FRADY'S ONE STOP FOOD STORE

Neighborhood po'boy spot **Frady's One Stop Food Store** (page 106), in the Bywater, serves the highest quality po'boys and plate lunches for the best prices.

>SOUTHERN

DOOKY CHASE'S RESTAURANT

There's nothing more New Orleans than the Afro-Creole **Dooky Chase's Restaurant** (page 244), which was created as a meeting and eating space at a time when there weren't many options for the city's black community. The home-style soul food, like fried chicken and gumbo, is perfectly executed.

FIORELLA'S CAFE

The original **Fiorella's Cafe** (page 260), a family-owned spot, wows folks in Gentilly and beyond with their fried chicken.

They've even been certified as the best at the New Orleans Fried Chicken Festival.

TOUPS SOUTH

This is a historical dining experience. Adjacent to the Southern Food and Beverage Museum is **Toups South** (page 218), an open-kitchen restaurant run by Cajun chef Isaac Toups, who branches out into other southern specialties here. Check out the heritage pork boudin, cracklin', seared redfish, and the cornmeal fried gulf oyster salad.

>SEAFOOD
CASAMENTO'S RESTAURANT

Raw oysters on the half shell, fried catfish and trout, seafood gumbo, soft shell crab dinner—at **Casamento's Restaurant** (page 169), you'll find Gulf seafood cooked simply and served fresh.

>VIETNAMESE
LILLY'S CAFÉ

Thanks to the significant Vietnamese immigrant population in New Orleans East and the Westbank, Vietnamese food is as much a part of New Orleans's culinary history as French, Italian, and German cuisine. **Lilly's Café** (page 139) is a no-frills place that's perfect for a bowl of pho or a banh mi. The food is fresh, delicious, traditional, and cheap.

TD SEAFOOD PHO HOUSE

With boiled seafood and delightful Vietnamese cuisine under one roof, **TD Seafood Pho House** (page 262) has it all.

>ECLECTIC
COQUETTE

Don't let the grand mahogany bar and crystal chandelier fool you: **Coquette** (page 139) is a deliciously playful and consistently excellent bistro.

MAYPOP

With influences from Goa, Sichuan, New Orleans, Lafayette, Dijon, Sicily, Korea, Bangkok, and the Mekong Delta, **Maypop** (page 75) serves creative dishes in harmonious ways, but doesn't take itself too seriously.

SAFFRON NOLA

Saffron Nola (page 172) captures the best of Louisianan and Indian cuisine—two culinary cultures that don't shy away from big flavors and spices.

>ITALIAN
IRENE'S

The Sicilian influence on New Orleans's culinary history is huge. **Irene's** (page 48) is one of the best examples of an old-school Creole-Italian restaurant, and serves dishes like shrimp and crab pappardelle, rosemary- and garlic-roasted chicken, and mussels marinara.

>LATIN AMERICAN
LA BOCA

La Boca (page 78) is a Latin American twist on the traditional steakhouse, and serves all sorts of delicious cuts of meat, some of which aren't as well-known as others. Since they're all prepared to perfection, you could

BEST FOR ROMANCE

EFFERVESCENCE
Champagne, the French drink of love and romance, flows in abundance at this strikingly decorated wine bar, set in a Creole cottage on the edge of the French Quarter. With an accompanying menu of oysters, caviar, and a grilled half wheel of cheese, this elegant spot is the perfect place to take that special someone (page 55).

N7
This mysterious bistro is like a lovely countryside French café, with twinkling lights, an outdoor patio, and a natural wine menu featuring small European vineyards. You and your paramour will feel like you're in your own world as you nibble on Japanese-influenced dishes like sake-cured salmon tartine and escargot tempura (page 107).

CRESCENT PARK
Nothing's more romantic than ambling by the river hand in hand through a park filled with greenery and pristine pathways. It's also not as well-known as the riverfront parks in the French Quarter, so it's a more intimate experience (page 119).

SYDNEY AND WALDA BESTHOFF SCULPTURE GARDEN
Behind the New Orleans Museum of Art, you can wind your way through a path filled with sculptures and outdoor art, under oak trees, and around a small pond. There's even a replica of the Philadelphia *Love* statue here (page 210).

PARK VIEW HISTORIC HOTEL
Surrounded by mature live oaks, this hotel offers rooms filled with antiques, making it easy to imagine being in another time (page 309).

just close your eyes and point to something on the menu and have a divine steak experience.

MANGÚ
Food from the Dominican Republic isn't something you might think to seek out while in New Orleans, but a visit to **Mangú** (page 264) will yield authentic flavors, dynamic dishes, and a friendly staff.

>SWEET TREATS
HANSEN'S SNO-BLIZ
Hansen's Sno-Bliz (page 176), a multi-generational family business, has been doling out frozen fluffy flavored ice since long before air-conditioning was a common thing, providing cooling relief on those sticky summer days.

ANGELO BROCATO
One visit to **Angelo Brocato** (page 204) can bring happiness for just a few dollars. Try a cool, tart, flavorful lemon ice or a filled-to-order crunchy, creamy cannoli.

PLANNING YOUR TRIP

WHEN TO GO

There's a local joke that insists that the almost-always warm New Orleans actually does have four seasons: winter is Mardi Gras and parade season, spring is crawfish season, summer is snowball (a shaved-ice treat) season, and fall is football season. Of course, there's also festival season, usually between March and May; the holiday seasons (Halloween, Christmas, Thanksgiving, and Easter); and the very hot and humid season, late May through early October. **High season** starts when parades do, in February or March, and continues through festival season, with early April's French Quarter Fest and late April/early May's Jazz Fest as the highlights.

Things tend to simmer down for the **low season** once June (and hurricane season) hits, with a brief uptick for Essence Fest during the Fourth of July weekend, Southern Decadence over Labor Day weekend, and Tales of the Cocktail in between. Mid-October through early December is usually **terrific weather.** During this time, Saints football fever is in high gear, so there may be crowds and hotel crunches during home games.

the Krewe of Bacchus during Mardi Gras

Crescent City Connection bridge

Once late December and January hits, there's a bit of a lull before Mardi Gras, when there's the potential for some damp and cold weather.

Hotels are more expensive during the high season, especially during Mardi Gras, French Quarter Fest, and Jazz Fest. In the low season, there are deals to be found with accommodations, and some restaurants, who very much need business during the slow summer months. Some local businesses will take summer vacation for a week or two, so it's good to check before heading over.

ENTRY REQUIREMENTS

International travelers are required to show a **valid passport** upon entering the United States. The U.S. government's **Visa Waiver Program** allows tourists from many countries to visit without a visa for up to 90 days. All other international travelers are required to secure a **nonimmigrant visa** before entering Louisiana. For more information, consult the U.S. Department of State's Bureau of Consular Affairs (202/663-1225, www.travel.state.gov).

TRANSPORTATION

New Orleans is served by **Louis Armstrong New Orleans International Airport** (MSY, 1 Terminal Dr., Kenner, 504/303-7500, flymsy.com), 15 miles west of downtown via I-10.

The city's **streetcar** network covers limited, although popular routes: the entire length of St. Charles Avenue, the entire length of Canal Street (with a spur to City Park and the Fairgrounds), and from the Superdome to Elysian Fields on Loyola Avenue and North Rampart Street.

Bus service is unreliable and spotty, so **taxis** or **ride-hailing**

DAILY REMINDERS

- **Monday:** Monday is when the city eats traditional red beans and rice, found on specials boards all over town; get some for free at Gris-Gris in the Lower Garden District. Several museums and attractions, such as the New Orleans Museum of Art, the New Orleans Jazz Museum, The Cabildo, The Historic New Orleans Collection, all Audubon Institute sights, and the visitors center of Jean Lafitte National Historical Park and Preserve, are closed, along with some restaurants and shops. At cocktail bar Twelve Mile Limit, you can get a free dinner.

- **Tuesday:** The Crescent City Farmers Market Uptown runs from 9am to 1pm. Some restaurants are closed on Tuesdays.

- **Wednesday:** During the spring you can check out the free concert series YLC Wednesday at the Square in Lafayette Square.

- **Thursday:** The Crescent City Farmers Market Mid-City runs from 3pm to 7pm. Jazz in the Park is a free concert series in Louis Armstrong Park that runs through the fall. The Ogden Museum of Southern Art hosts live music events called After Hours from 6pm to 8pm.

- **Friday:** The Newcomb Art Museum offers free tours on the first Friday of the month. During the summer, admission to Tipitina's is free on Fridays.

- **Saturday:** The Crescent City Farmers Market Downtown runs from 8am to noon. On the first Saturday of the month, there are gallery openings in the Julia Street Arts District.

- **Sunday:** Sundays mean Saints football games during the fall (along with some Thursday and Monday nights). This is also the day for second lines in Central City or the Tremé (except during the summer).

programs like Lyft and Uber are the best ways to get around the city. You can **rent a car,** though it can be challenging to find parking in parts of the city.

All public transportation costs $1.25 (exact change, please) or you can purchase a **Jazzy Pass** for 1, 3, 5, or 31 days at any Walgreens in the city or using ticket vending machines on Canal Street. You can opt to use the **GoMobile app** (which you can also use to purchase single tickets).

RESERVATIONS

Hotel reservations and **restaurant reservations** are essential for places you really want to go to. During the two weekends before Mardi Gras, as well as during French Quarter Fest, Jazz Fest, and other

festivals, they can be tough to come by at the last minute.

PASSES AND DISCOUNTS

There are several sights that can be seen for free at any time, like the Sydney and Walda Besthoff Sculpture Garden, The Historic New Orleans Collection, and the Lower Ninth Ward Living Museum. For Louisiana residents, the New Orleans Museum of Art in City Park is free on Wednesdays, the Contemporary Arts Center is free on Sundays, and the Ogden Museum of Southern Art is free on Thursdays.

The **New Orleans Pass** (neworleanspass.com) is a one-stop pass to more than 25 of the area's biggest attractions, like Blaine Kern's Mardi Gras World, The National WWII Museum, the Audubon Aquarium, Insectarium and

Zoo, the Pharmacy Museum, the Southern Food and Beverage Museum, and Longue Vue House and Gardens, as well as various walking, boat, and bus tours. Check the website for prices for single- and multi-day adult and child passes.

If you or a friend has a **New Orleans Public Library Card,** all branches of the library have **museum passes** available for the Ogden Museum of Southern Art, Longue Vue House and Gardens, the Southern Food and Beverage Museum, The National WWII Museum, the New Orleans Museum of Art, and all the Audubon sights.

It's worthwhile to check out the **French Quarter Visitor Center** (419 Decatur St., 504/589-3882, ext. 221, nps.gov/jela/french-quarter-site.htm; 9am-4:30pm Tues.-Sat., free) for the **Jean Lafitte National Historical Park and Preserve.** There are daily history talks at 9:30am with a park ranger as well as free events.

Take a mule and carriage to check out the French Quarter.

GUIDED TOURS

You can tour the city by foot, bus, bike, mule-led carriage, or Segway (often with drink in hand).

Popular tour topics include general history, ghosts and spooky stuff, music, food, and cocktails.

To get an understanding of New Orleans history through a cocktail and booze lens, the **Drink & Learn cocktail tour** (504/578-8280, drinkandlearn.com; 6pm Fri. and 10am Sat.; $55) is perfect. It also includes four cocktails.

Keith Abel of **Abel Tours** (504/252-0469, abeltours.com; 2-3 departures per day; $25) adds a ton of local character to his music-history walking tour, which goes through the Faubourg Marigny, French Quarter, and the Tremé.

The **New Orleans Black Heritage and Jazz Tour** (504/457-9439, allaboutdat.com; 10am Mon., 10am and 2pm Wed.-Fri., 2pm Sat.-Sun.; $55) is a bus tour that delves into African American history with a focus on jazz, the Tremé, slavery and resistance, the Freedom Fighters of the Civil Rights era, voodoo, and current black-owned businesses.

If you're lucky, Alaina Rene will be doing a **Bulbancha Decolonizing New Orleans tour,** which talks about pre-colonization New Orleans (known as Bulbancha to the indigenous people of the area). This walking tour provides a much-needed deconstruction of colonized history and delves deep into the natural resources and rich traditions that made the area so appealing, as well as what happened to the indigenous culture after the French arrived on the scene. Check the Bulbancha: Decolonizing New Orleans Facebook page to see what's scheduled.

WHAT'S NEW?

- **South Market District:** The last several years have seen a huge uptick in what's being called the South Market District, an area that's bounded by O'Keefe Avenue, South Rampart Street, Julia Street, and Poydras Street. Several multi-use buildings house residents and restaurants, revitalizing this once desolate area of downtown.

- **Food Halls:** St. Roch Market in the Faubourg Marigny kicked off the trend of housing multiple food businesses under one roof. Now there's also the **Auction House Market** and the **Pythian Market.**

- **Bayou Road:** Technically, Bayou Road is one of the oldest traveled routes in the country, but a recent revitalization of this area off Broad Street in the Fairgrounds neighborhood has brought new, mostly Black-owned businesses, public art and murals, and the new location of the Southern Rep Theatre.

- **Relocation of the Louisiana Children's Museum:** After 30 years in the Warehouse District, the Louisiana Children's Museum has moved to a larger, more interactive space in City Park. It has several outdoor elements and exhibits, including a floating classroom, a sensory garden, and a wetland education area.

- **Expansion of The Historic New Orleans Collection:** The new exhibition center, which opened in 2019 after 15 years of planning and construction, is across the street from the original spot on Royal Street, combining the old and the new. Expect to find more interactive opportunities, including using virtual reality binoculars to see what the historic building once looked like and how it was used when it was built. Everything is still free.

- **Sazerac House:** The Sazerac distillery has taken the Sazerac theme and run with it in this multi-level museum, working distillery, and bar. Visitors can take a self-guided tour of the facility.

- **Ride-Hailing Services:** Lyft and Uber's presence in New Orleans has given people more options for transportation, especially outside the French Quarter. It's much easier to get into outlying neighborhoods now.

- **The New MSY:** In late 2019, a new airport terminal opened, offering more local food and beverage options, along with live music.

CALENDAR OF EVENTS

JANUARY-MARCH

Mardi Gras season (mardigrasday.com) starts on January 6, leading into parades and celebrations in February (and sometimes early March). After Mardi Gras, March serves up **St. Patrick's Day, St. Joseph's Day** (mardigrasneworleans.com), **Super Sunday,** and the **Tennessee Williams Literary Festival** (tennesseewilliams.net).

APRIL-JUNE

In April, festival season begins in earnest with **French Quarter Fest** (fqfi.org/frenchquarterfest) early on, followed by the **New Orleans Wine and Food Experience** (nowfe.com), and **Jazz Fest** (nojazzfest.com) at the end of the month. Jazz Fest runs into the first weekend of May, and the month closes out with the **Bayou Boogaloo** (thebayouboogaloo.com) and the **New Orleans Greek Festival** (greekfestnola.com).

In June, don't miss the **New Orleans Oyster Festival** (nolaoysterfest.org), the **Creole Tomato Festival** (frenchmarket.org), and the **Louisiana Cajun/Zydeco Festival** (jazzandheritage.org).

St. Patrick's Day parade

JULY-SEPTEMBER

July brings **Essence Fest** (essence.com/festival) and **Tales of the Cocktail** (talesofthecocktail.com), and in August, check out **Satchmo SummerFest** (fqfi.org) and the **Hancock Whitney White Linen Night** (cacwhitelinennight.com).

September is officially fall, but still feels like summertime, with **Southern Decadence** (southerndecadence.com), the **New Orleans Burlesque Festival** (neworleansburlesquefest.com), and **NOLA On Tap** (nolaontap.org).

OCTOBER-DECEMBER

October's cooling temps bring the **Crescent City Blues & BBQ Festival** (jazzandheritage.org), **Oktoberfest** (oktoberfestnola.com), **Voodoo Music + Arts Experience** (worshipthemusic.com), and of course, **Halloween.** November brings three of the best food festivals: **Boudin, Bourbon & Beer** (boudinbourbonandbeer.com), **Oak Street Po-Boy Festival** (poboyfest.com), and the **Tremé Creole Gumbo Festival** (tremegumbofest.com).

In December, check out City Park's **Celebration in the Oaks** (neworleanscitypark.com) and **NOLA Christmas Fest** (nolachristmasfest.com) in the Convention Center, as well as taking part in **Réveillon** meals and holiday customs like caroling in St. Louis Cathedral Square.

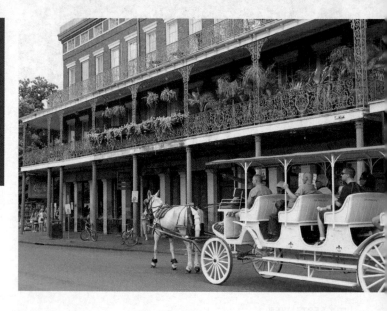

French Quarter

Map 1

This is the OG New Orleans neighborhood. It's filled with **history** and ghosts, as well as hotels, **great eats,** galleries, shops, bars, and tourists. Wander the streets to see the **wrought iron balconies** and gates that New Orleans is known for and slip into **tiny shops** that offer everything from masks to parasols to voodoo dolls. The Quarter is home to well-preserved historic buildings, local institutions, and many attractions oriented to visitors.

This is by no means an exhaustive list of all there is to do, see, eat, and drink in the French Quarter. Rather, these are the **hidden gems, local favorites,** and **under-the-radar spots.** These French Quarter

suggestions will provide a genuine, entertaining, and funky flavor of New Orleans—just don't stay here too long, OK?

TOP SIGHTS

- Best Multi-Purpose Museum:
  **New Orleans Jazz Museum at the
  Old U.S. Mint** (page 43)

TOP RESTAURANTS

- Where to Find Brandy Cocktails and
  Gumbo: **Jewel of the South** (page 47)
- Best Late-Night Eats: **Palm
  & Pine** (page 48)

TOP NIGHTLIFE

- Most Sought-After Bloody Mary:
  Bar Tonique (page 52)
- Where to Feel Like a Regular:
  Erin Rose (page 53)

TOP ARTS AND CULTURE

- Best All-Ages Live Music Venue:
  Preservation Hall (page 56)
- Most Drool-Inducing Art: **Modernist
  Cuisine Gallery** (page 57)

TOP RECREATION

- Where to See the Mighty Mississippi:
  Woldenberg Park (page 59)

TOP SHOPS

- Where to Drink Tea and Have a
  Psychic Reading: **Bottom of the
  Cup Tea Room** (page 61)
- Best Antiques Shop with a Secret Room:
  M.S. Rau Antiques (page 61)

GETTING THERE AND AROUND

- Streetcar lines: Riverfront (2), Canal
  (47, 48), Rampart-St. Claude (49)
- Major bus routes: 5, 10, 16, 55, 57, 88, 91

SEE MAP 8

Louis Armstrong Park

VIEUX CARRÉ

Jackson Square

River

Dumaine

Ursulines

Beauregard-Keyes House

Old Ursuline Convent and Museum

New Orleans Jazz Museum at the Old U.S. Mint

French Market

SEE MAP 3

SIGHTS

11	J&M Recording Studio	55	Audubon Butterfly Garden and Insectarium
46	The Cabildo	64	New Orleans Jazz Museum at the Old U.S. Mint
50	Beauregard-Keyes House		
51	Old Ursuline Convent and Museum		

RESTAURANTS

3	Palm & Pine	37	Green Goddess
5	Jewel of the South	38	Sobou
7	Arrow Cafe	39	Irene's
12	Meauxbar	49	Croissant d'or Patisserie
14	Killer Poboys	54	Cleo's French Quarter
15	GW Fins	59	Manolito
18	Bayona	61	Dian Xin
22	Felix's Restaurant & Oyster Bar	63	Small Mart
28	Longway Tavern		

NIGHTLIFE

8	Black Penny	20	Good Friends Bar
9	700 Club	23	21st Amendment Bar at La Louisiane
10	Bar Tonique	24	Patrick's Bar Vin
13	Effervescence	43	One Eyed Jack's
16	Erin Rose	56	Tiki Tolteca
19	Bourbon O Bar	60	Santos

ARTS AND CULTURE

4	Mardi Gras Museum of Costumes and Culture	30	Preservation Hall
25	Modernist Cuisine Gallery	31	Rodrigue Studio
27	The Historic New Orleans Collection	34	Gallerie Vinsantos
		42	Pharmacy Museum
		45	Le Petit Théâtre du Vieux Carré

RECREATION

| 6 | Flambeaux Bicycle Tours | 65 | Woldenberg Park |

SHOPS

17	Dauphine Street Books	40	Lost and Found
21	Bourbon Pride	41	Bottom of the Cup Tea Room
26	Leah's Pralines	44	Louisiana Loom Works
29	M.S. Rau Antiques	47	Faulkner House Books
32	Boutique Du Vampyre	48	Maskarade
33	Bourbon French Parfums	58	Ma Sherie Amour
35	No Rules Fashion	62	The Tahyo
36	Idea Factory		

HOTELS

1	The Saint Hotel	53	Le Richelieu
2	City House Hostel	57	Bienville House Hotel
52	Soniat House Hotel		

FRENCH QUARTER WALK

TOTAL DISTANCE: 2 miles (3.2 kilometers)
WALKING TIME: 45 minutes-1 hour

The French Quarter is so compact, it's easy to cover a lot of ground in a day or two. This walk takes you by sights, food, drinks, shopping, and art. The walk itself will take around 45 minutes to an hour, but there will be so many spots (both mentioned here and ones you'll discover for yourself) to stop at that you could easily set aside several hours. This is a good walk for the later morning, after you've had some coffee and are ready to go exploring. During the week, daytime in the Quarter is generally low-key; weekends will be a little crazier. Weekends are also when the majority of street musicians come out to play.

1 Start your walk at **Modernist Cuisine Gallery,** only a couple of blocks from Canal Street, on Royal Street. Check out the crazy food photography of Nathan Mhyrvold.

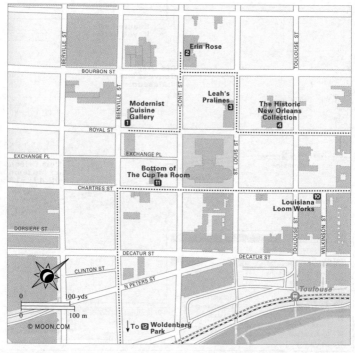

2 Take a left leaving the gallery and continue northeast up Royal one block to Conti Street. Take a left onto Conti, walk a block and a half, and pop into the **Erin Rose** for a frozen Irish coffee or Bloody Mary, either for here or to go. If you're feeling peckish, a po'boy from Killer Po-Boys (serving from the back room starting at 10am) is perfect for a late breakfast or early lunch.

3 From the Erin Rose, double back to Bourbon Street and turn left. After one block, turn right onto St. Louis Street. Walk a half block to **Leah's Pralines** for a sweet treat or souvenir shopping.

4 Take a right out of Leah's, head southeast to the next cross street, which is Royal, then turn left. Walk a half block and go check out **The Historic New Orleans Collection,** which you can peruse for free. (There are also guided tours.) The rotating exhibits focus on the history of New Orleans and its environs.

5 Continue strolling up Royal for three blocks to the intersection of Royal Street and St. Ann Street. Turn left onto St. Ann and you'll come across the **Boutique Du Vampyre,** full of goth-inspired goods for fun browsing.

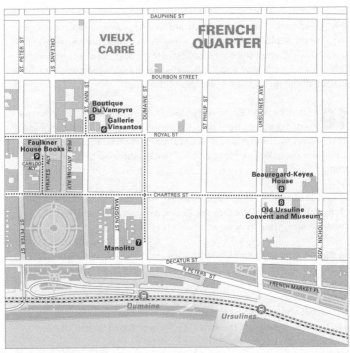

a 1908 advertisement from The Historic
New Orleans Collection

6 Double back to Royal and head northeast for a half block to hit **Gallerie Vinsantos** for some freaky, creative art in the form of glitzy, dramatic dolls made out of clay.

7 Now it's time to rest a little and refuel. Continue to the end of the block and turn right onto Dumaine Street. Walk two blocks to the Cuban-influenced **Manolito** for a daiquiri and a snack.

8 From Manolito, head back down Dumaine the way you came. Turn right onto Chartres and walk two blocks. As soon as you hit the intersection with Ursulines Avenue, you'll see the **Beauregard-Keyes House** on the left and the **Old Ursuline Convent and Museum** on the right. Check out one or the other (or both) to learn a little bit about some of the people who lived here back in the day.

9 Head back down Chartres toward Ursulines Avenue and continue for three blocks to St. Louis Cathedral and Jackson Square. Facing the cathedral, you'll see a small side street running down its left-hand side. That's Pirate Alley, and **Faulkner House Books** is located there. Stop in to pay homage to the storytellers of the South.

10 Head back on Pirate Alley toward Jackson Square. Just past the cathedral, turn right onto Chartres Street. A block down, just past Wilkinson Street, you can count the kitties through the window of **Louisiana Loom Works.** Head inside if textiles (or shop cats) are your thing.

11 Head another three blocks down Chartres Street and check out the **Bottom of the Cup Tea Room,** a cool shop that offers psychic readings and interesting varieties of tea.

12 Continuing down Chartres, take your next left onto Bienville Street. You'll walk two blocks, then cross North Peters Street, and continue past a couple parking lots and across the train tracks. You'll know you've arrived at **Woldenberg Park** when you see the Mississippi River. Just ahead of you is the Holocaust Memorial. Enjoy the river views and the cool breeze off the water. You're near Canal Street for easy transportation to other parts of the Quarter or city.

Sights

Audubon Butterfly Garden and Insectarium

The Audubon Butterfly Garden and Insectarium contains the largest collection of insects in the United States—about 900,000 species in all. The attraction is housed in part of the stately U.S. Custom House, an intimidating gray structure that occupies an entire city block.

Here, you can touch all kinds of creatures, like millipedes and beetles, although many others (like cockroaches) are presented in clever displays from a safe distance. Even the museum's Tiny Termite Café has insect-themed decor—and the glass-topped tables are actually terrariums, so you might find yourself eating directly over a live tarantula.

The museum's bug-cooking demonstration "café," Bug Appétit, illustrates how people around the world routinely snack on insects as an excellent source of protein. Less harrowing for squeamish visitors is the massive butterfly room set within a Japanese-style garden. The Audubon Butterfly Garden and Insectarium is closed most Mondays in fall, winter, and spring.

Audubon Insectarium

MAP 1: 423 Canal St., 504/524-2847 or 800/774-7394, auduboninstitute.org; 10am-4:30pm daily summer, 10am-4:30pm Tues.-Sun. fall-spring; $23 adults, $20 seniors, $18 children 2-12, children under 2 free

Beauregard-Keyes House

Opposite the Old Ursuline Convent stands the Beauregard-Keyes House, one of relatively few raised cottages in the French Quarter; the entrance and main floor are one level above the street. After the Civil War, the handsome mansion, which was finished in 1826, became the home of the Confederate general P. G. T. Beauregard. Over the years that followed, the house had a number of owners, and by the mid-1920s, it was nearly slated for demolition before a group of women campaigned to save it. In 1944, novelist Frances Parkinson Keyes took possession of the house and hired a firm to restore it. She lived here until 1969 and wrote several of her 50-odd books here. Today, her extensive collections of antique dolls, fans, and folk costumes are on display, and some of her books are available in the on-site gift shop.

One of the main attractions is the formal garden, designed by the wife of Switzerland's consul to New Orleans, who owned the house in the 1830s. From beyond the outer wall, you can see the ornamental garden through brick "windows" fashioned with iron grills. A stroll through this lovely space is included in any of the guided **house tours** (45

41

the historic Cabildo

minutes, free), which depart every hour on the hour. Roses, daylilies, crape myrtle, azaleas, sweet olive trees, irises, magnolia trees, and evergreen shrubs blend and bloom in one of the Quarter's loveliest gardens.

MAP 1: 1113 Chartres St., 504/523-7257, bkhouse.org; 10am-3pm Mon.-Sat.; $10 adults, $9 seniors and students, $7.50 military, $4 children 6-12, children under 6 free

The Cabildo

On the upriver side of the St. Louis Cathedral stands the Cabildo, the building in which the formal transfer of Louisiana to the United States took place after the Louisiana Purchase. The Spanish first constructed the Cabildo as their seat of government in the 1770s, but it and its replacement were destroyed during two major city fires in the late 18th century. The current structure, made of brick and stucco and built in the Spanish style with Moorish influences, was erected in 1794. It served as the Louisiana Supreme Court headquarters for much of the 19th and early 20th centuries, and it was where the *Plessy v. Ferguson* decision (which legalized segregation) originated in 1892.

Many prominent visitors have been officially received in the Cabildo, from the Marquis de Lafayette to Mark Twain. Today, the building looks more French than Spanish, because the original flat-tile roof was replaced with a Second Empire mansard roof in the late 1840s.

Part of the Louisiana State Museum since 1908, the Cabildo contains a fascinating exhibit tracing the history of Louisiana through the past two centuries, beginning with the region's Native Americans and ending with Reconstruction. Each section uses maps, photographs, drawings, historical documents, and narrative signs to describe the period and theme. The museum is closed on state holidays.

MAP 1: 701 Chartres St.,
504/568-6993 or 800/568-6868,
louisianastatemuseum.org;
10am-4:30pm Tues.-Sun.; $9 adults, $7 seniors, students, and military, children under 7 free

⚙ New Orleans Jazz Museum at the Old U.S. Mint

Fashioned with a granite facade and made of stucco and Mississippi River mud brick, the Old U.S. Mint was constructed in 1835. This is the only building in the country to have functioned as both a U.S. and a Confederate mint. It also housed Confederate troops for a time during the Civil War. With the Union occupation, the mint was shut down until Reconstruction, at which time it resumed service.

In 1909, the mint was decommissioned, and in 1981, it was added to the state museum system. Today, it's home to the New Orleans Jazz Museum, which features a variety of music-related artifacts, such as sheet music and instruments, like the cornet that Louis Armstrong learned to play on and Dr. John's piano. The thoughtful exhibits, like one dedicated to the life and work of Professor Longhair or an exploration of the history of women in jazz, are always changing, so check the website to see what's on. The Jazz Museum also hosts live performances and interviews with musicians.

A small display is dedicated to the building's architect, William Strickland, and historical information and objects related to its U.S. Mint days. It's also home to

inside the New Orleans Jazz Museum at the Old U.S. Mint

sculptures at the Old Ursuline Convent

the **Louisiana Historical Center,** an archive open to the public that contains a priceless collection of colonial-era maps and manuscripts. Note that the entire building is closed on state holidays.

MAP 1: 400 Esplanade Ave., 504/568-6993 or 800/568-6868, nolajazzmuseum.org; 10am-4:30pm Tues.-Sun.; $6 adults, $5 students, seniors, and military, children under 7 free

J&M Recording Studio

Although Cosimo Matassa's J&M Recording Studio, on the corner of North Rampart and Dumaine Streets, is recognized as a pivotal place in the history of rock 'n' roll, the building is now a laundromat called Hula Mae's Tropic Wash. Plaques adorn the exterior, marking it as the spot where Matassa worked with musicians like Fats Domino, Little Richard, Professor Longhair, Ray Charles, Jerry Lee Lewis, and Bobby Charles. Inside,

next to the dryers, are headshots of the many musicians that recorded here. Cosimo Matassa is a huge, yet often overlooked, influence on the musical history of New Orleans.

MAP 1: 840 N. Rampart St., no phone; 8:30am-6pm Mon.-Fri., 8:30am-3pm Sat.; free

Old Ursuline Convent and Museum

To understand New Orleans, it's important to understand the role of Catholicism in its founding and history. The Ursuline convent is the oldest existing building in New Orleans, having survived two city fires and as many wars. Today, the convent-turned-museum tells the story of some of the first women living in the city. It's run by the Archdiocese of New Orleans as its Catholic Culture Heritage Center, so the rooms house information and artifacts from neighboring St. Louis Cathedral as well. The convent has also served as an archbishop's residence, a boy's Catholic school, a public school, and the seat of the Louisiana legislature.

The museum hosts rotating exhibits, like an overview of Catholicism in New Orleans and how it shaped the city. Another focused on the life and legacy of Henriette Delille, a black Creole woman who founded the Sisters of the Holy Family, a Catholic order for free women of color, in the mid-19th century. The exhibits have been placed in the convent's former classrooms, dormitory, dining room, and

workroom. Many of the original features of the property are still on display, like the front staircase and the pine-and-cypress ceiling beams. The outdoor gardens are beautifully maintained, creating a quiet opportunity to rest and reflect. Connected to the convent complex is the still-active St. Mary's Church, built in 1845.

MAP 1: 1100 Chartres St., 504/529-3040, oldursulineconventmuseum.com; 10am-4pm Mon.-Fri., 9am-3pm Sat.; $8 adults, $7 seniors, $6 students and military

Restaurants

PRICE KEY

$	Entrées less than $15
$$	Entrées $15-30
$$$	Entrées more than $30

CAJUN AND CREOLE
SoBou $$

SoBou (short for "south of Bourbon") was created by the culinary experts behind Commander's Palace. The menus change throughout the day: You might find hot fried chicken with biscuits and gravy for breakfast, a cracklin' crusted pork belly steamed bun for lunch, or, for dinner, NOLA-style barbecue shrimp *pinchos* (small plates). Besides the main dining room—which is stylishly illuminated by shelves of glowing bottles—SoBou has an on-site bar (11:30am-close daily) and semi-private dining areas. During the Sunday "Legs and Eggs" brunch, enjoy the burlesque stylings of dancer Bella Blue along with

decadent dishes like the signature Legs & Eggs—a duck leg over grits with a crawfish-boil-spiced poached egg. The restaurant offers limited free parking at the nearby W New Orleans French Quarter.

MAP 1: 310 Chartres St., 504/552-4095, sobounola.com; 7am-10pm daily

PO'BOYS
Killer Poboys $

At Cam Boudreaux and April Bellow's Killer Poboys, the banh mi-inspired seared gulf shrimp sandwich is a signature dish that's been refined over the years for perfect flavors and textures. The roasted sweet potato po'boy is a hearty, somewhat healthy option, tastily teamed up with a black-eyed pea and pecan spread and braised greens. The pork belly they use is glazed with New Orleans rum and ginger cane syrup, the chorizo is house made, and the cheddar in the glorious take

45

on the grilled cheese is infused with Irish whiskey. The deli-style interior is always buzzing during lunch, with bottled sodas and canned beer available to go along with the sandwiches. This location is referred to as "Big" Killer Poboys; it's the sibling to "Little" Killer Poboys, inside the Erin Rose.

MAP 1: 219 Dauphine St., 504/462-2731, killerpoboys.com; 10am-8pm Wed.-Mon.

SEAFOOD
GW Fins $$$

Although many local dishes are offered at GW Fins, the kitchen specializes in fresh fish from all over the world, ranging from Canadian salmon to New Zealand John Dory. The setting, a converted warehouse with lofty ceilings, warm wood, and cushy booths, is contemporary and upbeat. Worthy specialties include Korean-spiced tempura fin wings (also known as fish collars), lobster dumplings, and the seasonally available "scalibut," a dish that combines New England scallops and Alaskan halibut. The menu is based on the day's catch, so it's subject to change. Reservations are recommended, and the dress code is business casual.

MAP 1: 808 Bienville St., 504/581-3467, gwfins.com; 5pm-10pm Sun.-Thurs., 5pm-10:30pm Fri.-Sat.

Felix's Restaurant & Oyster Bar $

Just off the insanity of Bourbon Street, Felix's Restaurant & Oyster Bar has been serving local seafood fanatics since the early 1900s. Though known for its oysters on the half shell, this super-casual joint prepares all of New Orleans's seafood favorites well, including shrimp rémoulade, blackened alligator, and oysters Bienville (baked oysters in a shrimp sauce).

MAP 1: 739 Iberville St., 504/522-4440, felixs.com; 10am-11pm Mon.-Thurs., 10am-1am Fri.-Sun.

ECLECTIC
Bayona $$$

A highly regarded restaurant on a quiet stretch of Dauphine, Bayona fuses traditions, recipes, and ingredients from a handful of cultures, namely American, French, Italian, Mediterranean, Asian, and North African. Award-winning chef Susan Spicer dreams up such imaginative combos as peppered lamb loin with a goat cheese-zinfandel sauce. Desserts are no mere afterthought, and there's a commendable wine list. The setting—an 18th-century Creole cottage filled with trompe l'oeil murals of the Mediterranean countryside, plus a lush courtyard—is the quintessence of romance, though the odd interior acoustics can make it rather loud.

MAP 1: 430 Dauphine St., 504/525-4455, bayona.com; 5:30pm-9:30pm Mon.-Tues., 11:30am-1:30pm and 5:30pm-9:30pm Wed.-Sat.

Green Goddess $$

An oasis down a quaint alleyway, Green Goddess sounds like it would be a great vegetarian spot for those seeking to escape the meat- and seafood-heavy menus of the French Quarter. And it is vegetarian- and vegan-friendly, but also serves meat and seafood for a perfectly omnivore experience. The dishes, ingredients, and flavors at Green

Enjoy the fresh food at Green Goddess.

cocktail menu, and the food menu always has some variation of gumbo on it. The 1830s-era Creole cottage the tavern resides in has two floors for eating and drinking, as well as a private courtyard.

MAP 1: 1026 St. Louis St., 504/265-8816, jewelnola.com; 6pm-midnight Mon.-Fri., 7pm-midnight Sat.-Sun.

Longway Tavern $$

The small plates at Longway sound pretty simple on the menu—fried calamari, shrimp toast, chicken sandwich, bread and butter—but the flavors and techniques used to create what are actually sophisticated and exciting yet approachable dishes will have you ordering more before you even finish your first round. Longway Tavern is a narrow space with a long bar on one side, booths on the other, and courtyard seating in the back. It's laidback and completely unpretentious, with a badass cocktail menu that's also deceptively simple.

MAP 1: 719 Toulouse St., 504/962-9696, longwaytavern.com; 4pm-midnight Mon.-Thurs., 11:30am-midnight Fri.-Sun.

Goddess are exciting and quirky, but also taste good. Service is generally unhurried, so prepare for a languid lunch or dinner. There are only a half dozen or so tables inside; most of the seating is outside, so this is the perfect spot on a sunny day. Try the sweet potato biscuits with wild mushroom gravy or the manchego *patatas bravas* (fried cubed potatoes) at lunch, the chimichurri brisket (or mushrooms) at dinner, and the signature rolled *uttapam* (an Indian-style lentil pancake) or freekeh salad anytime.

MAP 1: 307 Exchange Pl., 504/301-3347, greengoddessrestaurant.com; 11am-9pm Wed.-Sun.

✪ Jewel of the South $$

The minds behind the Latin flavors of Manolito have created a uniquely New Orleans tavern steeped in history. It's named for a mid-1800s-era saloon owned by unsung cocktail hero Joseph Santini, who created the Brandy Crusta cocktail, a drink made with cognac, curacao, and lemon juice. His establishment was also the first to serve gumbo to the public. Both those achievements are honored by the inclusion of the almost-forgotten classic on the

Meauxbar $$

Meauxbar serves up creative takes on French dishes like escargot, roasted chicken, and fried oysters, as well as a gussied-up version of the New Orleans corner store classic *yaka mein,* a local hangover cure similar to beef ramen. The space has a quasi-midcentury modern feel, with atomic-burst-shaped pendant lights, but its rustic hardwood floor, simple seating, and cozy simplicity evoke a quiet French bistro, low on pretense and high on charm.

MAP 1: 942 N. Rampart St.,
504/569-9979, meauxbar.com;
5pm-10pm Mon.-Thurs., 10am-2pm and
5pm-midnight Fri.-Sat., 10am-2pm and
5pm-10pm Sun.

✪ Palm & Pine $$

Jordan and Amarys Herndon are married chefs with years of fine dining experience (Jordan at Ralph's on the Park, Amarys at Bayona). In recent years, they've also experimented with pop-up kitchens; their late night Vietnamese crawfish boils at the Black Penny were legendary. With Palm & Pine, they finally have their own spot—and it's as good as their pedigrees suggest. There's a casual vibe, a large open dining room with blonde wood and shades of green and pink, and a gorgeous kitchen bar where guests can watch the chefs at work. The cuisine at Palm & Pine is "The South, and South of that," so there's tons of Latin American, Caribbean, and Tex-Mex influences, but dishes like the "corner store crudo," which combines raw tuna with shrimp puffs, pineapple slices, and a sweet and salty sauce made from pineapple soda and *nam pla,* defies classification. Try the tasty and gluttonous fried chicken livers accompanied by house-made seasonal preserves.

MAP 1: 308 N. Rampart St.,
504/814-6200, palmandpinenola.com;
5pm-1am Sun.-Mon. and Wed.-Thurs.,
5pm-2am Fri.-Sat.

ITALIAN
Irene's $$

At this French Quarter gem, the aromas of garlic and rosemary hit you as soon as you walk through the door. The food is high-end Italian with a focus on roasted meat and seafood, and the space is elegant and high-ceilinged. The antipasto plate is a stunner, and longtime favorites oysters Irene (baked oysters with bacon and bell pepper), cioppino, and rosemary- and garlic-roasted chicken bring comfort and joy to both regulars and new acolytes.

MAP 1: 529 Bienville St., 504/529-8811,
irenesnola.com; 5:30pm-10pm Mon.-Sat.

MEDITERRANEAN
Cleo's French Quarter $$

A restaurant that provides healthy, high-quality food and service for every one of the 24 hours its open, Cleo's on Decatur is an outpost of Cleo's Market at 940 Canal Street, but with a greatly expanded menu and a wood fired oven for made-to-order pita bread. A bright, modern spot with gold touches, the restaurant feels warm and welcoming at any time of the day. The menu takes its cues from all over the Middle East and Mediterranean, with lots of tabbouleh, hummus, falafel, zaatar, and olives. Even though the menu is limited during late-night hours, you can't go wrong even with the simplest items. No booze is served, but they have a lovely menu of fresh juices and other non-alcoholic mocktails.

MAP 1: 117 Decatur St., 504/616-3773;
24 hours daily

ASIAN
Dian Xin $

One of the few spots in New Orleans to serve authentic dim sum, Dian Xin's opening in 2019 sparked an unanticipated hunger for soup dumplings and steamed *bao* (filled dumplings). The popularity of the tiny spot means you'll likely have to wait during popular times. Luckily, you can leave your number and someone will call you when your table's ready, meaning you can window shop or grab a drink while you wait. Aside from dim sum, they also have a variety of larger dishes, as well as noodle soups and *jianbing* (Chinese-style crepes).

MAP 1: 1218 Decatur St., 504/266-2828; 3pm-10pm Tues.-Thurs. and Sun., 3pm-11pm Fri.-Sat.

LATIN AMERICAN
Manolito $

With so many places to eat in New Orleans, grazing is the way to go so that you can try as many spots as possible, and Manolito is perfect for a quick bite. The brainchild of local cocktail legends Chris Hannah and Nick Deitrich, Manolito's small plates are simple but tasty; both the food and beverage menus are love letters to the flavors and traditions of Cuba. Try one of the excellent made-to-order frozen cocktails. The space itself is small and cozy, but inviting, with a couple tables downstairs and another half dozen up in the loft area, as well as a few bar stools. There's a nice collection of photographs taken in Cuba by Hannah himself.

MAP 1: 508 Dumaine St., 504/603-2740, manolitonola.com; 4pm-11pm Mon.-Tues., 11am-11pm Wed.-Sun.

VEGETARIAN
Small Mart $

This tiny Upper Quarter spot is easy to miss. It looks every inch the typical convenience store from the outside but inside, it sells inexpensive but house-made international street food, like *chana chaat* (an Indian snack made with chickpeas and potatoes), a vegetable curry of the day, a Jamaican veggie patty, and a po'boy with tandoori marinated tofu or fried veggie pakora. They also carry authentic New York bagels, vegan chai and coffee drinks, gluten-free baked goods, kombucha on tap, and self-serve drip coffee for $1, all in a friendly, progressive, bodega-style atmosphere. It's small, so plan to take your food to go. The kitchen is open from noon to 6pm.

MAP 1: 1303 Decatur St., 504/309-2288; 8am-8pm daily, kitchen noon-6pm daily

CAFÉS AND LIGHT BITES
Arrow Cafe $

This homey, hip, and slightly ragtag spot has flyers on the walls, random New Orleans-made items for sale, and delicious baked goods provided by pastry chef Ryan Universe and local baker Wretchin' Gretchin's. They host monthly pop-ups to show off products from these and other New Orleans-based bakers and makers, making it a convenient spot to grab a cup of coffee while checking out one-of-a-kind, locally created products. Oh, and the coffee's good, too: They use Extracto beans from Portland, Oregon, as well as locally roasted Congregation Coffee and pull a hell of an espresso. There are also lots of vegan-friendly options to eat and drink.

MAP 1: 628 N. Rampart St., no phone; 8am-5pm daily

Croissant d'Or Patisserie $

A source of delightful pastries and sweets, from napoleons to dark

Croissant d'Or Patisserie

chocolate mousse, Croissant d'Or is a classic French bakery that also serves delicious sandwiches, fresh salads, and yummy breakfasts. Situated in the Lower Quarter, not far from the Old Ursuline Convent, this spacious café—with plenty of tables, local artwork, and a simply furnished courtyard. Be prepared for long lines, especially in the morning.

MAP 1: 617 Ursulines Ave., 504/524-4663, croissantdornola.com; 6am-3pm Wed.-Mon.

Nightlife

LIVE MUSIC

21st Amendment at La Louisiane

21st Amendment at La Louisiane honors the Prohibition era of the 1920s, when both the mafia and speakeasies thrived in the United States. Decorated with black-and-white images of the country's most notorious mobsters, including Al Capone, this cozy bar occupies part of a 19th-century building that was once owned by local mobsters Diamond Jim Moran and Carlos Marcello. Today, you can savor a delicious cocktail made from home-made syrups and infused spirits while listening to live old-time jazz and blues music, which is offered nearly every afternoon and evening.

MAP 1: 725 Iberville St., 504/378-7330, 21stamendmentlalouisiane.com; 2pm-11pm Mon.-Wed., 2pm-midnight Thurs., noon-2am Fri.-Sat., 11am-11pm Sun.; no cover

Santos

Brought to you by the same folks who run the Saint in the Lower

SNOWBALL STANDS

(Contributed by Megan Braden-Perry, who literally wrote the book on snowballs, *Crescent City Snow*. She loves guiding people to the right stands and flavors. Below are a few of her off-the-beaten-path snowball stand recommendations, all of which are open year-round. Find Megan at crescentcitysnow.com and @crescentcitysnow on social media.)

snowball in the summertime

Snowball stands are microcosms of New Orleans, serving scrumptious yet affordable treats to friendly people of diverse backgrounds. It's flavored ice, but so much more than that: The ice is shaved, making the texture soft and fluffy. Bring cash and don't hesitate to ask other guests at the stand for their favorite flavor combos.

- **Ike's** (520 City Park Ave., 504/208-9983, ikessnowballs.com): Ike's serves perfect snowballs. They have a wide variety of flavors, including a half dozen sour ones. The best thing about Ike's is the consistency. The flavors are always mixed perfectly (some stands add too much sugar, which makes the snowball lose flavor) and the ice is smooth.

- **The Original New Orleans Snoball and Smoothie** (4339 Elysian Fields Ave., 504/283-8370): Since this stand is open year-round, is centrally located, and has been open for nearly 30 years, it's probably the most visited of all stands. The cream flavors here are outstanding.

- **Sno-La Uptown** (8108 Hampson St., 504/327-7669, snolasnowballs.com): Just off the St. Charles streetcar line, Sno-La Uptown is a land of innovation. Sno-La created the first cheesecake-stuffed snowball and the beignet-flavored snowball, held the first snowball gender reveal and the first all-you-can-eat tasting, and much more. The Beam Me Up Mikey (banana and chocolate stuffed with peanut butter cheesecake) is my go-to.

- **Brain Freeze** (10816 Hayne Blvd., 985/290-5195): If you've got your own car, it's worth the drive to check out Brain Freeze, on the southeastern shore of Lake Pontchartrain. When friends come to town, this is where I take them. The snowballs are exactly what they should be, but this stand is also attached to Castnet Seafood and Walker's BBQ, so it's a one-stop shop of deliciousness.

- **Rodney's** (9231 Lake Forest Blvd., 504/241-2035): Also a haul from the central part of the city, Rodney's is my favorite stand of all time. Every flavor they serve is delightful, but my favorites are the sour apple and the cotton candy cream. This stand is also designed well, with easy parking and exiting, a covered patio, and separate order and pickup windows.

Garden District, Santos is a rock club that features everything from indie rock and metal to the occasional jazz or brass band. Regardless of who's playing, it's a fun, friendly, and super cool vibe with good drinks at decent prices. The space is a snug brick-walled spot with lots of corners to lean into. Note that a portrait of Lemmy, the late founder of Motorhead, occupies a prominent spot behind the bar, much like a patron saint.

MAP 1: 1135 Decatur St., 504/605-3533, santosbar.com; 4pm-5am Mon.-Fri., 2pm-5am Sat.-Sun.; cover $5-20

COCKTAIL BARS
✪ Bar Tonique

This cozy, unassuming bar may not look like it makes the best cocktails in town, but it does. Behind the U-shaped bar, bartenders create every drink from scratch with painstaking perfection, which means you might need to wait a little while for your cocktail. (They also have a good beer list if you're in a rush.) From the heartily shaken Ramos Gin Fizz to the icy mint julep, there's a cocktail for everyone. Pro tip: Their Bloody Marys have bacon, cost five bucks, and are only available on Saturdays.

MAP 1: 820 N. Rampart St., 504/324-6045, bartonique.com; noon-2am daily

Bourbon O Bar

Run by longtime cocktail mixologist Cheryl Charming, the Bourbon O is the only bar I recommend on Bourbon Street, partly for the antique Ramos Gin Fizz shaker machine, which makes the famed drink by automatically shaking it for six minutes. They also serve the whole gamut of New Orleans classic cocktails, including the Sazerac and the French 75. This is where to come to get an authentic glass of absinthe, served the traditional way. The bar itself is dark and gleaming, a haven from the shenanigans just outside. There's also live music every night.

Black Penny

MAP 1: 730 Bourbon St., 504/571-4685, bourbono.com; noon-midnight Sun.-Thurs., noon-1am Fri.-Sat.

Tiki Tolteca

The "tiki trail" of North Peters and Decatur Street begins at Tiki Tolteca, an upstairs hideaway over Felipe's Mexican Taqueria. It's sort of like you stumbled into someone's basement bar, if that someone had a lot of time and money to dedicate to a shrine to tiki culture. Tiki Tolteca is unique in its use of Latin American flavors and ingredients, like pisco or mezcal, to go along with the rum-heavy classic tiki cocktails. Be sure to try the boozy gummy bears.

MAP 1: 301 N. Peters St., 2nd fl., 504/288-8226, tikitolteca.com; 5pm-11pm Mon.-Thurs., noon-2am Fri.-Sat., noon-11pm Sun.

BARS AND LOUNGES

Black Penny

The Black Penny is a Southern Gothic dive bar with a huge selection of canned beer, great cocktails, and a local-hangout vibe. It's a neighborhood bar, with a convivial air and frequent food pop-ups, in a two-room carriage house with high ceilings and vintage decor. The S-shaped wooden bar sneaks through both rooms, so there's plenty of space to belly up.

MAP 1: 700 N. Rampart St., 504/304-4779; noon-4am daily

✪ Erin Rose

This neighborhood bar just off Bourbon Street is the place to be when you just want a drink, to listen to a great jukebox, to hang out with friends, or to just do some people

watching. The interior is a little dark and dive-y, and the ceiling and brick walls are festooned with New Orleans and Irish memorabilia. The frozen Irish coffee is a lifesaver on warm days, and the Bloody Mary is one of the best in the city (the secret is a splash of Guinness). If you need a bite to eat, grab a sandwich from Little Killer Poboys in the back.

MAP 1: 811 Conti St., 504/522-3573, erinrosebar.com; 10am-7am daily

LGBTQ VENUES

700 Club

This popular gay bar provides great drinks, delightful service, and an adventurous food menu (try the PB&J wings and the Brussels sprouts). The high ceilings with chandeliers scream shabby chic and the many television screens play music videos from back in the day. It can get crowded during and after French Quarter events like the Red Dress Run, Decadence, and Easter, but it's also a great spot to slip into for some day drinking on an average day.

MAP 1: 700 Burgundy St., 504/561-7095, 700nola.com; noon-4am Mon.-Fri., 11am-4am Sat.-Sun.

Good Friends Bar

The mellow, longstanding Good Friends Bar isn't too loud or too flashy. It's just a casual, pet-friendly neighborhood watering hole, where you'll find a pool table, affordable beer and cocktails, a slightly fancier upstairs area, and attentive bartenders. Saints fans come here, as do low-key locals, and no matter your sexual orientation, you're welcome to join in the karaoke fun every Tuesday night (9pm-midnight).

BOURBON STREET SURVIVAL TIPS

When visitors think of New Orleans, the first thing that comes to mind is Bourbon Street. It's the epitome of what people think this city is - drinking to excess, lewd behavior, loud music. Although Bourbon Street isn't my destination of choice in the city, there are a few restaurants, bars, shops, and clubs that may be of interest to folks. (For example, there are a lot of LGBTQ-friendly spots that have been around a long time the farther upriver/east you go.) For those of you who want to brave Bourbon, here's my advice on navigating the most infamous nine blocks in New Orleans:

Toast to staying happy and healthy on Bourbon Street.

- Do not wear flip-flops or open-toed shoes anywhere in the vicinity of Bourbon Street. There's all sorts of effluvia that puddles up and you do not want it touching your feet.
- Speaking of shoes…. If someone comes up and wants to bet that they know where you got your shoes, either ignore the person or say, "on my feet" and walk away. It's a scam: The person will use word play to try and trick you out of your money.
- Don't eat a Lucky Dog. The cheerful hot dog stands seem to be on every block, but partaking might make your stomach very, very unhappy.
- Don't drink a Hand Grenade. If you're going to have a weirdly colored, sugar saturated, grain-alcohol based beverage, have something fun like a Shark Attack or a Purple Drank or a crazy flavor of frozen daiquiri. Same great hangover, but you look less ridiculous than if you carry around the tall, neon-green plastic cup that Hand Grenades are served in.
- Don't flash for beads. It perpetuates a tiresome stereotype about New Orleans. Beads are only meant to be thrown during Mardi Gras season, no matter what the dudes on Bourbon Street are hooting and hollering at you.

MAP 1: 740 Dauphine St., 504/566-7191, goodfriendsbar.com; 24 hours daily; no cover

DANCE CLUBS

One Eyed Jack's

One Eyed Jacks is a spacious, bordello-style venue, with red walls, curious paintings, and mood lighting. Beyond the intimate front bar, revelers will encounter a large showroom, which features a horseshoe-shaped bar, limited seating, an ample stage, and oodles of room for dancing. While live concerts are common here, regulars also come for themed events, like 1980s-style dance parties, burlesque shows, and vaudeville nights, which often include comedy sketches, old-fashioned jazz performances, acrobatics, and sexy dance routines.

MAP 1: 615 Toulouse St., 504/569-8361, oneeyedjacks.net; hours and cover vary by event

Effervescence

WINE BARS

Effervescence

This pristine and elegant converted French Quarter residence with its own courtyard is perfectly suited for its bubbles-heavy wine menu. The space features hardwood floors with tile accents and high ceilings. Effervescence has more than 30 sparkling wines available by the glass or half glass, and of those, about a dozen are true Champagnes. They also offer an array of bubbly flights and bubbly-based cocktails. The food menu is a bit fancy-pants, with several preparations of caviar, a stunning cold Gulf seafood platter, and wagyu beef. But there are also more casual (and affordable) options, like pommes frites, crispy brussels sprouts, and a grilled half wheel of cheese. Beer, still wine, whiskey, and other booze are all available as well.

MAP 1: 1036 N. Rampart St., 504/509-7644, nolabubbles.com; 4pm-11pm Wed.-Thurs., 3pm-1am Fri.-Sat., 1pm-8pm Sun.

Patrick's Bar Vin

This elegant, cozy spot boasts wine lockers, antique reproduction furniture, and a courtyard. Patrick Van Hoorebeek, the owner and host, is an engaging bon vivant who is passionate about wine. He's Belgian, which explains the selection of classic Belgian beers from Duvel and Chimay—as well as the miniature *Manneken Pis* statue in the courtyard (the original can be found in Brussels). A number of vintage wines from all around the world are available by the bottle; Patrick's Bar Vin provides an excellent opportunity to enjoy them in a relaxing setting.

MAP 1: 730 Bienville St., 504/200-3180, patricksbarvin.com; 4pm-midnight Mon.-Thurs., noon-1am Fri., 2pm-1am Sat., 2pm-midnight Sun.

Arts and Culture

LIVE MUSIC VENUES
✪ Preservation Hall

Since 1961, Preservation Hall has been one of the city's top places to hear true New Orleans jazz. The house band and the venue were formed expressly to keep the legacy of the city's distinctive style of jazz music alive for generations to come, and visiting musicians continue to perform in the surprisingly intimate concert hall, sitting in with the Preservation Hall Band. Housed within a weathered, 1750s-era house, Preservation Hall is a charming, laid-back place, with vintage wooden benches, folding chairs, and a good bit of standing room. Be sure to get here early, as the line forms quickly for the nightly concerts (8pm, 9pm, and 10pm). If you'd rather skip the line altogether, consider the limited "Big Shot" seating option ($35-50). After the all-too-brief concerts (usually less than an hour), feel free to stroll along the carriageway to the landscaped courtyard for a breath of fresh air.

MAP 1: 726 St. Peter St., 504/522-2841, preservationhall.com; 8pm-11pm daily; tickets $15-20

GALLERIES
Gallerie Vinsantos

Much of this gallery is dedicated to the work of artist-owner Vinsantos, who creates commissioned dolls

Preservation Hall

that fuse various artistic techniques and are inspired by his personal history as a musician and drag performer. The 18- to 36-inch-tall dolls, made from clay and show-cased each in its own custom-built wood box, have a Tim Burton aesthetic, with giant eyes and haunted faces, but they also have a hyper-glam style depicting personas like divas, buskers, and circus perform-ers. All the dolls' faces are sculpted by hand and then decorated with an abundance of jewels, feathers, and glitter. The gallery also dis-plays art by a dozen other artists, which ranges across expressions, formats, mediums, and themes. They're all daring, exciting works and everything in the gallery is uniquely, gloriously weird.

MAP 1: 811 Royal St., 504/603-6038, gallerievinsantos.com; 11am-7pm daily; free

✪ Modernist Cuisine Gallery

Scientist and photographer Nathan Myhrvold is well-known in the culi-nary world for his photographs and explorations of food. His gallery on Royal Street features close-up photographs of ordinary foods like raspberries and kale, inviting dis-cussions about food on a micro level. Myhrvold uses motion technology to catch instants of spills and other movement, freezing a moment in time that is usually lost to the naked eye. It's playful but takes the subject of food (in all its forms) seriously. It's art that anyone who eats can re-late to.

MAP 1: 305 Royal St., 504/571-5157, modernistcuisinegallery.com; 10am-6pm Sun.-Wed., 10am-8pm Fri.-Sat.; free

Rodrigue Studio

Although the famous Cajun "Blue Dog" artist George Rodrigue passed away in 2013, you can still visit his studio on Royal Street, situated in a warmly lighted space not far from the St. Louis Cathedral. Here, you can buy everything from inexpen-sive gifts to original oil paintings, de-picting the "Blue Dog" amid swamps, cemeteries, and other picturesque places. The inspiration for these works was twofold: a Cajun legend about the loup-garou (werewolf) and the owner's terrier, Tiffany, who had died several years before Rodrigue started painting her.

MAP 1: 730 Royal St., 504/581-4244, georgerodrigue.com; 10am-6pm Mon.-Sat., noon-5pm Sun.; free

MUSEUMS
The Historic New Orleans Collection

Amid the art galleries of Royal Street lies one of the city's most un-derrated attractions. The Historic New Orleans Collection (THNOC) is an interconnected complex of buildings that includes the Greek Revival-style Merieult House. Built in 1792, the house now contains the Williams Gallery, featuring rotating history exhibits, and the Louisiana History Galleries, 13 chambers that each explore a specific period of the state's history with displays of authentic maps, books, furni-ture, and artwork. This impressive complex also includes three struc-tures on Toulouse Street: a former banking house, a Creole cottage, and the Louis Adam House, where Tennessee Williams once boarded. Make time for the museum shop in the Merieult House, where you'll find everything from local novels and history books to vintage maps and iconic jewelry.

Several different tours ($5) of the compound are offered. They're great for folks who want to get a close-up view of life in the French Quarter. Tours run four times a day Tuesday through Saturday, and three times a day on Sunday.

THNOC also oversees the **Williams Research Center** (410 Chartres St., 504/598-7171; 9:30am-4:30pm Tues.-Sat.; free), a Beaux Arts-style brick structure containing an extensive library of roughly 35,000 documents and manuscripts, plus more than 300,000 photographs, drawings, prints, and paintings about the history of New Orleans.

MAP 1: 533 Royal St., 504/523-4662, hnoc.org; 9:30am-4:30pm Tues.-Sat., 10:30am-4:30pm Sun.; free

Mardi Gras Museum of Costumes and Culture

Mardi Gras Museum of Costumes and Culture

Step inside to get the lowdown on Mardi Gras through its costumes. Here you can find extravagantly decorated costumes for many different Mardi Gras groups, like the Mardi Gras Indians, krewe royalty (people who are chosen each year to ride in the front of their krewe's parade), and walking krewes (participants in smaller parades that are on foot, or those who walk between driven floats during larger parades). Other items on display include traditional Cajun country Mardi Gras costumes (which resemble rag doll outfits) and the beaded bodices from the all-female walking krewe Dames de Perlage. This is a great place for kids as well: The museum offers a variety of hands-on costume-crafting classes, and there's a room where the whole family can dress up in Mardi Gras finery. The docent-led tour ($3) brings the textiles together with Mardi Gras history through the decades—it's a great way to better understand Mardi Gras traditions, and well worth the extra three bucks.

MAP 1: 1010 Conti St., 504/218-4872, themardigrasmuseum.com; 10am-5pm daily; $12 adults, $10 seniors, students, military, and Louisiana residents

Pharmacy Museum

This museum occupies a former apothecary shop from the 1820s. Original shop owner Louis J. Dufilho Jr. was the first licensed pharmacist in the United States. Displays show what a period pharmacy looked like, including rows of hand-carved mahogany cabinets filled with everything from

Pharmacy Museum

1855 Italian marble soda fountain. Guided tours are offered Tuesday through Friday at 1pm.

MAP 1: 514 Chartres St., 504/565-8027, pharmacymuseum.org; 10am-4pm Tues.-Sat.; $5 adults, $4 seniors and students, children under 6 free

PERFORMING ARTS

Le Petit Théâtre du Vieux Carré

Founded in 1916 and relocated to its current spot near Jackson Square in 1922, Le Petit Théâtre du Vieux Carré is one of America's oldest community theaters. Le Petit houses both a highly regarded Louisiana Creole restaurant (Dickie Brennan's Tableau) and a comfortable place for patrons to watch a wide range of dramas, comedies, musicals, and intimate concerts.

MAP 1: 616 St. Peter St., 504/522-2081, lepetittheatre.com; hours and cost vary by show

established drugs to gris-gris voodoo potions. Exhibits tell the story of Louisiana's development in medicine and health care. Interesting features include an assortment of bloodletting equipment, a medicinal herb garden in the courtyard, and an

Recreation

PARKS AND PLAZAS

✪ Woldenberg Park

Lovely Woldenberg Park is a 16-acre green space and redbrick promenade that extends along the riverfront from the aquarium to St. Peter Street. It's along this stretch that New Orleans was established in 1718. Crape myrtle and magnolia trees shade numerous park benches, affording romantic views of the Mississippi River. One of the original quays, Toulouse Street Wharf, is home to the palatial riverboat, the Steamboat *Natchez*. Fringing the park is the Moonwalk, a wooden boardwalk that stretches along the riverfront between St. Philip and St. Peter Streets.

Within the park are several significant sculptures. The stunning, 20-foot-tall *Monument to the Immigrant,* by noted New Orleans artist Franco Alessandrini, commemorates New Orleans's role as one of the nation's most prolific immigrant ports throughout the 19th century. It's fashioned from white Carrara marble. Other sculptures include Robert Schoen's bizarre *Old Man River,* an 18-foot tribute to the Mississippi River, and John

waterfront Woldenberg Park

Scott's *Ocean Song*, a series of slender, 10-foot-tall, stainless-steel pyramids, topped by a grid of rings. Don't miss the mesmerizing **New Orleans Holocaust Memorial** (holocaustmemorial.us), created by Israeli artist Yaacov Agam, featuring nine colorful panels that meld to form different images depending on where you're standing.

MAP 1: Riverfront, from Canal St. to St. Peter St.; 24 hours daily; free

BICYCLE TOURS
Flambeaux Bicycle Tours
Flambeaux offers bicycle tours led by the passionate New Orleans natives who run this locally owned business. The tours are interesting because they often encompass more than the usual tourism spots. The Creole Odyssey tour is wide ranging, as it goes from the French Quarter to the Tremé to Esplanade Ridge, City Park, and Bayou St. John. You'll learn lots of interesting history and see beautiful scenery. There's also a tour that's more focused on the French Quarter, which includes jaunts into the Tremé and Faubourg Marigny. The tours are three hours long and cover 6-10 miles. The bikes are comfy European cruisers with hand brakes. Bottled water and a helmet rental are included. Flambeaux offers walking tours.

MAP 1: 626 N. Rampart St., 504/321-1505, flambeauxtours.com; 9am-5pm daily; tours $50

Shops

OCCULT AND VOODOO

✪ Bottom of the Cup Tea Room

Besides offering more than 100 varieties of fine tea, this cozy shop has been giving psychic readings since 1929. In fact, the name of the store is derived from its early days, when the resident psychic would read the tea leaves left at the bottom of a customer's cup. The house psychics still offer tea leaf readings, but mostly they do tarot card readings. The all-organic tea selection is the largest in the country; there are some really interesting blends to try. (Tea is included with the cost of a reading but can also be purchased separately for $3.) This is also a good spot to purchase tarot cards and quirky gifts like crystals, amulets, and wands.
MAP 1: 327 Chartres St., 800/729-7148, bottomofthecup.com; 10am-6pm daily

Bottom of the Cup Tea Room

Boutique Du Vampyre

This intriguing boutique, opened in 2003, has a lot of vampire- and Goth-related art, jewelry, and accessories for sale, most created by local artists. There's a fortune teller box, as well as shrines to several spirits, like the French Quarter Monster and the Boudreaux Mule. There's a lot of cool art on the walls and coffin-shaped backpacks and purses to consider. This is also the place to get custom-made vampire fangs. And, if you're lucky, you'll get the password for their secret speakeasy that's at a different location. An employee should tell you as you leave, but you can always ask.
MAP 1: 709 St. Ann St., 504/561-8267, boutique-du-vampyre.myshopify.com; 10am-9pm daily

Boutique Du Vampyre

ANTIQUES AND VINTAGE

✪ M.S. Rau Antiques

A family-owned, French Quarter landmark since Max Rau opened the doors in 1912, M.S. Rau Antiques is one of the oldest antiques shops in New Orleans. Today, the showroom

the "secret" door at M.S. Rau Antiques

houses a stupendous collection of 19th-century paintings and sculptures, exquisite clocks and music boxes, and striking bedroom and dining sets. If you're looking for a special piece of jewelry, you might find it here: Precious items include Pope Paul VI's diamond ring and diamond cross, Colombian emerald rings, and bangle bracelets courtesy of Tiffany & Co. Ask about arranging a tour of the secret room of practically priceless paintings and furniture for a museum experience in an already storied antique shop.
MAP 1: 630 Royal St., 888/711-8084, rauantiques.com; 9am-5:15pm Mon.-Sat.

SPECIALTY FOOD
Leah's Pralines
Family owned and operated since 1944, Leah's offers the city's signature confection, the praline, made with Louisiana sugar, Alabama pecans, cream, milk, and butter. The shop also offers fudge, brittle, and chocolate, all made in-house daily, and all from the recipes passed down through three generations of Leah's

family. The pralines are delicious, but if you're a brittle fan, check out some of the varieties on offer: The peanut-and-coconut and the bacon-pecan brittle are both winners. Pralines make for a uniquely New Orleans gift, but they're also good for eating while walking the streets of the Quarter.
MAP 1: 714 St. Louis St., 504/523-5662, leahspralines; 10am-6pm Wed.-Mon.

GIFTS AND SOUVENIRS
Bourbon French Parfums
Since the 1840s, this aromatic perfumery has been creating custom-blended fragrances. Schedule a one-hour private sitting with a specialist who will analyze your body chemistry, assess your personality, and record your preferred scents. Once your secret formula is created, you can order an entire set of toiletries, including perfume, lotion, and foaming bath gel. If you lack the time or patience, you can just as easily choose from the perfumes, musk oils, and voodoo potions available on-site. Also on display are elegant perfume bottles, decorated with everything from frogs to fleurs-de-lis.
MAP 1: 805 Royal St., 504/522-4480, neworleansperfume.com; 10am-5pm daily

Bourbon Pride
This somewhat raunchy shop is on the edge of the Bourbon Street craziness and is the only Pride-themed, LGBTQ-specific store in Louisiana. They design and print all their own T-shirts, so you're sure to find something unique. It's also perfect for picking up beads,

sunglasses, sex toys and accessories, boas, and a myriad of other fun and feisty items.

MAP 1: 909 Bourbon St., 504/566-1570, bourbonpride.com; 10am-10pm Mon.-Wed., 10am-11pm Thurs.-Sun.

Ma Sherie Amour

Located right off Jackson Square, this store calls itself a "nature-inspired gift shop." The walls and shelves at Ma Sherie Amour are lined with unique home accessories, jewelry (men's and women's), masks, and even some clothing items. Due to its location, it's usually pretty crowded.

MAP 1: 517 St. Ann St., 504/598-1998, ma-sherie-amour.business.site; 10am-5:30pm daily

Maskarade

If it's masks you want, Maskarade delivers in spades. They stock masks of all styles, materials, and price points. You can find Venetian bird masks, Mexican sugar skull masks, animal masks, masks for people who wear glasses—I could go on. They sell both handcrafted items and masks sold in bulk for parties. They even commission custom masks, if what you need is not found within their walls. The handmade masks come from more than 20 local and international artists. They also sell fascinators and other fun hair accessories. This is a great place to browse and explore.

MAP 1: 630 St. Ann St., 504/568-1018, themaskstore.com; 10am-5pm daily

The Tahyo

This shop, along with Tahyo Tavern (1140 Decatur St. 504/301-1991, thetahyotavern.com; 11am-11pm Tues.-Sun., 11am-8pm Mon.) on the next block, supports the non-profit Villalobos Rescue Center, featured on the Animal Planet show *Pit Bulls & Parolees*. The shop sells lots of goodies for dogs, along with some human stuff, like T-shirts, hand-crafted jewelry, and art. Every purchase directly benefits the dogs at the nearby rescue center, so it's a win-win.

MAP 1: 1224 Decatur St., 504/218-8337, shoppe.thetahyo.com; 11am-6pm Sun.-Thurs., 11am-7pm Fri.-Sat.

BOOKS AND MUSIC

Dauphine Street Books

This is the kind of bookstore that requires agility and a love of digging around for the perfect book. There are so many books in this tiny shop that many are in unsteady piles on the floor, and moving around them to get to the shelves is an adventure. A true book lover knows there's nothing like finding a literary needle in a haystack. There's a lot of New Orleans history books for sale here.

The Tahyo

MAP 1: 410 Dauphine St., 504/529-2333; noon-7pm daily

Faulkner House Books

Hidden in an alley between the Cabildo and the St. Louis Cathedral, this small bookstore occupies the same space that novelist William Faulkner inhabited in 1925, when he first arrived in New Orleans as a young poet. It was here, in fact, that he wrote *Soldiers' Pay*. Operated by a knowledgeable staff, frequented by writers and collectors alike, and only closed on Mardi Gras Day, this charming place sells new and used books, including rare first editions, titles about Southern Americana, and literature by Faulkner, Tennessee Williams, and Walker Percy.

MAP 1: 624 Pirate's Alley, 504/524-2940; 10am-5:30pm daily

Faulkner House Books

CLOTHING AND SHOES

Lost and Found

This funky vintage women's clothing and accessory shop has something for everyone. Everything here is high quality, prices are affordable, the shopkeepers are welcoming and laid-back, and a lot of the products come from local artists and crafters. There's a great variety of ladies' plus size dresses, as well as one-of-a-kind items such as hand-crafted headbands and jewelry. The folks running the place will be happy to tell you the story behind each piece.

MAP 1: 323 Chartres St., 504/595-6745; 10am-6pm Sun.-Thurs., 10am-7pm Fri.-Sat.

No Rules Fashion

Come here to get your freak on. This is the place to find daring and provocative dresses, corsets, thigh-high boots, and anything else you can think of in steampunk, boho, goth, rockabilly, and burlesque styles, for both men and women. It's perfect if you're looking for something unique for Mardi Gras, Jazz Fest, Halloween, or just for a day ending in "y." The stock shifts seasonally.

MAP 1: 927 Royal St., 504/875-4437, norulesfashion.com; 10am-8pm daily

ARTS AND CRAFTS

Idea Factory

A great spot for kids and adults, the Idea Factory creates and sources handcrafted toys, games, tools, and the like, all made of wood. The items on display are gorgeous. The collection of cribbage boards might call out to you, or one of the puzzle boxes, and you're likely to get an enthusiastic backstory on any piece that piques your interest. Before you know it, you've been in here for an hour. The shop was originally a wood-working gallery back in 1974.

MAP 1: 924 Royal St., 504/524-5195, ideafactoryneworleans.com; 10am-6pm daily

Louisiana Loom Works

This spot has a huge loom upon which rugs are custom crafted. The shop also has many of those rugs available to peruse and purchase, and about a half dozen cats curled up in various corners, on the loom, between the rugs, or anywhere else. The cotton-woven rugs are painstakingly created by hand; if you're lucky, one of the shopkeepers might be working on one when you stop in. They produce rugs of varying colors, patterns, and sizes, and all are machine washable.

MAP 1: 616 Chartres St., 504/566-7788, customragrugs.com; 11am-6pm Thurs.-Tues.

Central Business District and Warehouse/Arts District Map 2

Across Canal Street from the French Quarter is the Central Business District (CBD), where merchants and traders once set up shop. Today it's a visual history of **commerce,** as many of those original structures still stand. It's also home to **hotels, cafés,** and **restored theaters.** Heavily trafficked Poydras Street is the boundary between the CBD and the once industrial Warehouse District.

Within the Warehouse District is the Arts District, spanning four blocks of **Julia Street.** The neighborhood also houses culinary insti-

tutions like the flagship restaurants of Emeril Lagasse, Donald Link, and Adolfo Garcia, as well as one of the most culturally significant venues in the city: the **Superdome,** where the New Orleans Saints play for more than 76,000 fans.

TOP SIGHTS

- Best for History Buffs: **The National WWII Museum** (page 73)

TOP RESTAURANTS

- Best Multi-Fusion Food: **Maypop** (page 75)
- Where to Find Unique Cuts of Beef: **La Boca** (page 78)
- Best Coffee Program: **Mammoth Espresso** (page 81)

TOP NIGHTLIFE

- Best Bar to Try Before You Buy: **Victory** (page 84)

TOP ARTS AND CULTURE

- Where to Watch Artists at Work: **New Orleans Glassworks & Printmaking Studio** (page 86)
- Best Downtown Gallery for African American Art: **Stella Jones Gallery** (page 87)
- Best Combination of History and Art: **Ogden Museum of Southern Art** (page 87)

TOP RECREATION

- Best Spot for Free Live Music: **Lafayette Square** (page 89)
- Where to See Team Spirit in Action: **New Orleans Saints** (page 90)

TOP SHOPS

- Most Old-School Timepieces: **The Clock & Watch Shop** (page 93)

GETTING THERE AND AROUND

- Streetcar lines: St. Charles (12), Canal (47, 48), Rampart-St.Claude (49)
- Major bus routes: 10, 11, 15, 16, 39, 91, 101, 102, 106, 115

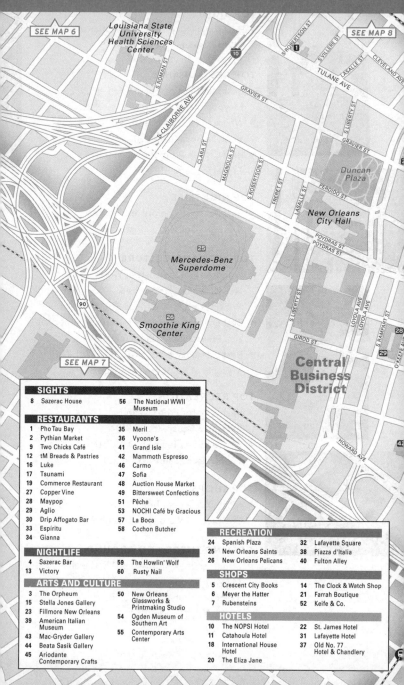

SEE MAP 6
SEE MAP 8

Louisiana State University Health Sciences Center

S TONTI ST
S VILLERE ST
S ROBERTSON ST
LASALLE ST
CLEVELAND AVE
TULANE AVE
S CLAIBORNE AVE
GRAVIER ST
S LIBERTY ST
GRAVIER ST
CLARA ST
MAGNOLIA ST
S ROBERTSON ST
FRERET ST
LASALLE ST
Duncan Plaza
PERDIDO ST

New Orleans City Hall
POYDRAS ST
POYDRAS ST

Mercedes-Benz Superdome

Smoothie King Center

S LIBERTY ST
LOYOLA AVE
LOYOLA AVE
S RAMPART ST
O'KEEFE AVE

GIROD ST

SEE MAP 7

Central Business District

HOWARD AVE

SIGHTS
8	Sazerac House
56	The National WWII Museum

RESTAURANTS
1	Pho Tau Bay
2	Pythian Market
9	Two Chicks Café
12	tM Breads & Pastries
16	Luke
17	Tsunami
19	Commerce Restaurant
27	Copper Vine
28	Maypop
29	Aglio
30	Drip Affogato Bar
33	Espiritu
34	Gianna
35	Meril
36	Vyoone's
41	Grand Isle
42	Mammoth Espresso
46	Carmo
47	Sofia
48	Auction House Market
49	Bittersweet Confections
51	Pêche
53	NOCHI Café by Gracious
57	La Boca
58	Cochon Butcher

NIGHTLIFE
4	Sazerac Bar
13	Victory
59	The Howlin' Wolf
60	Rusty Nail

ARTS AND CULTURE
3	The Orpheum
15	Stella Jones Gallery
23	Fillmore New Orleans
39	American Italian Museum
43	Mac-Gryder Gallery
44	Beata Sasik Gallery
45	Ariodante Contemporary Crafts
50	New Orleans Glassworks & Printmaking Studio
54	Ogden Museum of Southern Art
55	Contemporary Arts Center

RECREATION
24	Spanish Plaza
25	New Orleans Saints
26	New Orleans Pelicans
32	Lafayette Square
38	Piazza d'Italia
40	Fulton Alley

SHOPS
5	Crescent City Books
6	Meyer the Hatter
7	Rubensteins
14	The Clock & Watch Shop
21	Farrah Boutique
52	Keife & Co.

HOTELS
10	The NOPSI Hotel
11	Catahoula Hotel
18	International House Hotel
20	The Eliza Jane
22	St. James Hotel
31	Lafayette Hotel
37	Old No. 77 Hotel & Chandlery

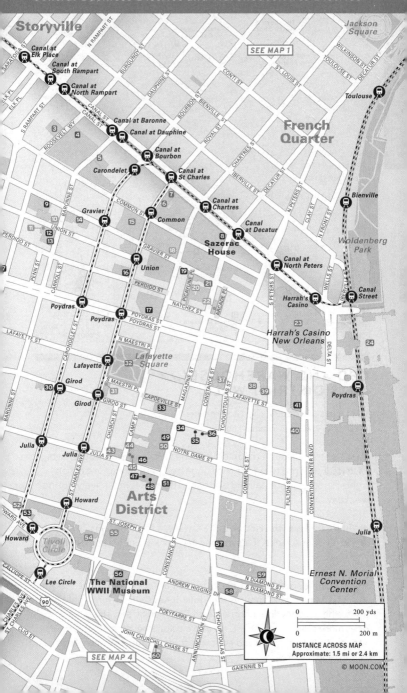

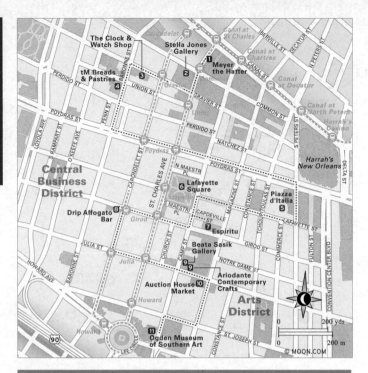

CBD AND WAREHOUSE/ ARTS DISTRICT WALK

TOTAL DISTANCE: 2.2 miles (3.5 kilometers)
WALKING TIME: 45 minutes-1 hour

This is a stroll through the middle of the CBD and Warehouse/Arts District. Feel free to go off the suggested path to explore other sights, shops, and restaurants or bars. The area is most lively during weekdays.

1 Start at **Meyer the Hatter,** just a few steps south of Canal Street on St. Charles Avenue. If it's a sunny day, think about getting a hat for your walk.

2 Continue south up St. Charles for half a block to get to the Place St. Charles, which houses the **Stella Jones Gallery.** Turn right to get to the gallery's direct entrance on Common Street. This gallery does more than showcase art; it's also a cultural resource that supports African American artists and educates students about African American culture and history.

3 Exit onto St. Charles Avenue, turn right, walk south for one block, and turn right onto Gravier Street. Walk a block and a half to **The Clock & Watch Shop** to browse luxury timepieces and vintage pocket watches.

4 Continue west down Gravier and then take your next left onto Baronne Street. Walk a block; once you pass Union Street, duck into **tM Breads & Pastries** for a snack and a caffeinated beverage.

5 Continue south on Baronne for two blocks until you get to Poydras Street. Take a left onto Poydras and walk six blocks east, taking in the sculptures along Poydras's neutral ground (the New Orleanian name for the median). If you see one that intrigues you, you can find a corresponding plaque with info about the piece on the sidewalk across from it. Once you reach South Peters Street, turn right, walk one block, and take a right onto Lafayette Street, then take a rest at the soothing **Piazza d'Italia,** with its oasis of water fountains and Italian architecture.

6 From the plaza, continue west up Lafayette Street for four blocks till you get to **Lafayette Square.** Even if there's not a concert or festival currently going, it's a nice urban green space with statues of Henry Clay, John McDonogh, and Benjamin Franklin scattered throughout.

Lafayette Square Park

Ogden Museum of Southern Art

7 It's time for a taco and a margarita! Head to the southeast corner of the square, where Camp Street and South Maestri Street intersect. Turn south onto Camp, then take a quick left onto Capdeville Street to get to **Espíritu.**

8 After you're properly sated, take a left out of Espíritu onto Capdeville, and back to Camp Street. Turn left onto Camp, and then, one block down, turn right onto Girod Street. Walk two blocks to Carondelet Street and you'll see **Drip Affogato Bar** on the southwestern corner. Have a little sugar and/or caffeine to offset the margarita from earlier.

9 Head south on Carondelet and walk one block to Julia Street. Turn left and check out a bunch of galleries like the **Beata Sasik Gallery** and **Ariodante Contemporary Crafts** over the next three blocks.

10 Continue east on Julia to Magazine Street. Take a right to reach the front entrance of the **Auction House Market,** which is just past the corner. Get a juice, a snack, a cocktail, an empanada, or some raw oysters at this food hall and take a load off.

11 Leaving the Auction House, take a right to continue down Magazine Street for a block, then take a right onto St. Joseph Street, then a left onto Camp Street, where the **Ogden Museum of Southern Art** awaits you on that block.

Sights

Sazerac House

The Sazerac is the city's signature cocktail, and the Sazerac House exists to tell you all about it, on a journey through New Orleans history as told through its cocktails. Visitors pay no fee to take the self-guided tour, which includes interactive, multi-media exhibits on rum, Peychaud's bitters, and a history of the French Quarter. Cheerful and helpful staff members are at every exhibit to give context for what you're seeing.

Sazerac-brand rye whiskey is distilled and bottled onsite, making this the first distillery in the Central Business District. Visitors can watch the process and see the custom-made still that distills the whiskey. If you're 21 or over, you'll get a small sample of a Sazerac during the tour, as well as a taste of the distillery's other products, like rum, coffee liqueur, and praline liqueur.

MAP 2: 101 Magazine St., 504/901-0107, sazerachouse.com; 10am-6pm daily; free

✪ The National WWII Museum

This museum opened to the public on June 6, 2000, the 56th anniversary of the amphibious World War II invasion and it's the only museum in the United States dedicated to this event. The building that houses the museum was originally a factory that built ships during World War II, including some of the very vehicles that transported infantrymen to Normandy.

A visit here can be an all-day (or multiday) affair; it might take that long to absorb the enormous collection of exhibits documenting the Allied victory in World War II in both the Pacific and European theaters. You'll want to check out the interactive "Final Mission: The USS *Tang* Submarine Experience" (9:35am-4:35pm daily; $7 pp). The experience allows visitors to relive the last epic battle of the most successful submarine in World War II by placing 27 people at a time inside a replica of the sub and recreating the skirmish. You can also watch the immersive 4-D, Tom Hanks-narrated documentary *Beyond All Boundaries* (10am-4pm Sun.-Thurs., 10am-5pm Fri.-Sat.; $7 pp) in the 250-seat Solomon Victory Theater. If you have time, consider a meal at the on-site restaurant, The American Sector (11am-9pm daily), or an old-fashioned dinner theater experience in the Stage Door Canteen (hours vary).

MAP 2: 945 Magazine St., 504/528-1944, nationalww2museum.org; 9am-5pm daily; $28 adults, $24 seniors, $18 military, students, and children 5-17, children under 5 free

Restaurants

PRICE KEY

$	Entrées less than $15
$$	Entrées $15-30
$$$	Entrées more than $30

CAJUN AND CREOLE

Cochon Butcher $

Situated just around the corner from its well-known and well-respected sibling Cochon Restaurant, the aptly named Cochon Butcher makes some of the city's most delectable sandwiches. Its small but eclectic menu ranges from classics like pastrami and sauerkraut on rye, to local twists like the Cajun pork dog on a pretzel bun, to more exotic fare such as the Moroccan spiced lamb with cucumbers, tzatziki, and chili oil on flatbread. The muffuletta and the Cubano are highly recommended. Given the eatery's proximity to the convention center, it's a popular spot at lunchtime.

MAP 2: 930 Tchoupitoulas St., 504/588-7675, cochonbutcher.com; 10am-10pm Mon.-Thurs., 10am-11pm Fri.-Sat., 10am-4pm Sun.

SEAFOOD

Grand Isle $$

Food options around the convention center and casino are mostly overpriced and not that great. Fortunately, Grand Isle, an unassuming spot tucked between a brewpub and a bowling alley, provides great food in a pleasant atmosphere. It's a restaurant that appeals to tourists, conventioneers, locals, large groups, families (thanks to its great kids' menu), and raw oyster lovers. There's nothing too off the chain here, but that's not a bad thing. You'll see well-executed classics like redfish on the half shell, boiled shrimp, shrimp and grits, and gumbo. There are a few standouts as well, like the smoked fried oysters and the shrimp *caminada* po'boy (with spicy citrus butter, fresh herbs, and slaw). The happy hour (4pm-6pm Mon.-Fri.) is awesome, with 75-cent oysters, a mini shrimp boil for $7, and half-price cocktails, wines by the glass, and draft beer. Get a seat at the marble bar and watch the oyster shucking, or get a table by one of the large windows to watch the world go by.

MAP 2: 575 Convention Center Blvd., 504/520-8530, grandislerestaurant.com; 11am-2pm and 4pm-10pm Mon., 11am-10pm Tues.-Thurs. and Sun., 11am-11pm Fri.-Sat.

Luke $$

This German-French-Creole bistro is well known for its gorgeous raw bar and excellent happy hour (3pm-6pm daily) that boasts 75-cent raw oysters and $1.25 fried oysters. They also have a lot of great snacks and dishes, like pâté of Louisiana rabbit and chicken livers, fried chicken & waffles, and Flammenkuchen (an Alsatian onion, bacon, and cheese tart). There's a nicely priced small seafood platter for those that don't want to go all in on the grand seafood tower, and if you sit at the raw bar, you might get tossed a free oyster or two. The dark wood bar, with its pillars supporting an antique wooden canopy, dominates the main dining room, which also has a pressed-tin ceiling and parquet floors. It can get a little crazy here, due to its location at St. Charles and Poydras, especially during happy hour.

MAP 2: 333 St. Charles Ave.,
504/378-2840. lukeneworleans.com;
7am-11pm daily

Pêche $$

This is the place to be to get an ever-changing selection of fresh-caught fish, oysters, and other seafood. It's got a rustic fish shack theme, although it's pretty upscale. The raw bar is great—the oysters are divine, and the crab claws with pickled chilies are a high point as well. The catfish with pickled greens and chili broth and the spicy ground shrimp and noodles are regulars on the small-plate menu. There are different fish specials every day. My recommendation? Get a whole grilled fish for the table and supplement with sides and small plates. Note that the high ceilings and hard surfaces can result in a significant amount of background noise.

MAP 2: 800 Magazine St.,
504/522-1744, pecherestaurant.com;
11am-10pm Sun.-Thurs.,
11am-11pm Fri.-Sat.

VIETNAMESE
Pho Tau Bay $

Pho Tau Bay is only open during the week, providing worker bees from nearby offices or the neighboring hospital complex with pho, banh mi, spring rolls, *café sua da* (iced Vietnamese coffee), and *da chanh muoi* (salt preserved limeade). The restaurant is owned by a Vietnamese and an American family, which creates an authentic but approachable experience for the diner. Apparently, it's New Orleans celebrity chef Emeril Lagasse's favorite Vietnamese restaurant, which certainly merits some culinary investigation. Two walls of windows let in plenty of natural light, and there's counter seating in addition to the tables available. The space features tasteful dark wood, white marble tabletops, exposed brick, and mid-century modern accents.

MAP 2: 1565 Tulane Ave.,
504/368-9846, photaubayrestaurant.com;
10am-7pm Mon.-Fri.

ECLECTIC
✪ Maypop $$$

Bringing the bounty of the Mississippi and the Mekong Rivers together, along with his skill in pasta-making and French cooking techniques, chef Michael Gulotta has created a unique menu of perfectly prepared plates of bold flavor combinations. The creativity of the dishes is matched only by the impeccable execution. Even though some of the dishes sound off-the-wall, like fried hot chicken in vindaloo curry, they will be delicious, eye-opening, and mind-bending. The cocktail list has a distinctly Southeast Asian vibe, and the non-traditional weekend dim sum, like "The Baodin," a boudin-stuffed *bao* (filled dumpling), or the headcheese and blue crab soup dumplings, are also excellent reasons to stop by. Check out the happy hour with select wine, beer, cocktails, and snacks, all under

$10. The high ceilings and minimalist modern dark wood furnishings create a feeling of casual, simple elegance.

MAP 2: 611 O'Keefe Ave., 504/518-6345, maypoprestaurant.com; 11am-10pm Sun.-Thurs, 11am-11pm Fri.-Sat.

Meril $$

Small plates! So many small plates here at Meril, Emeril Lagasse's newest restaurant in New Orleans. The menu fleshes out flavors from New Orleans, Europe, Latin America, and Southeast Asia in dishes both traditional and creative. Must-tries include the turkey necks, candied pork ribs, and linguine and clams. There are some truly interesting spirit combinations at play on the cocktail menu as well. The space is huge, with clean, modern lines and aqua- and agricultural-themed art on the walls. Be sure to tell your server if it's your birthday—they'll bring out some house-spun cotton candy for you and your dining companions.

MAP 2: 424 Girod St., 504/526-3745, emerilsrestaurants.com/meril; 11:30am-10pm Sun.-Thurs., 11:30am-11pm Fri.-Sat.

Carmo $

Carmo's tropical focus encompasses Southeast Asia, West Africa, the Caribbean, and South America. It has a very strong vegan and vegetarian menu, but also serves many dishes with meat and seafood. Carmo's provides ample seating space (order at the register), a coffee bar, a raw bar, a bar bar, a gallery, and a reading nook. Salads are flavorful and creative, the

the bar at Maypop

the daily specials at Carmo

ceviche list is top-notch, and if you have a hankering for *pão de queijo* (Brazilian cheese bread), this is the place for it. Carmo's version is even gluten-free.

MAP 2: 527 Julia St., 504/875-4132, cafecarmo.com; 9am-10pm Mon.-Sat.

FRENCH

Vyoone's $$$

Vyoone's offers a romantic dining experience. The inside is dark and cozy, with wood floors and brick walls. A corridor of twinkling lights reveals a path to a traditional New Orleans courtyard. Congregate and converse over a glass or bottle of wine and treat yourself to beautifully prepared, traditional French dishes, from escargot to cassoulet. The French onion soup is rumored to be the best in town. It's a great spot for a quiet date—the atmosphere, the food, and the drinks certainly deliver on *la vie amour.*

MAP 2: 412 Girod St., 504/518-6007, vyoone.com; 11am-10pm Tues.-Thurs., 11am-11pm Fri., 10:30am-11pm Sat.

ITALIAN

Gianna $$

This gorgeous, spacious restaurant has a dark wood, marble-topped bar that divides the restaurant into lounge-style seating up front, four-top tables and chairs in the center of the room, and booths to the side. There's also an open kitchen; the wood-burning pizza oven and pasta making station are visible from where you're eating. There are a variety of plate sizes: small antipasti (the *panelle* chickpea fritters with honey are a must-order); small plates (the creamy polenta with lamb sausage gravy will satisfy a need you didn't even know you had); pasta, all fresh and handmade; and the rustic, flavorful entrées, including a rarely seen *tummula,* a layered casserole with rice, chicken, and sausage. The cocktails are creative and fabulous.

MAP 2: 700 Magazine St., 504/399-0816, giannarestaurant.com; 11am-10pm Sun.-Thurs., 11am-11pm Fri.-Sat.

Sofia $$

If you like eating Italian bistro food while looking at photos of Sofia Loren, this is the place for you. The space has a hip, sophisticated air about it (just like its namesake) and the pizzas and pastas are beautifully made. Try the brassica—charred broccoli and brussels sprouts with rosemary-browned-butter vinaigrette, apple-aged provolone, and toasted pumpkin seeds. The risotto is made with aged Carnaroli rice and blue crab. You'll see the wood-fired oven in the corner next to one of the large communal tables. Don't forget about the creative cocktails and stellar Italian wine list.

MAP 2: 516 Julia St., 504/322-3216, sofianola.com; 4pm-10pm Tues.-Thurs., 5pm-11pm Fri.-Sat.

JAPANESE
Tsunami $$

Tsunami takes their sushi seriously. The quality of ingredients and gorgeous plating might make you think you're in Los Angeles, but you're actually tucked in the bottom of a big office building. Besides a long list of rolls and nigiri, Tsunami's specialties elevate it from great to "OMG." Try the smoked salt escolar, or the Sunflower, sashimi slices of tuna in ponzu with two types of roe, and quail egg. There's a great happy hour here, as well (3pm-6pm Mon. and Wed.-Fri., 3pm-10pm Tues.), where you can get fresh nigiri for 99 cents; they also offer several specials for half off.

MAP 2: Pan American Life Center, 601 Poydras St., suite B, 504/608-3474, servingsushi.com; 11am-10pm Mon.-Thurs., 11am-11pm Fri., 4pm-11pm Sat., 5pm-9pm Sun.

LATIN AMERICAN
✪ La Boca $$$

Although this Argentinean steakhouse from Chef Adolfo Garcia offers traditional American-style steakhouse cuts like rib eye, filet, and NY strip, the ones to get are hanger, skirt, flank, and the *bife la boca*, a bottom sirloin flap marinated in lime and garlic. Also necessary for an authentic and delicious experience are the house-made morcilla pork blood sausage, the empanadas, and the crispy grilled sweetbreads. It's pricy, as steakhouses tend to be, but if you have a true love of beef, this spot

will satisfy your soul. The exposed brick and dim lighting of the dining room is punctuated with pops of bright color, and the round bar in the middle of the room is a sight to behold. This is the kind of place where locals and visitors alike come back again and again, either to work their way through the menu or to enjoy the dish they can't get anywhere else.

MAP 2: 870 Tchoupitoulas St., 504/525-8205, labocasteaks. com; 5:30pm-10pm Mon.-Wed., 5:30pm-midnight Thurs.-Sat.

Espíritu $

This Mexican joint calls itself a *mezcaleria,* which means it has a lot of different mezcals and isn't afraid to use them. Mezcal is an agave-based spirit brewed outside the universally recognized tequila regions. The flavors vary significantly from traditional tequila, and Espíritu's cocktail program and mezcal selection are eager to showcase the varieties. Try a spicy-sweet Mezcalrita, made with house-made syrups and fresh ingredients, or a Mexican 75, a refreshing blend of mezcal and sparkling wine. The food is straightforward and authentic, with options that include tacos and *tortas* (sandwiches). Don't miss the street corn, which is served off the cob.

MAP 2: 520 Capdeville St., 504/267-4975, espiritunola. com; 11:30am-10pm Mon.-Thurs., 11:30am-midnight Fri., 4:30pm-midnight Sat.

GASTROPUBS
Copper Vine $$

This spacious and relaxing restaurant serves up great food along with

VEGETARIAN AND VEGAN OPTIONS

New Orleans cuisine, and Southern food in general, has historically been very meat- and seafood-forward. Many vegetarians and vegans who come to town are rightfully concerned that the only things they will be able to consume are side salads and beer. But the city has come a long way in the past decade or so. Local fruits and vegetables are readily available, and chefs enjoy making use of them. Add in the increased attention to global cuisines that are less meat-focused, and there are lots of tasty options in New Orleans these days.

For pure vegan experiences, check out Seed (1330 Prytania St., seedneworleans.com), Breads on Oak (8640 Oak St., 504/324-8271, breadsonoak.com), or Sweet Soulfood (page 244).

For spots that offer meat and fish dishes alongside thoughtful vegetarian and vegan options, head to Green Goddess (page 46), Bearcat Café (2521 Jena St., 504/309-9011, bearcat.cafe), Sneaky Pickle (4017 St. Claude Ave., 504/218-5651, yousneakypickle.com), Carmo (page 76), or Trilly Cheesesteaks (4413 Banks St., 504/784-8169, trillycheesesteaks.com), which makes a vegan version of every sandwich it offers.

There's also a growing number of Middle Eastern restaurants, which rely heavily on vegan and vegetable-based specialties such as hummus, falafel, and baba ghanoush. A few high-end options are Saba (page 171) and Shaya (4213 Magazine St., 504/891-4213, shayarestaurant.com). Casual spots include Cleo's French Quarter (page 48), Mona's (multiple locations; monascafeanddeli.com), Tal's (4800 Magazine St., 504/267-7357, ordertalsonline.com), Kebab (page 108), and 1000 Figs (page 245).

One last tip: If you go to a restaurant (especially if it's on the fancy side), just tell them your dietary restriction and 9 times out of 10, the chef may just whip up something special for you if there's nothing on the menu that qualifies.

30 taps of wine and an impressive collection of bottles. The flatbreads and crab-topped deviled eggs are solid choices, along with Chef Mike Brewer's chicken and boudin gumbo and the pork belly with cornbread pudding. Copper Vine has one of the best outdoor spaces in the CBD. The enclosed downstairs patio feels like an oasis, and the upstairs balcony is a great vantage point to overlook the heart of the city. Check out the weekday happy hour (3:30pm-5:30pm Mon.-Fri.) for $5 glasses of house wine and snacks starting at $5, including duck fat fries with garlic aioli.
MAP 2: 1001 Poydras St., 504/208-9535, coppervinewine.com; 11am-10pm Mon.-Thurs., 11am-11pm Fri., 10:30am-11pm Sat., 10:30am-10pm Sun.

DINERS
Commerce Restaurant $
A breakfast diner until 11am, with cafeteria-style lunch from 11am to 2:30pm, Commerce is the type of place that's easy to walk by without noticing. This is where the employees call everyone "my baby" and regulars swear by their roast beef po'boy, fried shrimp po'boy, and muffuletta. For breakfast, have one of their homemade biscuits with whatever you order, or just get the signature Commerce Breakfast Biscuit, topped with a spicy, cheesy sausage gravy and over-easy eggs. The wood-paneled interior seems stuck in the '50s, especially with the antique cash register, but don't worry, they take credit cards.

MAP 2: 300 Camp St., 504/561-9239, commercerest.com; 7am-2:30pm Mon.-Fri.

FOOD HALLS
Auction House Market $
This food hall has a large, square bar in the center, surrounded by plenty of seating and an international hodgepodge of great food stalls skirting the building. Those looking for authentic Indian cuisine will find it here, at Tava Indian Streetfood. There are empanadas at Empanola, gluten-free and vegan sweet treats from Mac & Moon, and one of the city's most consistent raw bars, Elysian Seafood, for a seafood tower or just a half dozen oysters on the half shell. It's easy to nibble here and there, so try a little something from as many stalls as you can.
MAP 2: 801 Magazine St., 504/372-4321, auctionhousemarket. com; 7am-10pm Sun.-Thurs., 7am-11pm Fri.-Sat.

Pythian Market $
Originally built in 1908 by the Colored Knights of the Pythias, this former civil rights and community center has been restored and repurposed as a food hall with a diverse stable of vendors, including 14 Parishes (Caribbean), Eat Well (Vietnamese), Little Fig (Middle Eastern), and La Cocinita (Latin American). It's got a bright central bar and eating area in the front, anchored by Bar 1908, a great spot to grab a frozen drink or a beer. There are also options for vegetarian, vegan, and gluten-free eaters. The Pythian also has a rotating roster of pop-up vendors that brings goodies like barbecue, baked goods,

and donuts around every once in a while.
MAP 2: 234 Loyola Ave., 504/481-9599, pythianmarket.com; 8am-9pm Sun.-Thurs., 8am-10pm Fri.-Sat.

CAFÉS AND LIGHT BITES
Aglio $
This Italian deli/casual restaurant/ bar is easy to overlook, especially since it's surrounded by other worthy quick-service choices. But duck in, and your curiosity will be well rewarded. Try the T.A.S.T.E., a sandwich with fried turkey, avocado, sprouts, tomato, and a fried egg on local ciabatta, or the Godfather, a gussied-up meatball sub. Salads are huge and flavorful, and there are a variety of proteins to top them, like pork shoulder, shrimp and lobster, or fried portobello mushrooms. The bar is well stocked with local beer on tap and a creative cocktail list. Their happy hour (3pm-6pm daily) includes snacks for under $10.
MAP 2: 611 O'Keefe Ave., suite C-8, 504/827-1090, aglionola.com; 11am-9pm Mon.-Sat.

NOCHI Café by Gracious $
The NOCHI Café differs from the other locations of Gracious Bakery (in Mid City, the Garden District, and Uptown) in that it combines its pastries and breads with a chef-focused menu, located on the ground floor of one of the city's cooking schools, the New Orleans Culinary and Hospitality Institute (NOCHI). There are a lot of popular items from the other locations (including tarragon chicken salad, the meatloaf sandwich, quiches, cakes, and pies), as well as chef Michael

Doyle's elevated plates like grilled Gulf fish salad, a short rib "debris" sandwich, and seared butternut squash over lentils. The industrial warehouse vibe of the café is offset by the warm employees.

MAP 2: 725 Howard Ave., suite 102, 504/635-0033, nochi.org/cafe; 7am-7pm Mon.-Fri., 7:30am-4pm Sat.

Two Chicks Café $

This cozy, cheerful café is a good place to sneak in some healthy choices for breakfast or lunch. They've got a nice fresh-squeezed juice and smoothie list (try the Ginger Sun, with fresh squeezed grapefruit, apple, and ginger) and they serve breakfast all day, from omelets, Benedicts, and fried egg sandwiches to sweet and savory buckwheat crepes. After 11am, they also have a good selection of sandwiches, like the Thai shrimp po'boy, and salads like quinoa or a well-loaded mixed greens salad. The decor is colorful and homey, with painted chairs and art on the walls. You'll see tourists here at breakfast, businesspeople at lunch, and groups of friends catching up at any time.

MAP 2: 920 Gravier St., 504/218-7400, twochickscafe.com; 7am-3pm Wed.-Mon.

COFFEE AND DESSERTS

Bittersweet Confections $

This is the perfect spot to jump in and grab a drink or a sweet pick-me-up. The handmade macarons and chocolate truffles are always a hit, and the baked goods (both sweet and savory) also please the palate. There's a small but satisfying breakfast and lunch menu, and the old-timey ice cream parlor atmosphere is perfect for chilling out and relaxing for a while. They serve beer, wine, and booze, too. During Carnival season, check out their to-die-for chocolate king cake.

MAP 2: 725 Magazine St., 504/523-2626, bittersweetconfections. com; 7am-5:30pm Mon.-Fri., 7am-4pm Sat., 7:30am-2pm Sun.

Drip Affogato Bar $

There isn't much that can't be improved with the addition of ice cream, and coffee is no different. The Italians have known this forever, because they created the *affogato*—espresso poured over gelato for a cold-hot, sweet-bitter treat. At Drip Affogato, there are several options of both ice cream and hot beverages to select from, resulting in options like the Matcha, Matcha, which pairs matcha ice cream with matcha tea, or the Cookie Monster, which tops mint chocolate chip ice cream and cookie crumbles with a hot chocolate pour-over. The best bet is the affogato flight, which provides four different combinations.

MAP 2: 703 Carondelet St., 504/313-1611, dripaffogatobar.com; 10am-10pm daily

✪ Mammoth Espresso $

Keep your eyes peeled for this unassuming coffee shop, because the quality of coffee at Mammoth, regardless of how it's prepared, is sublime. Get a single source pour-over (their pour-over equipment is really cool), an expertly pulled espresso drink, or a signature beverage like an espresso tonic, a cardamom latte, or the "Sweet Little Thing," a double shot of espresso

THE BEAN SCENE

Cafe au lait and coffee with chicory are drinks that only scratch the surface of the history of coffee in New Orleans. As a thriving port, New Orleans once received and distributed more coffee than anywhere else in the world. The coffee break was invented here: It came from a very New Orleans philosophy of stepping away from work and socializing with friends while drinking a well brewed cup of coffee.

New Orleans today is home to a growing number of independent, small-batch roasters, like French Truck (multiple locations, frenchtruckcoffee.com), Mojo Coffee House (page 144), Hey! Café (4332 Magazine St., no phone, heycafe.biz), and Congregation (240 Pelican Ave., 504/265-0194, congregationcoffee.com; 7am-5pm daily).

The third-wave coffee trend has rolled through town, too. Many shops create a list of curated espresso drinks by carefully sourcing their beans, educating their staff and consumers, and adding new flavor-forward processes like the pour-over, *oji* drip, and cupping. Some of the best spots in town include Mammoth Espresso (page 81), HiVolt (1829 Sophie Wright Pl., 504/324-8818, hivoltcoffee.com), Coffee Science (page 205), and Arrow Cafe (page 49). CLOSED

combined with vanilla, half and half, and Bitterman's Burlesque bitters, served over ice. They also bake all their sweet treats and snacks on-site every morning, providing the perfect accompaniment for whatever coffee drink you decide on.

MAP 2: 821 Baronne St., 504/475-4344, mammothespresso.com; 7am-5pm Mon.-Fri., 7am-3pm Sat.-Sun.

tM Breads & Pastries $

The minimalist design of this bakery-boulangerie allows the edible works of art to take center stage. The front case is crammed with perfectly browned, flaky croissants, scones with bright pops of fruit, tantalizing cinnamon buns, and the intriguingly named Stuffed Strudel Parcels, filled with various fruits. The freshly baked baguettes, loaves of ciabatta, and round boules are arrayed behind the front counter. Buy a loaf to take with you or have them make you a sandwich on the bread that calls your name. There's a small but decent coffee list; the cold brew is especially good.

MAP 2: 335 Baronne St., 504/302-7234, tmbreadsandpastries.com; 7am-4pm Mon.-Sat., 7am-2pm Sun.

Mammoth Espresso

Sazerac Bar

Nightlife

LIVE MUSIC
The Howlin' Wolf

For the most part, you'll catch top blues and funk acts at the Howlin' Wolf, a cavernous nightclub in the Arts District, not far from the convention center. This is indeed one of the Big Easy's largest and most prominent live music venues, which has been known to host rock, alternative, pop, and R&B bands, too. Over the years, some of the more famous performers have included Alison Krauss, Harry Connick Jr., and the Foo Fighters.

MAP 2: 907 S. Peters St., 504/522-9653, howlin-wolf.com; 5pm-2am daily; cover varies

COCKTAIL BARS
Sazerac Bar

In this hushed, art deco-style, dark-wood-paneled spot, it's easy to envision the Southern gentlemen who once patronized the space. One such person was Huey P. Long, the famously corrupt Louisiana politician. The Sazerac Bar was once known as "Huey's Office," as this is where the governor held many of his meetings. The cocktails are pricey, but it's worth it to sit at the enormous gleaming African walnut wood bar surrounded by murals created by 1930s artist Paul Ninas and drink a Sazerac.

MAP 2: Roosevelt Hotel, 130 Roosevelt Way, 504/648-1200, therooseveltneworleans.com; 11am-2am daily

BEST HAPPY HOURS

Eating and drinking in New Orleans is practically a full-time commitment, so when we can make our dollar stretch, that's something to celebrate! (Ideally with half-priced drinks.)

There are so many happy hour spots in the city that there's no way to list them all here. Instead, I've listed my favorites at both restaurants and bars, along with a handful of places that aren't otherwise mentioned in this guide. To get the live scoop on what's cheap where, download the Drinkers Edition app (available on Android and iPhone).

MY FAVORITE RESTAURANT HAPPY HOURS

- 1000 Figs (page 245)
- Araña Taqueria and Cantina (page 141)
- Avo (page 171)
- Blue Oak BBQ (page 201)
- Copper Vine (page 78)
- Grand Isle (page 74)
- Gris-Gris (page 137)
- Luke (page 74)
- Lula Restaurant-Distillery (page 141)
- Maypop (page 75)
- Tsunami (page 78)

MY FAVORITE BAR HAPPY HOURS

- Bakery Bar (page 145)
- Cure (page 178)
- Oak (page 180)

✪ Victory

This is one of the first modern New Orleans cocktail bars offering exciting, creative, and delicious cocktails, a swanky (but not off-puttingly so) atmosphere, and a free sample of the cocktail du jour. Step into the richly colored, part-Arabian Nights, part-Bollywood atmosphere, sip a cocktail, and try some of the addictive truffle popcorn. It's great for an after-work meet-up, a pre-dinner or pre-theater drink, or a romantic date. Owner Daniel Victory also offers one-day mixology classes through his program New Orleans Drink Lab, for fun hands-on opportunities to meet new people and learn new things.

MAP 2: 339 Baronne St., 504/522-8664, victorynola.com; 4:30pm-midnight Sun.-Thurs., 4:30pm-2am Fri.-Sat.

BARS AND LOUNGES
Rusty Nail

The Rusty Nail is a neighborhood bar that's wedged between neighborhoods. On the very edge of the Warehouse District, in the shadow of the Crescent City Connection, it's not a place you'll easily stumble upon, but an intentional visit is a great time. They've got an excellent international whiskey selection and a nice variety of classic and creative cocktails, including six different kinds of Mules. The indoor and outdoor spaces

OTHER SPOTS WITH GREAT HAPPY HOURS

The listings for these spots don't have much information about their happy hours, so I've listed out the most pertinent details here.

- Espíritu (page 78): 3pm-6pm Mon.-Fri.; $6 hand shaken margaritas and $2 tacos
- Meril (page 76): 4pm-6pm daily; $5 glasses of wine and $5 flatbreads
- Rusty Nail (page 84): 4pm-7pm Mon.-Wed., 2pm-7pm Fri.; half off bottles of wine, $3 Abita beers, $6 mules, $5 Disco Lemonade and well drinks, along with daily specials
- SoBou (page 45): 3pm-6pm daily; great selection of food and booze ranging $3-6
- Toups South (page 218): 3pm-6pm Mon.-Sat., bar area only; ever-changing selection of signature cocktails for $6, wine by the glass (2-for-1 on Wed.), and small plates for $4-5

Finally, here are a few great happy hours at spots that aren't listed in this guide:

- Cane & Table (1113 Decatur St., 504/581-1112, caneandtablenola.com; happy hour 3pm-6pm Mon.-Fri.): Classic cocktails and food specials.
- Compere Lapin (535 Tchoupitoulas St., 504/599-2119, comperelapin.com; happy hour 3pm-6pm Mon.-Fri.): Classic cocktails for $6 and a bunch of snacks for $5 each.
- Half Shell on the Bayou (2517 Bayou Rd., 504/558-4403, halfshellonthebayou. business.site, happy hour 4pm-6pm Wed.-Thurs.): The happy hour window is limited, but if you catch it, it's great. Order a dozen oysters and get a half dozen free.
- Sake Cafe (2830 Magazine St., 504/894-0033, sakecafeonmagazine.com; happy hour 3pm-6pm daily): Sushi and sashimi for $3.50 per order, hot snacks like edamame and *gyoza* (dumplings) for $3-5, cocktails for $4, and sake, wine, and beer for $2.50-4.50.

are great. This is a local spot for watching football. On days that the Saints play at home, they open at 9am.

MAP 2: 1100 Constance St., 504/525-5515, rustynailnola.com; 4pm-1am Mon.-Thurs., 2pm-3am Fri., 11am-3am Sat., noon-1am Sun.

Arts and Culture

GALLERIES

Ariodante Contemporary Crafts

If you've ever felt that art galleries are too fancy, this is the perfect spot. Ariodante works with artists and crafters to showcase a variety of artwork, like traditional wall hangings, sculpture, jewelry, and even candles from talented emerging artists. The mediums used are delightfully diverse—metal, canvas, wood, clay, and glass, to name a few—and the gallery owners encourage patrons to take photos (which is forbidden at many other galleries) to enjoy and share. Pro tip: Check out the bathroom, it will likely be the best shopping you do near indoor plumbing.

MAP 2: 535 Julia St., 504/524-3233, ariodantegallery.com; 9:30am-4pm Mon.-Sat., 9:30am-1:30pm Sun.

Beata Sasik Gallery

Step inside the Sasik Gallery and prepare to lose yourself in a sea of bright colors, bold strokes, and passion that seeps out of every palette-knife-created oil painting you see. Beata Sasik is a long-time painter, originally from Poland, who has recently ventured into jewelry creation with the same intensity that she applies to her paintings. She posts behind-the-scenes videos on her Instagram account (@sasikgallery), as well.

MAP 2: 541 Julia St., 504/309-4249, sasikart.com; 10am-5pm Mon.-Sat., by appointment Sun.

Mac-Gryder Gallery

The sweeping white walls that show off the framed art inside may seem intimidating, but the friendly owners and the converted warehouse ambience will have you relaxing and enjoying the works of the modern masters like Françoise Gilot, Roland Golden, and Dean Mitchell on display. Owners Jill McGaughey and Garlyn Gryder are happy to discuss the work within their four walls, the state of modern art in general, and the history of the Arts District.

MAP 2: 615 Julia St., 504/322-2555, macgrydergallery.com; 10am-6pm Mon.-Sat. and by appointment

✪ New Orleans Glassworks & Printmaking Studio

In this massive space, you can observe highly skilled glassblowing, torch-working, printmaking, metalworking, and stained-glass artisans in action. Besides browsing their wares, you can also learn how to create your own glasswork, jewelry, and paper arts by taking one

Ariodante Contemporary Crafts

of the studio's exceptional classes, which range from two-hour courses on paper marbling to six-week workshops about Venetian glassblowing. MAP 2: 727 Magazine St., 504/529-7279, neworleansglassworks. com; 10am-5pm Mon.-Sat.

New Orleans Glassworks & Printmaking Studio

✪ Stella Jones Gallery

The Stella Jones Gallery has been promoting Black art and artists since its opening in 1996. It displays mixed and traditional media pieces that speak to local Black history, such as exhibits dedicated to Mahalia Jackson, the "Queen of Gospel Music," and the city's now-razed Calliope public housing development. The gallery also shows the work of Black artists around the country. It's well worth a stop, especially considering the gallery is only steps away from Canal Street and St. Charles Avenue. The direct entrance is on Common Street, inside the Place St. Charles building.

MAP 2: 201 St. Charles Ave., 504/568-9050, stellajonesgallery.com; 10am-5pm Tues.-Sat., by appointment Sun.

MUSEUMS

American Italian Museum

Inside the American Italian Cultural Center, you'll find the American Italian Museum, which, via family histories, photographs, and other memorabilia, chronicles the history and cultural influence of American Italians in southeastern Louisiana. Visitors who often associate New Orleans with French, Spanish, and Caribbean cultures may find the Italian contributions to the city's cuisine, music, festivals, and demographics especially surprising. The center also supports a comprehensive research library, containing numerous oral histories, immigration records, books, and photographs, located in the East Bank Regional Library (4747 W. Napoleon Ave., Metairie).

MAP 2: 537 S. Peters St., 504/522-7294, americanitalianmuseum.com; 10am-4pm Tues.-Fri.; $8 adults, $5 seniors and students, children under 11 free

✪ Ogden Museum of Southern Art

This museum contains one of the country's largest collections of artwork related to the American South. The impressive complex comprises the contemporary, five-story Stephen Goldring Hall, the restored Howard Memorial Library, and the Clementine Hunter Education Wing, named for the famous Louisiana folk artist who grew up on a cotton plantation in Cloutierville and produced about 4,000 works during her storied career. The art here includes all mediums and spans the 18th to 21st centuries, representing artists from 15 Southern states as well as Washington DC. On Thursday evenings, the museum reopens for "Ogden After Hours," presenting live music 6pm-8pm. Docent-led tours are available at 2pm on the first and third Saturdays of each month. Louisiana residents are entitled to free admission to the museum every Thursday.

MAP 2: 925 Camp St., 504/539-9650, ogdenmuseum.org; 10am-5pm Wed.-Mon., 10am-5pm Thurs.; $13.50 adults, $11 seniors, students, teachers, and military, $6.75 children 5-17, children under 5 free

CULTURAL CENTERS
Contemporary Arts Center

The Contemporary Arts Center (CAC) is a multipurpose venue that houses an innovative art gallery as well as performing arts spaces. In addition to staging lectures, performances, and concerts, the CAC often serves as a main location for the New Orleans Film Festival and other annual events. Stop by the on-site café (10am-5pm Mon.-Fri., 11am-5pm Sat.-Sun.) for refreshments. Louisiana residents can enjoy the gallery for free on Sundays.

MAP 2: 900 Camp St., 504/528-3800 or 504/528-3805, cacno.org; art gallery 11am-5pm Wed.-Mon.; event hours vary; $10 adults, $8 seniors and students, children under 18 free; ticket prices vary for shows and events

PERFORMING ARTS
Fillmore New Orleans

Opened in 2019, the Fillmore New Orleans is a music venue that can support crowds too big for House of Blues but in a more intimate setting than the Superdome—think Lizzo, Duran Duran, Garbage, or the Avett Brothers. The Fillmore is on the second floor of Harrah's Casino, and combines some of the offbeat touches of the original Fillmore in San Francisco, with giant chandeliers studding the space, but has a very New Orleans sensibility as well, with tin ceiling tiles, wrought iron, and a mural of Louis Armstrong in the lobby. It's a standing theater, meaning there's space to dance, and there's a kicking VIP lounge. Music lovers will appreciate the pristine sound engineering, and booze lovers will appreciate the multiple bars (though the prices are rather high). There's a decent food menu available, too.

MAP 2: 6 Canal St., 504/881-1555, fillmorenola.com; hours and ticket prices vary

The Orpheum

This gorgeously restored beaux-arts style theater is the home of the

Contemporary Arts Center

Louisiana Philharmonic Orchestra (504/523-6530, lpomusic.com) as well as the site for other concerts and shows. You can see anything from RuPaul's Drag Race: Werq the World Tour, to the orchestra's performance of Beethoven's Symphony No. 7, to Death Cab for Cutie, to a performance of *Cinderella* by the New Orleans Ballet Theater.

Architecture nerds might like to know that the terra-cotta ceiling and plasterwork in the lobby were restored carefully by hand, matching the color scheme to its heyday in 1921.

MAP 2: 129 Roosevelt Way, 504/274-4870, orpheumnola.com; box office 10am-4pm Wed., hours and ticket prices vary

Recreation

PARKS AND PLAZAS

✪ Lafayette Square

South of Poydras Street lies the attractive Lafayette Square, which was laid out in the late 18th century. Bound by St. Charles Avenue, Camp Street, and North and South Maestri Places, it is named in honor of the Marquis de Lafayette, who visited the city in 1825. With its ample park-bench seating, the shaded, landscaped park—one of the CBD's few patches of greenery—is a pleasant place to relax, read a newspaper, or listen to live music. In fact, you can catch free concerts by some of the city's top bands and musicians every Wednesday at 5pm, from late March to mid-June. Known as the YLC Wednesday at the Square (504/585-1500, wednesdayat-thesquare.com), this 12-week concert series has featured the likes of Tab Benoit, Marcia Ball, and The Iguanas. Local bars and restaurants sell food and drinks to benefit the Young Leadership Council.

MAP 2: St. Charles Ave. and Lafayette St., lafayette-square.org; 24 hours daily

Piazza d'Italia

Not far from the American Italian Cultural Center, you'll encounter the picturesque Piazza d'Italia, which is dedicated to the city's Italian American community and its indelible influence on New Orleans. Designed in 1978 by the renowned postmodernist architect Charles Moore, the plaza serves as a gathering place for residents, a relaxing spot for a lunch break, and the site of St. Joseph's Day celebrations. The white marble statuary and fountain create a serene place to relax.

MAP 2: Lafayette St. and Commerce St.; 24 hours daily

Spanish Plaza

Between the Audubon Aquarium of the Americas and The Outlet Collection at Riverwalk, this pleasant square is an ideal spot to gaze at the bustling Mississippi. The square was rededicated by Spain in 1976 to commemorate its influence on the Crescent City's history and to serve as an ongoing promise of fraternity.

As a symbolic reminder, the seals of Spanish provinces encircle the central fountain. Spanish Plaza is a common gathering place for residents and tourists alike, as well as the site of food festivals and free public concerts throughout the year.

MAP 2: 1 Poydras St.; 24 hours daily

SPECTATOR SPORTS
New Orleans Pelicans

The New Orleans basketball team, originally knowns as the Hornets, were renamed the Pelicans in 2013 and have amassed a pretty decent following in New Orleans, considering that football has claimed the hearts and souls of the folks living here. They've advanced to the playoffs seven times in the team's history. In their home at the Smoothie King Center (504/587-3822, smoothiekingcenter.com), an arena

next door to the Superdome, the team is known in part for its mascots: When regular mascot Pierre the Pelican was debuted, he frightened fans so much the team had to immediately redesign the costume. During Carnival season, the creepiest mascot in the entire league, the King Cake Baby, is on the court freaking folks out. Pelicans games are much more relaxed than Saints games: The team is good enough that people show up to support them, but without the crazy obsessive nail-biting going on.

MAP 2: Smoothie King Center, 1501 Dave Dixon Dr., 504/587-3663, nba.com/pelicans; Oct.-May; tickets $10-150

✪ New Orleans Saints

Y'all, if you don't know within an hour of hitting New Orleans, no matter what time of year it is, how

Piazza d'Italia

BEST BARS FOR SAINTS FANS

Saints games are always sold out, thanks to fanatic season ticket holders. Although it's possible to grab a ticket through a friend or ticket reseller service, it's always fun to find a spot to hang out with like-minded Who Dats (Saints fans) and watch the game. (Beer will be a lot cheaper than at the Dome, too.)

Uptown, check out Rusty Nail (page 84), Cooter Brown's (page 179), and Tracey's (2604 Magazine St., 504/897-5413, traceysnola.com).

In Mid-City, your best bets are Mid City Yacht Club (440 S. St. Patrick St., 504/483-2517, midcityyachtclub.com), which is not an actual yacht club, or the Bayou Beer Garden (326 N. Jefferson Davis Pkwy., 504/302-9357, bayoubeergarden.com) which also has an adjoining wine garden.

Downtown, check out the combination sports shrine, bar, and restaurant Manning's (519 Fulton St. 504/593-8118) in Fulton Place behind Harrah's Casino. For a neighborhood/dive bar experience, head to Markey's Bar (page 115) and J&J's Sports Lounge (page 114) in the Bywater.

important the Saints NFL football team is to the city's soul, then you're not paying attention. The Saints play in the Mercedes-Benz Superdome (504/587-3822 or 800/756-7074, superdome.com), the largest domed stadium in the world, holding more than 76,000 fans. Game days are gleefully celebrated, with longtime season ticket owners tailgating in a nearby parking lot and rubbing elbows with folks lucky enough to get a ticket, even if they support the other team. (Except Atlanta. Don't mention the Atlanta Falcons.) Games have been sold out on a season-ticket basis since the team's triumphant return to New Orleans in 2006, but if you poke around reseller sites or have a season-ticket-holding friend, you might be able to experience the roar of the crowd and the loud as hell defense noisemaking by Saints fans, the best fans in the league.

MAP 2: Mercedes-Benz Superdome, 1500 Sugar Bowl Dr., 504/558-6260, neworleanssaints.com; Sept.-Jan.; tickets $375-400

BOWLING
Fulton Alley

With 12 bowling lanes, foosball tables, and cornhole in the enclosed courtyard, Fulton Alley is great for games, but it manages to offer all these things in a sleek, sophisticated space that has plenty of room for adult beverages, great food, and social gatherings. Try a taco, flatbread, or slider. They also have an extended menu of classic and craft cocktails to enhance your gaming experience.

MAP 2: 600 Fulton St., 504/208-5569, fultonalley.com; 4pm-11pm Mon.-Thurs., 4pm-1am Fri., 11am-1am Sat., 11am-11pm Sun.

Shops

SPECIALTY FOOD AND DRINK

Keife & Co.

For your inner spirits nerd, Keife & Co. offers not only an extensive collection of wine, liquors, liqueurs, fortified wine, and bitters, but also an expert guide to get you what you need. Or what you really want, which could also be cheese, charcuterie, and other specialty foods. Service is terrific, but sometimes you'll have to wait as employees help other customers. Luckily, there are lots of interesting items to browse in the meantime.

MAP 2: 801 Howard Ave., 504/523-7272, keifeandco.com; 10am-8pm Tues.-Sat.

BOOKS AND MUSIC

Crescent City Books

This bookshop, right off Canal Street, is easy to overlook from outside, and is surprisingly large on the inside. Aside from a chill cat named Isabelle (she has her own seat where she can usually be found lounging), Crescent City Books is home to new and used titles in a wide range of subjects. There are several antique and vintage books on display, and there's an unusually far-reaching antique map print selection to peruse. It's easy to lose a couple hours in here.

MAP 2: 124 Baronne St., 504/524-4997, crescentcitybooks.com; 10am-7pm Mon.-Sat., noon-6pm Sun.

CLOTHING AND SHOES

Farrah Boutique

This fun, chic shop for women's fashion offers clothes for all sizes, plus shoes, jewelry, and seasonal accessories. The look is upscale, but casual. The space itself is large and easy to navigate, with an attentive and friendly staff on hand to assist. It's definitely worth a look even if you're not usually into perusing boutiques.

MAP 2: 301 Magazine St. #106, 504/372-5450, farrahboutique.net; 10:30am-5pm Tues.-Sat.

Meyer the Hatter

Established by Sam H. Meyer in 1894 as Meyer's Hat Box, this family-run business has since moved into a much bigger space. It now boasts the South's largest collection of headwear, from stylish Stetsons and satin top hats to jazz band caps and black-and-gold Saints visors. Thankfully the staff are proactive in helping you find the right choice, since the store is jammed floor to ceiling with hats, hats, and more hats.

MAP 2: 120 St. Charles Ave., 504/525-1048 or 800/882-4287, meyerthehatter.com; 10am-5:45pm Mon.-Sat.

Rubensteins

If you need a men's jacket for your dinner at Commander's Palace, consider Rubensteins, a classic, family-owned outfitter carrying such exclusive lines as Hugo Boss, Ralph Lauren, and Brioni. Situated in the CBD since 1924, this well-respected emporium is considered one of the finest men's specialty stores in the country, featuring suits, sweaters, jeans, and fine footwear. Special services include complimentary valet parking, expert alterations, and personal shoppers.

MAP 2:102 St. Charles Ave.,
504/581-6666,
rubensteinsneworleans.com;
10am-5:45pm Mon.-Thurs.,
10am-6pm Fri.-Sat.

The Clock & Watch Shop

JEWELRY AND ACCESSORIES
✪ The Clock & Watch Shop

Remember when people used watches and clocks instead of cell phones to tell the time? If you'd like to get back to that (or, if you never left), this is the place for you, with hundreds of luxury watches, including an amazing selection of vintage pocket watches and a wall full of cuckoo clocks. This is also the perfect place to get your timepiece repaired. The shop has been in this location since 1958 and is a family business with two generations of master watch and clock makers.

MAP 2: 824 Gravier St., 504/525-3961,
theclockwatchshop.com;
9am-5pm Mon.-Fri., 10am-2pm Sat.

Faubourg Marigny and the Bywater

Map 3

To the east of the French Quarter, Faubourg Marigny and the Bywater offer a **funky, bohemian vibe** with lots of **corner bars** and **hip restaurants.** (Some might say too hip.) Brightly colored **Creole cottages** line the streets between St. Claude Avenue and the river.

The Faubourg Marigny (the Marigny for short) was New Orleans's first suburb. The Bywater is "down river" (east) of the Marigny. As the neighborhood closest to the French Quarter, the Marigny gentrified more rapidly than the Bywater. It has a more established **music scene** on **Frenchmen Street** and **St. Claude Avenue** and houses fewer dive bars.

TOP RESTAURANTS

- Best Neighborhood Po'boy Shop: **Frady's One Stop Food Store** (page 106)
- Best NY-Style Pizza: **Pizza Delicious** (page 107)
- Best On-the-Go Breakfast: **Bywater Bakery** (page 110)

TOP NIGHTLIFE

- Best Outdoor Music: **Bacchanal Fine Wine & Spirits** (page 112)
- Best Karaoke: **Kajun's Pub** (page 115)
- Best Use of the Go-Cup: **Brieux Carré Brewing Co.** (page 116)

TOP ARTS AND CULTURE

- Most Intense Gallery Experience: **Studio Be** (page 118)

TOP RECREATION

- Best Food or Drink on Wheels: **Confederacy of Cruisers** (page 119)

TOP SHOPS

- Best 24-Hour Shopping: **Mardi Gras Zone** (page 122)

GETTING THERE AND AROUND

- Streetcar lines: Rampart-St. Claude (49)
- Major bus routes: 5, 55, 84, 88

I-10

N PRIEUR ST

FAUGER ST

TOURO ST

ELYSIAN FIELDS AVE
ELYSIAN FIELDS AVE

N JOHNSON ST

ST ROCH AVE

ST ROCH AVE

N PRIEUR ST

PAINTERS ST

N ROMAN ST

N DERBIGNY ST

MARIGNY ST

MANDEVILLE ST

MUSIC ST

N CLAIBORNE AVE
N CLAIBORNE AVE

N ROBERTSON ST

N ROBERTSON ST

ARTS ST

FRANKLIN AVE
FRANKLIN AVE

SEE MAP 6

N ROBERTSON ST

N VILLERE ST

N VILLERE ST

ST ROCH AVE

FRENCHMEN ST

SPAIN ST

URQUHART ST

URQUHART ST

MARIGNY ST

MARAIS ST

FAUGER ST

MARAIS ST

5

8

11

6

9 10

13

1

ST. CLAUDE AVE

3

4

7

12

2

N RAMPART ST

25

26

SPAIN ST

28

ST ROCH AVE

MUSIC ST

FRENCHMEN ST

ELYSIAN FIELDS AVE
ELYSIAN FIELDS AVE

29

24

BURGUNDY ST

27

**FAUBOURG
MARIGNY**

MANDEVILLE ST

FRANKLIN AVE

PORT ST

23

DAUPHINE ST

*Washington
Square
Park*

MARIGNY ST

41

40

ROYAL ST

KERLEREC ST

36

37

ESPLANADE AVE

30

34

32 33

35

38

ARCHITECT
ALY

31

39

SPAIN ST

54

BOURBON ST

BARRACKS ST

52

DECATUR ST

53

PORT ST

ST FERDINAND ST

DECATUR ST

51

CHARTRES ST

DECATUR ST

N PETERS ST

**FRENCH
QUARTER**

*The Old
U.S. Mint*

**French
Market**

*Mandeville Street
Wharf*

*Esplanade Avenue
Wharf*

*Gov. Nicholls Street
Wharf*

Mississippi River

SEE MAP 1

Ursulines

Dumaine

RESTAURANTS

7	Arabella Casa di Pasta	45	Frady's One Stop Food Store	
8	Kebab	47	Bywater Bakery	
9	Shank Charcuterie	50	Jack Dempsey's Restaurant	
11	St. Roch Market	53	Paladar 511	
13	Morrow's	54	Bao & Noodle	
14	Poke-Chan	55	Bywater American Bistro	
15	N7	57	The Country Club	
18	Red's Chinese	60	Bratz Y'all	
22	Sólo Espresso	61	Pizza Delicious	
39	New Orleans Cake Café & Bakery			
43	Capulet			

NIGHTLIFE

1	Sidney's Saloon	32	D.B.A.
5	Hi-Ho Lounge	33	The Spotted Cat Music Club
16	Junction	48	J&J's Sports Lounge
17	The Domino	49	Vaughan's Lounge
19	Saint-Germain	52	Brieux Carré Brewing Co.
20	Saturn Bar	58	Markey's Bar
23	Buffa's	63	Parleaux Beer Lab
26	The Phoenix Bar	64	Bacchanal Fine Wine & Spirits
29	Marie's Bar and Kitchen		
31	Three Muses		

ARTS AND CULTURE

3	The AllWays Lounge & Theater	41	Marigny Opera House
12	Cafe Istanbul	42	Studio Be
21	New Orleans Art Center	56	Dr. Bob's Folk Art

RECREATION

5	Crescent City Cat Club	35	Alex's Bikes
34	Confederacy of Cruisers	62	Crescent Park

SHOPS

2	Second Vine Wine	40	Mardi Gras Zone
10	Island of Salvation Botanica	44	Bargain Center
25	Loretta's Authentic Pralines	46	Anchor & Arrow Dry Goods Co.
36	Crescent City Conjure	51	Louisiana Music Factory
		59	Euclid Records

HOTELS

24	Madame Isabelle's House in New Orleans	30	Royal Street Inn and R Bar
27	Hotel Peter and Paul	37	Royal Street Courtyard
28	Auld Sweet Olive Bed & Breakfast	38	B&W Courtyards

N CLAIBORNE AVE

DESIRE ST

N ROBERTSON ST

BARTHOLOMEW ST

St. Vincent de Paul Cemetery

N VILLERE ST

ALVAR ST

PRESS ST

4

URQUHART ST

15

16

MARAIS ST

To 22

18   20

17

MARTINIQUE ALY

19

ST. CLAUDE AVE
ST. CLAUDE AVE

N RAMPART ST

21

MAZANT ST

FRANCE ST

MONTEGUT ST

ROSALIE ALY

BURGUNDY ST

LOUISA ST

PIETY ST

43

DAUPHINE ST

BYWATER

2

44   45

N RAMPART ST

CLOUET ST

58

56   57

61

ROYAL ST

DESIRE ST

GALLIER ST

46   47

60

59

CONGRESS ST

INDEPENDENCE ST

PAULINE ST

ALVAR ST

BARTHOLOMEW ST

MAZANT ST

FRANCE ST

LESSEPS ST

48

49

CHARTRES ST

50

63

POLAND AVE

64

Pauline Street Wharf

	0	200 yds
	0	200 m

DISTANCE ACROSS MAP
Approximate: 1.9 mi or 2.9 km

Poland Avenue Wharf

© MOON.COM

FAUBOURG MARIGNY WALK

TOTAL DISTANCE: 1.7 miles (2.7 kilometers)
WALKING TIME: 45 minutes

This is a daytime walk. At night, it's pretty easy to find your own way up and down Frenchmen Street and St. Claude Avenue to check out all the music. This walking tour passes some of the hidden treasures of the Marigny (including brightly painted Creole cottages, public art, and a lot of cats). There's lots of stuff to see, so keep your eyes open. There's also a lot of stuff to eat, so bring your appetite.

1 Start at the foot of Frenchmen Street, just below where it intersects with Decatur Street. Head into **Louisiana Music Factory** to browse some records and listen to some groovy local tunes.

2 Head north on Frenchmen Street and make a quick right onto Decatur. After a block, turn left onto Elysian Fields Avenue. Make the first right onto Chartres Street. Walk three blocks to **New Orleans Cake Cafe & Bakery** and grab a coffee, snack, or cupcake. Keep an eye out:

On the left-hand side of Chartres is where jazz pioneer Jack Laine once lived.

3 Facing Spain Street, turn left and walk up Spain one block to Royal Street. Turn left onto Royal and walk one block to **Crescent City Conjure** to learn a little something about hoodoo practices.

4 Take a right onto Mandeville Street and walk two blocks north to Burgundy Street. Turn left onto Burgundy and behold the **Hotel Peter and Paul,** a gorgeous restoration of an ecclesiastical complex including a church, Catholic school, rectory, and convent that dates back to 1860. Pop into the on-site **Elysian Bar** with its various sitting rooms and courtyard. Grab a beverage or plate of something if the spirit moves you. Checking out the bar is a great way to get the feel of the hotel without actually staying here.

5 Take a left out of Elysian onto Burgundy and walk for three blocks to St. Roch Avenue. Turn left onto St. Roch, walk two blocks, and cross St. Claude Avenue to **St. Roch Market.** Inside this food hall is whatever you need right now, be it coffee, fresh squeezed fancy juice, raw oysters, cocktails, or the food of several overseas regions. Or just a seat to relax for a few minutes.

6 Leaving the food hall, cross St. Claude and turn left. Walk two blocks east and turn right onto Franklin Avenue. Stay on Franklin for three blocks. Turn left onto Dauphine Street and then take a right onto St. Ferdinand Street two blocks later. On the left side of that block you'll see the **Marigny Opera House.** It looks dilapidated outside (in a cool way), but if you can poke your head inside, you'll see that it has a gorgeous interior.

7 Continue down St. Ferdinand for the rest of the block and turn right onto Royal Street. On that first block you can check out the **Mardi Gras Zone** for a unique browsing experience. Head upstairs to check out all the Carnival-themed goodies.

8 Take a right out of Mardi Gras Zone, walk two blocks, cross Homer Plessy Way and the railroad tracks, and you'll see a giant yellow mural of a young girl on your left. That's **Studio Be,** the gallery of graffiti and mural artist Brandan "B-Mike" Odoms. You can just admire the murals from the outside (there's another one on the other side of the building) or go in and pay $10 for the full experience (which I recommend). From here, you can continue exploring the area by taking the **Bywater Walk** (page 100).

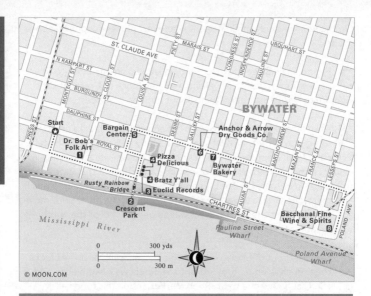

© MOON.COM

BYWATER WALK

TOTAL DISTANCE: 2 miles (3.2 kilometers)
WALKING TIME: 1 hour

This walk can be done independently or in conjunction with the **Faubourg Marigny Walk** (page 98). There are so many cool houses, weird decorations, and fun art pieces around the Bywater that the journey is half the fun of this walking tour. This is a good early or mid-afternoon walk, which will get you to your final destination before dark. Have a light lunch or snack before starting, since there will be opportunities to get a more substantial afternoon meal during the walk.

1 Starting from the intersection of Royal Street and Montegut Street, head down Montegut Street (toward the river). Walk a block and turn left onto Chartres Street. About halfway down that block is **Dr. Bob's Folk Art.** Check out the quirky signs and funky paintings of narrow shotgun houses, gators, and bayou landscapes.

Dr. Bob's

Bratz Y'all

2 Continue east on Chartres and walk 2.5 blocks until you get to Piety Street. On your right will be the **Rusty Rainbow Bridge,** which will carry you up and over the railroad tracks so you can enjoy unfettered views of the river in a peaceful setting at **Crescent Park.** Note: Crossing the bridge requires climbing a bunch of stairs.

3 After wandering around the park, climb back up and over the bridge to the corner of Chartres and Piety. Right in front of you is **Euclid Records,** perfect for all your vinyl-browsing, music-listening needs.

4 With your back to the river, head up Piety Street just a few steps. Next door to each other you'll find **Bratz Y'all,** a beer garden where you can sip a beer while eating a pretzel, and **Pizza Delicious,** for those who want a cocktail on draft with a New York-style slice of pizza.

the Rusty Rainbow Bridge to Crescent Park

5 Continue up Piety to the next cross street, which is Royal. Turn left and after one block turn right onto Louisa. Walk another block to the **Bargain Center.** Lose yourself in their massive selection of furniture, old Mardi Gras throws, and other vintage ephemera. (It's cash only.)

Bacchanal Fine Wine & Spirits

6 Take a right out of the Bargain Center and turn onto Dauphine Street. Walk four blocks to Congress Street, to the very cool and hipster **Anchor & Arrow Dry Goods Co.** Investigate the shop's cowboy boots and ukuleles, among other fun things.

7 Turn right, back onto Dauphine, and grab a coffee or a pastry at **Bywater Bakery** on the next corner. Bywater Bakery is open till 3pm most days (it closes at noon on Wednesday and is closed all day Thursday). If you miss them, consider grabbing a drink or snack at Paloma Café across the street from the Bargain Center, because it's a bit of a trek to get to the next stop.

8 It'll be a seven-block walk down Dauphine to the end of the Bywater, which is lined with colorful shotgun houses (narrow structures with rooms set one behind the next), Creole cottages, corner stores, and neighborhood bars. When you hit Poland Avenue, the last street on this side of the Industrial Canal, turn right and walk two blocks to **Bacchanal Fine Wine & Spirits,** a combination wine bar, retail shop, and live music venue. Rest up, drink some wine, and call for a ride back from whence you came—or take the #5 bus, which stops on Chartres right in front of Bacchanal.

Restaurants

PRICE KEY

$	Entrées less than $15
$$	Entrées $15-30
$$$	Entrées more than $30

CAJUN AND CREOLE

The Country Club $$

The name of this spot is tongue in cheek: This is no stuck-up country club. Instead, it's a historically LGBTQ-friendly restaurant and bar, once known as the spot where clothing-optional swimmers splashed around the pool area. The Country Club has honed its menu with a jump-start from former Commander's Palace sous chef Chris Barbuto; it's a fun place for a great meal. There's a bit of classic French technique in some of the preparations, like the chateaubriand for two, but the New Orleans influence comes through loud and clear in the crab meat beignets, crispy Gulf oysters, and shrimp & tasso au gratin. It's a an approachable yet still adventurous menu. Brunch is great, and not just for the food—enjoy the long-running drag show on Saturdays.

MAP 3: 634 Louisa St., 504/945-0742, thecountryclubneworleans.com; 10am-9pm Sun.-Thurs., 10am-10pm Fri.-Sat.

Jack Dempsey's Restaurant $$

This old school New Orleans restaurant has been around since 1980, and from the outside it looks like a hard 40 years. Don't let that dissuade you. Inside, you'll find a delightfully dated but well-kept dining room and bar with red neon signage taking center stage. Here's your chance to enjoy excellent takes on classic local cuisine and fantastic service, with standards like fried frog legs, NOLA-style baked macaroni and cheese, and blackened fish. It's like stepping through a time machine in all the best ways.

MAP 3: 738 Poland Ave., 504/943-9914, jackdempseys.net; 11am-2pm Tues., 11am-8pm Wed.-Thurs., 11am-9pm Fri., noon-9pm Sat.

Morrow's $$

At the mother-son endeavor Morrow's, you can grab some New Orleans favorites like fresh oysters (raw, chargrilled, or fried), fried catfish, grilled redfish, and crawfish étouffée or Korean dishes like bibimbap. The happy hour (4pm-7pm Mon., 3pm-6pm Tues.-Fri.) is killer, with 50 percent off premium alcohol, $3 shots, and $3 beer. Be warned that there's often a wait to get seated at this sleek but cozy bistro-style spot, especially on weekends. The authenticity of the New Orleans cuisine and the Korean dishes make Morrow's a great place to experience the wide diversity of the city.

MAP 3: 2438 St. Claude Ave., 504/827-1519, morrowsnola.com; 4pm-10pm Mon., 11am-10pm Tues.-Thurs, 11am-11pm Fri.-Sat., 10:30am-4pm Sun.

EXPLORE THE LOWER NINTH WARD

Lower Ninth Ward Living Museum

The Lower Ninth Ward, on the eastern side of the Industrial Canal, was made famous by the devastation wrought after Hurricane Katrina and the levee failures in
2005. As the area stretches away from the Mississippi River, it feels more desolate,
with abandoned properties and vacant lots. This is because only about a third of
the neighborhood's population was able to return and rebuild after the flooding.
Today, you can visit the still-recovering neighborhood and learn about its resilient
community.

If you have a car, you can easily spend an hour or more visiting the Lower
Ninth after hitting the Bywater. Going by bike would work, too, but I don't recommend this as a walking tour; the sights are too spread out. No matter how you get
around, be careful. The streets and sidewalks are in disrepair and can damage your
car—or you!

Follow the driving tour described here, or opt for a guided tour with Ninth
Ward Rebirth Bike Tours (504/400-5468, ninthwardrebirthbiketours.com; 9:30am
Fri.-Sat., other days by request; $65). This bicycle tour is perfect for getting the in-
side perspective and an authentic experience of talking to locals and hearing their
stories. The tour's route and stops are flexible, depending on the interests of the
group. Call or email ahead to book a spot.

To get to the Lower Ninth Ward (and St. Bernard Parish just beyond), take the St.
Claude Bridge, which begins at the easternmost point of the Bywater, across the
canal. (Pray you don't get stuck in the traffic that occurs when it's raised!)

1. CHECK OUT THE DOULLUT STEAMBOAT HOUSES

After you've crossed the St. Claude bridge, take the third right onto Egania Street.
Head all the way down to the river till you can't drive any farther, then get out and
take a gander at both of the Doullut Steamboat Houses (400 and 503 Egania St.).

The houses were built by a riverboat pilot father and son and were inspired by
the steamboats they captained. Captain Milton P. Doullut built his home, the one
closer to the river, in 1905, then built a second one nearby, in 1913, for his son Paul.
The buildings' pagoda-esque lines, hexagonal shape, and wraparound balconies
with railings are all unique features that stand out from the other homes in the
area. The houses were also built to withstand flooding: The ground floor is covered

in ceramic, inside and out, making for easy cleanup. The homes are privately owned, but it's easy to get a good glimpse of the exteriors.

2. EAT AT CAFÉ DAUPHINE

From the Doullut houses, turn around and head back up Egania for three blocks. Stop at Café Dauphine (Map 9: 5229 Dauphine St., 504/309-6391, www.no-lacafedauphine.com; 11am-8pm Mon. and Wed.-Thurs., 11am-9pm Fri.-Sat., 11am-5pm Sun.) and eat with gusto.

This casual comfort-food eatery is really the only restaurant in the area, so it's good that it's so damn delicious. The seafood-heavy menu offers all the bounty of the Gulf in fried, grilled, baked, and broiled forms. The friendly service and cheerful, yellow interior also add to the appeal. It's a neighborhood joint through and through. When I left after gobbling down the crawfish corn bisque and the house specialty, fried crab-and shrimp-stuffed peppers, I was jovially interrogated by the restaurant's next door neighbor: He wanted to know how my meal was because his nephew's the chef.

3. LEARN AT THE LOWER NINTH WARD LIVING MUSEUM

After lunch, continue up Egania till you're back at St. Claude. Turn left onto St. Claude and drive five blocks, being careful to stay to the right of the bridge, so you don't get on it. Drive parallel to the bridge for a few blocks. Turn right onto Deslonde Street, drive for two blocks, and you'll spot the Lower Ninth Ward Living Museum (Map 9: 1235 Deslonde St., 504/220-3652, www.l9livingmuseum.org; noon-5pm Tues.-Sun.; free, donations welcome) on the corner of Deslonde and Urquhart Streets.

This six-room shotgun house is dedicated to the history of the Lower Ninth Ward, a chronicle of various disasters (up to and including Katrina) that have affected the neighborhood. It provides helpful context as to why the cultural contributions of the community are important, and why they're now critically endangered due to governmental neglect and corruption. The destruction of the Bayou Bienvenue has, over the course of years, removed any natural barriers to storms; officials admit that the Lower Ninth Ward won't survive another catastrophic event. It's important to hear the stories of the people who live here, have struggled to rebuild, and are trying to save their neighborhood. Listening to the oral history audio and video recordings provides a whole new perspective. The exhibit on the devastation caused by Hurricane Betsy in 1965 is especially chilling.

4. CELEBRATE AT THE HOUSE OF DANCE & FEATHERS

Get some joy by visiting Ronald Lewis's House of Dance & Feathers (Map 9: 1317 Tupelo St., 504/957-2678, houseofdanceandfeathers.org; call for appointment; free, donations welcome). You'll need to call Mr. Lewis ahead of time to visit. (Consider calling just before you sit down at Café Dauphine.) Drive down Urquhart, away from the canal for two blocks, turn right onto Reynes Street, and then left onto St. Claude two blocks after that. After about three-quarters of a mile (12 blocks) down St. Claude, turn left onto Tupelo, and drive two and a half blocks to the House of Dance and Feathers.

Mr. Lewis has been educating people about New Orleans African American history in the back house on his property since 2003, to keep alive the traditions and spread knowledge of Mardi Gras Indians, social aid and pleasure clubs, the Skull and Bones Gang, and the Baby Dolls. Come on into the small building crammed full of Mardi Gras Indian suits, parasols for second lines, headdresses, and costumes, and Mr. Lewis will tell you all about the traditions they represent—and won't mince words about why those traditions are in danger today.

It's time to say goodbye to the Lower Ninth. Return down Tupelo, turn right onto St. Claude, and take the bridge back over to the Bywater.

PO'BOYS
✪ Frady's One Stop Food Store $

Frady's has been around since 1972 as a family-run corner store, and the folks who run it know what they're doing. Frady's is cash-only, but they have an ATM onsite, though almost everything is under $10. The real find is breakfast: try the "Grumpy Old Man" (two eggs, meat, potatoes or grits, and toast) for $5.50. Don't pass by the homemade plate specials, which rotate daily, but may include jambalaya, meatloaf with mashed potatoes, and baked pork chops. There's no place to sit and eat inside the store, but there are several tables set up outside under the side awning.
MAP 3: 3231 Dauphine St., 504/949-9688; 7:30am-6pm Mon.-Fri., 9am-3pm Sat.; cash only

Frady's One Stop Food Store

GERMAN
Bratz Y'all $$

Looking for an authentic German beer garden? This is the spot for you, with long communal outdoor tables shaded by sun umbrellas, bunting fluttering in the breeze, and folks hefting steins of German ale while eating brats, schnitzels, pretzels, and the like. They also deviate a little from standard German fare with dishes like gravlax Flammkuchen or the NOLA Schnitzel, a deep-fried pork loin or chicken breast with crawfish-remoulade slaw, served on a muffuletta bun. German beers are the way to go here—there's a great selection of imports—but they also have an intriguing selection of German wines and liqueurs. It's the perfect place to enjoy a fine-weather day or night.
MAP 3: 617-B Piety St., 504/301-3222, bratzyall.com; 11am-10pm Tues.-Thurs., 11am-11pm Fri., 11am-midnight Sat., 11am-9pm Sun.

NEW AMERICAN
Bywater American Bistro $$

The second restaurant from Chef Nina Compton, Bywater American Bistro is more laid-back than her flagship Compere Lapin in the Warehouse District—but just as flawlessly conceived and executed. The menu is always changing, but don't overlook the "rice, grains, noodles" section on both the dinner and brunch menus; there's always something there that's satisfying to the soul. The cocktail list is fantastic as well, especially the house bottled Negroni and the thoughtful twists on the classic martini.
MAP 3: 2900 Chartres St., 504/605-3827, bywateramericanbistro. com; 5pm-10pm Wed.-Fri., 10:30am-2pm and 5pm-10pm Sat.-Sun.

ECLECTIC
N7 $$

N7 is like a secret garden of delight where you can find French-Japanese fusion dishes, natural wines, and fancy pâtés. Try the sake-cured salmon tartine, escargot tempura, or soy-sauce crème brûlée in this intimate, romantic setting. N7 feels like an old-school European roadside restaurant. Decorated with antique Michelin guides inside and with a red vintage Citroen parked outside, it's a reflection of the owners, and feels wildly cinematic and personal, like a backyard party in your most sophisticated friend's home.

MAP 3: 1117 Montegut St., no phone, n7nola.com; 6pm-10pm Mon.-Thurs., 6pm-11pm Fri.-Sat.

Capulet $

Capulet's industrial loft building feels much more spacious than you'd expect from a neighborhood café that's generally only open for weekday breakfast and lunch. That's because this bar/café becomes an event space at night and on weekends (complete with a rooftop deck). Menu items like the kimchi BLT and Bloody Mary roast beef sandwich have become local favorites. Capulet also serves probiotic cocktails with ingredients like shrubs, kombucha, kimchi, and pickled fruits and vegetables. My favorite thing to do is order a cherry shrub and soda and a breakfast bagel sandwich and hang out on one of the comfy chairs next to the huge wall of windows.

MAP 3: 3014 Dauphine St., 504/507-0691, capuletbywater.com; 9am-3pm Mon.-Wed. and Fri., 9am-7pm Thurs.

ITALIAN AND PIZZA
Paladar 511 $$

This under-the-radar, semi-fancy restaurant provides gorgeous versions of pizza, pasta, and seasonally inspired, Italian-influenced dishes. It also has a great drinks list, a rustic loft-like space with art on the walls and an open kitchen, and excellent service. It's a really lovely dining experience without being stuffy in the slightest. Although the entire menu is great, the starters really shine, with vegetable preparations that reflect what's growing nearby, as well as versions of crudo, carpaccio, and the house-made *raviolo* (a single large ravioli), which I highly recommend. All pastas are made from scratch and rolled out by hand, so make sure to check those out as well.

MAP 3: 511 Marigny St., 504/509-6782, paladar511.com; 5:30pm-10pm Mon. and Wed.-Thurs., 5:30pm-10:30pm Fri., 10am-2pm and 5:30pm-10:30pm Sat., 10am-2pm and 5:30pm-10pm Sun.

✪ Pizza Delicious $$

Owners Mike and Greg started Pizza D as a pop-up when they wanted to fill a NY-style pizza-shaped hole in the local food scene. The successful pop-up led to this always-busy brick and mortar spot. You can get a pie with delicious and fancy toppings, like garlic-sautéed mushrooms and pancetta, a white pie with bechamel, roasted potatoes, and rosemary—or just pick up a giant slice of plain cheese or pepperoni for under $3. They also have pastas and salads, and there's always a vegan option. The specialty pizzas and toppings rotate throughout the week and seasonally, so come with an open mind.

MAP 3: 617 Piety St., 504/676-8482, pizzadelicious.com; 11am-11pm Tues.-Sun.

Arabella Casa di Pasta $

For those who love fresh hand-rolled pasta and have opinions about what the perfect bowl of pasta looks like, the casual and affordable Arabella offers seven different shapes, types, and flavors (including a couple of vegan options), as well as seven different sauces. Pick your faves along with any extras (like meatballs, mushrooms, and Gulf shrimp) and you've got exactly what you want. For those who don't have anything specific in mind, order from their signature menu, which includes sauces and add-ons that aren't on the à la carte menu, like the John Belu-Cheese, a creamy Jack Daniels whiskey sauce with chicken, blue cheese crumbles, green onion, and fried chicken cracklin' over rigatoni; or the Lambotomy, which combines spicy tomato pesto, ground lamb, feta cheese, and basil over roasted red pepper rigatoni. Arabella also serves small plates and desserts. It's been described as the "apex of chill," with a great bar that features local beer on draft and cocktail specials, as well as music that reflects the bartender's mood. It's great for solo dining, casual dates, and group outings.
MAP 3: 2258 St. Claude Ave., 504/267-6108, arabellanola.com; 4pm-10pm Sun.-Thurs., 4pm-11pm Fri.-Sat.

MIDDLE EASTERN
Kebab $

Kebab serves locally sourced chicken and pork that's grilled, placed on their freshly made bread (baked every hour), and slathered with explosively flavorful fresh herb sauces. The vegetarian options are just as thoughtful and shine on their own, like the feta-stuffed roasted portobello mushroom sandwich and the falafel, which can be ordered as a sandwich, plate, or side. Kebab's funky lower-level location has a small open kitchen, local art on the walls, and a collection of video and pinball games. Always check out their specials board before ordering.
MAP 3: 2315 St. Claude Ave., 504/383-4328, kebabnola.com; 11am-11pm Sun.-Mon. and Wed.-Thurs., 11am-midnight Fri.

ASIAN
Red's Chinese $$

Playful versions of Chinese-American standards rule at Red's, like the craw rangoon (made with crawfish tails instead of crab), pork buns with pork belly and kimchi mayo, and the Kung Pao pastrami sandwich. The cocktails are fun, too, with drinks like the Smoke Thai Everyday (rum, mezcal, Curacao, and orgeat) and Bangcock Knights (gin, chili simple syrup, fresh cucumber juice, lemongrass, Thai basil, and fresh lime). The cozy, grungy interior is low ceilinged and neon-lit, with an open kitchen, bar seating, and deep-red walls, and there's a very nice patio in back. The service can be a bit hit or miss, but on the whole it's friendly and fun.
MAP 3: 3048 St. Claude Ave., 504/304-6030, redschinese.com; noon-11pm daily

Bao & Noodle $

This unassuming converted corner store turns out some of the best *bao*

(a Chinese filled bun or dumpling) and hand-pulled noodle dishes in town. The *bao* comes in vegan or pork versions (including *rousong bao*, which is a scallion bun with pork floss). The cumin-braised lamb with *biang biang* noodles is revelatory. This is a great place to scratch the itch for Chinese comfort carbs.
MAP 3: 2266 St. Claude Ave., 504/272-0004, baoandnoodle.com; 11:30am-2pm and 5pm-10pm Tues.-Sat.

Poke-Chan $

Multiple people will tell you that Poke Chan is their favorite of the several poke eateries in the city. It's in a converted Creole cottage and retains the building's original hardwood, plaster walls, and fireplace, but the kitchen area is sparkling white and stainless steel. Poke options here include raw seafood, vegetarian, and even cooked seafood. Try the Kinda Hawaiian for raw tuna with sesame oil, mangoes, and seaweed salad over fried wonton chips, or the Karaage Don, with Japanese fried chicken, kimchi, sesame seeds, and spicy mayo over white rice.
MAP 3: 2809 St. Claude Ave., 504/571-5446, poke-chan.com; 11am-9:30pm Sun.-Thurs, 11am-10pm Fri.-Sat.

FOOD HALLS
St. Roch Market $

Perched on the edge of the St. Roch neighborhood, which is sandwiched between the Tremé and the Marigny, is this cavernous, high-ceilinged edifice, a refurbished gathering place for foodies and families. With its white, minimalist decor, plentiful indoor and outdoor seating, and assorted

Bywater Bakery

food stalls offering everything from cold-pressed juices and savory crepes to raw oysters and Haitian dishes, it's a welcome addition to the local food scene. It's also a decent place to pick up coffee, pastries, specialty meats, fresh produce, and wine.

MAP 3: 2381 St. Claude Ave., 504/609-3813, strochmarket.com; 7am-10pm Sun.-Thurs., 7am-11pm Fri.-Sat.

CAFÉS AND LIGHT BITES

✪ Bywater Bakery $

This cheerful café provides "breakfast go-cups" filled with bacon and eggs, shrimp and grits, or yogurt and granola. They also have gorgeous salads, tartines, and soup specials for lunch. The sweet and savory baked goods are diverse and delightful, with boudin-stuffed sandwiches, petit fours, and Chantilly cakes to name just a few. Don't miss bagel Wednesdays, the only day they make and sell bagels between 7am and noon (or until they're sold out). There's often live music, too.

MAP 3: 3624 Dauphine St., 504/336-3336, bywaterbakery.com; 7am-noon Wed., 7am-3pm Thurs.-Tues.

CHARCUTERIE AND DELIS

Shank Charcuterie $

Part butcher shop, part takeout joint, and part low-key café, Shank offers a revolving supply of beef, pork, poultry, and other charcuterie items. The small menu is subject to change, but if you spot the meatball sub, try it. The size of the hanger steak in the steak and eggs dish must be seen to be believed. This is where meat adventures happen, so don't miss the boat.

MAP 3: 2352 St. Claude Ave., 504/218-5281, shankcharcuterie.com; 11am-7pm Tues.-Sat., 11am-5pm Sun.

COFFEE AND DESSERTS

New Orleans Cake Cafe & Bakery $

To satisfy your sweet tooth, venture to this homey café in the Faubourg Marigny that prepares to-die-for treats, such as red velvet cake with cream cheese frosting, plus specialty cupcakes flavored with champagne, mimosas, and chocolate mousse. This well-regarded spot also serves delicious breakfast and lunch items. You can get a cupcake for $1 with the purchase of any meal. The service is friendly and easygoing, and the crowd is a comfortable mix of students, retirees, artists, and hipsters. Be prepared for long lines, especially during weekend brunch.

MAP 3: 2440 Chartres St., 504/943-0010, nolacakes.com; 7am-3pm Wed.-Mon.

Sólo Espresso $

The baristas at this hideaway coffee shop on the edge of the Industrial Canal are effusively friendly, helpful, and pull a great espresso. In addition to espresso, drip coffee, and cold brew, Sólo offers two types of manual brews: Clover full immersion and Chemex pour-over. They also host a pop-up that serves Latin American- and Asian-inspired vegan dishes at lunchtime during the week. On the weekends, grilled to order breakfast tacos are

available. Their house-made baked treats are great, too, including oat bars, tarts, and biscuits served with butter and jam. The wood-paneled interior creates a tranquil atmosphere for drinking coffee, working, and meeting friends.
MAP 3: 1301 Poland Ave., 504/408-1377, soloespressobar.com; 7am-3pm Mon.-Sat., 8am-2pm Sun.

Nightlife

NIGHTLIFE DISTRICTS

Frenchmen Street
When people talk about the music scene on Frenchmen Street, they're talking about a three-block stretch of musical excess—over a dozen bars and music clubs are jammed in together here. When it gets busy (weekends, Jazz Fest, Mardi Gras), it's wall-to-wall people. For the best experience, pop in from club to club. Most places don't charge a cover, but if you stay and listen, tip the band and buy a drink. You can find old-school big band jazz, brass band, traditional jazz, R&B, klezmer, rock, acoustic folk... you name it, you'll find it—sometimes all in the same bar if you stay in one place long enough.

There are some great late-night

Frenchmen Street

entrance for the Hi-Ho Lounge

snacks to be had along Frenchmen, too, and there's even an **artists market** between Royal Street and Chartres Street that's open every night till midnight or 1am. There are always lots of street musicians and vendors out and about.

MAP 3: Frenchmen St., spanning Decatur St. to Dauphine St.

LIVE MUSIC
✪ Bacchanal Fine Wine & Spirits

Bacchanal is at once a unique live music venue, a wine bar and retail shop, a cheese shop, and an international bistro. There's nothing like listening to jazz with a glass of chilled rosé while eating a beautifully arranged cheese plate. Bacchanal has a show every day at 7:30pm, with late afternoon shows (starting 4pm-5pm) from Friday through Sunday. All the musicians are local, and include acts like the Jesse Morrow Trio, John Zarsky, and

Nutria. The music spans different genres of jazz, from classic to modern, so this spot is as New Orleans as it gets. If you want to sit outside, come early to stake your space: This gem is not as hidden as it used to be. There's also a small indoor bar here for cocktails. The kitchen usually closes around 11pm.

MAP 3: 600 Poland Ave., 504/948-9111, bacchanalwine.com; 11am-midnight Sun.-Thurs., 11am-1am Fri.-Sat.; no cover

d. b. a.

Located in a late-19th-century building, this dimly lit, hipster hangout is a good place to meet locals, hear live rock and blues bands, and, on occasion, catch performances from the likes of Jimmy Buffett and Stevie Wonder. The drink selection encompasses about a zillion beers (including plenty of imported options), plus many types of whiskey and tequila, and the crowd is young and laid-back, with a touch of style.

MAP 3: 618 Frenchmen St.,
504/942-3731, dbaneworleans.com;
5pm-4am Mon.-Wed., 5pm-5am Thurs.,
4pm-5am Fri.-Sat., 4pm-4am Sun.; cover
$0-20

Hi-Ho Lounge

Hi-Ho is a great spot for comedy, belly-dance performances, burlesque, and live local music. Though it's dark and kind of rundown inside, it has great bartenders, fairly priced drinks, and a food pop-up in the back courtyard. The small space means you can get up close with the music and it makes for a great experience. Be sure to check out No Lye Comedy, a lineup of Black women comics.

MAP 3: 2239 St. Claude Ave.,
504/945-4446, hiholounge.net;
5pm-1am Sun.-Thurs., 5pm-2am Fri.,
5pm-4am Sat.; cover $5-20

Saturn Bar

If you passed by the Saturn Bar in the light of day, you'd assume it was long abandoned. That all changes at night, when it's a bustling bar and music/dance club. The welcoming, inclusive spot encourages booty shaking to the highest degree; expect to get sweaty. Thankfully, cheap, ice cold beers are plentiful. (But the bathrooms look like they haven't been maintained since the '80s.) On Wednesdays from 3pm to midnight, they roll out a tiki-themed cocktail menu.

MAP 3: 3067 St. Claude Ave.,
504/949-7532, saturnbarnola.com;
3pm-close Wed.-Mon.; cover $5-10

The Spotted Cat Music Club

This cozily cramped, dark, and sweaty dance hall offers a long happy hour, a nice selection of specialty martinis, and terrific live bands. Although you'll occasionally hear rock, blues, bluegrass, salsa, and other dance-worthy musical styles, modern and traditional jazz are the mainstays here. Local favorite Meschiya Lake and the Little Big Horns, known for their old-time jazz performances, often pack in the crowds and inspire old-fashioned dancing among the regulars. There's a one-drink minimum here.

MAP 3: 623 Frenchmen St.,
504/943-3887, spottedcatmusicclub.
com; 2pm-2am daily; no cover

Three Muses

This is probably the only spot in the city where you can make a reservation to listen to live music, and one of the few all-ages live music venues. It's a full-scale restaurant, too, so you can eat and drink very well while enjoying the show. Tables can only be occupied for 90 minutes, so plan accordingly. (They are also quick to give your table away if you're late for your reservation, so be prompt.) The music is mostly traditional New Orleans jazz and blues. The cocktail list has some great concoctions.

MAP 3: 536 Frenchmen St.,
504/252-4801, 3musesnola.com;
5pm-10pm Mon.-Wed., 5pm-11pm
Thurs. and Sun., 5pm-midnight Fri.-Sat.;
no cover

Vaughan's Lounge

Vaughan's is like if a honkytonk and a second line had a baby in a sketchy-looking, sweaty bar. It's awesome! Thursday nights see live music, courtesy of Corey Henry and the Treme Funktet, along with free red beans and rice. Other acts stop by as well, like Jamaican Me Crazy Breakfast Club or Malevitus. When the joint's not a-jumping, it's a low-key dive bar, great for day drinking, night drinking, or sports watching.

MAP 3: 4229 Dauphine St., 504/947-5562; noon-2am daily; cover $0-10

BARS AND LOUNGES

Buffa's

Situated between the French Quarter and the Faubourg Marigny since 1939, Buffa's feels like a well-kept secret, despite its obvious location on Esplanade. A popular neighborhood hangout, the front room of Buffa's offers a variety of vittles and libations 24 hours a day. The real treat is the back room, which hosts live music performances. Here, patrons can listen to traditional jazz every day of the week.

MAP 3: 1001 Esplanade Ave., 504/949-0038, buffasrestaurant.com; front bar 24 hours daily, back room open for performances, generally 6pm-11pm Mon.-Fri., 11am-midnight Sat., 10am-10pm Sun.; no cover

The Domino

The Domino is a cozy neighborhood bar with low ceilings, a great circular bar in the back, and tons of board games (with an emphasis on dominos). The game theme even extends to the gorgeous booth tables, which have various game boards (checkers/chess, backgammon, and Settlers of Catan) custom painted on the tops. There are great wines by the glass, but also cocktails and beer, and the kitchen makes delicious versions of Gen-X snacks like Lunchables and bagel bites.

Vaughan's Lounge

MAP 3: 304 St. Claude Ave., 504/354-8737, dominonola.com; 3pm-2am daily

J&J's Sports Lounge

One of many neighborhood bars in the Bywater, J&J's distinguishes itself with a variety of local draft beer options and a hands-on husband and wife ownership team. Even though the place does have a focus on sports (especially Saints and LSU football), at its heart it's a funky, dive-y, friendly bar with cheap drinks on offer all day long. Bonus: It's cat friendly. Keep an eye out for the feline bouncer at night.

MAP 3: 800 France St., 504/942-8877, jjssportslounge.com; 9am-4am daily

Junction

Beer and burgers are the focus of the geniuses at Junction. The interior is art deco style with a bright red wall behind the 40-tap bar. The jukebox features obscure local bands and old hardcore punk, and there's a menu of burgers that are named for famous railroad lines. Junction is a place that satisfies an itch you didn't even know you had. The beer leans heavily toward local and regional options, with a variety of styles and breweries represented. If you're hungry, try the Central Vermont, with applewood smoked bacon, white cheddar, grilled apple, and maple sauce, or the Boston & Maine, a fried fish sandwich.

MAP 3: 3021 St. Claude Ave., 504/272-0205, junctionnola.com; 11am-2am daily

Marie's Bar & Kitchen

Marie's Bar & Kitchen

Of all the bars in the Marigny, Marie's is one of the best places to grab a Bloody Mary and take in the vibe of the neighborhood from the café-style sidewalk seating just outside the bar's door. The kitchen is only open weekend nights (5pm-midnight Fri.-Sun., cash only), but it's worthwhile to make a stop for pork-rind nachos, build your own mac & cheese, gumbo, or burgers. Be sure to check out the drink special of the day.

MAP 3: 2483 Burgundy St., 504/267-5869, maries-bar.business.site; 10am-2am daily

Markey's Bar

The only Bywater bar with shuffleboard and a dart league, Markey's also has 27 beers on tap. The same family has been running the place since 1947. The kitchen puts out top-notch bar food favorites like wings and sandwiches. It's definitely an old-school spot with beer memorabilia and an Irish vibe. Don't miss their crawfish boils in season on Fridays and Sundays.

MAP 3: 640 Louisa St., 504/943-0785, markeysbar.com; 2pm-2am Mon.-Thurs., noon-2am Fri.-Sat.

Sidney's Saloon

Sidney's is a neighborhood bar with a great beer list, a pool table, and live music on the weekends (cover ranges from free to $5). It looks like a dive from the outside, but the interior is faded in a comfortable way, like your favorite pair of jeans. Behind the S-shaped bar is a long list of beers as well as their house cocktails, which run around $6 each.

MAP 3: 1200 St. Bernard Ave., 504/224-2672, sidneyssaloon.com; 3pm-3am daily

LGBTQ VENUES

✪ Kajun's Pub

This isn't a gay bar so much as a 24-hour karaoke bar that's a safe port in a storm for LGBTQ locals and visitors. The world-famous karaoke is only in the evening, starting at 5pm. In the days immediately following Katrina, owner and proud trans woman JoAnn Guidos kept Kajun's open to provide a haven to whoever needed it. Nowadays, Kajun's is a boisterous spot packed with locals, karaoke lovers, visitors doing an informal St. Claude Ave. bar crawl, Saints fans, and anyone who knows about the "777 Happy Hour," which serves up drink specials from 7am to 7pm, seven days a week. That's a happy 12 hours.

MAP 3: 2256 St. Claude Ave., 504/947-3735, kajunpub.com; 24 hours daily

The Phoenix Bar

This spot is very focused on big ol' bears and leather play—it's not for the faint of heart. This is a fun, outrageous, community-focused spot with DJs and saucy dancing. The interior of the barroom is dark and dive-y; the upstairs bar is darker still—as in, no lights whatsoever. (No cell phones are allowed upstairs.) The ownership is hugely supportive of dialogue and activism in these topsy-turvy times, but at the end of the day, it's all about the leather. This spot is cash only.

MAP 3: 941 Elysian Fields Ave., 504/945-9264, phoenixbarnola.com; 24 hours daily; no cover

BREWERIES
✪ Brieux Carré Brewing Co.

This tiny taproom with an airy courtyard and beer garden is near the foot of Frenchmen Street, so this is the perfect place to grab a beer to go while wandering the area, or an oasis to take a load off and try one of the brewery's many styles of beer, ranging from traditional to WTF. The Pomeranian Fight Club is one of their flagships, a sour saison with hibiscus, lavender, and rose hips. They also have other entertainingly named beers like Wookie Sounds (dry-hopped saison), Dad Jokes (New England-style double IPA), and Come Drink Your Caraway (a spiced amber ale). Regular food pop-ups, fun events, and tons of board games makes this the perfect place to hang out for a beer or an entire day.

MAP 3: 2115 Decatur St., 504/304-4242, brieuxcarre.com; 11am-10pm daily

Parleaux Beer Lab

Parleaux, which loosely translates to "by the water," is indeed situated in the Bywater. Hang out in Parleaux's easy-going, expansive beer garden and drink well-crafted beers like the refreshing Czuck Pils and the hazy as hell Foggy Glasses IPA. The tap list is always different, since the mad scientists at this beer lab are constantly experimenting, but there's always something for every taste. They also have a great variety of food tucks and pop-ups, or you can get some Pizza Delicious delivered while you drink.

MAP 3: 634 Lesseps St., 504/702-8433, parleauxbeerlab.com; noon-10pm Sun.-Mon. and Thurs.-Fri., 11am-10pm Sat.

WINE BARS
Saint-Germain

Don't be confused: Although the neon sign outside this tiny wine bar/restaurant says Sugar Park, this is the right place for an impressive by-the-glass wine selection, lovely cocktails, and light snacks. The long bar in the narrow space stretches out almost to the soothing courtyard in the back. As the sun sets, and the wine kicks in, it's a peaceful New Orleans experience. The small front room is reserved for Saint-Germain's dinner service.

MAP 3: 3054 St. Claude Ave., 504/218-8729, saintgermainnola. com; 3pm-midnight Mon.-Tues. and Thurs., 3pm-2am Fri., noon-2am Sat., noon-midnight Sun.

Parleaux Beer Lab

Arts and Culture

GALLERIES

Dr. Bob's Folk Art

Enter through the driveway and make your way around to Dr. Bob's workshop and gallery, where local Louisiana scenes and sayings are painted on different sized and shaped pieces of wood. His admonishment to "Be Nice or Leave" joins funky paintings of iconic shotgun houses, po'boys, gators, and bayou landscape scenes, among other things. You really need to get there in person to see his larger than life technique and artistic voice.

MAP 3: 3027 Chartres St., 504/945-2225, drbobart.com; 10am-5pm daily

New Orleans Art Center

The largest of the galleries on the St. Claude art corridor, the New Orleans Art Center hosts rotating multimedia and ethnographic exhibitions that dig into global diversity and feature local artists. Browse and discover traditional canvases;

Dr. Bob's Folk Art

sculptures made with clay, wood, and nontraditional textiles; and found-object art. If you're an artist yourself, check out their weekly live drawing classes on Monday nights. The owners and staff are incredibly sweet and helpful, eager to answer any questions but not hovering or using high-pressure sales tactics.

MAP 3: 3330 St. Claude Ave., 504/383-4765, theneworleansartcenter. com; noon-6pm daily

✪ Studio Be

Brandan "B-Mike" Odoms is a New Orleans graffiti and mural artist who focuses on public art that creates a dialogue about the intersection of art and resistance. His medium of choice is spray paint and his inspiration is Black history. His murals can be found throughout New Orleans, but Studio Be is where he's created his *Ephermal. Eternal* exhibition, with original murals, large-scale installations, and reconstructed murals salvaged from the walls of the New Orleans's Florida Housing Development before its demolition in 2014. The gallery is unusual in that it charges admission, but it's more of a museum-type of experience. The intensity of Odoms's images will have you thinking for a long time.

MAP 3: 2941 Royal St., 504/252-0463, ephermaleternal.com; 2pm-8pm Wed.-Sun.; $10 adults, $8 teachers, students, and military

PERFORMING ARTS

The AllWays Lounge & Theater

From peep show to burlesque to a "jockstrap cabaret," The AllWays is committed to sex-positive expressions of music, dance, theater, and writing. Enjoy burlesque routines set to live blues music, improv classes, LGBTQ storytelling, and erotic readings by local writers. Sunday nights are relatively low-key, with free swing dance lessons followed by live music, and no cover. Go with an open mind and you'll undoubtedly learn something new about the city—or yourself.

MAP 3: 2240 St. Claude Ave., 504/218-5778, theallwayslounge. net; 6pm-2am Sun.-Thurs., 6pm-4am. Fri.-Sat.; cover varies by show

Cafe Istanbul

Occupying a performance hall in the rear of the New Orleans Healing Center, Cafe Istanbul does a lot to foster local performance art. In addition to presenting live concerts, dance and theatrical performances, and comedy shows, Cafe Istanbul offers poetry readings, film screenings, and an upper gallery dedicated to visual arts, particularly the paintings and photography of local artists.

MAP 3: 2372 St. Claude Ave., 504-975-0286, cafeistanbulnola.com; 7pm-2am daily; cover varies by show

Marigny Opera House

The imposing structure that now houses the Marigny Opera House once served as the Holy Trinity Catholic Church, which was founded in 1847 for German Catholics, built in 1853 by architect Theodore Giraud, and is known for its excellent music. Perhaps it's fitting, then, that the Marigny Opera House considers itself a "church of the arts." Home to the Marigny Opera Ballet, a professional contemporary ballet company founded in 2014, the Opera House also hosts various musical concerts, spotlighting everything from classical to jazz, as well as other cultural events.

MAP 3: 725 St. Ferdinand St., 504/948-9998, marignyoperahouse.org; show times and ticket prices vary by performance

Recreation

PARKS AND PLAZAS
Crescent Park

Since Crescent Park opened in February 2014, the 1.4-mile-long, 20-acre strip has lured countless recreationists. Besides scenic views of the New Orleans skyline and the Mississippi River, you'll find picnic areas and a network of paths suitable for walking, jogging, and biking. A parking lot is situated near Piety and Chartres Streets, where you'll also spot the Piety Street Bridge, a rusted steel arch (known as the "Rusty Rainbow Bridge") that safely delivers pedestrians over the active riverfront railroad tracks. Certain activities, such as cooking, swimming, and littering, are not allowed, and neither are skateboards, motorcycles, and glass bottles.

MAP 3: Crescent Park Trail, 504/636-6400, crescentparknola.org; 6am-7:30pm daily

BIKING
Alex's Bikes

Handsome bike shop owner Alex (he requested that description) presides over this well laid out bicycle kingdom tucked away on a Marigny side street, where he rents, sells, and repairs bikes. The rental rates are very reasonable ($5 per hour, with a maximum charge of $20, or $30 if

you keep it overnight and return it the next business day), and each bike comes with a helmet, lock, basket, and lights. The customer service is excellent—friendly but relaxed, and it's a great neighborhood business to support.

MAP 3: 607 Marigny St., 504/327-9248, alexsbikes.com; 10am-6pm Tues.-Fri., 10am-5pm Sat., noon-5pm Sun.

bike tour in the Bywater

✪ Confederacy of Cruisers

This bike tour company offers several themed journeys: a culinary bike tour, which is four hours of riding around the city, learning about its food traditions, and eating at various local spots; a cocktail tour, which has the special touch of drink holders affixed to each bike and includes a bartender-led tour with five beverage stops; and the standard Creole bike tour, which covers six miles in the Marigny, Bywater, Esplanade Ridge, and the Tremé.

MAP 3: 634 Elysian Fields Ave., 504/400-5468, confederacyofcruisers. com; 9am-5pm daily

Crescent City Cat Club

PET/ANIMAL SERVICES
Crescent City Cat Club
Whether you miss your cat, or just want some kitten time, Crescent City Cat Club is a great place to unwind. The CCCC is a rescue agency and all the cats in the house are available for adoption. It's a great activity for kids and adults alike, and you haven't lived until you've had half a dozen tiny kittens trying to climb up your legs simultaneously. No food or drink is for sale, but you can bring in your own beverages or snacks while visiting with your new feline friends.

MAP 3: 1021 Marigny St., 504/833-6652, crescentcitycatclub. com; noon-6pm or by appointment Thurs.-Sun.

Shops

OCCULT AND VOODOO
Crescent City Conjure
This real-deal hoodoo, witchcraft, and spirituality store is run by Sen Elias, a self-described preacher and healer. He can and will talk about the carefully handmade gris-gris bags, conjure oils, candles, and curios in great detail, so that customers know what each one means. This is a place to go if you're serious about hoodoo or are just starting out and are curious about the culture and practice. It's not a souvenir store as much as a place to realize your intentions. Readings and other spiritual services are also available.

MAP 3: 2402 Royal St., 504/421-3189, conjurecityconjure.us; 11am-10pm Wed.-Mon.

Island of Salvation Botanica
Run by longtime voodoo practitioner Sallie Ann Glassman, this spiritual supply shop is a good place to find herbs, oils, specialty candles, and Haitian artwork. You can even purchase custom-made gris-gris bags, made with various herbs, stones, and other materials—including a clipping of your own hair or nails. Housed within the New Orleans Healing Center, the Island of Salvation Botanica also provides readings and healings.

MAP 3: 2372 St. Claude Ave., Ste. 100, 504/948-9961, islandofsalvationbotanica.com; 10am-5pm Tues.-Sat.

ANTIQUES AND VINTAGE

Anchor & Arrow Dry Goods Co.

With a curated hipster vintage vibe, Anchor & Arrow delivers on a great stock of clothing, cowboy boots, books, and musical instruments. There's also quite a bit of local art scattered throughout. They also host artist events, crafting workshops, and other pop-ups. Be sure to ask what a "Nudie Suit" is—don't worry, the answer is PG!

MAP 3: 3528 Dauphine St., 504/302-7273, anchor-arrow-dry-goods-co.business.site; 11am-7pm daily

Bargain Center

The name may not blow you away, but the size of the store and the amount of awesome stuff they're selling surely will. For those who love thrifting and antiquing, this is a must-visit. From furniture to old Mardi Gras throws to knickknacks and other vintage ephemera from throughout the decades, this is a place to dig into. Note that it's cash only, but there's an ATM up the block at Frady's.

MAP 3: 3200 Dauphine St., 504/948-0007; 11am-5pm daily

SPECIALTY FOOD AND DRINK

Loretta's Authentic Pralines

Loretta loves making and selling pralines and beignets. The standard beignets are delightful, but you can

Loretta's Authentic Pralines

also get them stuffed with sweet or savory fillings. There's a lovely selection of pralines (the creamy version and the rum flavor are my two faves) as well as preserves and syrups made from local fruit. There are tables to sit and relax while enjoying your treat.

MAP 3: 2101 N. Rampart St., 504/944-7068, lorettaspralines.com; 9am-5pm Tues.-Fri., 9am-3pm Sat.

Second Vine Wine

This spot on a quiet block in the Marigny works to make wine accessible to everyone—regardless of previous knowledge, gender, or age. The owners and staff are effusively friendly, and treat customers like valued guests. This is a place that you can get comfy with your wine after you choose it—they've got seating out front, leather couches around a TV inside, and a hidden tasting bar in the back that hosts wine tastings, book signings, happy hours, and private events. The majority of their bottles are in the $15-30 range, and you'll find a lot of interesting grapes from unexpected places.

Euclid Records

MAP 3: 1027 Touro St., 504/304-4453; 2pm-10pm Mon.-Wed., noon-11pm Thurs.-Sat.

GIFTS AND SOUVENIRS
✪ Mardi Gras Zone

Mardi Gras Zone sells *everything*. Masks, beads, souvenirs, prepared food, booze, and lots of groceries. And it's open 24 hours a day so you can run out and get a pint of gelato or loaf of bread any time of the day or night. Just browsing the place is an experience that everyone should have at least once. The huge space has two stories. Head upstairs to find the selection of Mardi Gras beads, costume pieces, and masks.

MAP 3: 2706 Royal St., 504/947-8787, mardigraszone.com; 24 hours daily

BOOKS AND MUSIC
Euclid Records

Euclid is a record store heaven for nerding out in the stacks or with the staff; it's a testament to the most hardcore of vinyl geeks and jazz lovers. Most of the shop's two floors are dedicated to row upon row of LPs and 45s, but there is some other media if you poke around. There are several music-listening stations as well, so you can try some records before you buy.

MAP 3: 3301 Chartres St., 504/947-4348, euclidnola.com; 11am-7pm daily

Louisiana Music Factory

The Louisiana Music Factory is in the Marigny, just a stone's throw from the famous music clubs of Frenchmen Street. This noted music

FARMERS MARKETS

Farmers markets are great places to pick up local, seasonal produce as well as pre-pared foods and baked goods. They can be found all through the city. The organization Crescent City Farmers Market (CCFM, www.crescentcityfarmersmarket.org) holds seven weekly farmers markets in various locations over five different days of the week.

TUESDAY

The uptown CCFM Tuesday Market (200 Broadway St.; 9am-1pm Tues.) by the river is excellent and is where a lot of local chefs buy their produce. There's also a local food vendor selling hot plates every week; the vendor changes monthly.

WEDNESDAY

There are two CCFM Wednesday Markets. One is the Bywater Market (Chartres St. at Piety St.; 3pm-7pm Wed.) by the Rusty Rainbow Bridge. This market hosts musicians. The other is the Ochsner Market (Ochsner Rehabilitation Hospital, 2614 Jefferson Hwy.; 3pm-7pm Wed.) in Jefferson Parish. This market partners with Ochsner Hospital, so there's an emphasis on healthy foods. There's also a nutritionist on-site every week.

THURSDAY

The Mid-City Market (American Can Company, 3700 Orleans Ave.; 3pm-7pm Thurs.) is cleverly placed right next to the retail shops at the American Can Company, so you can also grab a cup of coffee or bottle of wine. It started in 2002 and is one of CCFM's longest-running markets.

FRIDAY

CCFM's Bucktown Market (Bucktown Harbor, 325 Metairie-Hammond Hwy.; 3pm-7pm Fri.) is held right on the edge of Lake Pontchartrain.

SATURDAY

One of the best market experiences is the Downtown Farmers Market (750 Carondelet; 8am-noon Sat.) in the Warehouse District. There are usually cooking demonstrations and live entertainment. The Rivertown Saturday Market (LaSalle's Landing; 9am-1pm Sat.) in Kenner is a new addition to the CCFM markets. It brings some well-deserved attention to the Rivertown historic district.

For the adventurous early riser, the Vietnamese Farmers Market (14401 Alcee Fortier Blvd.; 5:30am-9am Sat.) is out in New Orleans East. This is a hard-core ethnic Vietnamese market with a focus on seafood and Asian vegetables. Don't expect everyone here to speak English.

shop offers a great selection of local and regional blues, jazz, funk, R&B, gospel, Cajun and zydeco, reggae, swamp pop, rock, and hip-hop. This is an especially great place if you're looking for Mardi Gras music, performers of which range from brass bands to Mardi Gras Indians to the Neville Brothers. You'll find both used and new CDs, plus vinyl records, books, DVDs, videos, and T-shirts. This popular store also has occasional in-store live performances.

MAP 3: 421 Frenchmen St., 504/586-1094, louisianamusicfactory.com; 11am-8pm Sun.-Thurs., 11am-10pm Fri.-Sat.

Garden District and Irish Channel

Map 4

The scenic Garden District, south of Central City, is filled with historic mansions and the oldest cemetery in the city. There's plenty of diverse, cosmopolitan flare here, too, with **hip bars,** cafés prime for people-watching, and **indie boutiques** all sitting side by side along Magazine Street and St. Charles Avenue. Eateries range from hipster sandwich spots to the famous **Commander's Palace.** Between the Garden District and the Pontchartrain Expressway is the **Lower Garden District** (LGD), a neighborhood with decidedly **punk vibes.** You'll find funky stores, **dive bars,** and casual ethnic restaurants.

South of the Warehouse District and the Pontchartrain Expressway, along the banks of the Mississippi, is the Irish Channel. **Historic churches** and pubs honor the Irish and German roots of this formerly working-class neighborhood.

TOP SIGHTS

- Where It's Mardi Gras Year-Round: **Blaine Kern's Mardi Gras World** (page 133)
- Where to Learn about Catholic History in New Orleans: **St. Alphonsus Church Art and Culture Center** (page 133)

TOP RESTAURANTS

- Best Updated Creole Classics: **Commander's Palace** (page 137)
- Best Elegant Comfort Food: **Coquette** (page 139)
- Where to Satisfy Your Cravings: **Turkey and the Wolf** (page 141)

TOP NIGHTLIFE

- Where to Find Rare Belgian Beer 24 Hours a Day: **The Avenue Pub** (page 145)
- Where to Pair Cocktails and Cake: **Bakery Bar** (page 145)
- Most Cave-Like Whiskey Bar: **Barrel Proof** (page 145)

TOP ARTS AND CULTURE

- Best Gallery for Homespun Signage: **Simon of New Orleans** (page 148)

TOP SHOPS

- Best NOLA Gear that Supports the City: **DNO** (page 151)
- Where to Spot an Up-and-Coming DJ: **NOLA Mix Records** (page 152)
- Best Shop for a New Orleans Necessity: **Bella Umbrella** (page 152)

GETTING THERE AND AROUND

- Streetcar lines: St. Charles (12)
- Major bus routes: 11, 27, 91

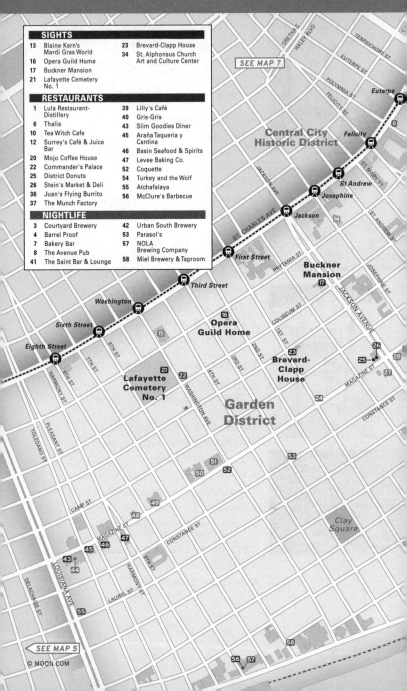

SIGHTS

13	Blaine Kern's Mardi Gras World	23	Brevard-Clapp House
16	Opera Guild Home	34	St. Alphonsus Church Art and Culture Center
17	Buckner Mansion		
21	Lafayette Cemetery No. 1		

RESTAURANTS

1	Lula Restaurant-Distillery	39	Lilly's Café
6	Thalia	40	Gris-Gris
10	Tea Witch Cafe	43	Slim Goodies Diner
12	Surrey's Café & Juice Bar	45	Araña Taqueria y Cantina
20	Mojo Coffee House	46	Basin Seafood & Spirits
22	Commander's Palace	47	Levee Baking Co.
25	District Donuts	52	Coquette
26	Stein's Market & Deli	54	Turkey and the Wolf
36	Juan's Flying Burrito	55	Atchafalaya
37	The Munch Factory	56	McClure's Barbecue

NIGHTLIFE

3	Courtyard Brewery	42	Urban South Brewery
4	Barrel Proof	53	Parasol's
7	Bakery Bar	57	NOLA Brewing Company
8	The Avenue Pub	58	Miel Brewery & Taproom
41	The Saint Bar & Lounge		

SEE MAP 7

Euterpe

Central City Historic District

Felicity

St Andrew

Josephine

Jackson

First Street

Third Street

Washington

Sixth Street

Eighth Street

Opera Guild Home

Buckner Mansion

Brevard-Clapp House

Lafayette Cemetery No. 1

Garden District

Clay Square

SEE MAP 5

© MOON.COM

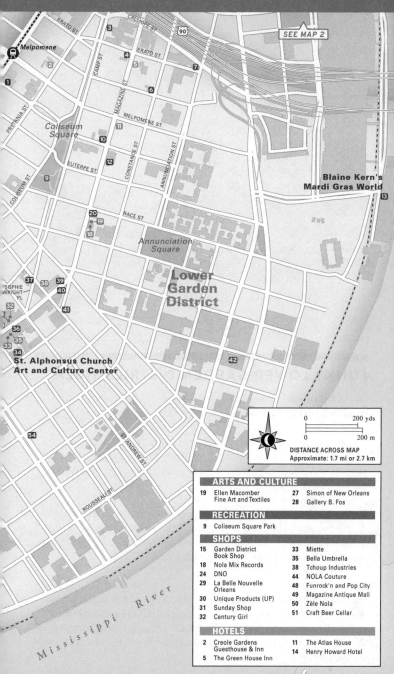

ARTS AND CULTURE

19 Ellen Macomber Fine Art and Textiles
27 Simon of New Orleans
28 Gallery B. Fos

RECREATION

9 Coliseum Square Park

SHOPS

15 Garden District Book Shop
18 Nola Mix Records
24 DNO
29 La Belle Nouvelle Orleans
30 Unique Products (UP)
31 Sunday Shop
32 Century Girl
33 Miette
35 Bella Umbrella
38 Tchoup Industries
44 NOLA Couture
48 Funrock'n and Pop City
49 Magazine Antique Mall
50 Zèle Nola
51 Craft Beer Cellar

HOTELS

2 Creole Gardens Guesthouse & Inn
5 The Green House Inn
11 The Atlas House
14 Henry Howard Hotel

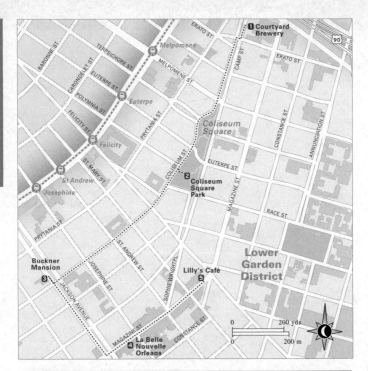

FUNKY LOWER GARDEN DISTRICT WALK

TOTAL DISTANCE: 1.3 miles (2.1 kilometers)
WALKING TIME: 30-45 minutes

This area is filled with shops, cafés, restaurants, and plenty of opportunities for people-watching, especially on the neighborhood's
stretch of Magazine Street. This is a great post-lunch afternoon
walk.

1 Start at **Courtyard Brewery,** grabbing a malty drink to-go before
turning left and walking to the intersection of Magazine and Erato
Streets, the gateway to Uptown. Turn left and head up Magazine Street,
with the Mississippi River on your left and the Crescent Connection
span bridge to your back.

2 Walk up Magazine Street for two blocks before turning right onto
Melpomene Street. Walk another block to **Coliseum Square Park,**
a peaceful urban oasis, to take a breath for a moment. Walk south along
Coliseum Street to check out the architecture of the houses surrounding the park.

3 Keep heading up Coliseum Street (with the river on your left) for five and a half blocks, continuing to admire the historic architecture of the homes in the area. At the intersection with Jackson Avenue, you'll come upon the famed **Buckner Mansion,** an enormous and lavish building. After taking it in, take a left onto Jackson.

4 Continue on Jackson for three blocks before hitting Magazine Street again. Take another left onto Magazine. You'll quickly come across the intriguing **La Belle Nouvelle Orleans,** which is crammed full of antiques that range from rundown and downright weird to mint condition rarities.

5 Walk down Magazine Street for another four blocks, checking out the many shops, boutiques, galleries, and restaurants. If you're peckish, **Lilly's Café** will fuel your shopping with restorative pho or inexpensive banh mi sandwiches. If you just need a beverage, opt for a refreshing *cafe sua da* (Vietnamese iced coffee) or tropical juice. It's about eight blocks back down Magazine to return to the starting point or keep shopping till you drop!

the Buckner Mansion

GARDEN DISTRICT AND IRISH CHANNEL WALK

TOTAL DISTANCE: 2.4 miles (3.9 kilometers)
WALKING TIME: 1-1.25 hours

Where Magazine Street crosses Jackson Avenue, the neighborhood shifts from the Lower Garden District to the Garden District (on the right) and the Irish Channel (on the left side). The side-by-side districts pack a lot of different atmospheres into a small area. This is a great walk for the late morning, culminating in a lovely lunch.

1 Start at **District Donuts,** just a few steps west on Magazine Street from its intersection with Jackson Avenue. Grab a birthday cake donut or savory breakfast sandwich and a coffee.

2 After fueling up, head back to the intersection of Magazine and Jackson, and take a right on Jackson. In half a block you'll see Antiques on Jackson; behind that shop is **Simon of New Orleans,** an offbeat outdoor art gallery of a very New Orleans-style character. Peruse

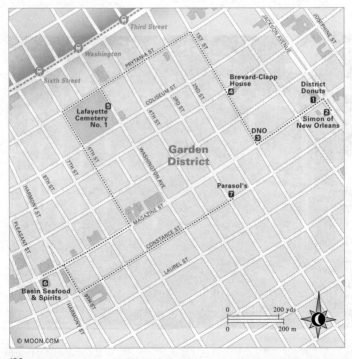

colorful houses in the Irish Channel

the artist's fun signs and decide whether you need to take one home as a souvenir.

3 From Simon's, head back to Magazine Street and take a left. At First Street, cross Magazine and peruse the progressive, fiercely New Orleans-centric T-shirts, notebooks, and local products at **DNO.**

4 Continue up First Street for two blocks in order to check out the exterior of the **Brevard-Clapp House** and see where Anne Rice used to live (and where she set her *Mayfair Witch* trilogy).

5 Walk two more blocks on First Street before taking a left on Prytania Street. Walk for four blocks under stately oak trees and past historic houses, before reaching **Lafayette Cemetery No. 1** on the corner of Prytania Street and Washington Avenue. Cross over Washington and you'll find the entrance on the left, halfway down the block. There will likely be several guides offering their services at the entrance; if you want to know about the specific "residents" of the cemetery and how they tie into the greater history of New Orleans, opt for a tour.

6 After exiting the cemetery, turn left back onto Prytania Street, then make the first left onto Sixth Street. Walk down Sixth Street among the unique and vintage Garden District homes for four blocks before taking a right onto Magazine Street. Window shop your way up the street for four blocks until you hit **Basin Seafood & Spirits** on the left. Slurp some "ersters" on the half shell (half price on Monday!) and some gumbo.

DNO

7 Leaving Basin, head out to the right for a block and a half and turn down Ninth Street. Walk down one block. Turn left onto Constance Street and walk for six blocks, checking out the architecture and neighborhood vibe. You'll see double shotguns, Creole cottages, folks sitting out on their porches, and locals going about their days. At the corner of Constance and Third Streets you'll see the famous Irish neighborhood bar and po'boy shop **Parasol's.** Grab a well-deserved beer and chat it up with the locals. You're a block below Magazine Street; the #11 bus can take you uptown or downtown from here.

GARDEN DISTRICT

NEIGHBORHOOD WALKS

22

Sights

✪ Blaine Kern's Mardi Gras World

The top reason that families venture to the Port of New Orleans is to visit Blaine Kern's Mardi Gras World, the largest builder of Carnival sculptures and parade floats in the country. A visit here consists of a one-hour guided tour of the cavernous warehouse facility, strolling amid kaleidoscopic floats and the artists working on them: you might see them shaping the oversized frames with wire and plaster or painting the entire float to bring the art to life. Though Mardi Gras takes place over a relatively short period each winter, this place hums with activity every day of the year. The last tour begins at 4:30pm, and a complimentary shuttle is available for visitors coming from the CBD or French Quarter. Mardi Gras World is right on the river between the CBD and the Garden District.

MAP 4: 1380 Port of New Orleans Pl., 504/361-7821, mardigrasworld.com; by guided tour 9:30am-5:30pm daily; $22 adults, $17 seniors and students, $14 children 2-11, children under 2 free

Blaine Kern's Mardi Gras World

✪ St. Alphonsus Church Art and Culture Center

In the early 1840s, German and Irish immigrants, many of whom were Catholic, began to arrive in the area. St. Mary's Assumption was constructed on Josephine Street, becoming the state's first Catholic church for Germans. By the late 1850s, there were three permanent churches here: St. Alphonsus, serving the Irish parishioners; a second St. Mary's Assumption, which replaced the original; and the Romanesque Notre Dame de Bon Secours, intended for the French-speaking Catholics. These buildings comprised what's known today as Ecclesiastical Square. Notre Dame de Bon Secours was demolished in 1925; St. Mary's Assumption is still an active parish.

St. Alphonsus was abandoned in the 1970s but restored (and deconsecrated) 20 years later as a cultural center. The altar, the baptismal font, and a statue known as *Jesus Entombed* have since been restored. The space often hosts concerts, community meetings, and art exhibitions. During the holiday season, the former church is filled with elaborate crèche scenes for visitors to look at. The stained-glass windows are the work of famed German artist F. X. Zettler.

If you stop by on one of the days the church is open, you'll likely receive an informal tour of the space by one of the Friends of St. Alphonsus, who have historic knowledge of not only the church

St. Alphonsus Church Art and Culture Center

and Ecclesiastical Square, but the entire neighborhood. They love answering questions, so keep them coming.

MAP 4: 2025 Constance St., 504/524-8116, friendsofstalphonsus.org; 10am-2pm Tues., Thurs., and Sat.; free, donations accepted

TOP EXPERIENCE

Lafayette Cemetery No. 1

Dating back to 1832, this cemetery is the oldest of New Orleans's municipal cemeteries and takes up an entire city block. Its proximity to the working-class Irish Channel neighborhood ensured that a wide variety of individuals and families made the Lafayette Cemetery their final resting place. It's non-denominational and non-segregated, with immigrants from over 25 different countries and natives of 26 states interred in its tombs over the centuries. There are tombs for volunteer firemen, orphans, and the wealthy "Southern Yankees" who made

their fortunes in cotton after the Louisiana Purchase.

There's a whole lot to learn about the city by reading the cemetery's various engravings. There are paths and tombs every way you look, which makes for a fun hour or so of self-guided exploration. To enhance your visit, there are multiple opportunities to take a tour. You can book one in advance with Save Our Cemeteries (saveourcemeteries.org; tours 9am and 11am Mon. and Thurs., 9am Tues.-Wed., 9am, 10am, and 11am Fri.-Sat.; $25), the non-profit organization that maintains the city's cemeteries. All proceeds of these tours support their work. If you didn't make advance reservations for a tour, there are usually independent guides waiting outside, eager to show you around.

MAP 4: 1416-1498 Washington Ave., 504/658-3781, saveourcemeteries.org; 7am-3pm daily

Opera Guild Home

Built in 1859 by William A. Freret, this eye-catching, Greek Revival-style mansion became the home of the Women's Guild of New Orleans Opera Association in 1965. It's particularly noted for its small octagonal tower, though the color scheme—all white with dark-green shutters—plus the manicured lawn and wrought-iron fencing all make for a lovely photograph. Furnished with 18th- and 19th-century European and American furniture, artwork, and collectibles, this well-appointed Garden District home is the frequent site of wedding ceremonies and receptions.

Drop in for a tour on Monday

Opera Guild Home

afternoons, where a squad of docents will be happy to show you around. There are no advance reservations or set times for tours. Tours are about a half-hour long, and cost $15 (cash only). This is the only private home in the Garden District open to the public.

MAP 4: 2504 Prytania St., 504/267-9539; by tour only, 11am-3pm Mon. Labor Day-Memorial Day; $15

Brevard-Clapp House

This Greek Revival townhouse with Italianate details housed and inspired horror novelist Anne Rice for 15 years, but even before that it was a Garden District historic home of note. It was built in 1857 for wealthy merchant Albert Hamilton Brevard, who lived in it until 1869 and then sold it to Reverend Emory Clapp, who kept it in the family until 1935. Anne Rice, whose best-selling novel *Interview with a Vampire* (1976) put her on the literary map, was born in New Orleans in 1941 and lived in the Big Easy for the first 16 years of her life. She eventually returned and

Lafayette Cemetery No. 1

lived in the Brevard-Clapp House from 1989 to 2004. During that time, it served as the inspiration for Mayfair Manor, the fictional home of Rice's Mayfair Witches.

MAP 4: 1239 1st St., closed to the public

Buckner Mansion

You may recognize this enormous plantation-style mansion from several television shows and movie sets, including *American Horror Story: Coven*. It was originally erected in 1853 by Henry Sullivan Buckner, who wanted to own the largest house in New Orleans. It hasn't been open to the public since 1983, but if you and your 10 closest friends are so inclined, it's available to rent for $20,000 per month.

MAP 4: 1410 Jackson Ave., closed to the public

the Bloody Mary bar at Atchafalaya

Restaurants

PRICE KEY

$	Entrées less than $15
$$	Entrées $15-30
$$$	Entrées more than $30

CAJUN AND CREOLE

Atchafalaya $$$

Look for the enormous homage to the Southern cooking staple, the cast iron skillet, on the exterior wall of Atchafalaya, a spot that brings raucous brunch and sophisticated dinner experiences to the Irish Channel. The restaurant is set in a converted Creole cottage, with design elements repurposed from materials found in post-Katrina New Orleans. The brunch menu, which is served Thursday through Monday, includes hearty, rich dishes that may require an immediate nap, aided by the build your own Bloody Mary bar and a selection of elegant craft cocktails. Enjoy live jazz music on Saturday and Sunday. The dinner menu offers a take on fine dining, thanks to the talents of Chef David Barbeau, who applies innovative techniques to Southern ingredients. At night, the restaurant is softly lit, making it perfect for a romantic or celebratory occasion.

MAP 4: 901 Louisiana Ave., 504/891-9626, atchafalayarestaurant. com; 10am-2:30pm and 6pm-10pm Thurs.-Mon., 6pm-10pm Tues.-Wed.

✪ Commander's Palace $$$

Open since 1880, you might fear that Commander's Palace is resting on its laurels, but nothing could be further from the truth. Chef Tory McPhail's "Haute Creole" cuisine coaxes bold flavors out of locally sourced meat, seafood, and seasonal produce, and the classics—turtle soup, pecan-crusted Gulf fish, and a sinful bread pudding soufflé with whiskey sauce—have kept their well-deserved place. Servers attend to every need in the warren of dining rooms. The famous jazz brunch is still a must-do. Lunch is great, too, especially with 25-cent martinis on the menu. Reservations are recommended—all three meals tend to fill up fast. If you plan on going, wear something nice. Jackets for men aren't required (although collared shirts and closed-toe shoes are), but are preferred. Shorts, T-shirts, sweatshirts and -pants, and flip-flops are out, along with ripped jeans. (They discourage regular jeans, but they aren't banned.)

MAP 4: 1403 Washington Ave., 504/899-8221, commanderspalace. com; 11:30am-1:30pm and 6pm-10pm Mon.-Fri., 11am-1pm and 6pm-10pm Sat., 10am-1:30pm and 6pm-10pm Sun.

Gris-Gris $$

Sit downstairs at the 15-seat kitchen counter in a striking, industrial-style space for an intimate experience. Here, you can watch elevated homestyle Southern and Creole/Cajun dishes being made right in front of you, like Oysters BLT, with pork belly, microgreens, and tomato jam, or Mama's Chicken & Dumplings. The entire menu is also served upstairs, which has a sleek, casual contemporary vibe with

fried chicken plate at McClure's Barbecue

a more traditional bar and high-top tables and outdoor seating on a wraparound deck overlooking Magazine Street. Don't skimp on the great cocktails. The daily happy hour (4pm-7pm) offers deals on cocktails, craft beer, and wines by the glass.

MAP 4: 1800 Magazine St., 504/272-0241, grisgrisnola.com; 11am-10pm Mon.-Sat., 11am-9pm Sun.

The Munch Factory $$

Southern faves and comfort Creole food made from scratch are big draws at this spacious, high-ceilinged dining room with friendly service and fun cocktails. On the lunch menu, burgers and salads sit side by side with locally inspired creations, like the Oysters Gentilly—fried oysters on creamed spinach topped with caramelized onions—or the hot sausage patty melt. For dinner, add elevated entrées like chicken in a creamy herb sauce or classics like blackened redfish. In 2017, Beyoncé and Jay-Z stopped in here the day after playing the Superdome, supporting this minority-owned Creole-soul restaurant.

MAP 4: 1901 Sophie Wright Pl., 504/324-5372, themunchfactory. net; 11:30am-9pm Tues.-Thurs., 11:30am-10pm Fri.-Sat., 11am-2:30pm Sun.

BARBECUE
McClure's Barbecue $$

Neil McClure serves his smoked meats with a wide variety of regional barbecue sauces (Kansas City, North Carolina, Alabama, etc.). Get a plate of meat with sides, a smoked meat sandwich, or a surprisingly excellent burger. The specials, like buttermilk fried chicken or house-smoked pastrami, are insanely delicious. McClure's is the house kitchen for NOLA Brewing's taproom, so there are plenty of beers with which to wash your 'cue down.

MAP 4: 3001 Tchoupitoulas St.,
504/301-2367, mccluresbarbecue.com;
11am-10pm daily

STEAK AND SEAFOOD
Basin Seafood & Spirits $$

This well-located restaurant, tucked into a busy block on Magazine Street, offers innovative and traditional Louisiana seafood dishes like seafood gumbo, crawfish mac & cheese, stuffed crab beignets, and chargrilled or raw oysters on the half shell. The cocktail menu is terrific. Besides the indoor dining area, Basin has a lush rear courtyard as well as sidewalk seating along the bustling street out front, ideal for people-watching. Happy hour alert: They offer 50-cent oysters on Mondays.

MAP 4: 3222 Magazine St.,
504/302-7391, basinseafoodnola.com;
11:30am-10pm Mon.-Sat., 11:30am-9pm
Sun., no lunch Tues.-Thurs. June-Sept.

Lilly's Café

VIETNAMESE
Lilly's Café $

Craving some pho or a traditional banh mi? Head up Magazine Street to the small and bustling Lilly's Café, a casual spot where locals, celebrities, and visitors alike flock for the healing power of lovingly made Vietnamese food. It's a traditional menu with some surprises; check out the *pho ga* (chicken pho) served with poached quail eggs, the spicy shrimp pho, or Lilly's spring rolls made with shrimp, pork, avocado, and strawberry.

MAP 4: 1813 Magazine St.,
504/599-9999; 11am-9pm Mon.-Sat.

ECLECTIC
✪ Coquette $$

A neighborhood bistro with farm-to-table and classic Southern elements, Coquette coalesces into an elegant experience with beautiful food that delivers in both flavor and creativity. Chef co-owners Michael Stoltzfus and Kristen Essig, along with their stellar team, offer up dishes like smoked catfish dip, as well as gulf seafood stew with Spanish chorizo and okra. There are also creative cocktails and thoughtful wine and beer lists. The service is hospitable and friendly, making this a great place to celebrate a special occasion or just sit at the bar.

MAP 4: 2800 Magazine St.,
504/265-0421, coquettenola.com;
5:30pm-10pm Tues.-Sun.

Thalia $$

This cozy, bright space has yellow walls and light wood accents. With an ever-changing menu built around sustainable food practices, Thalia's hearty and straightforward dishes are prepared perfectly, and are augmented with culinary themes like Pasta Night on Thursdays or Steak Night on Saturdays. Conceived, built, and run by the team behind the more formal bistro Coquette, Thalia sits on the former site of one of the city's last segregated bars

BAHN MI: THE NEW PO'BOY

bahn mi sandwich

After the fall of Saigon in 1975, hundreds of Vietnamese refugees, many of them Catholic, sought haven in the United States. The Archdiocese of New Orleans resettled new arrivals in communities in New Orleans East and on the Westbank (across the Mississippi River from New Orleans proper). The similarities in climate and the abundant fishing, shrimping, and farming opportunities made for a somewhat familiar environment for the first wave of Vietnamese immigrants.

Although Vietnamese residents and their culinary traditions have existed in this area for several decades, they mostly stayed within Vietnamese communities. But post-Katrina, those areas recovered more quickly than others. During the months when grocery stores and restaurants were few and far between, Vietnamese cuisine began making its way into the greater New Orleans culture. Soon enough, the traditional banh mi—a French bread roll filled with cold cuts, pâté, aioli, herbs, and pickled vegetables—became known as the "Vietnamese po-boy."

As more people have developed a taste for the rich, fresh, crunchy, spicy sandwich, banh mi spots have opened throughout the city. Restaurants serving banh mi, pho, and other Vietnamese standards like *bun* (rice noodles) or *com* (rice) range from no-frills to upscale. A good banh mi can be found for less than $5-6, especially if you go to the dish's original stomping grounds: New Orleans East (Dong Phuong) or the Westbank (Tan Dinh).

The banh mi melds perfectly into the already strong po'boy game New Orleans offers; it's even served on the same kind of bread. Some spots around town, like McClure's Barbecue and Killer Poboys, use Dong Phuong's rolls for their po'boys, and fancy fusion banh mi (irreverently called "po-mi sandwiches") can be found at Mopho, where fillings like pulled pork, fried oysters, and roast duck are prepared with house mayo, pickled vegetables, fresh herbs, and jalapeños. Namese in Mid City also does crossover banh mi with meatballs and one called "The Ducky Cuban." Cafe Minh, also in Mid-City, offers variations with sautéed wild mushrooms and tempura-fried five-spice chicken.

and looks to overcome that history with a welcoming and inclusive atmosphere. They offer limited reservations.

MAP 4: 1245 Constance St., 504/655-1338, thalianola.com; 5pm-10pm Tues.-Sat.

LATIN AMERICAN
Araña Taqueria and Cantina $

Traditional and innovative Mexican fare (and a whole lot of tequila) come together at Araña, a fun, hip spot with a giant spider web on the wall complete with an oversized spider (*araña* means "spider" in Spanish) and an enormous "Tequila" sign over the bar. It's part of a new New Orleans generation of funky, cool, casual Mexican restaurants. You'll find superior taco and *torta* (sandwich) options, like the *torta cubana* and the spinach, mushroom, almond, and potato taco. The tequila selection is world-class, so aficionados should certainly stop by for one of the six flights offered. The happy hour is a doozy: From 3pm to 7pm Monday through Friday, all tacos and drinks are half price.

MAP 4: 3242 Magazine St., 504/894-1233, aranataqueria.com; 11am-10pm daily

Juan's Flying Burrito $

Juan's has anchored the Lower Garden District since well before the vast majority of trendy and tasty businesses moved in. It's got a grungy edge, manifested in its menu, decor, and sometimes-surly servers. The food is cheap and hearty and hits the spot before or after an evening of drinking—or the morning after. Art covers the brick walls, and loud music fills this joint. The fare is a mod take on Tex-Mex, with pork 'n' slaw tacos, bacon and blue cheese quesadillas, and the Veggie Punk burrito, stuffed with potatoes, jalapeños, and pinto beans. There are lots of vegetarian options and even some vegan dishes. The margaritas are a must. There are now several locations in the city: Mid-City (4724 S. Carrollton Ave.), which is a little less funky but has a dedicated parking lot; in the CBD (515 Baronne St.); and Uptown (5538 Magazine St.).

MAP 4: 2018 Magazine St., 504/569-0000, juansflyingburrito.com; 11am-10pm daily

GASTROPUBS
Lula Restaurant-Distillery $

Louisiana's only distillery-restaurant, Lula is like a brewpub bumped up to the next level, with a gleaming copper still visible in the large, high-ceilinged warehouse. The cuisine has a rustic bent to it, featuring dishes like boudin egg rolls, sugarcane pork skewers, and a seasonal seafood boil. Of particular note is the all-you-can-drink vodka bar at Saturday and Sunday brunch, as well as the weekday happy hour (4pm-7pm Mon.-Thurs.), which features $5 cocktails and appetizers.

MAP 4: 1532 St Charles Ave., 504/267-7624, lulasnola.com; 11am-10pm Mon.-Thurs., 11am-11pm Fri., 9am-11pm Sat., 9am-10pm Sun.

CAFÉS AND LIGHT BITES
✪ Turkey and the Wolf $

Mason Hereford just wanted a place to make sandwiches with the ingredients and flavors he loved from childhood. What he created was this

lunch at Turkey and the Wolf

nationally lauded lunch spot (voted #1 New Restaurant in America in 2017 by *Bon Appetit*) with menu items like a fried baloney sandwich, a collard melt, deviled eggs, and the most insane Cobb salad ever. The cocktail menu reads like a boozy Mad Libs, with the names of the drinks reflecting the personal stories of their creators. Order at the register and enjoy the '70s and '80s kitsch plates and salt and pepper shakers. The cinderblock walls are painted turquoise and the whole vibe is very upbeat and casual.

MAP 4: 739 Jackson Ave., 504/218-7428, turkeyandthewolf. com; 11am-5pm Mon. and Wed.-Sat., 11am-3pm Sun.

DELIS
Stein's Market & Deli $
You'll find two businesses for the price of one here: a popular Philly-style Jewish deli with classic and creative sandwiches, bagels, and meats and cheese by the pound; and

a jaw-dropping beer vendor with options from all over the world. Oddly, you're not allowed to drink any of the beer sold on site—so indulge in a Doc Brown's cream soda and a sandwich at the restaurant, and take your beer to go. Be sure to check out the daily special sandwiches. If weather permits, take a seat at one of the picnic tables out front: They're great for people-watching.

MAP 4: 2207 Magazine St., 504/527-0771, steinsdeli.com; 7am-7pm Tues.-Fri., 9am-5pm Sat.-Sun.

BREAKFAST AND BRUNCH
Slim Goodies Diner $
Conveniently located on Magazine Street, Slim Goodies provides the classic diner experience, with great breakfast plates, pancakes, omelets, and grilled sandwiches. With menu options like the Orleans Slammer (hash browns, bacon, eggs, and cheese served with toast), this is where to go if you need to fight off a

hangover. It's a staple of the community, having supported rescue and construction workers in the early recovery days after Hurricane Katrina.

MAP 4: 3322 Magazine St., 504/891-3447, slimgoodiesdiner.com; 6am-3pm daily

Surrey's Cafe and Juice Bar $

This eclectic breakfast spot features American, Southern, and Latin American dishes. Try the boudin, traditional *migas* (scrambled eggs with poblano peppers, cheese, and tortilla chips), bananas Foster pancakes, enormous biscuits, or the best grits beside your mama's. All meals go down great with the delicious fresh-squeezed juices. Surrey's is a great option when everyone in your party wants something different for breakfast or lunch—there are also vegan, vegetarian, and gluten-free

options. There's no booze served here, and there will likely be a line unless you head over relatively early (before 10am) during the week.

MAP 4: 1418 Magazine St., 504/524-3828, surreysnola.com; 7am-3pm daily

COFFEE AND DESSERTS

District Donuts $

District Donuts elevated New Orleans's donut scene with creative offerings like raspberry cheesecake, Nutter Butter, and wedding cake. But don't fret if you're more inclined toward savory breakfast pastries—there's an outstanding selection of *kolaches* (a Czech pastry filled with an assortment of savory items) and breakfast sandwiches served on fluffy biscuits (don't miss the chicken fried pork belly biscuit

the menu and specials at Stein's Market & Deli

143

with white gravy). For lunch and dinner there are delicious sliders, burgers, and salads.

MAP 4: 2209 Magazine St., 504/570-6945, districtdonuts.com; 7am-9pm daily

Levee Baking Co. $

This bakery consistently produces the finest from-scratch pastries, breads, and cookies made with local fruits and vegetables. The croissants are perfectly created, and the scones and hand pies come in both sweet and savory options, depending on what's at the farmers markets that week. Keep an eye out for the weekly bread; it tends to feature unusual ingredients and techniques. Grab a treat and a cup of coffee and enjoy the rustic communal wood tables in the airy space, where what's behind the glass is the real decoration.

MAP 4: 3138 Magazine St., 504/354-8708, leveebakingco.com; 9am-3pm Wed.-Sat., 10am-3pm Sun.

Mojo Coffee House $

Mojo has held down the corner of Magazine and Race Streets since 2006. Today it includes an in-house coffee roasting facility and serves an expansive menu of breakfast and lunch items. In addition to the standard array of pastries, Mojo offers yogurt bowls, heartily topped crispbreads (think avocado toast taken to the next level), sandwiches, and salads. There's plenty of room in this high-ceilinged space, warmed

up with cheerful orange walls and wood tables and counters. It's also one of the few coffee spots in the area that's open late. There's a second location at 4700 Freret Street.

MAP 4: 1500 Magazine St., 504/525-2244, mojocoffeehouse. com; 6am-11pm Mon. -Fri, 7am-11pm Sat.-Sun.

Tea Witch Cafe $

Although the Tea Witch Cafe offers several obscure forms of psychic readings (Lenormand, medicine cards, and ancestor work in addition to tarot), the focus of the proprietors is to provide the neighborhood with a cozy café seving dozens of low-caffeine tea options as well as more traditional coffee drinks. You can "get witchy" if you want to, and talk about the tea's spiritual properties, or you can just hang out sipping a unique hand-blended tea (hot or iced) in comfy chairs with free Wi-Fi and friendly service.

MAP 4: 1381 Magazine St., 504/407-0694, teawitchcafe.com; noon-6pm Wed.-Sun

espresso and avocado toast at Mojo Coffee House

Nightlife

BARS AND LOUNGES

✪ The Avenue Pub

Ask any local beer nerd where to find the best beer in the state, and they'll tell you to visit The Avenue Pub. The focus is on quality over quantity (although there are almost 50 taps between the two bars here). Owner Polly Watts has access to some of the finest beers in the world, and the Belgian, sour, and IPA selections are on point. It's also a long-time neighborhood corner bar that's open 24 hours a day, so it's not your typical beer bar. That lack of pretension only adds to the appeal of the place. They also have a serious whiskey selection in their upstairs balcony bar. Regardless of what you drink, there's nothing like watching the streetcar and New Orleans life go by on the balcony overlooking St. Charles Avenue.

MAP 4: 1732 St. Charles Ave., 504/586-9243, theavenuepub.com; 24 hours daily

✪ Bakery Bar

The Bakery Bar is what happens when cake makers collaborate with a seasoned local bartender. The team at Debbie Does Doberge and bartender Jeff Schwartz created a unique concept that excels on both sides of the equation, with a tight list of classic and unique cocktails and slices of *doberge* (a type of many-layered cake that originated in New Orleans). The excellent bartending staff will be happy to help you figure out the perfect cocktail to pair with your cake. There's also a delicious brunch menu served until 3pm, and savory snacks (plus more desserts) served in the evening. Happy Hour alert: From 5pm to 7pm every day, they have 5-6 rotating drinks available for $5-6.

MAP 4: 1179 Annunciation St., 504/265-8884, bakery. bar; 11am-midnight Tues.-Fri., 10am-midnight Sat.-Sun.

✪ Barrel Proof

The cave-like atmosphere of Barrel Proof makes you feel like an artist sipping whiskey, waiting for inspiration to flow from the glass of brown liquid in front of you. The bar's 300-plus whiskey selection backs up these flights of fancy, and locals and visitors alike benefit from the bar staff's deep breadth of both whiskey knowledge and life wisdom.

MAP 4: 1201 Magazine St., 504/299-1888, barrelproofnola.com; 4pm-1am Sun.-Thurs., 4pm-2am Fri.-Sat.

Parasol's

This unpretentious bar is more of a neighborhood institution than a dive. The front room has a bar that runs the length of the room, while the back dining room serves up assorted po'boys (roast beef, fried catfish, and firecracker shrimp are a few standouts). The vibe changes according to the crowd; some days it'll be quiet and reflective, and others it will be crowded and very merry. Parasol's co-hosts an insane

Irish Channel block party every St. Patrick's Day.

MAP 4: 2533 Constance St., 504/302-1543; 11am-2am daily

DANCE CLUBS
The Saint Bar & Lounge

At this late-night club, the party really gets going around midnight. There's a DJ, cheap drinks, and throngs of service industry folks just getting off work. Tikioke Tuesday is a long-standing tradition with tiki drink specials and karaoke starting at 11pm. It's a dive-y party and a New Orleans rite of passage. If you're not into the rowdy scene, go for the 7pm-9pm happy hour.

MAP 4: 961 St Mary St., 504/523-0050, thesaintneworleans.com; 7pm-4am daily; no cover

BREWERIES
Courtyard Brewery

This microbrewery makes some of the city's best beers, and the only place to find them is right here. San Diego native and NOLA transplant Scott Wood brought his love of IPAs and experimentation to his brewing to much success. It's like sitting in a friend's house or backyard, drinking great beer and engaging in boisterous conversation under twinkling lights. Folks from the neighborhood mingle with beer geeks from near and far, resulting in a low-key party-like atmosphere spilling out into the courtyard and beyond most nights. Be sure to check out Courtyard's other location (2745 Lafitte St.) if you're near the Lafitte Greenway.

MAP 4: 1160 Camp St., no phone, courtyardbrewing.com; 11am-10pm Sun.-Wed., 11am-11pm Thurs.-Sat.

NOLA Brewing Company

Miel Brewery & Taproom

Opened in 2018, Miel strives to be a community hangout that also happens to brew and sell beer. The converted warehouse space means noise bounces around inside; the dog-friendly courtyard beer garden is where it's at. *Miel* means "honey" in both French and Spanish, which reflects both owners' heritages. Co-owner and brewer Alex Peyroux's family manages a bee colony outside New Orleans, so the brewery has access to a lot of honey for making its beer. Note: Miel only takes credit or debit cards.

MAP 4: 405 6th St., 504/372-4260, mielbrewery.com; 2pm-10pm Mon.-Thurs., 11am-11pm Fri.-Sat., noon-8pm Sun.

NOLA Brewing Company

Open since 2009, NOLA Brewing was the first brewery in the city of New Orleans after Dixie Brewing closed in 2005. The brewery has an attached taproom that serves all its flagships, seasonals, limited releases, and taproom-only beers. NOLA Brewing embraces every aspect of New Orleans, and somehow captures all of that (and more) in every can and glass of its beer. The beers range from mild to hoppy to sour. The taproom is a spacious thing of beauty—spanning two floors with an outdoor patio upstairs, two bars, and rustic wooden furniture. On-site is McClure's Barbecue, which serves up barbecued meat, fried chicken, and burgers all day. Free tours of the production facility are offered on Friday afternoons.

MAP 4: 3001 Tchoupitoulas St., 504/896—9996, nolabrewing.com; 11am-11pm daily

Urban South Brewery

Located halfway between NOLA Brewing Company and Courtyard Brewery, Urban South's warehouse taproom bustles with beer aficionados, families, and dogs, all of whom sit at indoor picnic tables that have a clear sightline to the brewing equipment. The offerings include traditional German styles, hazy IPAs, fruited goses, and kettle-soured beer. There are also many experimental beers on tap, as well as a lot of packaged beers to go that can't be found anywhere else.

MAP 4: 1645 Tchoupitoulas St., 504/267-4852, urbansouthbrewery.com; noon-9pm Mon.-Fri., 11am-9pm Sat.-Sun.

Arts and Culture

GALLERIES

Gallery B. Fos

Artist Becky Fos likes bold, bright colors. A lot. Her gallery on Magazine Street in the Lower Garden District proves it, displaying canvases she painted with bright oils using the tip of a palette knife. Some work is abstract, but there are a lot of New Orleans inspired subjects in her style as well.

MAP 4: 2138 Magazine St., 504/444-2967, beckyfos.com; 10am-5pm Thurs.-Sat., noon-5pm Sun.

Ellen Macomber Fine Art and Textiles

This dazzling gallery resembles a funky gift shop. That's because Ellen Macomber works extensively with textiles, so her artwork, in the form of caftans, capes, and bags, can be worn as clothing or utilized in everyday life. The gorgeous glittering caftans all have pockets, making the art even more practical. She also works with cartography, so there are many items with artistic renderings of maps of New Orleans, including framed prints, postcards, and pillows.

MAP 4: 1518 Magazine St., 504/314-9414, ellenmacomber.com; by appointment only

✪ Simon of New Orleans

You'll find the long-haired, bearded Simon (pronounced the French

Gallery B. Fos

Simon of New Orleans

way, See-MONE) Hardeveld kicking around his outdoor studio filled with bold folk art. Simon is known for his stylized New Orleans-patois signs with sayings like "Be Nice or Leave," "Do You Know What it Means to Miss New Orleans?," and "Ain't Nothing that a Poboy Can't Fix." His signs are found all over town, but oddly, there's no sign denoting his artistic space, located obscurely in the yard of the Antiques on Jackson shop. Simon may hail from Cannes, France, originally, but he's a true New Orleans character—stop by and he'll tell you the stories behind all his signs and other artwork.

MAP 4: Antiques on Jackson, 1028 Jackson Ave., 504/524-8201, simonofneworleans.com; 10am-5pm Mon.-Sat.

Recreation

PARKS AND PLAZAS

Coliseum Square Park

Bordered by Coliseum, Race, and Camp Streets, this oddly shaped, semi-triangular park in the Lower Garden District offers a lush, peaceful place to read, picnic, or walk your dog. Filled with shady oak trees, inviting benches, and well-manicured lawns, the park also has a lovely fountain that is a popular spot to hang out with friends and neighbors. There are no public bathrooms.

MAP 4: Bounded by Coliseum St., Race St., and Camp St., 24 hours daily; free

Shops

SHOPPING CENTERS
Zèle NOLA

Dozens of local artists, artisans, and craftspeople have set up stalls at Zèle, so coming here is like visiting a ton of cool shops all in one place. Everything's unique; you'll find practical items like cutting boards and hairbands next to more artistic flights of fancy. The large open space is well laid out, bright, and inviting; every vendor has a section of their own, but nothing's isolated or cut off. This is the perfect stop for crossing multiple people off your gift list.

MAP 4: 2841 Magazine St., 504/450-0789, zelenola.com; 10:30am-6pm Mon.-Sat., noon-5pm Sun.

ANTIQUES AND VINTAGE
Century Girl

At Century Girl, you'll find upscale vintage clothing, shoes, and accessories for women. The merchandise and the decor will make you feel like you've stepped back in time to the 1950s, 1920s, or even earlier, as you take in the antique fabrics, garments, and accessories that not only appear on the sales racks but also on the walls. Prices are on the higher end, but the quality of the goods and the experience are worth it.

MAP 4: 2023 Magazine St., 504/875-3105, centurygirlvintage.com; 11am-5pm Mon.-Fri., 11am-5:30pm Sat., 11am-4pm Sun.

La Belle Nouvelle Orleans

This is one of those antique shops stuffed so full of old, random items that it's hard to move around or even reach many of the wares. But look closely and you may find the weird, cool thing you've been looking for your whole life.

MAP 4: 2112 Magazine St., 504/581-3733, labellenouvelle.tumblr.com; 10am-5pm daily

Magazine Antique Mall

If you like mining for antique treasure, this is the place for you. The Magazine Antique Mall is filled with dozens of vintage sellers displaying wares for sale on consignment. The building houses multiple stalls and makeshift corridors, and surprises lurk around every corner. Local artists also set up stalls here. It's a great place to spend some time, especially when it's raining or really hot outside.

La Belle Nouvelle Orleans

MAP 4: 3017 Magazine St., 504/896-9994; 10am-5pm Mon.-Sat., noon-5pm Sun.

SPECIALTY FOOD AND DRINK

Craft Beer Cellar

Whether you're looking for a six-pack, a single can to sip on while walking up Magazine Street, or a nerdy conversation about beer with the knowledgeable, passionate staff, the Craft Beer Cellar has you covered. They've got tons of local options, helpfully organized in "New Orleans," "Louisiana," and "The South" sections, as well as Belgians and a nice selection of ciders.

MAP 4: 2801 Magazine St., ste. D, 504/962-7870, neworleans. craftbeercellar.com; 10am-8pm Mon.-Sat., 10am-5pm Sun.

GIFTS AND SOUVENIRS

✪ DNO

T-shirts, hats, and stickers with DNO's iconic skull logo can be spotted all over town and you can buy one for yourself at this socially conscious, community-minded shop that's dedicated to New Orleans. Set on an unexpected residential corner, the shop also sells New Orleans- and Louisiana-focused books, art, beauty products, coffee mugs, and much more. A portion of the shop's proceeds are donated to local non-profits.

MAP 4: 1101 1st St., 504/941-7010, dno. la; 11am-6pm daily

Funrock'n and Pop City

This pair of conjoined shops are, as advertised, just plain fun. One shop sells costumes, custom-made T-shirts, and weird accessories, while the other offers geeky collectables and, like, whoopie cushions. It's the perfect place to grab anything from last-minute wigs to a gift for a friend (of any age and/or maturity level).

MAP 4: 3109-3118 Magazine St., 504/895-4102, nolapopcity.com; 11am-6pm Sun.-Thurs., 11am-7pm Fri.-Sat.

Miette

Miette

This store is crammed full of wares from New Orleans artists and makers. It's the place to find unusual and fun souvenirs like jewelry made from New Orleans water meters, giant wall hangings made by a Mardi Gras float artist, and stuffed voodoo dolls. Upstairs is an adults-only loft that features sexy art and other adult-themed products.

MAP 4: 2038 Magazine St., 504/522-2883, iheartmiette.com; 10am-7pm Mon.-Sat., 10am-6pm Sun.

Unique Products (UP)

Unique Products provides recycled and repurposed souvenirs for both locals and visitors. The store is a wonderland of creativity, dominated by the co-owners' colorful and vibrant lamp shades made from recycled Mardi Gras beads along with other fun, locally produced, New Orleans-focused products like hand towels, books, throw pillows, clocks, hand-painted matchboxes, voodoo gris-gris bags, and other objects d'art. It's fun for the whole family.

MAP 4: 2041 Magazine St., 504/237-4224, shopgreenneworleans.com; 11am-6pm Mon.-Sat.

BOOKS AND MUSIC
Garden District Book Shop

This is a bookstore designed to get lost in—both in its wide range of genres and in the shelves and stacks of books upon books. Over the last four decades, this new and used bookstore has become a staple in the community, hosting dozens of book signings by both local and nationally renowned authors each month.

MAP 4: Rink Shopping Center, 2727 Prytania St., 504/895-2266, gardendistrictbookshop.com; 10am-5pm Mon.-Sat., 10am-4pm Sun.

✪ NOLA Mix Records

Originally an organization to teach local kids how to spin records, NOLA Mix has become an entrenched part of the community. This Lower Garden District retail shop carries tons of new and used vinyl with categories like "bounce" and "experimental Cajun." There's a heavy emphasis on soul, funk, jazz, and gospel. On weekends, they spice it up with live music,

DJs, or art shows (note the local art on the walls).

MAP 4: 1522 Magazine St., 504/345-2138, nolamix.com; 11am-6pm Tues.-Sat., noon-5pm Sun.

Bella Umbrella

CLOTHING AND ACCESSORIES
✪ Bella Umbrella

Bella Umbrella is perfect for weathering one of New Orleans's frequent rainstorms, but it's also much more than that. Owner Jodell Egbert offers everything from standard travel umbrellas to reverse closure umbrellas to high-end imports from Italy. Egbert also rents out her collection of gorgeous vintage umbrellas for a reasonable price ($25 for a Thurs.-Mon. rental). And she designs and fabricates her own line of pagoda-inspired umbrellas that work both as fashionable parasols as well as waterproof umbrellas. Even if it's a sunny day, stop in, twirl some umbrellas, and take a selfie.

MAP 4: 2036 Magazine St., 504/302-1036, bellaumbrella.com; 11am-5pm daily

NOLA Couture

When you first walk into NOLA Couture, you'll see dog leashes on the left and men's ties on the right—setting the tone for this local, quirky boutique. Everything is designed in-house, so you can expect a lot of cool little New Orleans touches (the playful yet sophisticated prints feature everything from oysters to Mardi Gras masks). Gentlemen's accessories are the most popular items sold here, but there's also clothes and accessories for ladies.

MAP 4: 3308 Magazine St., 504/319-5959, nolacouture.com; 10am-6pm daily

Tchoup Industries

This bag- and backpack-maker uses local, repurposed, and natural materials like canvas to craft handmade, waterproof, and rugged bags and accessories. Whether you're looking for a backpack, messenger bag, wallet, or fanny pack, choose a color, pattern, and size or customize something to your exact specifications. Since every piece is handmade, prices can get up there, but they guarantee quality. Smaller items like pouches, patches, and travel accessory bags are also great purchases, and may fit your budget a little more easily.

MAP 4: 1115 St. Mary St., 504/872-0726, tchoupindustries.com; 11am-6pm Mon.-Sat., noon-5pm Sun.

HOME DECOR

Sunday Shop

Stepping into this aspirational home decor shop is like visiting a friend's beautifully decorated home. It's light, pretty, relaxing, and smells great (thanks to the small perfume selection in the back). There are both large and small pieces for sale (think furniture, rugs, and lamps), high-end lotions, linens, and ceramics. They also offer customers the chance to build custom bouquets stem by stem.

MAP 4: 2025 Magazine St., 504/342-2087, sundayshop.co; 11am-6pm Mon., Wed.-Sat., 11am-5pm Sun.

Uptown and Riverbend   Map 5

Uptown is a collection of smaller neighborhoods, the most prominent of which is Riverbend, also known as **Carrollton.** The area starts at Louisiana Avenue and moves westward to the curve of the Mississippi River; this marks the beginning of Riverbend. The southern boundary is the river (until it curves) and the northern boundary is South Claiborne Avenue. Uptown is bisected by the St. Charles Avenue streetcar line.

Locals, students from the nearby universities, and visitors all mingle on the bustling **Freret Street corridor,** known for its **diverse** and **affordable** food and drink offerings. Riverbend offers **Audubon**

Park, the zoo, and Tulane and Loyola Universities, plus **funky restaurants,** cafés, and shops on Oak Street. The area is home to students and long-time residents and is one of the most diverse in the Uptown area. Modern businesses and restaurants are found side by side with old-school sights and shops.

TOP SIGHTS
- Best Place to See Gators and Lions: **Audubon Zoo** (page 165)

TOP RESTAURANTS
- Where to Best Understand Creole Food: **Brigtsen's** (page 168)
- Intersection of Louisianan and Indian Flavors: **Saffron Nola** (page 172)
- Best Burger: **The Company Burger** (page 174)
- Where to Air-Condition Your Stomach: **Hansen's Sno-Bliz** (page 176)

TOP NIGHTLIFE
- Most Laid-Back Live-Music Venue: **Le Bon Temps Roule** (page 177)
- Where to See Serious Mixologists at Work: **Cure** (page 178)

TOP ARTS AND CULTURE
- Best Spot for Classic Films: **Prytania Theatre** (page 182)

TOP SHOPS
- Best Merchandise: **Hazelnut** (page 187)

GETTING THERE AND AROUND
- Streetcar lines: St. Charles (12)
- Major bus routes: 10, 11, 15

Jeannette
Willow
Oak
Carrollton
Carrollton Cemetary
Freret
Maple
South Carrollton
Fern
Burdette
Hillary
Black Pearl
Lowerline
Broadway
Greenville
Walnut
Tulane/Loyola
Calhoun
Webster
State
Nashville
Joseph

Tulane University
Loyola University

Uptown New Orleans Historic District

Mississippi River

Audubon Park Golf Course

Audubon Zoo
Audubon Park
The Fly

0   400 yds
0   400 m
DISTANCE ACROSS MAP
Approximate: 2.8 mi or 4.6 km

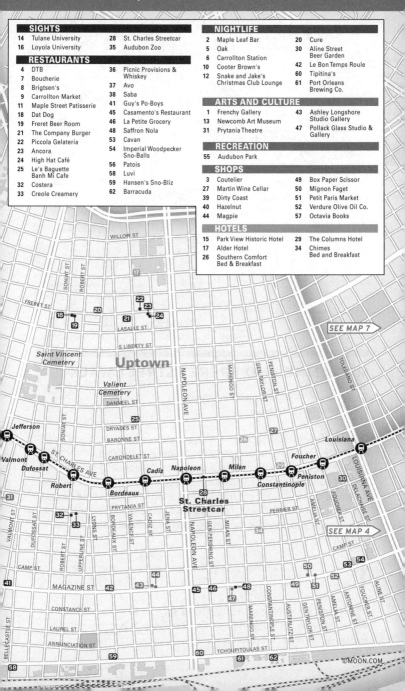

SIGHTS
14	Tulane University	28	St. Charles Streetcar
16	Loyola University	35	Audubon Zoo

RESTAURANTS
4	DTB	36	Picnic Provisions & Whiskey
7	Boucherie	37	Avo
8	Brigtsen's	38	Saba
9	Carrollton Market	41	Guy's Po-Boys
11	Maple Street Patisserie	45	Casamento's Restaurant
18	Dat Dog	46	La Petite Grocery
19	Freret Beer Room	48	Saffron Nola
21	The Company Burger	53	Cavan
22	Piccola Gelateria	54	Imperial Woodpecker Sno-Balls
23	Ancora	56	Patois
24	High Hat Café	58	Luvi
25	Le's Baguette Banh Mi Cafe	59	Hansen's Sno-Bliz
32	Costera	62	Barracuda
33	Creole Creamery		

NIGHTLIFE
2	Maple Leaf Bar	20	Cure
5	Oak	30	Aline Street Beer Garden
6	Carrollton Station	42	Le Bon Temps Roule
10	Cooter Brown's	60	Tipitina's
12	Snake and Jake's Christmas Club Lounge	61	Port Orleans Brewing Co.

ARTS AND CULTURE
1	Frenchy Gallery	43	Ashley Longshore Studio Gallery
13	Newcomb Art Museum		
31	Prytania Theatre	47	Pollack Glass Studio & Gallery

RECREATION
55	Audubon Park

SHOPS
3	Coutelier	49	Box Paper Scissor
27	Martin Wine Cellar	50	Mignon Faget
39	Dirty Coast	51	Petit Paris Market
40	Hazelnut	52	Verdure Olive Oil Co.
44	Magpie	57	Octavia Books

HOTELS
15	Park View Historic Hotel	29	The Columns Hotel
17	Alder Hotel	34	Chimes Bed and Breakfast
26	Southern Comfort Bed & Breakfast		

SEE MAP 7
SEE MAP 4
©MOON.COM

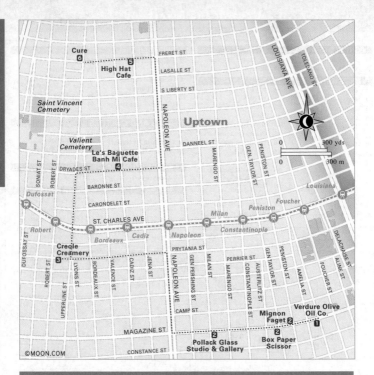

Cure 6
High Hat Cafe 5
FRERET ST
LASALLE ST
S LIBERTY ST
NAPOLEON AVE
Saint Vincent Cemetery
Uptown
DANNEEL ST
MARENGO ST
GEN TAYLOR ST
PENISTON ST
LOUISIANA AVE
TOLEDANO ST
0   300 yds
0   300 m
Valient Cemetery
Le's Baguette Banh Mi Cafe 4
SONIAT ST
ROBERT ST
DRYADES ST
BARONNE ST
CARONDELET ST
Louisiana
Dufossat
ST. CHARLES AVE
Foucher
Milan
Peniston
DUFOSSAT ST
Robert
Bordeaux   Cadiz   Napoleon
Constantinople
DELACHAISE ST
Creole Creamery 3
ROBERT ST
LYONS ST
UPPERLINE ST
DIBORDEAUX ST
VALENCE ST
CADIZ ST
JENA ST
PRYTANIA ST
NAPOLEON AVE
GEN PERSHING ST
MILAN ST
PERRIER ST
MARENGO ST
CONSTANTINOPLE ST
AUSTERLITZ ST
GEN TAYLOR ST
PENISTON ST
AMELIA ST
FOUCHER ST
ALINE ST
CAMP ST
Verdure Olive Oil Co. 1
Mignon Faget 2
MAGAZINE ST
Pollack Glass Studio & Gallery 2
Box Paper Scissor 2
CONSTANCE ST
©MOON.COM

MAGAZINE AND FRERET STREET WALK

TOTAL DISTANCE: 2.8 miles (4.5 kilometers)
WALKING TIME: 1-1.5 hours

This walk has it all: Shopping on Magazine Street, snacking and drinking on the go, and admiring the wide range of Uptown architecture. You'll cross between commercial shopping districts and residential areas, and some blocks that are both. Prepare to find lots of hidden treasures in the streets of Uptown. This is a great post-lunch walk but note that Sundays and Mondays (and occasional Tuesdays) find some shops and galleries closed, so take that into account as you're planning.

1 Start out at the intersection of Magazine and Antonine Streets, browsing at **Verdure Olive Oil Co.** for tasty local food souvenirs.

2 Head west up Magazine Street, checking out sophisticated and eclectic shops. **Mignon Faget** and **Box Paper Scissor** are good examples of the many shopping options you'll pass as you make your way

Le's Baguette Banh Mi Café

nine blocks to Napoleon Street. Keep an eye out for the various galleries along the way, like the **Pollack Glass Studio & Gallery.**

3 Turn right onto stately Napoleon Street. You can walk along the well-maintained neutral ground (wide median strip) to admire the houses and the slowly returning oak trees. Walk five blocks and turn left onto Prytania, then walk another 5.5 blocks to **Creole Creamery,** a cheerful, old-fashioned ice cream parlor with unique and local ice cream flavors. Then backtrack a half block to Upperline and turn left.

4 Take Upperline for five blocks, turn right onto Dryades, and walk three blocks to **Le's Baguette Banh Mi Cafe** for a Vietnamese iced coffee to get reenergized.

5 Take a left leaving Le's and walk two blocks to Napoleon. Turn left onto Napoleon and walk for another six blocks to Freret Street and turn left. Choose from the many restaurants and cafés for an early dinner, perhaps Southern cuisine at the **High Hat Cafe.**

6 A few blocks west on Freret, **Cure** can give you a cocktail experience you'll never forget. The drinks are creative and daring and the space is dramatic but cozy, with the tall backlit shelves of booze dominating the room of small tables and booths. This is a great place to kick back for the rest of the evening.

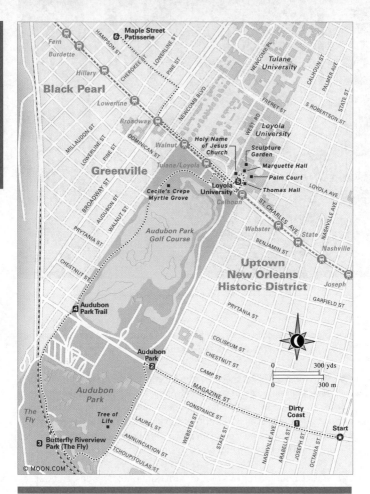

AUDUBON PARK AND RIVERBEND WALK

TOTAL DISTANCE: 5.2 miles (8.4 kilometers)
WALKING TIME: 1.75-2 hours

This walk is longer than the others in this guide, but it passes through some of the most beautiful landmarks in New Orleans. From the Fly to Audubon Park to the stately campus of Loyola to all the cafés and shops in the oak-lined Riverbend, it's a lovely way to wend away a morning or afternoon, even in the heat of the summer, since so much of the walk is shaded. Another option is to do this route as a bike tour. Pick up a bike from **Blue Bikes** (bluebikesnola.com), a New Orleans bike share program, at Magazine Street before Louisiana

Audubon Golf Course

Avenue, or rent one from **Mike the Bike Guy** (4411 Magazine St., 504/899-1344, mikethebikeguy.com; 10am-6pm Mon.-Fri., 10am-5pm Sat.), a little farther up Magazine, just past Napoleon.

1 Start on Magazine Street at Jefferson Avenue. Head three blocks west to check out some unique New Orleans flair from **Dirty Coast.**

2 Continue west on Magazine Street for seven blocks until you reach the edge of **Audubon Park.** Enter the park, take a left onto East Drive, and walk for about a quarter of a mile to check out the 300-year-old **Tree of Life,** which is also known as the Etienne de Boré Oak.

3 Continue south toward the river on East Drive. Take the first right and follow the trail to Tea Room Drive, then turn left to get a great view of the Mississippi at the **Butterfly Riverview Park,** or what residents call **The Fly.**

4 Turn right onto Riverview Drive and follow it for about half a mile to Magazine Street. Cross Magazine and continue onto the **Audubon Park Trail,** walking north, away from the river, until you get to St. Charles Avenue. You'll pass by the Hyams Fountain Gardens, the World War I Monument, the Newman Bandstand Terrace, the Audubon Golf Course and Clubhouse Café, and the Olmsted Lagoon (with the Hurst Street Bridge). There will also be sculptures peppered throughout the park along the paths. And, of course, lots of oak trees, Spanish moss, and crepe myrtles. In fact, just before you exit onto St. Charles Avenue, check out **Cecile's Crepe Myrtle Grove** to the left of the exit.

the Tree of Life at Audubon Park

5 Cross St. Charles Avenue and turn right to reach **Loyola University.** Walk up the right side of the horseshoe pathway and check out historic **Thomas Hall,** the first building on the right—it's part of the original Loyola campus, built in 1911. It used to be the chapel and residence of the local Jesuits, so you'll see stained-glass windows, marble floors, and a painted ceiling if you peek inside. Behind Thomas Hall is **Palm Court,** a shady courtyard ringed with palm trees (and home to parakeet flocks), and to the left is **Marquette Hall,** the oldest building on campus. Behind Marquette Hall is the **sculpture garden.** If you continue past Marquette Hall, you'll come to the **Holy Name of Jesus Church.** Keep heading down the horseshoe till you're back on St. Charles.

6 Turn right on St. Charles Avenue and walk for three blocks, turning right again onto Broadway. After three blocks, take a left onto Maple Street. Continue west for five blocks, passing by several Tulane student haunts—mostly bars and casual restaurants. Grab a quick caffeine or sugar boost at **Maple Street Patisserie.** To get back to where you started, turn left onto Adams Street and walk two blocks back to St. Charles Avenue. There's a streetcar stop one block over in either direction (at Burdette or Hillary). Get off at the Jefferson Avenue stop and walk eight blocks south to Magazine.

St. Charles Streetcar

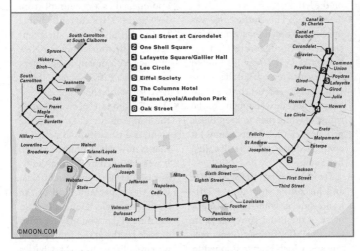

1. Canal Street at Carondelet
2. One Shell Square
3. Lafayette Square/Gallier Hall
4. Lee Circle
5. Eiffel Society
6. The Columns Hotel
7. Tulane/Loyola/Audubon Park
8. Oak Street

©MOON.COM

Sights

TOP EXPERIENCE

St. Charles Streetcar

The St. Charles Streetcar has been a New Orleans institution since 1835: You can't see any TV show or film set in the city without seeing the olive-green streetcars trundling along St. Charles Avenue. The streetcar runs 24 hours a day, and costs $1.25 (exact change only). The route begins on Canal Street at St. Charles Avenue, and goes the entire length of the avenue before banking to the right at South Carrollton Avenue, where it turns around at South Claiborne Avenue. Then it comes back down Carrollton and St. Charles, switching to Carondelet Street at Lee Circle to move with the one-way flow of traffic. Below is a quick list of the most significant

stops and sights you'll see on a streetcar ride.

- **Canal Street at Carondelet:** Folks like to jump on the streetcar at this intersection because it's close to the end of the line, so you've got a better chance of getting a seat. (Another option: Wait till it swings up St. Charles and grab it at Common Street.)
- **One Shell Square:** On the right, at the Poydras Street stop (before crossing Poydras) is One Shell Square, the tallest building not only in New Orleans but in the state of Louisiana.
- **Lafayette Square/Gallier Hall:** Before getting to the following stop (St. Charles at Lafayette) you'll see historic Gallier Hall (originally built as City Hall) on the right and Lafayette Square (with a view of

the John McDonogh monument) on the left.

- **Lee Circle:** This traffic circle was once well-known for its towering statue of Confederate General Robert E. Lee. Today it's known for the city's removal of the statue and its refusal to continue to honor someone who fought for the rights of white men to keep Black people as chattel. There is now an empty pedestal, but it's still called Lee Square.

- **Eiffel Society:** At the St. Charles and Josephine stop, on the left-hand side is what looks like a piece of the Eiffel Tower. It is, in fact, the Eiffel Tower's former restaurant, which France shipped to New Orleans in the early 1980s, after realizing that its weight would contribute to the tower sinking into the ground. It was reassembled on St. Charles Avenue and opened as a restaurant from 1986 to 1989. It's currently home to the Eiffel Society, an event space. (The tourist bureau New Orleans & Company is right next door to the Eiffel Society, if you need some information.)

- **The Columns Hotel:** Just after the Peniston Street stop, on the right, is a beautiful old mansion that is now The Columns Hotel. It was designed by Thomas Sully, one of New Orleans's architects, who was especially fond of the Italianate style. Depending on the time of day, you may see folks outside on the grand front porch, watching life go by on St. Charles over a cocktail or cup of coffee.

- **Tulane/Loyola/Audubon Park:** There's a lot going on at the Tulane/Loyola stop, with the two

the St. Charles streetcar

white tiger at Audubon Zoo

universities on the right and the entrance to Audubon Park on the left. This is a great spot to get off and explore a little—all three properties are photogenic and fun to wander.

- **Oak Street:** If you decide to continue (or get off and get back on in the outbound direction), you'll see the stately former bank, now coffee shop, Rue de la Course on the left: That's Oak Street, where restaurants, cafés, and shops abound. Check it out and wait for the streetcar to come back heading downtown.

Note: the St. Charles Ave streetcar is not air-conditioned, so keep that in mind when deciding when to take your ride. Afternoons might be uncomfortably warm if the temperature or humidity is high. The ride will take around 45-50 minutes unless there are traffic disruptions (which is more likely during morning and evening rush hours).

MAP 5: St. Charles Ave. and S. Carrollton Ave., spanning Canal St. to S. Claiborne Ave., 504/248-3900, norta.com; 24 hours daily; $1.25

✪ Audubon Zoo

Below Magazine Street lies the Audubon Zoo, a significant part of the larger Audubon Park. Established in 1914, the zoo contains historic buildings, notable sculptures, and nearly 2,000 animals from around the world. This relatively small zoo is a wonderful place to stroll, watch the animals' antics, and explore verdant gardens rife with nearly every species of flora known to Louisiana.

The award-winning **Louisiana Swamp exhibit** is the next best thing to taking a swamp tour—and even better in one respect: You're guaranteed to see marsh wildlife up close and personal. The swamp exhibit is a recreation of a Depression-era Cajun swamp settlement, complete with old bayou shacks and

165

a trapper's cottage. It's hard to leave this part of the zoo—the albino alligators never cease to amaze and the ever-frisky river otters are endlessly amusing.

Another highlight of the zoo is the Jaguar Jungle exhibit, which recreates a Mayan rain forest and houses two dignified yet powerful jaguars, along with toucans, spider monkeys, and sloths. The display features realistic reproductions of the stone carvings at the famed Chichén Itzá and Copán archaeological sites.

The zoo has plenty of free parking. If you're taking the St. Charles streetcar, disembark at the Audubon Park stop. From fall through spring, the zoo has shorter operating hours and is closed most Mondays.

MAP 5: 6500 Magazine St., 504/861-2537 or 800/774-7394, auduboninstitute.org; 10am-5pm Mon.-Fri., 10am-6pm Sat.-Sun.; $19 adults, $15 seniors, $14 children 2-12, children under 2 free

Tulane University

Tulane was originally built in the 1890s and has grown into a prestigious university, which is reflected in the architecture of this sprawling urban campus. Between St. Charles Avenue and Freret Street are turn-of-the century historic academic buildings, including Gibson Hall (at the St. Charles entrance), established in 1894 as the College of Technology, now the School of Engineering. Facing Gibson, to the left is Tilton Hall, originally built in 1902 as the university's library, and Dinwiddie Hall, on the right, houses anthropological research and Central American studies. Past

Gibson Hall, there's an open-air green space—the Academic Quad, which is surrounded by stately academic buildings and patios, and usually filled with students during the school year.

Erected in 1929 and named after the first and only president of Newcomb College, the Italian Renaissance-style Dixon Hall houses music classrooms, practice and listening rooms, and a 1,000-seat auditorium that usually features jazz and classical music concerts, plus musical theater performances—most of which are free.

Since 2014, the Tulane Green Wave, Tulane University's football team, has been playing at the 30,000-seat Benson Field at Yulman Stadium (333 Ben Weiner Dr., 504/861-9283, tulanegreenwave. com).

MAP 5: 6823 St. Charles Ave., 504/865-5000, tulane.edu

Loyola University

Opposite verdant Audubon Park stands Loyola University. Established by the Jesuit order in 1904 as Loyola College, the school became a full-fledged private university in 1912. Over the years, it grew and expanded, eventually becoming one of the most well-respected universities in the South, open to all faiths and currently nurturing 5,000 students annually. Visitors are free to wander amid the school's stately red-brick buildings and gardens, built in the Tudor Gothic style; it's also not a bad place to catch concerts and sporting events. Check out the original campus buildings, Marquette Hall and Thomas Hall,

Loyola University

the tree-lined **Palm Court,** and the **sculpture garden.**

Something interesting is often happening at the **Nunemaker Auditorium** (Calhoun St. and Marquette Pl., 3rd fl., 504/865-2074), a 400-seat lecture and concert hall where students of the school's College of Music and Fine Arts present recitals, solo and ensemble performances, and live opera productions. Next door is the 600-seat **Louis J. Roussel Performance Hall** (504/865-2074, http://cmfa.loyno.edu) on the second floor. There, you can enjoy free concerts of the university's chamber orchestra, symphony orchestra, jazz band, and concert band.

Loyola offers a variety of spectator sports in the form of its Wolf Pack Athletics program, including a men's basketball team that dates to 1945 and a much newer women's basketball team. Both teams hold their home games at **The Den** (Loyola Recreational Sports Complex, Freret St. and Engineering Rd., 5th fl., 504/864-7225, wolfpack.loyno.edu; tickets $6 adults, $3 seniors and children), a facility on the fifth floor of the university's massive sports complex.

MAP 5: 6363 St. Charles Ave., 504/865-3240 or 800/456-9652, loyno.edu

Restaurants

PRICE KEY

$	Entrées less than $15
$$	Entrées $15-30
$$$	Entrées more than $30

CAJUN AND CREOLE
✪ Brigtsen's $$$

One of the first eateries to lure tourists to the Riverbend area, Brigtsen's occupies a Victorian cottage with a warm, homey dining room, enhanced by soft lighting and lovely wallpaper. The restaurant is perhaps most famous for its delicious and ever-changing seafood platter, which might include grilled redfish with crabmeat pesto sauce, baked oyster LeRuth (with shrimp and crabmeat), or shrimp cornbread with jalapeno smoked corn butter.
MAP 5: 723 Dante St., 504/861-7610, brigtsens.com, 5:30pm-10pm Tues.- Sat.

Boucherie $$

Since 2008, Boucherie has been combining Cajun comfort food with a Southern sensibility and a dash of Latin American and Southeast Asian influence. Set in a purple Creole cottage, the cozy restaurant resembles a rabbit warren, which adds to the considerable charm of chef Nathanial Zimet's confident preparations. The menu has a few outstanding staples, like the smoked Wagyu beef brisket with garlic-Parmesan fries and the blackened shrimp and grits cake with warm bacon dressing, which are interspersed with seasonal specialties like applewood smoked scallops with beet pastrami, ever-changing crudo fish preparations, and crawfish coconut bisque. Save room for the Krispy Kreme bread pudding.
MAP 5: 8115 Jeannette St., 504/862-5514, boucherie-nola.com; 5:30pm-9:30pm Mon., 11am-3pm and 5:30pm-9:30pm Tues.-Fri., 10:30am-2:30pm and 5:30pm-9:30pm Sat., 10:30am-2:30pm Sun.

DTB $$

The food at DTB (which stands for Down the Bayou) is as beautiful as it is delicious, and as creative as it is playfully unexpected. The DTB team offers fun fusion takes on coastal Cajun cuisine and make the flavors accessible to all palates and preferences. The vegetarian in your life will want to try DTB's mushroom boudin balls; the traditionalists will be drawn to the seasonal gumbo; the daring will find the blue-crab-topped squid ink tagliatelle irresistible. The space is cheerful and lively. Don't overlook the intriguing cocktail list or dessert menu.
MAP 5: 8201 Oak St. #1, 504/518-6889, dtbnola.com; 5pm-10pm Mon.-Thurs.,11:30am-4pm and 5pm-11pm Fri., 10:30am-2:30pm and 5pm-11pm Sat., 10:30am-2:30pm Sun.

PO'BOYS
Guy's Po-Boys $

Guy's is a po'boy shop with no hype, just great sandwiches. It does a brisk take-out business, since seating options are limited, but if you choose to eat in, you'll likely end up sharing a table with a local who works or lives nearby. The blazingly bright-blue exterior paint gives way to a no-frills interior that's half kitchen, half seating. The smell of the roast beef po'boy will have you drooling, so go ahead and order that, and be sure to grab plenty of napkins.

MAP 5: 5259 Magazine St., 504/891-5025; 11am-4pm Mon.-Sat.

SOUTHERN
Carrollton Market $$$

An open kitchen is one thing, but when you see how small the kitchen is at Carrollton Market, you'll be amazed at how precisely the team of chefs (headed by chef-owner Jason Goodenough) executes the food at this Southern bistro set in a converted Creole cottage. It's like magic. The cinnamon rolls are a sight (and taste) to behold on the brunch menu (unsold leftovers are used in the pan-seared foie gras dinner appetizer). This is the place for both special occasions and neighborhood weekday meals.

MAP 5: 8132 Hampson St., 504/252-9928, carrolltonmarket.com; 5pm-10pm Tues.-Thurs., 11am-1:30pm and 5pm-10pm Fri., 10am-2pm and 5pm-10pm Sat., 10am-2pm Sun.

Picnic Provisions & Whiskey $

A collaboration between the folks who helm Commander's Palace and the ones who run the Reginelli pizza empire, this restaurant is what happens when James Beard-award winning chef Tory McPhail starts to wonder, "How do you make the perfect fried chicken?" After much research, Picnic Provisions is the result, serving the owners' platonic ideal of spicy fried chicken (the secret ingredient is crab boil spice). They also expanded the restaurant's concept to include rustic dishes and Southern comfort food, which means delights like smoked fish-collar dip, pimento cheese, and *cochon de lait* (suckling pig). This is also where to find the perfect Old Fashioned. The cozy corner spot at Magazine and State Streets is cheerful enough to replicate picnic weather no matter what's happening outside.

MAP 5: 741 State St., 504/266-2810, nolapicnic.com; 11am-10pm Sun.-Thurs., 11am-11pm Fri.-Sat.

SEAFOOD
Casamento's Restaurant $

You need to pay close attention to the day of the week and time of year you plan to go to Casamento's because the schedule is capricious at best. They're closed for three months in the summer, and when they're open, it's only half of the week (Thurs.-Sun.). However, the research necessary to pounce on a Casamento's meal is well worth it, from the moment you walk in and see the green and white tile decor with a tiled oyster bar in the tight front room, where the eye is drawn to the shuckers working fast and furiously. Oysters on the half shell, the oyster loaf sandwich, and the seafood gumbo are the items not to miss.

MAP 5: 4330 Magazine St., 504/895-9761, casamentosrestaurant.com; 11am-2pm and 5:30pm-9pm Thurs.-Sat., 5pm-9pm Sun. Sept.-May; cash only

VIETNAMESE
Le's Baguette Banh Mi Cafe $

Part all-American café (breakfast sandwiches, eggs, and espresso drinks are all available), and part Vietnamese street food stand (with banh mi, pho, spring rolls, and vermicelli), this place adds up to awesome. Take your five-spiced barbecue pork belly banh mi or noodle bowl to one of the tables in the cozy café or out back to the courtyard, wash it down with an iced coffee (cold brew or Vietnamese-style with condensed milk), and read or do some work using Le's free Wi-Fi.

MAP 5: 4607 Dryades St., 504/895-2620; 10am-9pm Mon.-Sat., 10am-5pm Sun.

ECLECTIC
Cavan $$

Housed in a deteriorating 19th-century Victorian home on Magazine Street (how Gothic!), Cavan is the perfect place to celebrate the past and present of New Orleans and Louisiana cuisine. From zucchini beignets to crab-fat fried rice, and from fried oyster puttanesca to shrimp and cabbage, dining satisfaction is just around the corner. The front garden is an elegant vantage point from which to eat, drink, and people-watch on Magazine Street.

MAP 5: 3607 Magazine St., 504/509-7655, cavannola. com; 4pm-10pm Mon.-Thurs., 10:30am-3:30pm and 4pm-midnight Fri.-Sat., 10:30am-3:30pm and 4pm-10pm Sun.

FRENCH
La Petite Grocery $$$

The century-old building's history is what informs this restaurant's name, since it was the site of the first full-service grocery store in the city in the early 1900s. One of the only upscale Uptown restaurants open for lunch, it's easy to schedule a stop at this elegantly appointed former corner store to enjoy creative takes on New Orleans dishes, like blue crab beignets and turtle Bolognese. The exterior's cheery yellow draws passers-by inside, and the gorgeous wood bar creates and serves equally beautiful cocktails. Chef-owner Justin Devillier's French techniques and influences shine in more traditional dishes like steak tartare, pan roasted scallops with braised leeks, and roasted lamb loin with a lentil ragout.

MAP 5: 4238 Magazine St., 504/891-3377, lapetitegrocery. com; 5:30pm-9:30pm Mon., 11:30am-2:30pm and 5:30pm-9:30pm Tues.-Thurs., 11:30am-2:30pm and 5:30pm-10:30pm Fri.-Sat., 10:30am-2:30pm and 5:30pm-9:30pm Sun.

Patois $$$

This bistro-style restaurant is tucked away on the corner of a residential neighborhood way Uptown, so it kind of feels like you're going to someone's house for a meal—a really, really good meal. It's a casual Louisiana-French bistro, combining Continental fine food techniques with Louisiana ingredients. The grilled lamb ribs with green tomato relish and the pecan-crusted sweetbreads are mainstays on the menu, which mostly shifts seasonally. The intimate space can be quiet or raucous on the turn of a dime, depending on how many craft cocktails or glasses of wine have been drunk.

MAP 5: 6078 Laurel St., 504/895-9441, patoisnola.com; 5:30pm-10pm Wed.-Thurs., 11:30am-2pm and 5:30pm-10:30pm Fri., 5:30pm-10:30pm Sat., 10:30am-2:30pm Sun.

ITALIAN
Ancora $$

If wood-fired pizzas made to the exact standards of Neapolitan traditions are your jam, you're going to love Ancora. From the cheese-free marinara to the no-sauce *bianca* topped with cheese, green olives, capers, garlic, basil, and sweet chilies, it's all incredible. All cured meats are made in-house (you can see the various cuts of meat through the window at the back of the dining room). The under-the-radar star, however, is the bruschetta, made with bread that's baked in-house. They have a couple standards on the menu, and will always have a daily special that incorporates the chef's creativity and seasonal ingredients. Ancora has an open kitchen, and the brick pizza oven dominates the rustic space. Sit at the bar and have an aperitif and a chat with the bartender.

MAP 5: 4508 Freret St., 504/324-1636, ancorapizza.com; 11:30am-9pm Sun.-Thurs., 11:30am-10pm Fri.-Sat.

Avo $$

There is a historically strong Sicilian influence on the food and music culture of New Orleans, and Chef Nick Lama's Avo is the 21st-century version of that. This isn't the red-sauce-heavy Creole Italian, but a regional menu with an emphasis on seafood, authentic flavors, quality ingredients, and techniques that showcases the chef's talent in everything from the simplest spaghetti with spicy tomato sauce to more complex dishes involving rabbit, octopus, or escargot. The restaurant is divided into two sections: the crisp white main dining room with a Carrara marble-topped bar, and a more casual area that's reminiscent of a romantic garden courtyard. Avo has a happy hour (4pm-7pm Mon.-Thurs.) that includes half-off wines by the glass, $6 classic cocktails, and $9 plates of pasta.

MAP 5: 5908 Magazine St., 504/509-6550, restaurantavo.com; 4pm-10pm Mon.-Thurs., 5pm-10pm Fri.-Sat., 10:30am-2pm Sun.

MIDDLE EASTERN
Saba $$

Alon Shaya's high-end Israeli restaurant, under the supervision of chef de cuisine Cara Peterson, will make you look at hummus and pita bread in a whole new light. The bright and airy space lets in lots of light and the royal blue stripes, reminiscent of the adornment on a rabbi's tallit shawl stand out on the white walls. The pita comes out hot from the wood fired oven, and diners eat it with a variety of hummus preparations as well as small plates called *salatim* (the savory fruit preparations in particular are horizon-broadening). It's hard to go wrong with anything on the menu but know that this is not your average Mediterranean restaurant.

MAP 5: 5757 Magazine St., 504/324-7770, eatwithsaba.com; 11am-10pm Sun. and Wed.-Thurs., 11am-11pm Fri.-Sat.

an impressive raw fish preparation at Luvi

ASIAN
Luvi $$

This blue house next to the Tchoupitoulas shopping center is a haven of Asian flavors. Shanghai expat Chef Hao Gong provides versions of the comfort food he enjoyed as a child, but makes use of the knife skills and delicate sensibilities of Japanese raw fish preparation that come from his training as a sushi chef. He offers a gorgeous and reasonably priced *omakase* (chef's menu) as well, which costs only $45 for a mix of raw and cooked dishes or $60 for an all-raw preparation. Inside is as colorful and cheerful as outside; it's a small spot, but the minimalist wood tables and chairs create an illusion of space. The food is obviously not the typical New Orleans Creole/Cajun flavors, but the joy in which it's produced and presented encapsulates the local love of food.

MAP 5: 5236 Tchoupitoulas St., 504/605-3340, luvirestaurant. com; 11am-2:30pm and 5pm-9pm Tues.-Thurs., 11am-2:30pm and 5pm-10pm Fri.-Sat.

INDIAN
✪ Saffron Nola $$$

This upscale, trendy spot serves riffs on Indian classics, often with local ingredients and a fusion with the Creole/Cajun culinary tradition. Everything's meticulously crafted, from the unique cocktails (like their twist on a bourbon milk punch, I Ain't Sari, made with bourbon, yogurt, roasted chili peppers, and topped with salted caramel popcorn) to the curried seafood gumbo and rum-soaked lamb chops. Save room for dessert, though, because they're based in tradition but innovative and delicious, like the Jammin' Jamun, which takes the classic syrup-soaked *jamun* donut and adds a house-made fig-date-praline ice cream.

MAP 5: 4128 Magazine St., 504/323-2626, saffronnola. com; 5pm-9:30pm Tues.-Thurs., 5pm-10:30pm Fri.-Sat.

LATIN AMERICAN
Barracuda $

Authentic Mexican street tacos are the focus of this tiny, counter-service eatery with a large outdoor eating space. The ingredients are sourced ethically and the tortillas (both flour and blue corn varieties) are made fresh daily, along with house-made chorizo, salsa, agua fresca, and damn near everything else. Check out their Deluxe

Saffron Nola

Nacho happy hour (3pm-6:30pm Mon.-Fri.), which features ballpark-style nachos made with queso, salsa verde, pickles, and pepitas. Try subbing out your tortilla chips for crispy, airy chicharróns.

MAP 5: 3984 Tchoupitoulas St., 504/266-2961, eatbarracuda.com; 11am-10pm Tues.-Fri., 9am-10pm Sat.-Sun.

SMALL PLATES
Costera $$

This Spanish-inspired restaurant sits among the shops and cafes of Prytania Street, offering a welcome sit-down, full-service respite in the rustic exposed-brick-and-reclaimed-wood dining room and bar. Pops of orange and mint green liven up the space, and the majority of food served is tapas-style, concentrated hits of flavor on small plates—there are a few larger dishes like seafood paella or braised lamb shank, but they're also meant to be shared. Traditional tapas like *jamon Iberico* (cured ham) and *gambas al ajillo* (garlic shrimp) share the menu with more daring dishes like roasted cauliflower with pickled raisins and hazelnuts, or Louisiana blue crab salad.

MAP 5: 4938 Prytania St., 504/302-2332, costerarestaurant.com; 11am-10pm Sun.-Mon. and Wed.-Thurs., 11am-10:30pm Fri.-Sat.

GASTROPUBS
Freret Beer Room $

The city's first and only beer-focused eatery, the Freret Beer Room pairs a small but diverse selection of the best beers available with beer-friendly dishes that defy expectations of what typical pub grub can be. Everything on the menu is a winner, but special attention should be paid to the smoked brisket mac 'n' cheese. The bar is beautiful, with gleaming silver taps that extend from the ceiling down toward the bar, and the rest of the space is filled with comfy chairs and sofas between exposed brick walls and well-worn hardwood floors.

MAP 5: 5108 Freret St., 504/298-7468, freretbeerroom.com; 11am-10pm Sun.-Mon. and Wed.-Thurs., 11am-11pm Fri.-Sat.

CLASSIC AMERICAN
✪ The Company Burger $

Frequently hailed as home of the city's best burger, The Company Burger grinds its own meat, cuts its own fries, and makes everything fresh to order. The eponymous Company Burger is owner Adam Biederman's ideal burger: a double patty with American cheese, pickles, and grilled onions. No lettuce and no tomato (except during Louisiana's Creole tomato harvest season). If that doesn't do it for you, TCB also offers a lamb burger, a turkey burger, and a fried chicken sandwich, all of which are excellent. The location is a relatively bare bones affair, with white walls and blue accents, a chrome counter that overlooks an open kitchen, and scuffed but sturdy wooden tables and chairs. Condiment geeks: Check out the mayo bar in the back for a wide variety of flavored mayo sauces.

MAP 5: 4600 Freret St., 504/267-0320, thecompanyburger.com; 11am-10pm daily

Dat Dog $

This is the original outpost of the New Orleans weiner chain. Actually, the original outpost is across the street in the tiniest food retail spot on Freret,

High Hat Cafe

but they outgrew that space and moved to the converted gas station where they currently thrive, selling gourmet hot dogs and sausages, beer, and fries. The indoor and extensive outdoor spaces reflect Dat Dog's flippant, irreverent sensibilities with brightly

Creole Creamery

colored walls and locally painted signs. Select a traditional pork sausage or nontraditional options like crawfish, duck, or alligator weiners and lay on your choice of toppings, or try one of the house specials like the Bacon Werewolf, which tops a Slovenian-style sausage with bacon, sauerkraut, dill relish, tomatoes, grilled onions, and Creole mustard. They also have a happy hour (4pm-7pm Mon.-Fri.) that includes half-price well drinks, $3.50 Abita Amber drafts, and a selection of $5 dogs. There are two other locations in town, on Magazine Street and on Frenchmen Street, as well as in nearby Lafayette, and in College Park, Texas.

MAP 5: 5030 Freret St., 504/899-6883, datdog.com; 11am-10pm Mon.-Sat., 11am-9pm Sun.

DINERS
High Hat Cafe $

This cozy, vintage diner-style spot is the perfect place to get your Southern food fix, with regional dishes like pimento cheese (which they also use to make their mac 'n' cheese), Delta-style hot tamales, and fried catfish plates with slaw and hushpuppies. They also have an unswerving commitment to pie, with seasonal selections alongside chocolate chess pie, which is always on the menu. The weekly specials (which includes a brunch menu on the weekends) are always excellent—check out the fried chicken on Tuesday or the roasted pork debris with poblano peppers for brunch. Don't overlook drinks; not only is the cocktail program swinging, but the seasonally enhanced lemonade and iced tea options are stellar. Service is always friendly and attentive, and the decor exudes warmth with its colorful, casual, and completely Southern vibe.

MAP 5: 4500 Freret St., 504/754-1336, highhatcafe.com; 11am-9pm Sun.-Thurs., 11am-10pm Fri.-Sat.

COFFEE AND DESSERTS
Creole Creamery $

This old-timey ice cream parlor only accepts cash. In exchange, it doles out some of the best ice cream in the city. The pink walls and vintage booths and tables call to mind a couple sharing a malted after the sock hop. The flavors are always changing, and the creative seasonal specialties use local ingredients. In the summer, the shop serves a variety of options inspired by herb and flower gardens, incorporating thyme, lavender, rose, magnolia, jasmine, basil, and violet. New Orleans-themed flavors abound as well, with the iconic Creole Cream Cheese flavor being a year-round fave, along with Cafe au Lait. Thank heavens they offer a sampler platter, where you can get four or seven mini-scoops of different flavors. Creole Creamery has been a local favorite since 2004, when it took over the iconic but defunct McKenzie's Bakery space—you can still see the sign.

MAP 5: 4924 Prytania St., 504/894-8680, creolecreamery.com; noon-10pm Sun.-Thurs., noon-11pm Fri.-Sat.; cash only

✪ Hansen's Sno-Bliz $

Most summer afternoons will see a line snaking out the door of Hansen's Sno-Bliz, a family operation currently in its third generation. Classic snowball flavors adored for decades, like Cream of Nectar, Bubblegum, and Strawberry are on the menu, but it's the special syrups like ginger, cardamom, satsuma, and honey-lavender that make this place stand out. They're still made by hand and dispensed in at least 3-4 different layers with the snow-like shaved ice (founder Ernest Hansen invented his version of the machine in 1939, and it's still in use today). The spot is tiny and not much has changed throughout the more than seven decades that the Hansens have been serving this New Orleans treat—you can see the history told in faded newspaper clippings and photographs posted on every inch of wall space. You'll have time to check it all out while in line.

MAP 5: 4801 Tchoupitoulas St., 504/891-9788, snobliz.com; 1pm-7pm Tues.- Sun. Mar.-Nov.

Imperial Woodpecker Sno-Ball $

New Orleans native Neesa Peterson grew up with the snowball traditions known to all New Orleans kids, and when she moved to New York City as an adult, she brought that piece of home with her and opened the Imperial Woodpecker snowball stand in the Big Apple. She found her way back to the Crescent City a couple years later and although the NYC location closed, in 2013 she brought Imperial Woodpecker to a small outpost on Magazine Street. In addition to all the fruity and creamy standard flavors, Peterson has also created a dozen of her own house-made flavors that are beloved by both locals and visitors, like Earl Grey cream, cream of chicory coffee, strawberry-basil, and pineapple-cilantro.

MAP 5: 3511 Magazine St., 504/366-7777, iwsnoballs.com; noon-sunset daily Mar.-mid-Oct.

Maple Street Patisserie $

At first glance you might overlook this quiet bakery on bustling Maple Street—there's a Starbucks next door that's always busy, making it even more of a hidden gem by comparison. The European-style baked goods reflect master-baker-and-pastry-chef Ziggy Cichowski's studies abroad in both eastern and western Europe. It's a cozy spot with a nice mix of students and locals.

MAP 5: 7638 Maple St.,
504/304-1526, cargocollective.com/
maplestreetpatisserie; 6am-5pm
Tues.-Sat., 6am-noon Sun.

Piccola Gelateria $
This comfy spot overlooks Freret
Street, with a large front window
and patio tables, and they serve
authentic gelato that will make
you swoon. Everything's made in-
house; with flavors like Amarena
Cherry, Salted Caramel, and Toffee,
you'll want to sink into the comfy
couch or armchair and stay all day.
They also offer espresso drinks,
crepes, and Italian *piadinas*—rustic flatbreads that are sandwiched
around a variety of breakfast and
lunch ingredients.
MAP 5: 4525 Freret St.,
504/493-5999, piccolagelateria.com;
noon-7pm Tues.-Thurs.,
noon-10pm Fri.-Sat.

Nightlife

LIVE MUSIC
✪ Le Bon Temps Roule
This neighborhood juke joint is open
24 hours a day. In addition to presenting the Soul Rebels brass band
every Thursday night, it also hosts
funk DJs, local bands, trivia nights,
fundraisers, and free oysters on
Friday evenings (starting at 7pm till
they run out, usually around 9pm).
Remember to tip your server! This is
the quintessential New Orleans experience: hanging out in a somewhat
shabby but lively 24-hour bar, slurp-
ing oysters with beer (or one of their
excellent Bloody Marys), and listening to live piano music. In short, it's
NOLA perfection. The late-night
music in the back room is a jamming
scene, with local musicians and an
engaged crowd.
MAP 5: 4801 Magazine St.,
504/895-8117, lbtrnola.com; 24 hours
daily; cover $0-10

Maple Leaf Bar
One of Uptown's most popular live
music venues, the Maple Leaf Bar
serves up some of the best blues,
jazz, funk, rock, reggae, and zydeco
in the city. Established in 1974 and
now one of the Big Easy's longest-
running music clubs, the Maple Leaf
has played host to music students
from Tulane, local Grammy award-
winners like George Porter Jr., and
the Lost Bayou Ramblers. Every
Tuesday night at 11pm, the legendary Rebirth Brass Band is in residence to blow the roof off the joint.
MAP 5: 8316 Oak St., 504/866-9359,
mapleleafbar.com; 3pm-4am daily;
cover varies

Tipitina's
For catching rock (both hard-edged
and down-home), jazz, zydeco,
Cajun, and blues, there may be no
club in the city more acclaimed
or more festive than Tipitina's, a
longstanding venue in the heart of
Uptown. Purists may tell you that
Tip's has lost its edge and no longer presents the best—or at least the
most distinctive—local acts, but
anybody looking for an introduction

to the city's eclectic music scene should head here. Entertainment varies greatly, but no matter what's playing, you can probably dance to it.

MAP 5: 501 Napoleon Ave., 504/895-8477, tipitinas.com; hours and cover charges vary by show

COCKTAIL BARS
✪ Cure

This James Beard-award-winning cocktail bar has been widely credited for reviving not only the Freret Street neighborhood (it was one of the first food/beverage businesses that opened here post-Katrina), but the modern New Orleans cocktail movement as a whole. The bar is beautiful, although the space itself is dimly lit—keep your flashlight app ready to read the cocktail menu, because each drink has a list of ingredients that requires your full attention. The seasonal cocktails switch up, but they do keep a stable of their favorites on the menu. Drinks can be pricey ($10-12), so time your visit for the daily happy hour (5pm-7pm Mon.-Thurs., 3pm-7pm Fri.-Sun), when a dozen classic cocktails (including a Negroni, Sazerac, and the punch of the day) are available for $6 (along with discounted snacks, wine, and shot-and-a-beer specials). The friendly staff are true professionals and know their stuff. But do be patient; everything's made to order, and there's some complex stuff on the menu.

MAP 5: 4905 Freret St., 504/302-2357, curenola.com; 5pm-midnight Mon.-Thurs., 3pm-2am Fri.-Sat., 3pm-midnight Sun.

outside Cure on Freret Street

BARS AND LOUNGES
Aline Street Beer Garden

This spot combines the attitude of a German beer garden with the bonhomie of a neighborhood pub. You'll find an impressive number of German beers side by side with local brews and popular lagers. The bar takes up the front half of the space, and the kitchen is in the back, so most of the seating is outdoors at long, bright-orange tables and benches shipped here from Germany. Keep an eye out for various pop-up restaurants that serve food from small kitchen; check Aline Street's social media accounts to find out the schedule.

MAP 5: 1515 Aline St., 504/891-5774; 4pm-midnight Mon.-Thurs., 2pm-2am Fri., 11am-2am Sat., 11am-midnight Sun.

Carrollton Station

A great all-around neighborhood bar, the Station hosts live music, trivia nights (9pm Wed.), comedy nights (6:30pm Thurs.), and pop-up kitchens, and has a decent tap list and a friendly vibe. It's bigger than it appears when you first step inside—the second room goes all the way back and there's a large outdoor

courtyard with plenty of seating as well. Lots of locals hang out here, and it's a fun, friendly crowd.
MAP 5: 8140 Willow St., 504/865-9190, carrolltonstationbar.com; 4pm-3am Mon.-Sat., 2pm-3am Sun.

Cooter Brown's

This place is the epitome of "let's get a beer and watch the game!" with dozens of taps and 17 televisions, but this long-time anchor of the neighborhood, open since 1977, is much more than a typical sports bar. To wit: This is one of the best places to get trays of oysters on the half shell, which are half price on Tuesdays from 3pm to close. The back bar has hard-to-find beers—and folks who know how to talk about them. The decor is wood paneling everywhere, with caricature statuettes of national and local celebrities who have passed away.
MAP 5: 509 S. Carrollton Ave., 504/866-9104, cooterbrowns.com; 11am-2:30am Sun.-Thurs., 11am-3:30am Fri.-Sat.

Snake and Jake's Christmas Club Lounge

Open every day of the year—including Christmas—Snake and Jake's is one of the Crescent City's most legendary dive bars, with many a reveler stumbling out in the early morning light after a night of adventure (and drinking). Lit primarily with Christmas lights (of course), the vibe is dark and cozy. But for the sake of all that is good and decent, don't sit or lie down on the couches. Happy-hour specials are offered 7pm-10pm nightly.

Port Orleans Brewing Co.

MAP 5: 7612 Oak St., 504/861-2802, snakeandjakes.com; 7pm-7am daily

BREWERIES
Port Orleans Brewing Co.

This large brewery situated a couple blocks from Tipitina's provides a large variety of beer styles, elevated bar food, and a great space in which to enjoy it all. One of the founding partners of the brewery is former New Orleans Saints offensive tackle Zack Strief, so there's football everywhere, including beers named after coach Sean Payton and beloved former player Steve Gleason. It's family friendly and there are trivia nights, movie screenings, and of course football games are broadcast every Sunday. There's a great outdoor space perfect for good weather drinking as well as crawfish boils (when it's the season, that is).

MAP 5: 4124 Tchoupitoulas St., 504/266-2332, portorleans.com; 11am-10pm Wed.-Mon.

WINE BARS
Oak

This sophisticated but approachable wine bar on bustling Oak Street has its wines categorized by flavor profile instead of region, making it easy for even the novice wine drinker to figure out the right choice. It's got a nice cocktail list as well, live music on the weekends, and an outdoor patio shared with its sister beer bar, Ale on Oak. This is definitely a perfect spot to start the evening, with a daily happy hour from 5pm-7pm (and all night on Tuesday) that offers select wines by the glass, a cocktail of the day, and snacks like *frites* with aioli or buffalo cauliflower, all for $5 each. The full menu is great, too, with items like grilled flatbread, hanger steak, ricotta gnocchi, and fried shrimp tacos.

MAP 5: 8118 Oak St., 504/302-1485, oaknola.com; 5pm-midnight Tues.-Wed., 5pm-1am Thurs., 5pm-2am Fri.-Sat.

Arts and Culture

GALLERIES
Ashley Longshore Studio Gallery

Not for the faint of heart, Ashley Longshore's larger than life work is feminist, sexually explicit, inclusive, profane, provocative, and determined to get under the skin of American consumerism and pop culture. The space is bright, dazzling, and in-your-face, which is the point of her art. It's safe to say you won't experience anything else quite like this in New Orleans, let alone Uptown. The furniture collection is just as wild and fun. (Longshore also created the much-loved portrait of Lil Wayne that hangs in the august drawing room of the Pontchartrain Hotel outside of the Jack Rose restaurant.)

MAP 5: 4537 Magazine St., 504/333-6951, ashleylongshore.com; 10am-5pm Tues.-Fri., noon-4:30pm Sat.

Frenchy Gallery

Frenchy is well-known for painting on the fly—he goes to events and paints what he sees, capturing the

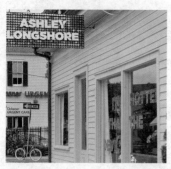

Ashley Longshore Studio Gallery

moment in time with his trademark energetic and bold brush strokes. His quest to communicate the beating heart of New Orleans and its people and culture has resulted in a collection of scenes of the city, making his local art some of the most vibrant ways to commemorate and honor the city. He's known as "The King of Oak Street." You can see him in action documenting events like Jazz Fest, French Quarter Fest, and Oak Street's own Po-boy Fest, and admire (and purchase) the results in his gallery and online. MAP 5: 8314 Oak St., 504/861-7595, frenchylive.com; 10am-10pm Tues., 10am-8pm Wed.-Sat., noon-6pm Sun.

Pollack Glass Studio & Gallery

Walking into this gallery is basically walking into an explosion of color and shapes, lit up by the sunbeams pouring through the front wall of windows. The glass techniques employed by artist Andrew Jackson Pollack combine bold colors and delicate shapes, and it's amazing what comes out of the studio—his work with birds, sea creatures, and goblets are especially impressive. He also sells smaller jewelry pieces like bracelets and pendants for those who prefer art they can wear. A rotating

Pollack Glass Studio & Gallery

Prytania Theatre

list of artists also bring their style and personality to the shop. Pollack also offers glassblowing classes.
MAP 5: 4132 Magazine St., 504/875-3627, pollackglassnola.com; 10am-6pm Tues.-Thurs., 10am-8pm Fri.-Sat., noon-5pm Sun.

MUSEUMS
Newcomb Art Museum

Opened in 1887, the Newcomb College Art School was once at the forefront of the American Arts and Crafts Movement, earning international fame for its unique pottery and for producing talented graduates like modernist Ida Kohlmeyer and fine jewelry creator Mignon Faget. Unfortunately, Hurricane Katrina forced the school's closure, but you can still see some amazing creations at the Newcomb Art Museum, which contains more than 400 examples of pottery, metalwork, embroidery, and bound books produced at Newcomb College from the late 19th through the early 20th centuries. Situated on Tulane University's campus, the museum's exhibits and programs are free to the public.
MAP 5: Woldenberg Art Center, Newcomb Circle, Tulane University, 504/865-5328, newcombartmuseum. tulane.edu; 10am-5pm Tues.-Fri., 11am-4pm Sat.; free

CINEMA
✪ Prytania Theatre

This old-fashioned movie house shows Hollywood blockbusters, classic films (check out the weekly classics series on Sunday and Wednesday mornings at 10am), and midnight movies on its massive single screen. It's also a principal venue for the annual New Orleans Film Festival (504/309-6633, www.neworleans-filmsociety.org) in the fall. Parking is sometimes hard to find in the residential neighborhood that surrounds the theater. Matinees (tickets $6) are a bargain.
MAP 5: 5339 Prytania St., 504/891-2787, theprytania.com; $11.75 adults, $9.75 children under 12, $6 matinee (starting before 5pm)

On the last Saturday of the month, the Palmer Park Arts Market (S. Claiborne Ave. at S. Carrollton Ave., 504/658-3200, artsneworleans.org/event/arts-market-of-new-orleans; 10am-4pm last Sat. of the month; free) features locally crafted art like ceramics, jewelry, photography, paintings, soap, and tons of other stuff from more than 80 artists. There's also live music and food to be had. During the holiday season, the Arts Market stretches into Sunday. It's a great place to get unique New Orleans gifts.

shop offers fun, witty, and unique T-shirt and souvenir options for kids and adults. Designs honor such iconic images as jazz musicians, above-ground cemeteries, and other unique aspects of the Big Easy, including historic moments like the Louisiana Purchase. You can also pick up po'boy posters, Saints hoodies, and enamel pins of NOLA-inspired food-stuffs, as well as coasters, mouse pads, and doormats emblazoned with images of the Crescent City's unique water-meter covers. There's a second location in the French Quarter (713 Royal St., 504/324-6730).

MAP 5: 5631 Magazine St., 504/324-3745, dirtycoast.com; 10am-6pm daily

BOOKS AND MUSIC

Octavia Books

Within easy driving distance of Audubon Park and Tulane University, and only a couple blocks south of Magazine Street, Octavia Books is especially popular among local residents and college students. Besides offering biographies, memoirs, and fiction, the store features plenty of local travel guides and cookbooks, as well as books about New Orleans's unique history, art, and celebrations. Stop by for regular in-store events like readings, signings, and book club meetings (there's a regular book club as well as one for science-fiction fans).

MAP 5: 513 Octavia St., 504/899-7323, octaviabooks.com; 10am-6pm Mon.-Sat., 10am-5pm Sun.

ACCESSORIES AND JEWELRY

Mignon Faget

Mignon Faget has an almost cult following among local devotees of fine jewelry. Not surprisingly, Faget has won countless awards for her creations, many of which incorporate icons and images familiar to Louisianians; there are oyster earrings, red-bean charm necklaces, depictions of the Crescent City Connection bridge, and locally themed cocktail glasses. You'll find other locations inside The Shops at Canal Place (504/524-2973), 4300 Magazine St. (800/375-7557), The Outlet Collection at Riverwalk (504/345-2679), and the Lakeside Shopping Center (504/835-2244).

MAP 5: 3801 Magazine St., 504/891-2005, mignonfaget.com; 10am-6pm Mon.-Sat., noon-5pm Sun.

ARTS AND CRAFTS

Box Paper Scissor

A truly eccentric shop that's not to be missed, Box Paper Scissor sells pens and stationery products, but also so much more, like locally created and imported art, tools, and jewelry. There's also high-end perfume, letter openers from Italy that are pieces of art, snake- and

Recreation

PARKS AND PLAZAS

Audubon Park

One of New Orleanians' favorite places for strolling is verdant Audubon Park, a 340-acre property that occupies the former estate of Etienne de Boré, the city's first mayor, and extends from St. Charles Avenue to the Mississippi River. Besides encompassing the Audubon Zoo, this beloved park features a pleasant lagoon, moss-draped live oak trees, and lush lawns with picnic areas. Named after ornithologist John James Audubon, who once lived in southern Louisiana, Audubon Park offers a slew of athletic facilities, including three playgrounds, a golf course, a swimming pool, and the Audubon Park Trail, a paved 1.8-mile path ideal for walking, jogging, and in-line skating. You can take horseback-riding lessons at Cascade Stables or view a variety of egrets, herons, and cormorants on Ochsner Island, which sits within the park's lagoon and is more commonly known as Bird Island.

The Fly is what the locals call the sliver of green space behind the zoo on the levee overlooking the Mississippi River, officially named Butterfly Riverview Park. It's where folks hang out, play Frisbee, and have impromptu cookouts, crawfish boils, and gatherings. Another popular meetup spot in

Audubon Park

the park is the centuries-old Tree of Life (officially known as the Etienne de Boré oak) that's just outside the walls of the zoo, near the giraffe habitat. Not only is it a peaceful place to meditate and people-watch, occasionally, a giraffe will peek its head over the wall and, well, that's just a great day right there.

MAP 5: 6500 Magazine St., 504/861-2537, auduboninstitute.org; 5am-10pm daily; free

Shops

SHOPPING DISTRICTS

TOP EXPERIENCE

Magazine Street

The Uptown stretch of Magazine Street has a steady stream of galleries, high-end interior design boutiques, vintage stores, gift shops, and jewelry designers, mostly locally owned. There are so many different kinds of businesses that if you picked any three blocks on this stretch, you'd find at least one or two places you love beyond all reason. You can find almost anything here: Need a wellness coffee drink while shopping for makeup? Drink Beauty (3424 Magazine St., no phone; 9am-5pm Mon., 7am-5pm Tues.-Sun.) has all you need. Shop for affordable clothing while helping animals at NO Fleas Market (4228 Magazine St., 504/900-1446, la-spca. org/nofleas; 10am-6pm Tues.-Sat., noon-5pm Sun.), a fantastic thrift store managed by the Louisiana SPCA. Check out Peaches Records (4318 Magazine St., 504/282-3322, peachesrecordsandtapes.com; 10am-7pm daily), a longtime New Orleans business, for local music on vinyl,

cassette, and CD, along with some very cool apparel.

Some of the blocks are more treelined than others; those are usually the ones that also have homes lining the street. Interspersed with all the shops are restaurants, cafés, neighborhood bars, and fitness studios. The #11 bus runs up and down Magazine, if you want to get a ride.

MAP 5: Magazine St., spanning Louisiana Ave. to Nashville Ave.

ANTIQUES AND VINTAGE

Magpie

A high-end yet approachable women's consignment shop, Magpie is great for vintage and estate-sourced jewelry, and other accessories, like handbags. They also carry hats, fascinators, fur stoles, and clothing. It's like browsing history you can wear. In addition to the antique and vintage items, Magpie carries locally designed contemporary pieces and costume jewelry.

MAP 5: 4529 Magazine St., 504/891-1333, magpievintagejewelry. etsy.com; 10:30am-5:30pm Mon.-Sat., noon-5pm Sun.

SPECIALTY FOOD AND DRINK

Martin Wine Cellar

There are several liquor shops around town that sell the ever-increasing brands of spirits and beer made in Louisiana, but Martin Wine Cellar is an Uptown fixture with the most space for perusal. It's also the perfect place to grab a bottle of wine and a sandwich or some cheese and charcuterie from the on-site deli/kitchen to eat there or take back to wherever you're staying. In addition to local libations, Martin's has gourmet products from New Orleans, Louisiana, and beyond. Put some of the most fun stuff together in a gift basket, or purchase individually for your own consumption.

MAP 5: 3827 Baronne St., 504/899-7411, martinwine.com; 10am-7pm Mon.-Fri., 9am-7pm Sat., 10am-3pm Sun.

Petit Paris Market

Petit Paris Market

Head here for chocolate, candies, dishware, jewelry, and more from the culinary capital of the world, Paris, France. This cheery, well-laid-out shop sparkles with Gallic joie de vie, and there are beautiful and delicious-looking treats wherever you look. It's an appropriate homage

to New Orleans's French though the first colonist way too rough and tumble egance on display at Petit

MAP 5: 3719 Magazine St., 504/891-1026, petitparismarket. noon-4pm Mon., 10am-5pm We 10am-6pm Sat.

spices at Verdure Olive Oil Co.

Verdure Olive Oil Co.

Not only does Vedure provide an astounding array of olive oils and vinegars to peruse, but it also offers locally produced spices, sauces, pickles, and jams, as well as books by New Orleans chefs. It's a great spot to purchase locally infused olive oil to take home (they offer TSA-friendly carry-on sizes) along with some of the spice blends with fun names like Pork Tchoup, Ragin' Cajun, and All Dat and Spuds Too!

MAP 5: 3634 Magazine St., 504/373-2848, verdureoliveoil.com; 10am-5:30pm Mon.-Sat., noon-5pm Sun.

GIFTS AND SOUVENIRS

Dirty Coast

Appealing to the fierce pride of locals—as well as curious tourists—the lovingly named Dirty Coast T-shirt

lizard-skin-covered notebooks, and candelabras. The owner is always excited to talk about what she has in stock—you'll see everything in a new light after chatting with her.

MAP 5: 3900 Magazine St., 504/891-4664, boxpaperscissor.com; 11am-5pm Tues.-Sat.

Box Paper Scissor

HOME DECOR
Coutelier

In a town full of restaurants and locals who love food, the most important tool to have in hand is a well-honed, high-quality knife. Coutelier goes around the world to source the best chef's knives—both Eastern and Western style—and bring them back for those who cook professionally and/or at home. Other kitchen products are available, in addition to a well-curated selection of knife-related products like sturdy knife rolls and cutting boards from a neighboring Uptown shop, NOLA Boards. If you don't want to pack your purchased knives in your checked luggage, the folks here will be happy to ship them home for you.

MAP 5: 8239 Oak St., 504/475-5606, couteliernola.com; 10am-6pm Mon.-Sat.

✪ Hazelnut

Whether you're a full-time New Orleans resident or a first-time visitor, you're sure to spot something you like at Hazelnut, an elegant, eclectic Uptown shop that presents exquisite gifts and home accessories, such as towels, linens, and trays emblazoned with the St. Louis Cathedral, the Steamboat Natchez, or any number of iconic local images. Other items include, but are certainly not limited to, clever salt-and-pepper shakers, eye-catching barware, and delicate chandeliers.

MAP 5: 5525 Magazine St., 504/891-2424, hazelnutneworleans.com; 10am-6pm Mon.-Sat.

Mid-City   **Map 6**

The Canal streetcar drives through the heart of this sprawling residential and commercial neighborhood, connecting the many **cemeteries** at the end of Canal at one end and **City Park** at the other. You'll find many small eateries on Carrollton Avenue and Banks Street.

Mid-City comprises multiple sub-neighborhoods, such as Bayou St. John, named after its eponymous waterway, and the evolving Tulane Street corridor, which is transitioning from seedy to **hip,** with **bars, hotels,** and **eateries.**

The area was hard hit by Hurricane Katrina and levee failure. Many

residences and businesses took on several feet of water, and neighborhood institutions underwent months and even years of rebuilding and renovation. It's fitting that the **New Orleans Katrina Memorial** is in Mid-City, among the graveyards along Canal Street and City Park Avenue.

Recreation

PARKS AND PLAZAS
Audubon Park

One of New Orleanians' favorite places for strolling is verdant Audubon Park, a 340-acre property that occupies the former estate of Etienne de Boré, the city's first mayor, and extends from St. Charles Avenue to the Mississippi River. Besides encompassing the Audubon Zoo, this beloved park features a pleasant lagoon, moss-draped live oak trees, and lush lawns with picnic areas. Named after ornithologist John James Audubon, who once lived in southern Louisiana, Audubon Park offers a slew of athletic facilities, including three playgrounds, a golf course, a swimming pool, and the Audubon Park Trail, a paved 1.8-mile path ideal for walking, jogging, and in-line skating. You can take horseback-riding lessons at Cascade Stables or view a variety of egrets, herons, and cormorants on Ochsner Island, which sits within the park's lagoon and is more commonly known as Bird Island.

The Fly is what the locals call the sliver of green space behind the zoo on the levee overlooking the Mississippi River, officially named Butterfly Riverview Park. It's where folks hang out, play Frisbee, and have impromptu cookouts, crawfish boils, and gatherings. Another popular meetup spot in

Audubon Park

the park is the centuries-old Tree of Life (officially known as the Etienne de Boré oak) that's just outside the walls of the zoo, near the giraffe habitat. Not only is it a peaceful place to meditate and people-watch, occasionally, a giraffe will peek its head over the wall and, well, that's just a great day right there.

MAP 5: 6500 Magazine St., 504/861-2537, auduboninstitute.org; 5am-10pm daily; free

Shops

SHOPPING DISTRICTS

TOP EXPERIENCE

Magazine Street

The Uptown stretch of Magazine Street has a steady stream of galleries, high-end interior design boutiques, vintage stores, gift shops, and jewelry designers, mostly locally owned. There are so many different kinds of businesses that if you picked any three blocks on this stretch, you'd find at least one or two places you love beyond all reason. You can find almost anything here: Need a wellness coffee drink while shopping for makeup? Drink Beauty (3424 Magazine St., no phone; 9am-5pm Mon., 7am-5pm Tues.-Sun.) has all you need. Shop for affordable clothing while helping animals at NO Fleas Market (4228 Magazine St., 504/900-1446, la-spca. org/nofleas; 10am-6pm Tues.-Sat., noon-5pm Sun.), a fantastic thrift store managed by the Louisiana SPCA. Check out Peaches Records (4318 Magazine St., 504/282-3322, peachesrecordsandtapes.com; 10am-7pm daily), a longtime New Orleans business, for local music on vinyl, cassette, and CD, along with some very cool apparel.

Some of the blocks are more treelined than others; those are usually the ones that also have homes lining the street. Interspersed with all the shops are restaurants, cafés, neighborhood bars, and fitness studios. The #11 bus runs up and down Magazine, if you want to get a ride.

MAP 5: Magazine St., spanning Louisiana Ave. to Nashville Ave.

ANTIQUES AND VINTAGE

Magpie

A high-end yet approachable women's consignment shop, Magpie is great for vintage and estate-sourced jewelry, and other accessories, like handbags. They also carry hats, fascinators, fur stoles, and clothing. It's like browsing history you can wear. In addition to the antique and vintage items, Magpie carries locally designed contemporary pieces and costume jewelry.

MAP 5: 4529 Magazine St., 504/891-1333, magpievintagejewelry. etsy.com; 10:30am-5:30pm Mon.-Sat., noon-5pm Sun.

SPECIALTY FOOD AND DRINK

Martin Wine Cellar

There are several liquor shops around town that sell the ever-increasing brands of spirits and beer made in Louisiana, but Martin Wine Cellar is an Uptown fixture with the most space for perusal. It's also the perfect place to grab a bottle of wine and a sandwich or some cheese and charcuterie from the on-site deli/kitchen to eat there or take back to wherever you're staying. In addition to local libations, Martin's has gourmet products from New Orleans, Louisiana, and beyond. Put some of the most fun stuff together in a gift basket, or purchase individually for your own consumption.

MAP 5: 3827 Baronne St., 504/899-7411, martinwine.com; 10am-7pm Mon.-Fri., 9am-7pm Sat., 10am-3pm Sun.

Petit Paris Market

Petit Paris Market

Head here for chocolate, candies, dishware, jewelry, and more from the culinary capital of the world, Paris, France. This cheery, well-laid-out shop sparkles with Gallic joie de vie, and there are beautiful and delicious-looking treats wherever you look. It's an appropriate homage to New Orleans's French history, although the first colonists here were way too rough and tumble for the elegance on display at Petit Paris.

MAP 5: 3719 Magazine St., 504/891-1026, petitparismarket.com; noon-4pm Mon., 10am-5pm Wed.-Fri., 10am-6pm Sat.

spices at Verdure Olive Oil Co.

Verdure Olive Oil Co.

Not only does Vedure provide an astounding array of olive oils and vinegars to peruse, but it also offers locally produced spices, sauces, pickles, and jams, as well as books by New Orleans chefs. It's a great spot to purchase locally infused olive oil to take home (they offer TSA-friendly carry-on sizes) along with some of the spice blends with fun names like Pork Tchoup, Ragin' Cajun, and All Dat and Spuds Too!

MAP 5: 3634 Magazine St., 504/373-2848, verdureoliveoil.com; 10am-5:30pm Mon.-Sat., noon-5pm Sun.

GIFTS AND SOUVENIRS

Dirty Coast

Appealing to the fierce pride of locals—as well as curious tourists—the lovingly named Dirty Coast T-shirt

AN UPTOWN ART MARKET

On the last Saturday of the month, the Palmer Park Arts Market (S. Claiborne Ave. at S. Carrollton Ave., 504/658-3200, artsneworleans.org/event/arts-market-of-new-orleans; 10am-4pm last Sat. of the month; free) features locally crafted art like ceramics, jewelry, photography, paintings, soap, and tons of other stuff from more than 80 artists. There's also live music and food to be had. During the holiday season, the Arts Market stretches into Sunday. It's a great place to get unique New Orleans gifts.

shop offers fun, witty, and unique T-shirt and souvenir options for kids and adults. Designs honor such iconic images as jazz musicians, above-ground cemeteries, and other unique aspects of the Big Easy, including historic moments like the Louisiana Purchase. You can also pick up po'boy posters, Saints hoodies, and enamel pins of NOLA-inspired food-stuffs, as well as coasters, mouse pads, and doormats emblazoned with images of the Crescent City's unique water-meter covers. There's a second location in the French Quarter (713 Royal St., 504/324-6730).

MAP 5: 5631 Magazine St., 504/324-3745, dirtycoast.com; 10am-6pm daily

BOOKS AND MUSIC
Octavia Books

Within easy driving distance of Audubon Park and Tulane University, and only a couple blocks south of Magazine Street, Octavia Books is especially popular among local residents and college students. Besides offering biographies, memoirs, and fiction, the store features plenty of local travel guides and cookbooks, as well as books about New Orleans's unique history, art, and celebrations. Stop by for regular in-store events like readings, signings, and book club meetings (there's a regular book club as well as one for science-fiction fans).

MAP 5: 513 Octavia St., 504/899-7323, octaviabooks.com; 10am-6pm Mon.-Sat., 10am-5pm Sun.

ACCESSORIES AND JEWELRY
Mignon Faget

Mignon Faget has an almost cult following among local devotees of fine jewelry. Not surprisingly, Faget has won countless awards for her creations, many of which incorporate icons and images familiar to Louisianians; there are oyster earrings, red-bean charm necklaces, depictions of the Crescent City Connection bridge, and locally themed cocktail glasses. You'll find other locations inside The Shops at Canal Place (504/524-2973), 4300 Magazine St. (800/375-7557), The Outlet Collection at Riverwalk (504/345-2679), and the Lakeside Shopping Center (504/835-2244).

MAP 5: 3801 Magazine St., 504/891-2005, mignonfaget.com; 10am-6pm Mon.-Sat., noon-5pm Sun.

ARTS AND CRAFTS
Box Paper Scissor

A truly eccentric shop that's not to be missed, Box Paper Scissor sells pens and stationery products, but also so much more, like locally created and imported art, tools, and jewelry. There's also high-end perfume, letter openers from Italy that are pieces of art, snake- and lizard-skin-covered notebooks, and candelabras. The owner is always excited to talk about what she has in stock—you'll see everything in a new light after chatting with her.

MAP 5: 3900 Magazine St., 504/891-4664, boxpaperscissor.com; 11am-5pm Tues.-Sat.

Box Paper Scissor

HOME DECOR
Coutelier

In a town full of restaurants and locals who love food, the most important tool to have in hand is a well-honed, high-quality knife. Coutelier goes around the world to source the best chef's knives—both Eastern and Western style—and bring them back for those who cook professionally and/or at home. Other kitchen products are available, in addition to a well-curated selection of knife-related products like sturdy knife rolls and cutting boards from a neighboring Uptown shop, NOLA Boards. If you don't want to pack your purchased knives in your checked luggage, the folks here will be happy to ship them home for you.

MAP 5: 8239 Oak St., 504/475-5606, couteliernola.com; 10am-6pm Mon.-Sat.

⊗ Hazelnut

Whether you're a full-time New Orleans resident or a first-time visitor, you're sure to spot something you like at Hazelnut, an elegant, eclectic Uptown shop that presents exquisite gifts and home accessories, such as towels, linens, and trays emblazoned with the St. Louis Cathedral, the Steamboat Natchez, or any number of iconic local images. Other items include, but are certainly not limited to, clever salt-and-pepper shakers, eye-catching barware, and delicate chandeliers.

MAP 5: 5525 Magazine St., 504/891-2424, hazelnutneworleans.com; 10am-6pm Mon.-Sat.

Mid-City   Map 6

The Canal streetcar drives through the heart of this sprawling residential and commercial neighborhood, connecting the many **cemeteries** at the end of Canal at one end and **City Park** at the other. You'll find many small eateries on Carrollton Avenue and Banks Street.

Mid-City comprises multiple sub-neighborhoods, such as Bayou St. John, named after its eponymous waterway, and the evolving Tulane Street corridor, which is transitioning from seedy to **hip,** with **bars, hotels,** and **eateries.**

The area was hard hit by Hurricane Katrina and levee failure. Many

residences and businesses took on several feet of water, and neighborhood institutions underwent months and even years of rebuilding and renovation. It's fitting that the **New Orleans Katrina Memorial** is in Mid-City, among the graveyards along Canal Street and City Park Avenue.

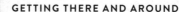

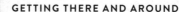

TOP SIGHTS

- Best Urban Retreat: **City Park** (page 194)

TOP RESTAURANTS

- Best Burgers and Wings:
  Fharmacy (page 202)
- Best Spot for Simple Pleasures:
  Angelo Brocato (page 204)
- Best Coffee Shop Food: **The
  Station** (page 205)

TOP NIGHTLIFE

- Best at Defying Categorization:
  Twelve Mile Limit (page 207)

TOP ARTS AND CULTURE

- Best Freebie: **Sydney and Walda Besthoff
  Sculpture Garden** (page 210)

TOP RECREATION

- Most Relaxing Way to See the City:
  Kayak-iti-Yat (page 211)

TOP SHOPS

- Best Place for Board Games: **Tubby &
  Coo's Mid-City Book Shop** (page 212)

GETTING THERE AND AROUND

- Streetcar lines: Canal Street to Cemeteries
  (47), Canal to City Park (48)
- Major bus routes: 27, 45, 90, 91

MID-CITY

Greenwood Cemetery 1

Delgado Community College

New Orleans Botanical Garden 5

City Park

3 4

7 8

6

Holt Cemetery

New Orleans Country Club

9 New Orleans Katrina Memorial

Cypress Grove Cemetery

St. Patrick Cemetery No. 1

St. Patrick Cemetery No. 2

Mid-City

Xavier University of Louisiana

12 13 14
11
10
20 21
17 18 19
27
22 25
23 24 26
30 31
32 33
34 36 3
10 35
45
44
41
42
43

0 500 yds
0 500 m
DISTANCE ACROSS MAP
Approximate: 2.9 mi or 4.6 km

SEE MAP 5

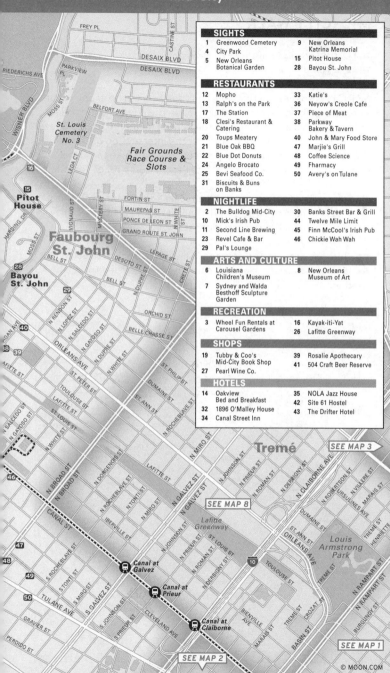

SIGHTS

1 Greenwood Cemetery
4 City Park
5 New Orleans Botanical Garden
9 New Orleans Katrina Memorial
15 Pitot House
28 Bayou St. John

RESTAURANTS

12 Mopho
13 Ralph's on the Park
17 The Station
18 Clesi's Restaurant & Catering
20 Toups Meatery
21 Blue Oak BBQ
22 Blue Dot Donuts
24 Angelo Brocato
25 Bevi Seafood Co.
31 Biscuits & Buns on Banks
33 Katie's
36 Neyow's Creole Cafe
37 Piece of Meat
38 Parkway Bakery & Tavern
40 John & Mary Food Store
47 Marjie's Grill
48 Coffee Science
49 Fharmacy
50 Avery's on Tulane

NIGHTLIFE

2 The Bulldog Mid-City
10 Mick's Irish Pub
11 Second Line Brewing
23 Revel Cafe & Bar
29 Pal's Lounge
30 Banks Street Bar & Grill
44 Twelve Mile Limit
45 Finn McCool's Irish Pub
46 Chickie Wah Wah

ARTS AND CULTURE

6 Louisiana Children's Museum
7 Sydney and Walda Besthoff Sculpture Garden
8 New Orleans Museum of Art

RECREATION

3 Wheel Fun Rentals at Carousel Gardens
16 Kayak-iti-Yat
26 Lafitte Greenway

SHOPS

19 Tubby & Coo's Mid-City Book Shop
27 Pearl Wine Co.
39 Rosalie Apothecary
41 504 Craft Beer Reserve

HOTELS

14 Oakview Bed and Breakfast
32 1896 O'Malley House
34 Canal Street Inn
35 NOLA Jazz House
42 Site 61 Hostel
43 The Drifter Hotel

© MOON.COM

MID-CITY WALK

TOTAL DISTANCE: 2.8 miles (4.5 kilometers)
TRAVEL TIME: 1 hour

Mid-City is so massive that you won't see everything in one excursion. This walking tour takes you through the commercial corridor of North Carrollton Avenue, to the Katrina Memorial, and to a few of City Park's attractions. It starts at the intersection of **North Carrollton and Bienville,** at the streetcar stop. (Take the Canal streetcar with the designation "City Park.") Come ready for lunch.

1 Start at **Bevi Seafood Co.** and grab some boiled crawfish if it's in season or have half a po'boy. This should satisfy your hunger, but will still leave room for other snacks along the walk.

2 Turn left onto North Carrollton, walk a half a block to **Angelo Brocato,** and get a cannoli or a frozen fruit ice, depending on the weather.

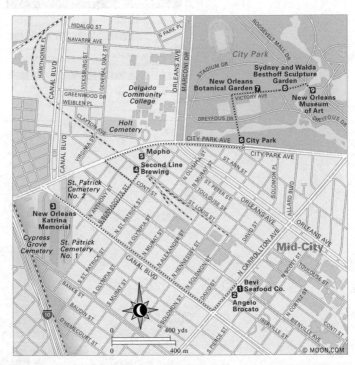

3 Continue down North Carrollton for a block and a half to the intersection of Canal and Carrollton. Take an outbound streetcar to "Cemeteries," which should be on the streetcar sign. Head to the last stop and with City Park Avenue ahead of you, turn left to cross to Canal Street to reach the **New Orleans Katrina Memorial.** The memorial is laid out to emulate the shape of a hurricane on radar. It's emblazoned with the names of all the people who died as a result of the storm and levee breach.

4 Outside the memorial, turn right onto Canal Street and head southeast for three blocks, turn left onto North Bernadotte Street and walk four blocks to check out the locally brewed beers in the beer garden at **Second Line Brewing.**

5 From Second Line, walk a block back down North Bernadette (going southwest) and turn right onto Conti. After two blocks, take a right onto City Park Avenue and walk a block to the mini strip mall where **Mopho** is. Depending on how hungry and weary you are, have some chicken wings or a bowl of pho. You've earned it.

6 Continue down City Park Avenue for about five blocks till you reach Ralph's on the Park. Cross City Park Avenue here, into **City Park** on Anseman Avenue.

7 After two blocks, turn right onto Victory Avenue. You'll pass the **New Orleans Botanical Garden** on your left. It was originally created in the 1930s as a rose garden, but now has so much more, including a Japanese garden, a butterfly garden, a native plant garden, and a small sculpture garden featuring the art of Enrique Alferez, a Mexican-American artist who created many sculptures throughout New Orleans.

8 Continue east on Victory Avenue. On the right is one of the entrances to the **Sydney and Walda Besthoff Sculpture Garden.** Check out the sculptures, created by a variety of artists. Eventually, you'll make your way across the lagoon and continue to Dueling Oak Drive.

9 If the sculpture garden whetted your appetite for art, turn to visit the **New Orleans Museum of Art.** You can't miss it: It's an imposing-looking building with columns and white marble, and it's well-known for its collection of American and French art (including several pieces by Degas). It's one of the finest art museums in the South. The museum's main exit leads out to Lelong Drive, which in turn leads to the park exit at North Carrollton and Esplanade Avenue. There's a streetcar stop just outside the gates. The streetcar will take you southwest down Carrollton and you'll be back where you started.

the Pitot House

Sights

✪ City Park

City Park is a haven for bikers, hikers, music lovers, art aficionados, and anyone looking to experience New Orleans's most captivating natural experiences. From the New Orleans Botanical Garden and the Sydney and Walda Besthoff Sculpture Garden to the beautifully designed bridges and walking paths, the thousands of lush and tangled oak trees (the nation's largest collection), and the wildlife that lives here, City Park is a gem that provides many hours of enjoyment. You can hit one feature for a quick stop, or make a day of it and explore as much as you can. Now that Cafe du Monde is open 24 hours near the sculpture garden, you'll have plenty

of fuel in the form of sweet beignets and creamy cafe au laits to keep you going.

Children are fond of the Carousel Gardens Amusement Park (hours vary seasonally; $5 admission, $4 per ride or $18 for unlimited rides), which features numerous attractions and a mini train that tours the park. Of particular note is the park's historic carousel, which since 1906 has been home to hand-carved and lovingly maintained animals including 53 horses (with real horsehair), a 500-pound lion, a giraffe, and a camel. The carousel's architecture is as stunning as the animals, with stained glass surrounding the circular building. In 2019, the park renovated the family-friendly Storyland (10am-5pm Tues.-Fri., 10am-6pm Sat.-Sun.; $4 pp), which features

New Orleans Museum of Art (page 209).

- Enjoy art outside at the **Sydney and Walda Besthoff Sculpture Garden** (page 210).
- Rent a bike from **Wheel Fun Rentals** (page 211).

Pitot House

Alongside the eastern bank of the peaceful Bayou St. John is one of the few surviving Creole colonial plantations in the South. The Pitot House Museum is named for an early occupant, James Pitot, the first mayor of New Orleans (after it was incorporated), who lived in the house in the early 1800s. At one time or another, lawyers, nuns, and other interesting New Orleanians have dwelled in this lovely home. With its early West Indies architectural style (one of the few such examples still remaining) and recreated rooms using period furniture pieces, the museum sheds light on the lifestyle of those who once lived alongside the bayou.

In the 1960s, the Pitot House was carefully restored to its appearance in the early 1800s, and filled with American antiques from that period. The colonial home's exterior is simple yet august, with sleek columns, wraparound balconies (also known as galleries), and large green plantation-style shutters. It's surrounded by trees, necessary to keep the house protected from the heat of the sun. The gardens, which extend significantly from the house, include plants commonly planted in the late 1700s to early 1840s—such as roses, okra, and sweet olive trees. Inside, low wooden-beam ceilings

fairytale inspired, larger-than-life sculptures and encourages interactive play through music and other means.

Daytime is the best time to explore the park, since you can traverse some of the smaller paths with more ease, and that's when most of the events and outdoor exhibits take place. Sometimes a particular space or attraction will have crowds over the weekend (especially if there's a festival, which also affects parking), but usually park-goers are spread throughout the many acres, walking, sitting on benches or on blankets on the ground, or partaking in the public art and music, so it never feels too crowded.

MAP 6: 1 Palm Dr., 504/482-4888, neworleanscitypark.com; hours vary seasonally; free

NEARBY

- Stop and smell the roses at the **New Orleans Botanical Garden** (page 196).
- Refuel at **Ralph's on the Park** (page 199).
- Play your heart out at the **Louisiana Children's Museum** (page 209).
- Check out the masterpieces at the

and wide plank-wood floors surround brightly colored plaster walls and period furniture. Admission is by guided tour only, and they run around 40 minutes. To reach the Pitot House, take the Canal streetcar. There's no off-street parking. MAP 6: 1440 Moss St., 504/482-0312, pitothouse.org; by guided tour only 10am-3pm Wed.-Sat.; $10 adults, $7 seniors, students, and children, children under 6 free

New Orleans Botanical Garden

Opened in 1936 as the City Park Rose Garden, this was the Big Easy's first public classical garden. A project of the Works Progress Administration (WPA), it was designed by landscape architect William Wiedorn and prolific local building architect Richard Koch to have several formal garden "rooms." It's one of the few remaining WPA-era public garden design projects that are still intact, and it's one of the best examples of the landscaping style. Rechristened the New Orleans Botanical Garden in the early 1980s, this lovingly tended sanctuary now contains more than 2,000 types of plants, including azaleas, camellias, and palm trees, all set within thematic gardens. Mexican American artist and New Orleans resident Enrique Alférez created all the statuary (16 pieces in total) in the 8,000 square foot sculpture garden.

Special attractions here include the colorful Butterfly Walk and Hummingbird Garden; the tranquil Yakumo Nihon Teien Japanese Garden; the Historic New Orleans Train Garden, in a fascinating, Paul Busse-designed layout that represents the city of New Orleans

New Orleans Botanical Garden

in the early 19th century; and the Conservatory of the Two Sisters, a gorgeous, glass-domed building erected in the 1930s.

Check out the native plant garden, which showcases the region's endemic flora with plants in both a wet swamp area and a dry prairie environment, along with the original WPA rose garden, where it all began. The staff provides tours by appointment for groups ($12-16 pp depending on group size) or individuals ($25) of the garden's grounds as well as a City Park-wide Ancient Oak Tree tour. The garden's entrance is near the Pavilion of the Two Sisters on Victory Avenue. Free parking is available in the nearby lot. Pets, bikes, and skates aren't permitted.

MAP 6: 1 Palm Dr., City Park, 504/483-9386, neworleanscitypark.com; 10am-4:30pm Tues.-Sun.; $8 adults, $4 children 3-12, children under 3 free

Greenwood Cemetery

Established in 1852, Greenwood, one of several aboveground graveyards in the city, is the site of New Orleans's first Civil War memorial, dedicated in April 1874, which marks the mass grave of 600 Confederate soldiers. Other impressive landmarks here include the Firemen's Monument, an Italian marble statue erected in 1887, and the marble tomb of Lodge No. 30 of the Benevolent and Protective Order of Elks, which was erected in 1912 by Albert Weiblen and is guarded by a majestic bronze elk. Several tombs are dedicated to fraternal organizations, such as the Police Mutual Benevolent Association, and to key New Orleanians, such as John Fitzpatrick, a 19th-century

mayor, and John Kennedy Toole, the Pulitzer Prize-winning author of *A Confederacy of Dunces.*

MAP 6: 5200 Canal Blvd., 504/482-8983, greenwoodnola.com; 8am-4:30pm daily; free

New Orleans Katrina Memorial

The New Orleans Katrina Memorial is tucked in the corner of the Canal Street cemetery area. Dedicated in 2008, the subtle memorial features a semi-circle of six stone mausoleums that contain the bodies of 83 people who were either never identified or were unclaimed after the devastating event. Though you may not realize it as you're wending through the space, the memorial is laid out in the shape of a hurricane as seen from above.

MAP 6: 5056 Canal St., 504/658-3200, 8am-2pm Mon.-Fri.; free

Bayou St. John

Bayou St. John runs along the eastern side of Wisner Boulevard, stretching from Lafitte Avenue all the way to Lake Pontchartrain. It was once linked to the Mississippi River, making it particularly attractive to early French explorers, traders, and trappers. This link to the Mississippi was part of the reason that the French established New Orleans where they did. Bayou St. John is said to have been the site of Marie Laveau's voodoo rituals in the 19th century. Today it's a picturesque, slow-moving body of water, lined by greenery and frequented by sunbathers, anglers, and residents of Mid-City. It's also the site of various annual events, such as the Mid-City Bayou Boogaloo in mid-May and the New Orleans Greek Festival in late

stand-up paddleboarders on Bayou St. John

May. It's a great place to walk and explore the crossroads of several neighborhoods (Tremé, Fairgrounds, and Mid-City), and the bayou's green banks are just calling out for sitting and/or picnicking. It's a significant piece of the fabric of New Orleans, and picturesque to boot.

Near the Pitot House and behind Cabrini High School, the pedestrian bridge known as the Magnolia, Bayou, or Cabrini Bridge underwent a significant renovation in 2019 and is now a bright blue beacon for all walkers and bicyclists to use when crossing over Bayou St. John. It rewards passers-by with a lovely view.

A worthwhile side trip for mid-century modern fans with a car is to head north about two miles to the intersection of Harrison and St. Bernard Avenues to cross the bridge to Demourelle Island, colloquially known as Park Island. It's got one street, Park Island Avenue, and almost all the homes are built overlooking the water. Most of the residences on the 28 lots were built at the same time, during the 1950s-1960s, in the era of Frank Lloyd Wright and the Mid-Century Modern architectural style. New Orleans native and Modernist star Albert Ledner designed two of the homes on the island, the Galatoire House and the Ash Tray House, the latter of which is adorned with thousands of amber square ashtrays inside and out.

MAP 6: Wisner Blvd., between Lafitte Ave. and Lake Pontchartrain

Restaurants

PRICE KEY

$	Entrées less than $15
$$	Entrées $15-30
$$$	Entrées more than $30

CAJUN AND CREOLE

Neyow's Creole Cafe $$

Neyow's is your friendly neighborhood Creole soul food restaurant, where everyone's welcome to partake in dishes like chargrilled oysters, gumbo, po'boys, and red beans any day of the week. This is a bustling, convivial restaurant with happy guests and attentive service. MAP 6: 3332 Bienville St. 504/827-5474, neyows.com; 11am-9pm Mon.-Thurs., 11am-11pm Fri.-Sat.

Ralph's on the Park $$

Located within steps of leafy City Park, the aptly named Ralph's on the Park is absolutely worth the trip. It's far from the madding crowds of the Quarter and the CBD, making for a relaxed, convivial dining experience. It's also set inside a lovely historic building that was constructed in 1860 as a coffeehouse and concession stand for the park. Then there's the elegant, innovative food, such as seared octopus, satsuma duck, and "shrimp skully," made with tempura shrimp, a hot sauce and pepper jelly reduction, and crispy smoked almonds. It's also one of the best brunch options in town, offering tasty dishes like turtle soup, crawfish Benedict, and Gulf shrimp and grits. Don't overlook the weekday happy hour (3pm-7pm Mon.-Fri.), where wines by the glass and all dips

and snacks, like sweet potato hummus and gumbo poutine, are $5, and craft beer is $3. MAP 6: 900 City Park Ave., 504/488-1000, ralphsonthepark.com; 5:30pm-9pm Mon., 11:30am-2pm and 5:30pm-9pm Tues.-Fri., 10:30am-2pm and 5:30pm-9pm Sat.-Sun.

Toups Meatery $$

With Meatery as part of the name, you have a pretty good idea what you're dealing with. Restaurateur and chef Isaac Toups (who also runs Toups South in Central City) brings his Cajun- and meat-loving sensibilities to New Orleans. You'll find rustic yet thoughtful duck, lamb, quail, Gulf seafood, and venison preparations alongside bold takes on more traditional meats like pork, chicken, and beef. The restaurant is a small spot with white walls and wood accents. But a large bar and substantial outdoor seating creates a space for everyone. No matter what, get the cracklin'. The chef's lunch is a winner too, with boudin balls, the Toups' burger, and a beer for $23. MAP 6: 845 N Carrollton Ave., 504/252-4999, toupsmeatery. com; 11am-2:30pm and 5pm-10pm Tues.-Thurs., 11am-2:30pm and 5pm-11pm, Fri.- Sat., 10am-3pm Sun.

Clesi's Restaurant & Catering $

This sibling-run boil house is the result of James Clesi's enormous popularity as a crawfish boil caterer, popping up in front of many a Mid-City bar offering spicy mudbugs to hungry revelers. There's indoor seating (and a gorgeous cypress wood-topped bar), but of course the communal outdoor vibe of the boils is what it's all about, so there's plenty of space on the patio. When crawfish aren't in season, shrimp and crab can be found alongside a selection of down-home dishes like burgers, boudin bites, po'boys, and fried seafood plates.

MAP 6: 4323 Bienville Ave., 504/909-0108, clesicatering.com; 11am-9pm Sun. and Tues.-Thurs., 11am-10pm Fri.-Sat.

Katie's $

This well-loved, family-owned neighborhood eatery is known for its friendly staff, easygoing atmosphere, and delicious food. The menu features both Creole-Italian and New Orleans-style cuisine, such as crawfish beignets, over-stuffed crab cakes, and a kalamata muffuletta. The Barge is an entire French bread loaf stuffed with fried shrimp, oysters, and/or catfish, which can serve up to four people. Katie's is also well known for its boisterous Sunday brunches with $15 bottomless mimosas, Bloody Marys, and sangria.

MAP 6: 3701 Iberville St., 504/488-6582, katiesinmidcity.com; 11am-9pm Mon.-Thurs., 11am-10pm Fri.-Sat., 9am-3pm Sun.

PO'BOYS

Avery's on Tulane $

This tiny spot decorated with Mardi Gras bead art and playing local brass band music serves up traditional po'boys, gumbo, and other regional treats, all made from scratch with fresh ingredients. Several of their dishes are unique to the Avery's kitchen, like their potato salad, which is made with bacon, formed into a ball, covered with Leidenheimer bread crumbs, and fried. It's a great accompaniment to either of the gumbos offered (chicken/sausage or seafood). The po'boys are the main draw though, and rightly so. Standard options like catfish, shrimp, oyster, and roast beef are on offer alongside choices like New Orleans-style barbecue shrimp, oysters Rockefeller, and something called "Fire in the Hole," with locally sourced hot sausage, pepper jack cheese, fried pickled jalapeños, and Sriracha mayo. Keep an eye out for their daily $8.75 plate specials and happy hour (2pm-4pm) with half price beer and wine. There's parking in the back.

MAP 6: 2510 Tulane Ave., 504/821-4110, averysontulane.com; 11am-4pm Mon.-Sat.

Parkway Bakery & Tavern $

Founded in 1911, the Parkway Bakery & Tavern is a terrific place to dine after exploring City Park. Despite the name, this popular eatery is mainly known for its delicious, well-stuffed po'boys, with fillings like pastrami, fried catfish, and alligator sausage. Patrons rave about the potato salad, the sweet potato fries, and the surf & turf po'boy, a winning combination of hot roast beef, fried shrimp, and gravy. The Parkway has a friendly staff and a nostalgic atmosphere—the walls are filled with old photographs and local memorabilia.

MAP 6: 538 Hagan Ave., 504/482-3047, parkwaypoorboys.com; 11am-10pm Wed.-Mon.

BARBECUE

Blue Oak BBQ $

This is some of the best barbecue in the city, if its many awards and trophies are to be believed. Believe them. Blue Oak has a fair bit of seating in its wood-paneled interior, with much more outside. The smokers do their meats justice—the ribs, brisket, and chicken legs are all on point. Most of the sandwiches are the standard combination of meat, slaw, pickles, and sauce, but there are a few original creations in the mix, too. Sides like the roasted garlic mac 'n' cheese, the ginger sesame slaw, and the Brussels sprouts are all justifiably popular, and the weekday happy hour (3pm-6pm Tues.-Fri.) offers up smoked wings, barbecue nachos, and barbecue sliders for very reasonable prices along with wine, beer, and cocktails for $4-5.

MAP 6: 900 N Carrollton Ave., 504/822-2583, blueoakbbq.com; 11am-9pm Tues.-Sun.

SEAFOOD

Bevi Seafood Co. $$

Bevi's Mid-City location is conveniently located on the corner of North Carrollton Avenue and Bienville Street and is a great place to get your boil on—including shrimp, crab, and crawfish (in season). This sparse space with cinderblock walls painted light blue and adorned with maritime-themed art also offers po'boys, in traditional seafood as well as more creative combinations like the Smokey Oyster, with fried oysters topped with smoked gouda and bacon or the Messi Swine, made with pork belly, *cochon de lait* (suckling pig), Chisesi ham, and bacon fat mayo. It's also a great place to try some New Orleans-style barbecue shrimp—their version is made with a sauce containing Canebrake, a local beer. They also carry a variety of local Louisiana beers on tap and infuse their own spirits for cocktails. There's another Bevi's at 4701 Airline Drive in Metairie.

MAP 6: 236 N Carrollton Ave., 504/488-7503, beviseafoodco.com; 11am-4pm Sun.-Mon. 11am-8pm Tues.-Sat.

VIETNAMESE

John & Mary's Food Store $

A stone's throw from Bayou St. John, John & Mary's Food Store is exactly what it sounds like: a corner store that also sells hot food. The primary focus is Vietnamese, with *chà giò* (Vietnamese egg rolls), pho, banh mi, and *gỏi cuốn* (spring rolls). However, they also serve up a few Chinese-American dishes, plate lunches, and Southern/New Orleans cuisine like red beans, white beans, gumbo, fried chicken, and, the best reason to check this place out, a decidedly pho-like take on the New Orleans noodle soup called *yakamein*. Like pho, there's a choice of which protein to include—the classic beef, of course, but also chicken, pork, shrimp, or a combination. This is Viet-Soul at its finest.

MAP 6: 3238 Orleans Ave., 504/484-3003; 7am-7:30pm Mon.-Sat.

Mopho $$

This irreverent take on fusing Louisiana and Vietnamese street food is chef Michael Gulotta's first spot which he opened in 2014 in a mini strip mall shared with a Burger King. (Only park in a Mopho-designated spot, or risk having your car towed.) Mopho serves up Vietnamese classics like pho and banh mi in a brightly colored spot, along with curries, chicken wings, rice bowls, and playful dishes like *nuoc mam* caramel chicken & waffles. On Saturdays, the kitchen roasts a whole hog outside in the cheerful courtyard (every third Saturday of the month it's lamb) and on Wednesdays the smoky pork pho is to die for. Gulotta also oversees a more upscale version of the same concept at Maypop in the Warehouse District.

MAP 6: 514 City Park Ave.,
504/482-6845, mophonola.com;
11am-10pm Sun.-Thurs., 11am-11pm
Fri.-Sat.

ECLECTIC
✪ Fharmacy $

Fharmacy is much more than it seems. It's run by two Vietnamese chefs from New Orleans East and the menu has some southeast Asian flavors (the mussels and frites with Asian steaming liquid is divine) but encompasses a wider culinary world of comfort food. Check out any and all of their wing flavors, the loaded fries or tots, the Cajun meat pies, the Chicago-style Italian beef sandwich, the lemongrass tacos, and, of course, the burgers. These burgers are consistently mentioned as some of the best in New Orleans, and not only can you get a standard cheeseburger, there are unique flavor combos like the Dr. Seuss burger with avocado aioli, ham, cheese, and egg, or the Fharmacy burger, with house-made *giardiniera* (Italian-style picked

Fharmacy

vegetable relish) and bacon jam. It's in a homey converted shotgun house with the chefs manning the grill from behind the lunch counter and cheerful, friendly service.

MAP 6: 2540 Banks St., 504/324-6090, fharmacyrestaurant.com; 11am-9pm Mon.-Sat.

Marjie's Grill $

New Orleanians are fiercely protective of this spot: Everyone wants to keep the cozy, unassuming restaurant a secret, but the food is so amazing that it's impossible to hide. It's nothing fancy, but the meat and seafood mains (and sides) are intensely flavored with Southeast Asian ingredients and cooked boldly, usually over a hot grill (there'll probably be good smelling smoke in the air), but sometimes fried or braised. There's something exuberant about the menu and the perfection of its execution that makes everyone who eats here a convert. Try a meat-and-three lunch plate with cornmeal fried chicken (with Thai chilies), charcoal-grilled Gulf shrimp, coal-roasted sweet potatoes, or grilled shishito peppers.

MAP 6: 320 S Broad Ave., 504/603-2234, marjiesgrill.com; 11am-2:30pm and 5pm-10pm Mon.-Fri., 4pm-10pm Sat.

Piece of Meat $

This is the place to go if you're looking for high-quality, well-butchered meat to have prepared for you or to take home to cook yourself. Beef and pork cuts along with a variety of house-made sausages and charcuterie are available from the cases, and a lovely menu of sandwiches and snacks graces the wall. Try the house-cured pastrami sandwich, the mind-blowing bologna sandwich, boudin egg rolls (a Cajun-country roadside favorite that's been almost impossible to find in New Orleans until now) and the charcuterie board. For vegetarians, they also have a selection of meat-free sandwiches and salads.

MAP 6: 3301 Bienville St., 504/372-2289, pieceofmeatbutcher. com; 11am-8pm Mon.-Tues. and Thurs., 11am-9pm Fri., 10am-9pm Sat., 10am-4pm Sun.

BREAKFAST AND BRUNCH

Biscuits & Buns on Banks $

There are several eateries on this stretch of Banks Street, but Biscuits & Buns is worth seeking out. It's tucked away in a converted shotgun-style house. Entering, the kitchen is immediately on the left but there are two spacious rooms in the back for diners, festooned with brightly painted New Orleans-themed murals on the walls. They serve a full range of espresso drinks, but their

Marjie's Grill

Angelo Brocato

drip coffee is strong and comes to grateful guests in large, bottomless mugs. Try the andouille sausage hash cakes or the Louisiana crab cake Benedict. The biscuits come with a choice of butter and preserves or andouille and chorizo gravy.
MAP 6: 4337 Banks St., 504/273-4600, biscuitsandbunsonbanks.com; 8am-3pm daily

Blue Dot Donuts $

Because Blue Dot was opened by two former NOPD cops, the jokes really write themselves, so instead let's focus on the high quality of the donuts and the variety of the flavors found in this bright-blue building. Yeast, cake, and buttermilk doughs are all used, with more than 40 toppings and fillings. Try the key lime pie crumb, the almond-flavored wedding cake, or the infamous "long john" yeast donut covered with maple icing and bacon. The retired cops sold Blue Dot to the bakery's longtime donut maker in 2017. The

decor is basic, but there are a few tables to sit and eat, though most folks take their donuts to go.
MAP 6: 4301 Canal St., 504/218-4866, bluedotdonuts.com; 6am-1pm Tues.-Sun.

COFFEE AND DESSERTS
✪ Angelo Brocato $

After a day of exploring City Park, head southwest on Carrollton, toward Canal Street, and take a snack-break detour at Angelo Brocato, an old-world bakery and ice cream parlor that's famous not only for its superb Italian pastries, such as biscotti and ricotta pie, but also for the tantalizing house-made ice cream, Italian ice, and gelato in all kinds of tempting flavors, such as spumoni, chestnut, and amaretto. The most popular treat is the lemon ice, a simple yet expertly blended concoction of water, granulated sugar, and fresh lemons. It even looks the part, with pastel pink walls and old-fashioned, soda-jerk-era chairs and marble-topped tables. The counter staff are friendly and helpful, but do like to keep the line moving along. Don't sleep on the cannoli—they're filled to order, decadent, and out-of-this-world.

MAP 6: 214 N Carrollton Ave., 504/486-0078, angelobrocatoicecream. com; 10am-10pm Tues.-Thurs., 10am-10:30pm Fri.-Sat., 10am-9pm Sun.

Coffee Science $

As could be concluded from its name, this is one of the geekiest coffee spots in town. The employees here have a passion for the bean and for teaching customers how to enjoy their coffee black (don't worry, they still have everything you might need to doctor your java). Along with the usual espresso drinks, owner Tom Oliver has put together a menu of specialty drinks like the Venetian Cream (with coconut milk), a Bavarian Cream iced coffee, and the frozen Mocha Frosted as an homage to Kaldi's, a long-lamented coffee shop in the French Quarter. Donuts, pastries, and bagels are on hand for munching, but keep an eye

out for the breakfast tacos, offered every now and then. The spacious and sunny back room and back deck overlook the small summertime pool (you gotta see it to understand it) and the very valuable customer parking lot.

MAP 6: 410 S Broad Ave., 504/814-0878; 7:30am-5:30pm Mon.-Fri., 8am-5pm Sat.-Sun.

✪ The Station $

With its bright purple A-frame roof, this coffee shop is nearly impossible to miss. Once inside, you'll find folks working on their laptops at tables or just relaxing with a coffee and a snack on the comfy couch and armchairs. The coffee and tea selection is extensive, as is the food menu. With sweet and savory options like the goat cheese, rosemary, and pecan danish, a shepherd's pie that's actually in pie form, or pear-butterscotch coffee cake, there's always something in the case that will excite you, even if you're vegan or gluten free.

MAP 6: 4400 Bienville St., 504/309-4548, thestation.coffee; 6:30am-7pm Mon.-Fri., 7:30am-5pm Sat.-Sun.

Nightlife

LIVE MUSIC

Banks Street Bar & Grill

This corner dive bar hosts live music a couple times a week—everything from rap to punk, rock and roll, and thrash. It underwent a recent renovation when neighboring Mid-City Pizza took it over (they'd gotten

their start in the back of the bar), so the bathrooms are in decent shape, the bar itself is sporting a new cypress wood top, and the whiskey and draft beer selections have been beefed up. It's a great spot to check out some music that's a bit off the beaten path for New Orleans.

The Station

4401 Banks St., 504/486-0258, banksstreetbarnola.com; 11am-4am daily; no cover

Chickie Wah Wah

This is one of the only music clubs outside of Frenchmen Street that has the same, laidback feel and that hosts a variety of local entertainers throughout the week. The cover charge here is reasonable—and all of it goes to the artist: musicians like Alex McMurry, Meschiya Lake, Paul Sanchez, Sharon Martin, and Phil DeGruy. Sets start at 6pm, so it's a great spot to wind down after a day in Mid-City or to ramp up for a night on the town.

MAP 6: 2828 Canal St., 504/304-4714, chickiewahwah.com; 5pm-midnight Mon.-Fri., 7pm till the end of the set Sat.-Sun.; cover varies by performance

COCKTAIL BARS
Revel Cafe & Bar

Chris MacMillan is rightly known as one of the best bartenders in the country. He and his wife Laura started the **Museum of the American Cocktail,** now housed in the **Southern Food and Beverage Museum.** Revel is right off the streetcar line, with a small, seated dining area at the front with plenty of natural light. Tucked in the back is a darker, classic wood bar with brass accents. Throughout the space are pressed tin ceilings. You won't get a drink quickly here, but you'll get it done right. MacMillan's Ramos Gin Fizz is a thing of beauty, and if you sit at the bar, he might tell you the history of this storied drink. The food menu is surprisingly interesting and excellent for a place that focuses on cocktails, with dishes like black garlic butter fries and crawfish grilled cheese.

MAP 6: 133 N Carrollton Ave., 504/309-6122, revelcafeandbar.com; 4pm-11pm Tues.-Thurs., 11am-11pm Fri.-Sat.

✪ Twelve Mile Limit

This place is like a dive bar mixed with a pool hall, a craft cocktail bar, a progressive safe space, and a hipster retreat—but in a good way. You can get a made-to-order classic or creative cocktail for a good price (everything's under $10) or a canned beer, enjoy the best jukebox in town, and play some pool. The kitchen serves up barbecue most nights, but keep an eye on their social media for announcements of brunch pop-up events.

MAP 6: 500 S Telemachus St., 504/488-8114; 5pm-2am Mon.-Fri., 10am-2am Sat., 10am-midnight Sun.

BARS AND LOUNGES

The Bulldog Mid-City

One of the oldest beer bars in the city, the Bulldog's Mid-City location (there's also one at 3236 Magazine St.) has a neighborhood, mellow vibe as well as a secluded dog-friendly patio. With 61 taps, several large-screen TVs, and a dark interior vaguely reminiscent of an English pub, it's a great place to watch the game, chill with friends, play with puppies, or just relax with a beverage.

MAP 6: 5135 Canal Blvd., 504/488-4180, bulldog-midcity.draftfreak.com; 11am-11pm or later daily

Finn McCool's Irish Pub

This is Mid-City's ground zero for all things soccer—or, football, as you should call it there. It's literally standing room only during the World Cup, and it's one of the city's St. Patrick's Day loci, given the boisterous nature and Irish roots of the regulars and staff. Otherwise, it's really more of a neighborhood spot,

Banks Street Bar & Grill

with regulars scattered all along the snaking, long, well-worn bar and local notices up on the walls. Get your Guinness on here.

MAP 6: 3701 Banks St., 504/486-9080, finnmccools.com; 11am-2am Mon.-Thurs., 9am-3am Fri.-Sun.

Mick's Irish Pub

A jovial corner bar dedicated to the pursuit of good times, Mick's offers a great place to drink and play. Pinball, video games, shuffleboard, and a pool table all await in the back rooms at Mick's, with plenty of space for socializing. The corner bar in the front room runs the length of two walls, with plenty of beer taps (including Guinness, of course) and booze bottles. The on-site kitchen Rum and the Lash serves up burgers and the like through their window in the back; don't sleep on the curry fries.

MAP 6: 4801 Bienville Ave., 504/482-9113; 11am-2am Mon.-Sat., 11am-midnight Sun.

Pal's Lounge

The rather conservative facade of this spot leads into a comfy bar with lots of regulars and friendly bar staff. They've got a reasonably priced list of original cocktails (including a sangria made with honey, rose, and a delicate house-made lavender syrup) as well as a pretty wide-ranging beer-and-a-shot pairing menu. The navy blue and gold exterior decor may seem fancy, but the inside is a little worn and faded from many nights of revelry. It's down to earth and a great place to mix it up.

MAP 6: 949 N Rendon St., 504/488-7257, palslounge.com; 3pm-4am daily

Twelve Mile Limit

BREWERIES

Second Line Brewing

This brewery, the only one in Mid-City, is convenient to City Park and the Canal streetcar line. Second Line is a fun, mostly outdoor, family-friendly space that serves up handcrafted beers (try the Alryte Alryte Alryte imperial rye IPA or the blood-orange-infused Saison Named Desire) and hosts food trucks, bands, and movie nights. It's a beer garden full of laughter—and beer.

MAP 6: 433 N. Bernadotte St., 504/248-8979, secondlinebrewing. com; 4pm-10pm Mon. and Wed.-Thurs., 2pm-10pm Fri., noon-10pm Sat., noon-8pm Sun.

Arts and Culture

MUSEUMS

Louisiana Children's Museum

Relocated to City Park in 2019, the Louisiana Children's Museum is a New Orleans institution that's been open since the 1980s and still feels fresh after more than 30 years. Its LEED-silver-certified location, north of the New Orleans Museum of Art, utilizes the natural elements already in City Park, with a floating classroom set over a lagoon, an edible garden, and a crawfish farm. At the much-loved exhibits on Louisiana food culture and industry, kids can "make groceries" and play restaurant with ingredients for classic Creole dishes. Exhibits on the many facets of the Mississippi River also provide localized education. The museum offers exhibits and programs for toddlers to older kids, both indoors and outdoors. Grown-ups will be impressed by the gorgeous campus as well as the on-site Acorn Café (15 Henry Thomas Dr., 504/218-5413, acorn-nola.com; 7am-5pm Tues.-Sun.), an elevated spot for food and drink.

MAP 6: City Park, 15 Henry Thomas Dr., 504/523-1357, lcm.org; 9:30am-4:30pm Tues.-Sun.; $14 adults and children over 1; $12 seniors and military

New Orleans Museum of Art

The vast holdings of the fabulous New Orleans Museum of Art (NOMA) total about 40,000 objects, spanning a variety of cultures and eras—from pre-Columbian, Native American, and Mayan artwork to French Impressionist paintings. The city's oldest fine arts institution is justly known for its excellent rotating exhibits, including everything from creative bookmarks to the 19th-century mass production of British decorative arts. The museum, in an imposing beaux arts-style building that dates to 1911, is also an architectural marvel.

The permanent collection is as eclectic as it is extensive. A few rooms are decorated with period 18th- and 19th-century American furnishings and decorative arts, as well as a survey of work by European and American artists.

New Orleans Museum of Art

Included are priceless Easter eggs and other items created by Peter Carl Fabergé; photographs by Ansel Adams, Diane Arbus, and Walker Evans; and works by Degas, Monet, Picasso, Chagall, Cassatt, and O'Keeffe.

NOMA offers ample free parking, but you can also reach the museum by bike, bus, or the Canal streetcar line. Each Wednesday, the museum is free to Louisiana residents. The last admittance to the museum occurs 45 minutes before closing.

MAP 6: City Park, 1 Collins C. Diboll Cir., 504/658-4100, noma.org; 10am-6pm Tues.-Thurs., 10am-9pm Fri., 11am-5pm Sat.-Sun.; $10 adults, $8 seniors and college students, $6 children 7-17, children under 7 free

✪ Sydney and Walda Besthoff Sculpture Garden

Behind NOMA, the peaceful Sydney and Walda Besthoff Sculpture Garden is peppered with magnolias, pines, and ancient, Spanish moss-draped live oaks and encompasses lagoons, pedestrian bridges, and more than 60 impressive sculptures. Noted works include sculptures by Pierre-Auguste Renoir, Ida Kohlmeyer, and Claes Oldenburg. A free cell-phone tour is available. Last entry is 30 minutes prior to closing.

MAP 6: City Park, 1 Collins C. Diboll Cir., 504/658-4100, noma.org; 10am-6pm daily summer, 10am-5pm daily winter; free

Recreation

PARKS AND PLAZAS
Lafitte Greenway

The Lafitte Greenway is a 2.6-mile pedestrian and bike trail that runs through the Tremé and Mid-City. Not only is it a place to walk and cycle away from cars, it also serves as a green space, with parks, recreation areas, gardens, and shade-providing trees. It's a great opportunity to explore an entire swath of the city in a safe and beautiful setting. If you're interested in biking the path, you can rent from any bike store mentioned in this guide, or grab one of the city's many **Blue Bikes** (bluebikesnola.com; $0.10/minute after initial $5 signup) at either end of (or along) the trail. Blue Bikes can be picked up and returned all over the city, so you're free to explore beyond the greenway. (Note that New Orleans drivers are surprisingly hostile to bicyclists, so exercise caution when riding elsewhere.)

MAP 6: Between Lafitte Ave. and St. Louis St., from the intersection of N. Alexander and St. Louis St. in Mid-City to Basin St. and St. Louis St. in the Tremé, 504/462-0645, lafittegreenway.org/greenway; 24 hours daily

BIKING
Wheel Fun Rentals at Carousel Gardens

Get biking on two, three, or four wheels—Wheel Fun has everything from cruisers ($12/hour) to multi-passenger surreys ($26-36/hour). You can also rent a tandem ($20/hour). Wheel Fun can also provide everything you need to take a **self-guided bike tour** ($25-30) from City Park to the French Quarter. A second location by City Park's Big Lake offers swan boats ($5-10/hour), kayaks ($15-22/hour), and canoes ($22/hour).

MAP 6: City Park, 7 Victory Ave., 504/252-5655, wheelfunrentals.com; 10am-sunset daily

CANOEING AND KAYAKING
✪ Kayak-iti-Yat

Choose from the two-hour Big Easy Bayou Tour ($45/pp, good for beginners); the four-hour Pontchartrain Paddle ($65/pp, good for more active folks, though kayak experience isn't necessary), which includes a dip in Lake Pontchartrain; or the Lake and Lighthouse Tour ($45/pp), during which you'll paddle for an hour and a half and spend a half hour at the New Canal Lighthouse Museum. Kids and dogs are welcome to take part in the fun.

MAP 6: 3494 Esplanade Ave., 512/964-9499, kayakitiyat.com; advance reservations required

Shops

SPECIALTY FOOD AND DRINK

504 Craft Beer Reserve

Part beer store, part beer bar, and part beer geek central, this spacious store has shelves filled with bottles and cans of beers lining the walls. You can buy any beer by the six-pack or individually. The beers running through the shop's 14 rotating taps can be purchased by the pint to sip while browsing or taken away in 32- or 64-ounce bottles. Flights are available, too, and in-store events like trivia nights and "Drinkin' wit da Breweries" happen regularly, along with special tasting classes. Plenty of New Orleans and Louisiana beers are available for sale, and the staff is knowledgeable and friendly.

MAP 6: 3939 Tulane Ave., 504/875-3723, 504craftbeer.com; 11am-9pm Sun.-Wed., 11am-11pm Thurs.-Sat.

Pearl Wine Co.

Pearl has a laid-back vibe and a stellar wine selection. A variety of styles are highlighted at the adjoining bar, so you can taste a new wine, talk about it with knowledgeable staff, and walk out with a bottle to enjoy at home. The selection is well-researched and curated, and you can also find lots of beer options and small-batch liquors. Every Thursday during the neighboring Crescent City Farmer's Market there's a free wine tasting from 5pm-7pm, and Mondays are great for multitasking with Manicure Mondays from 5:30pm-9pm, where you can sip, shop, and get your nails done. Keep an eye out for in-depth wine classes, which happen a couple times a month.

MAP 6: 3700 Orleans Ave #1C, 504/483-6314, pearlwineco.com; noon-10pm Sun.-Tues., noon-midnight Wed.-Sat.

BOOKS AND MUSIC

✪ Tubby & Coo's Mid-City Book Shop

This bookstore and proud nerd hangout boasts the motto "It's all geek to me," which perfectly encapsulates the product selection and general vibe of the place. Browse sci-fi and fantasy genre books, peruse and play their wide array of more than 250 board games, listen to their podcast, and hang out in a family-friendly, progressive, and welcoming environment, with people who are as passionate about this stuff as you are. Their board game club lets enthusiasts play all day for $5, or you can pay an annual fee ($25) to come in whenever you like.

MAP 6: 631 N. Carrollton Ave., 504/598-5536, tubbyandcoos.com; 10am-7pm Thurs.-Tues.

HEALTH AND BEAUTY

Rosalie Apothecary

Feeling under the weather? If pho, *yakamein,* or whiskey doesn't cure what ails you, get over to Rosalie Apothecary for herbs, oils, and tinctures to help with stress, clear

Tubby & Coo's Mid-City Book Shop

up your sinuses, or promote sleep. The apothecary also carries soothing bath salts, incense, tea blends, and books on herbalism. It's female focused, although all are welcome, and there are also classes in herbal medicine, fermented foods, tarot, and other related arts.

MAP 6: 3201 Toulouse St., 504/488-4425, rosalie-apothecary. myshopify.com; 10am-6pm Mon.-Sat., noon-6pm Sun.

Central City and Broadmoor

Map 7

These two often overlooked neighborhoods are in the middle of the city, an area that was flooded during Katrina. Since then, the many **mom-and-pop shops** and restaurants here have rebuilt. Central City, north of the Garden District, is an epicenter of **African American culture** and **history.** It was home to jazz musicians like Buddy Bolden and Professor Longhair. There's a proud **Civil Rights legacy,** with connections to Martin Luther King, Jr. and Oretha Castle Haley. Today, it's where to find Mardi Gras Indians parades, or to watch Sunday **second lines** dance through the streets.

After Hurricane Katrina, Broadmoor, northwest of Central City, has been finding its identity as it supports a thriving **artisan scene.** Broadmoor is known for **off-the-beaten-path eateries.**

TOP SIGHTS

- Civil Rights, Past and Present: **Oretha Castle Haley Boulevard** (page 218)

TOP RESTAURANTS

- Best Restaurants Disguised as Convenience Stores: **Heard Dat Kitchen** (page 220) and **CK's Hot Shoppe** (page 222)

TOP NIGHTLIFE

- Most Unexpected Tropical Getaway: **Portside Lounge** (page 223)

TOP ARTS AND CULTURE

- Where to Find Work by Important Black Artists: **McKenna Museum of African American Art** (page 226)

TOP SHOPS

- Where to Watch Chocolate Being Made: **Piety and Desire Chocolate** (page 228)

GETTING THERE AND AROUND

- Streetcar lines: St. Charles (12)
- Major bus routes: 16, 28

0 400 yds
0 400 m

DISTANCE ACROSS MAP
Approximate: 3.0 mi or 4.9 km

D'HEMECOURT ST
GRAVIER ST
PINE ST
DIXON ST
DREXEL DR
S PERDIDO S
S CLARK ST
HOWARD AVE
S REDONDO ST
S CLARK ST
CALLIOPE ST
EUPHROSINE ST
PALM ST
EDINBURGH ST
OLIVE ST
FERN ST
SHORT ST
S CARROLLTON AVENUE
FIG ST
COLAPISSA STREET
EARHART BOULEVARD
WASHINGTON AVE
OLIO STREET
WHITE STREET
APPLE STREET

South Carrollton
at South Claiborne

FONTAINEBLEAU DRIVE
CALHOUN STREET
NASHVILLE AVENUE
NAPOLEON AVENUE
S BROAD STREET
Broadmoor
WASHINGTON AVENUE
LOUISIANA AVENUE PARKWAY
DELACHAISE STREET
TOLEDANO STREE

SEE MAP 5

Uptown
SOUTH CLAIBORNE AVENUE

SIGHTS

19 Oretha Castle Haley
    Boulevard

RESTAURANTS

2   Ye Olde College Inn
3   Dunbar's Famous
    Creole Cuisine
4   Kin
8   El Pavo Real
11 Laurel Street Bakery
12 Cajun Seafood
16 Heard Dat Kitchen
17 Central City BBQ

18 Open Hands Cafe
20 Casa Borrega
21 Café Reconcile
22 Toups South
25 Cafe Porche
28 CK's Hot Shoppe
33 Mr. John's Steakhouse
34 Jack Rose
39 Maïs Arepas

NIGHTLIFE

5   Big Easy Bucha
6   Atelier Vie
9   Roulaison Distilling Co
10 Broad Street Cider & Ale
14 The Independent
    Caveau

15 Zony Mash Beer Project
29 Portside Lounge
30 Verret's Lounge
35 The Revolution

ARTS AND CULTURE

23 New Orleans
    Jazz Market
24 Ashé Cultural Arts
    Center

27 Southern Food and
    Beverage Museum
36 McKenna Museum of
    African American Art

SHOPS

1   Bellegarde Bakery
7   Crescent City Comics

13 Piety and Desire
    Chocolate
26 YEP Thrift Works

HOTELS

31 Grand Victorian
    Bed & Breakfast
32 Hotel Indigo

37 Pontchartrain Hotel
38 Auberge NOLA Hostel
40 The Quisby

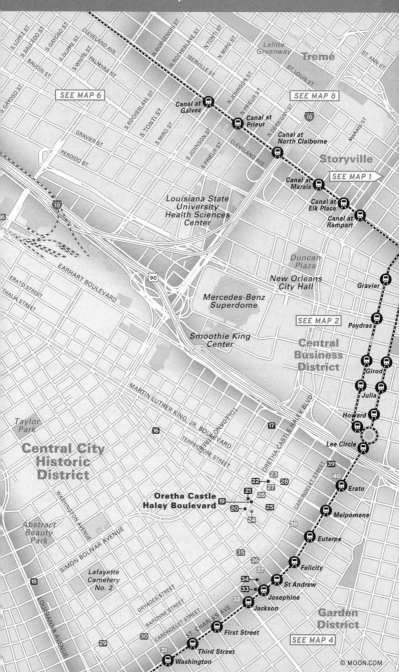

Sights

✪ Oretha Castle Haley Boulevard

Once a thriving shopping thoroughfare in the late 19th and early 20th centuries, this section of what was originally called the Dryades Street Commercial District, between Jackson and Calliope Streets, became the African American population's main shopping area during the Jim Crow era. It was abandoned by local businesses in the 1970s. The street has always functioned as a central rallying point for marches and protests supporting equality in New Orleans, imbued with energy from the surrounding community.

Oretha Castle Haley was a Civil Rights-era activist who played a major role in organizations like the Congress of Racial Equality (CORE) and the Freedom Riders in the early 1960s. The street was renamed for her in 1989, but it wasn't for another several decades that OCH Boulevard would begin to resemble its former bustling self. Today, community centers, non-profits, and eateries like Café Reconcile and the Ashe Cultural Arts Center line the blocks of OCH.

MAP 7: 1100-2100 blocks of Oretha Castle Haley Blvd., between Jackson St. and Calliope St.

Restaurants

PRICE KEY

$	Entrées less than $15
$$	Entrées $15-30
$$$	Entrées more than $30

CAJUN AND CREOLE

Toups South $$

Toups South is a spin-off restaurant from Isaac Toups, the chef-owner of Toups Meatery in Mid-City. This spot is adjacent to the Southern Food and Beverage Museum and offers a refined but rustic pan-Southern menu. It's a large space with a huge open kitchen in the back, with a chef's bar surrounding it. The restored 1851 wooden bar up front is from the beloved former New Orleans restaurant, Bruning's.

Toups South tips a cap to history, as befitting a museum eatery, but it also makes its own statement. This is not the place to worry about your cholesterol: The biscuits with crab fat butter and the cracklin' are both phenomenal. The cocktail program is top-notch (with happy hour 3pm-6pm Tues.-Sat.).

MAP 7: 1504 Oretha Castle Haley Blvd., 504/304-2147, toupssouth. com; 11am-10pm Mon. and Wed.-Sat., 10am-3pm Sun.

Ye Olde College Inn $$

An oft-overlooked New Orleans culinary institution, tucked in a sort of no-man's land between Mid-City, Broadmoor, and River Ridge,

Ye Olde College Inn has been serving up French-inspired Creole specialties since 1933. Enjoy house classics like Oysters Bleu (fried oysters with shredded iceberg lettuce, purple onion, and blue cheese oil); crawfish Delacroix, which ladles crawfish étouffée over Gulf fish; or the braised beef brisket, which comes with their signature onion rings as well as some of the best Brussels sprouts in the city (prepared with bacon, of course). Ye Olde College Inn has an on-site urban farm, which provides seasonal produce as well as fresh eggs, and inspires gorgeous specialty offerings.

MAP 7: 3000 S. Carrollton Ave., 504/866-3683, collegeinn1933.com; 4pm-11pm Tues.-Sat.

Cafe Porche $

This spot is tucked away between St. Charles Avenue and Oretha Castle Haley Boulevard, but it's worth seeking out for New Orleans home cooking. The heaping red beans and rice plate comes with lots of meat cooked into it, although the vegetarian version is highly recommended as well. Po'boys, smothered pork chops, and an amazing breakfast menu are other great reasons to check out this tidy and inviting café set back from the street with a pitched roof and lots of windows. The front building, called Snowbar (11am-7pm daily) serves snowballs and assorted snacks from the walk-up window. A vegan pop-up called Chef Ra's I-tel Garden is open for dinner Sunday through Thursday from 5:30pm to 9pm.

MAP 7: 1625 Baronne St., 504/930-4249; 7am-3pm daily

Café Reconcile $

Since 2000, the non-profit Café Reconcile has trained thousands of local at-risk youth and young adults in all aspects of restaurant operations. While the mission of this lunchtime café is indeed lofty, the real reason to check this place out is the great food. The gumbo, po'boys, and jerk chicken are all traditional and authentic—and don't overlook the sides, with options like smothered okra with shrimp, mashed sweet potatoes, and collard greens with pork.

MAP 7: 1631 Oretha Castle Haley Blvd., 504/568-1157, cafereconcile.org; 11am-2:30pm Mon.-Fri., 10am-3pm Sun.

Dunbar's Famous Creole Cuisine

Cajun Seafood $

This no-frills spot is the place to get boiled seafood and fixin's, fried shrimp and catfish po'boys, gumbo, and all the Cajun soul food you need. It's takeout only, so wait in line with the dozens of locals who love it, and get huge amounts of spicy food for cheap. Even when crawfish are out of season, Cajun Seafood will have frozen ones on hand to boil up, along with shrimp and crab. There are two other Cajun Seafood locations in the area (1479 Claiborne

Ave. and 1901 Almonaster Ave.) but this one is the easiest to access and it's the best of the three.

MAP 7: 2730 S. Broad Ave., 504/821-4722; 10:30am-9pm Mon.-Sat., 10:30am-8:30pm Sun.

Dunbar's Famous Creole Cuisine $

Dunbar's is known for its fried chicken and catfish, and the Creole-style gumbo is full of flavor, as well as crab claws and chicken pieces on the bone. Corn bread comes with every lunch and dinner meal, and the 99-cent breakfast (eggs, sausage, biscuit, and grits or hashbrowns) is a steal. Note: There's a pause in service between 10:30am (when breakfast finishes) and 11am (when lunch begins).

MAP 7: 7834 Earhart Blvd., 504/509-6287; 7am-9pm Mon.-Sat.

☸ Heard Dat Kitchen $

When the line cook shouts, "order up!" the dining room server yells back, "heard dat!" It's not clear which came first, the name of this soul food sensation or the kitchen banter, but behind an unassuming walk-up window and corner store is a cozy, great spot for New Orleans food. There's a bit of a spin on the usual Creole favorites—crawfish cream sauce on your fried chicken, for example, or a butter lemon sauce over your blackened fish and crab. Everything's delicious (try the bread pudding) and the service is warm and friendly.

MAP 7: 2520 Felicity St., 504/510-4248; 11am-9pm Mon.-Sat.

Open Hands Cafe $

When you walk into Ms. Katherine's Open Hands Cafe,

Central City BBQ

you'll feel the love right away. She's got a menu of fried fish plates, crawfish items (fries, pasta, pies, and nachos), and some of the best chicken wings in town, but she'll also be stirring up something on the stove behind the counter, whatever's calling to her that day. This is a neighborhood place where the kids stop by after school, retired folks come in to chat, and neighbors and visitors in the know come by for a plate and some conversation.

MAP 7: 3328 Lasalle St., 504/894-7072; 10am-6pm Wed.-Sat.

BARBECUE
Central City BBQ $

This huge shrine to smoked meats anchors the entrance to the Central City neighborhood from the Warehouse District. With its unmistakable exterior porcine paintings, Central City BBQ pays homage to the love of cooking meat with smoke. The pit here has several different kinds of smokers for different purposes and kinds of meat. It's hard to choose a favorite, but the brisket (and brisket burnt ends) is great, as is the corn spoonbread. But the boudin and pulled pork are high-quality as well.

MAP 7: 1201 S. Rampart St., 504/558-4276, centralcitybbq.com; 11am-9pm daily

STEAK AND SEAFOOD
Mr. John's Steakhouse $$$

Conveniently located on the St. Charles streetcar line, this high-end steak-and-seafood spot serves prime cuts basted in butter on sizzling plates alongside classic New Orleans dishes like barbecue shrimp, shrimp rémoulade, and pan-seared Gulf fish. The interior is appropriately dark and wood-paneled, with a bar busy making classic martinis and Sazeracs. It's a classy, old-school steakhouse with a quirky New Orleans twist.

MAP 7: 2111 St. Charles Ave., 504/679-7697, mrjohnssteakhouse.com; 5:30pm-9:45pm Tues.-Thurs. and Sat., 11:30am-2pm and 5:30pm-9:45pm Fri.

ECLECTIC
Jack Rose $$$

This place is a high-class hootenanny with quality food, excellent service, and whimsical yet elegant decor (think antique furniture paired with a portrait of Lil Wayne by Ashley Longshore). It's fun without being hokey, featuring creative dishes like octopus carpaccio and Black Angus daube. Don't miss the pimento cheese snack or the trademark Mile High Pie. Baller alert: at Friday lunch and Sunday brunch, enjoy bottomless Veuve Clicquot for $25 and Veuve Clicquot Rosé for $35 on the garden patio.

MAP 7: 2031 St. Charles Ave., 504/323-1500, jackroserestaurant. com; 3pm-10pm Wed.-Thurs. and Sat., 11am-2pm and 3pm-10pm Fri. and Sun.

JAPANESE
Kin $

Kin is a warm hug on a rainy day. It's all the best flavors in the world wrapped up in a dumpling. And it's where you attack your food while sitting elbow to elbow with your dining neighbor at the winding bar or the communal table that takes up most of the floor space. Everyone finishes their meal here and wonders, "Why am I not here every day?" The small menu encompasses an ever evolving menu of noodles, like a roasted chicken shoyu ramen and a pork shoulder udon bowl with mushrooms and greens. There's plenty of experimentation, so you never quite know what you're getting when you walk in. Check their social media accounts to get a hint of what's in store, or just prepare to be surprised.

MAP 7: 4600 Washington Ave., 504/304-8557; 11am-9:30pm Tues.-Thurs., 11am-10pm Fri.-Sat.

FILIPINO
☺ CK's Hot Shoppe $

This combination corner store and Filipino restaurant is a reminder that in New Orleans, it's often the most humble looking places that serve the best food. Filipino chef Crispin Pasia, who worked for 18 years with venerated Cajun chef Paul Prudhomme, brings the authentic flavors of his home to his customers. Try the *lumpia* (like narrow crispy spring rolls), pork and chicken adobo (a stew with a vinegar tang), and *halo-halo* (a traditional Filipino frozen dessert). Pasia makes every dish from scratch, so it can take a little while, especially with locals coming in for cold drinks and lottery tickets. The corner store atmosphere is informal and very enjoyable, though it's a little on the cramped side, so be ready to turn any table into a communal one.

MAP 7: 1433 Baronne St., 504/339-3867; 11am-3:30pm and 5:30pm-9pm Tues.-Sat., 11am-3:30pm Sun.

LATIN AMERICAN
Casa Borrega $

A longtime fixture on OCH Boulevard, Casa Borrega serves great mole, lamb (which is what *borrego* means in Spanish), and authentic Mexico City dishes (along with a few Tex-Mex options). It also pours one hell of a margarita and is a live music venue featuring Latin American artists. The shabby-chic interior is dominated by the wooden bar by the door, and the rest of the front dining room continues that wood decor along with some eclectic wall decorations featuring Mexican folk art and Día de los Muertos imagery.

MAP 7: 1719 Oretha Castle Haley Blvd., 504/427-0654, casaborrega. com; 11am-9:30pm Tues.-Thurs., 11am-10:30pm Fri.-Sat., 11am-3pm Sun.

El Pavo Real $

This cheerful, friendly neighborhood spot in Broadmoor serves authentic Mexican food for breakfast, lunch, and dinner. Standard preparations like tacos and enchiladas share the menu with *mole poblano* and the comforting *caldo de pollo* (chicken soup). Daily specials include dishes like Yucatan-style lentils with rice, avocado, and a poached egg. The low-frills setting feels a little like a diner, but the windows stretching around half the building and the colorful wall decor liven things up.

MAP 7: 4401 S. Broad Ave., 504/266-2022, elpavorealnola.com; 9am-9pm Tues.-Sat., 9:30am-3pm Sun.

Mais Arepas $

Arepas are cornmeal-based biscuits or cakes that are often stuffed with fillings, much like a sandwich. They serve as the basis for many of Mais Arepas's Colombian dishes. Grilled steak, shredded chicken, plantains, avocado, and pork belly number among the fillings, and everything's made to order. Mais Arepas also has the best ceviche in town, changing daily depending on the fresh fish, fruit, and vegetables available. Take a seat at a table or the sleek black and wood bar in this small but well laid-out and modern space.

MAP 7: 1200 Carondelet St., 504/523-6247; 11:30am-2:15pm and 6pm-9:45pm Tues.-Sat, 6pm-9:45pm Sun.

COFFEE AND DESSERTS

Laurel Street Bakery $

Laurel Street Bakery moved from Laurel Street to South Broad Avenue in 2013 and became the first of a cluster of shops to pop up in the area. It has a loyal following for its great coffee, pastries, and bagels. The bright, cozy spot harbors freelance workers, one-on-one meetings, and those who just want to sit with a café au lait and toasted everything bagel.

MAP 7: 2701 S. Broad Ave., 504/897-0576, laurelstreetbakery.com; 7am-2pm Mon.-Fri., 8am-2pm Sat.-Sun.

Nightlife

BARS AND LOUNGES

✪ Portside Lounge

Tiki in this neighborhood, who'd have thunk? The folks at Portside dub themselves "a remote island in Central City" and mix up Caribbean-style cocktails with top shelf rums, local spirits, hand-squeezed juices, and house-made bitters. They also have quite a collection of fun Polynesian and pirate-themed garnishes for your cocktail glass. Drinks are strong, cheap, and handcrafted. Portside frequently has pop-up food events, as well as regular live music and movie nights.

MAP 7: 3000 Dryades St., 504/503-0990, portsidenola.com; 5pm-2am Tues.-Fri., 3pm-2am Sat.-Sun.

Verret's Lounge

Verret's Lounge is all about keeping it real. You never know exactly what you'll find at this dimly lit bar—there could be live music, people grilling or smoking meat, a video game tournament, or just customers chilling in the red leather banquettes or at the red leather padded bar. The interior is cozy, but the space doubles once you take the large outdoor courtyard into consideration. There are several grills outside that

tiki drink at Portside Lounge

customers can use; just ask! Verret's is where diversity thrives—anyone's welcome as long as you aren't a jerk. It's a neighborhood dive with cheap drinks, but with its effusive staff, it's much more than that.

MAP 7: 1738 Washington Ave., 504/895-9640; 4pm-3am Mon.-Thurs., 4pm-4am Fri., 11am-4pm Sat., 11am-3am Sun.

DANCE CLUBS
The Revolution
The Revolution is where African American young professionals in New Orleans get their drink and dance on. It's pretty small inside, and tends to be dark and clubby—all the better for dancing, with DJs or live music most nights—but there's also a great outdoor space, for conversation and sipping drinks. They're open for Saints games on Sundays and sponsor a number of local pop-up kitchens, like Open Hands Cafe.

MAP 7: 1840 Thalia St., 504/265-5441, therevolutionnola.com; 4pm-11pm Thurs., 4pm-1am Fri.-Sat., 2pm-10pm Sun.; cover varies

BREWERIES AND DISTILLERIES
Atelier Vie
Jedd Haas, owner of Atelier Vie, has been able to make some of the area's best spirits with the city's most utilitarian still. It's a small distillery with homemade, piecemeal equipment that churns out creative, exciting, and world-class libations like Toulouse Red Absinthe Rouge and Euphrosine barrel-aged gin. Stop by on weekends to sample (for free!) the ever-expanding line of spirits, buy a bottle or two,

and hear the story of how Atelier Vie scrapped its way to award-winning greatness. The space is on the homespun industrial side, but in the carefully managed chaos, Haas and his small team are happy to share their passion along with the spirits. Check the website for detailed driving directions.

MAP 7: 1001 S. Broad St., 504/534-8590, ateliervie.com; 10am-2pm Sat.-Sun.

Big Easy Bucha
Big Easy Bucha is in a bright warehouse occupied by fermentation tanks as well as a space for folks to come in and learn about kombucha. A visit to the brewery includes free samples, information about the fascinating process of making kombucha, and the opportunity to purchase refillable 64-ounce jugs or 16-ounce "Geaux Cups" of the living liquid. This is very approachable kombucha, using Louisiana fruits and vegetables for flavors like the Cajun Kick, made with ginger, meyer lemon, and hibiscus, or the Streetcar Sipper, infused with satsuma tangerines. If you're curious about this probiotic, nearly non-alcoholic beverage (it's so low in alcohol content that there's no age restriction for tasting or purchase), Big Easy Bucha is the perfect place to give it a try. Plus, visitors get the first taste of their newest flavors. There's café-style seating and free Wi-Fi for getting comfy.

MAP 7: 4040 Euphrosine St., 504/407-0544, bigeasybucha.com; 10am-4pm Mon.-Thurs.

Broad Street Cider & Ale
Opened in 2017, New Orleans's first cidery plays around with different

Big Easy Bucha

as well as a tasting flight of five of Roulaison's rums. Booking in advance through the website is recommended, although they do accept walk-ins depending on availability. Roulaison is fun to investigate before or after a visit to Broad Street Cider & Ale, since it's right across the back patio.

MAP 7: 2727 S. Broad Ave., 504/517-4786, roulaison.com; 3pm-7pm Wed.-Fri., 1pm-7pm Sat.

yeasts and fruits to offer a unique cider experience. The vibe is like a British pub but bright and airy, with pale wood and plenty of natural light. Beers on tap are available alongside the house-made cider. The husband and wife duo that own and operate the place do so with much humor and an unwavering commitment to serving the highest quality products. Broad Street Cider & Ale plays around with different fermentation styles and unusual ingredients; there's always something new and interesting to try, like the Duchess of Devonshire, made with Earl Grey tea, or Gin Craze, which uses the spent gin botanicals from neighboring distillery Atelier Vie.

MAP 7: 2723 S. Broad Ave., 504/405-1854, broadstreetcider.com; 4pm-9pm Tues.-Thurs., 1pm-10pm Fri.-Sat.

Roulaison Distilling Co.

A small, rum-only distillery, Roulaison is growing fast. There's a cute vintage barrel-themed tasting bar to check out the various products. Tours ($10) are offered on Fridays (5:30pm) and Saturdays (3pm and 5pm) and include an in-depth look at the distilling process,

Zony Mash Beer Project

Set in a historic movie theater, this forward-thinking brewery offers innovative beers and a quirky, unique aesthetic. Head brewer Mitch Grittman has been lauded for his sour beers for years, and his attention to every detail shows. The beer menu is ever-changing, but there's always a saison, something hoppy, a radler, and plenty of different types of sours, like Groovy Shindig, made with watermelon, hibiscus, and local Gulf salt. Zony Mash offers entertainment most nights, like movies, stand up comedy, or burlesque trivia, and an on-site food truck.

MAP 7: 3490 Thalia St., 504/766-8868, zonymashbeer.com; 4pm-11pm Mon.-Fri., 11am-11pm Sat.-Sun.

tasting room at Roulaison Distilling Co.

WINE BARS

The Independent Caveau

Adding to the funky charm of Broadmoor is this fun wine bar with great cheese and charcuterie to nosh alongside reasonably priced wine. Their weekly blind wine tasting event is geared toward teaching wine drinkers to trust their own palate. The cheerful space has brightly colored wallpapered walls alongside the blonde wood of the bar. It's attached to a retail shop that sells the wine, cheese, and charcuterie you can try at the bar. This is the perfect spot for a date. It's convenient to get to from downtown or Mid-City, but its tucked-away location makes it feel like a secret spot.

MAP 7: 1226 S. White St., 504/275-4611; noon-10pm Mon.-Tues. and Thurs., noon-11pm Fri.-Sat.

Arts and Culture

MUSEUMS

✪ McKenna Museum of African American Art

This boutique museum houses the collection of New Orleans community leader Dr. Dwight McKenna. It contains 225 pieces of carefully curated art that showcases Black excellence and experience. The museum is small enough not to overwhelm, but chronicles decades of art from the perspective of African American history and culture. The docents are excellent at weaving a comprehensive story of New Orleans and the South that is seldom told. Be warned: The building housing the museum is a former slave holding area; there's no insulation, so it can get uncomfortably hot or cold, depending on the weather. The museum is only open to visitors via guided tour, which must be arranged in advance.

MAP 7: 2003 Carondelet St., 504/323-5074, themckennamuseum.com; tours by appointment only 10am-noon Thurs.-Fri.; $15

Southern Food and Beverage Museum

The Southern Food and Beverage Museum (SoFAB) is the only place of its kind in the region, a museum that explores the link between southern culture and food. It gives visitors the opportunity to understand southern history through an unusual and delicious lens. The interior of SoFAB is divided by state and then theme, but food culture tends to defy simple categorization; the museum feels a little like exploring someone's cluttered attic. There are some true treasures to be found, like a red-bean covered vintage car, and *La Galerie de l'Absinthe,* an exhibit that steps back in time to the heyday of absinthe drinking, with a vintage bar and absinthe bottles. The Museum of the American Cocktail is inside SoFAB, though it's supported by a different non-profit organization, and the two touch on similar themes.

THE SECOND LINE

A second line dances down the street.

Originally, a funeral procession in New Orleans had two parts. The "first line" of the procession consisted of the casket and the immediate family. Then came a brass band and all the mourners in the "second line," following and dancing. Second lines come from a Black New Orleans tradition dating back to the Jim Crow era, when newly freed slaves banded together in benevolent societies known as social-aid and pleasure clubs to help with funeral costs.

Today, these processions exist without a funeral as an excuse, put on by social-aid and pleasure clubs. The current idea of the second line is that it's made up of everyone who's dancing along with the band: the club's leadership in elaborate and gorgeous costumes, the club members, the band, and anyone and everyone who wants to join in at any point during the parade.

Second line season lasts from September through May (it's too hot to second line in the summer) and happens along routes in either Uptown-Central City or downtown in the Tremé-Ninth Ward. New Orleans's local music radio station WWOZ will usually have information on a second line's route, including the time and place it starts and all the stops it makes along the way.

If you're interested in checking out a traditional second line, stake out a spot at or near an announced stopping point and wait for the music and dancing to roll on by. Often there will be food and drinks for sale. Try to enjoy the moment instead of Instagramming it—and as it passes, if you feel the urge, just go ahead and dance along for a few blocks or so.

MAP 7: 1504 Oretha Castle Haley Blvd., 504/569-0405, natfab.org/southern-food-and-beverage; 11am-5:30pm Wed.-Mon.; $10.50 adults, $5.25 students, military, and seniors, kids under 12 free

CULTURAL CENTERS
Ashé Cultural Arts Center

Ashé always has something going on, whether it be an art exhibition, classes for kids or grown-ups, original theatrical productions, concerts, or spoken word events. This is the anchor of Oretha Castle Haley Boulevard, connecting, educating, and supporting the neighborhood and the local African American community. Check the schedule out online before heading over, or just stop in to see what's happening. MAP 7: 1712 Oretha Castle Haley Blvd, 504/569-9070, ashecac.org; 10am-6pm Mon.-Sat.; exhibit and event admission varies

New Orleans Jazz Market

Constructed in 2011, this is the only facility in New Orleans specifically designed to host and showcase local jazz. The Grammy-winning New Orleans Jazz Orchestra (NOJO), a 20-piece big band, plays a diverse repertoire in the acoustically perfect auditorium. The facility also hosts community gatherings, karaoke events, happy hours, and a Wednesday night jam session. There's a focus on shows that are appealing to a wide audience; recent performances have honored artists like Prince, Whitney Houston, and John Coltrane. The Jazz Market also has an archive of audio recordings, photos, and musical instruments that can be perused over a cocktail from the on-site bar (open only during events). The Wednesday Jam Sessions have a $5 cover; community events range from free to $65. Check their social media accounts for events happening during your stay. MAP 7: 1436 Oretha Castle Haley Blvd., 504/371-5849, thenojo.com; hours and cost vary by event

Shops

SPECIALTY FOOD AND DRINK

Bellegarde Bakery

Bellegarde breads have been available all over the city, thanks to the successful wholesale business that owner Graison Gill has cultivated since 2013. It wasn't until the summer of 2019, though, that Gill opened this small retail location for customers to come watch the milling and baking process, purchase loaves of bread not sold anywhere else, and even grab some of their freshly stone-milled flour made from wheat, rye, and corn. It's not a place to sit and linger—it's a place to browse, shop, and move along. MAP 7: 8300 Apple St., 504/827-0008, bellegardebakery.com; 8am-3pm Tues.-Sat.

✪ Piety and Desire Chocolate

Enter Piety and Desire and you'll find yourself in the lab of chocolate genius Chris Nobles. Behind the glass cases of colorful and gorgeous bonbons sold here is the production facility, so you can see exactly what happens during the process, from

Bellegarde Bakery

roasting and grinding cacao beans, to tempering the chocolate, to shaping and flavoring the results. Nobles loves collaborating with his neighbors—the Tiki Bar bonbon uses Roulaison rum, and the Apple Cider Caramel bonbon uses mulled cider from Broad Street Cider & Ale. The options are constantly changing, depending on the season and Nobles's mindset that day. If you can keep them cool, these are great options for gifts and souvenirs.

MAP 7: 2727 S. Broad Ave., 504/491-4333, pietyanddesirechocolate. com; 2pm-7pm Tues.-Sun.

BOOKS AND MUSIC
Crescent City Comics

Comic book nerds, assemble! And collectors of figurines or graphic novels, and folks looking for New Orleans-themed zines, comics, or other literature. This large space on Calhoun Street, near the Tulane stadium, is a big step up from their smaller, more merch- and game-focused location at 4916 Freret Street (504/891-3796; 1pm-7pm Wed.-Fri., 11am-7pm Sat., noon-6pm Sun.).

There's a lot to take in, for fans of old-school Marvel and DC, or Game of Thrones-type fantasy, or one of the thousands of super-cool independent comics, books, and accessories.

MAP 7: 3135 Calhoun St., 504/309-2223, crescentcitycomics.com; 11am-7pm Mon.-Sat., noon-6pm Sun.

THRIFT SHOPS
YEP Thrift Works

YEP Thrift Works is run by young adults in the non-profit Youth Empowerment Project, which teaches retail and customer service skills. All proceeds go to support the work of the non-profit, which means you can feel pretty good about rifling through racks of shoes, tuxes, and crystal dishware to find great deals. Thrift Works is set in a large space, with walls painted a bright white with the lime green logo attracting foot traffic. They also run a bike shop down the block.

MAP 7: 1626 Oretha Castle Haley Blvd., 504/702-8070, youthempowermentproject.com; 10am-6pm Mon.-Sat.

Tremé and Fairgrounds   Map 8

The Tremé is the oldest African American neighborhood in the nation. It's a **vibrant historic area** that too many visitors miss. **Small museums** celebrate local culture, narrow shotgun houses and **Creole cottages** line the streets, and the food is of the highest comfort. The Tremé is bisected by the Pontchartrain Expressway overpass.

Next to the Tremé is the Fair Grounds Race Course & Slots, where **Jazz Fest** is held. Bayou Road, in the Fairgrounds area, was once the path that native peoples and early traders and settlers would take after navigating Lake Pontchartrain to Bayou St. John.

It's now an important area for **small businesses.** The safety of this neighborhood is no better or worse than any other in the city. Like you would anywhere, make good choices, don't walk around after dark, and stay aware of your surroundings.

TOP SIGHTS

- Most Musically Historic Park: **Louis Armstrong Park** (page 240)
- Where to Understand the Joy and Pain of New Orleans History: **St. Augustine Catholic Church and the Tomb of the Unknown Slave** (page 242)

TOP RESTAURANTS

- Longest Post-Katrina Comeback: **Gabrielle Restaurant** (page 243)

TOP NIGHTLIFE

- Oldest Live Music Venue in the Tremé: **Candlelight Lounge** (page 247)

TOP ARTS AND CULTURE

- Most Important Museum Tour: **Le Musée de f.p.c** (page 249)

TOP SHOPS

- Only Black-Owned Bookstore in New Orleans: **Community Book Center** (page 253)

GETTING THERE AND AROUND

- Streetcar lines: Rampart-St. Claude (49)
- Major bus routes: 32, 84, 91, 94

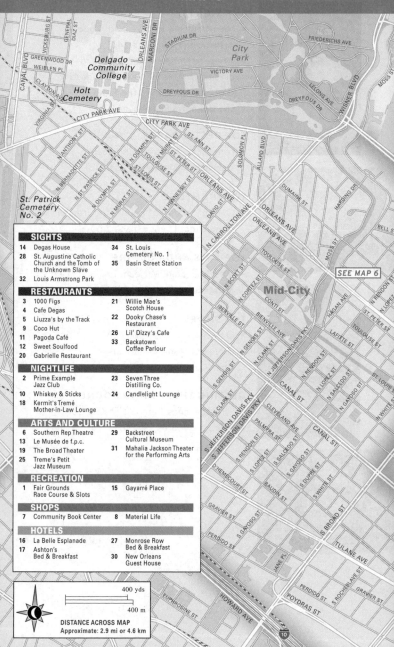

SIGHTS

14 Degas House
28 St. Augustine Catholic Church and the Tomb of the Unknown Slave
32 Louis Armstrong Park

34 St. Louis Cemetery No. 1
35 Basin Street Station

RESTAURANTS

3 1000 Figs
4 Cafe Degas
5 Liuzza's by the Track
9 Coco Hut
11 Pagoda Café
12 Sweet Soulfood
20 Gabrielle Restaurant

21 Willie Mae's Scotch House
22 Dooky Chase's Restaurant
26 Lil' Dizzy's Cafe
33 Backatown Coffee Parlour

NIGHTLIFE

2 Prime Example Jazz Club
10 Whiskey & Sticks
18 Kermit's Tremé Mother-in-Law Lounge

23 Seven Three Distilling Co.
24 Candlelight Lounge

ARTS AND CULTURE

6 Southern Rep Theatre
13 Le Musée de f.p.c.
19 The Broad Theater
25 Treme's Petit Jazz Museum

29 Backstreet Cultural Museum
31 Mahalia Jackson Theater for the Performing Arts

RECREATION

1 Fair Grounds Race Course & Slots

15 Gayarré Place

SHOPS

7 Community Book Center

8 Material Life

HOTELS

16 La Belle Esplanade
17 Ashton's Bed & Breakfast

27 Monrose Row Bed & Breakfast
30 New Orleans Guest House

400 yds
400 m

DISTANCE ACROSS MAP
Approximate: 2.9 mi or 4.6 km

SEE MAP 7

Fair Grounds
Race Course & Slots
1

Faubourg
St. John

Degas
House

Tremé

Lafitte
Greenway

Louis
Armstrong
Park

Louis
Armstrong
Park

St. Augustine
Catholic Church
and the Tomb of
the Unknown Slave

French
Quarter

Basin Street
Station
St. Louis
Cemetery No. 1

Louisiana State
University
Health Sciences
Center

SEE MAP 2

SEE MAP 3

SEE MAP 1

© MOON.COM

TREMÉ WALK: EAST OF THE UNDERPASS

TOTAL DISTANCE: 1.5 miles (2.4 kilometers)
WALKING TIME: 30-45 minutes

This is on the side of I-10 that's closest to the French Quarter. Taking the Rampart-St. Claude streetcar extension will drop you off right on the border of the two neighborhoods. Head away from the river to get to Tremé. Start this tour after breakfast, brunch, or lunch—there aren't many places to stop for food along the way.

1 Start at the entrance of **Louis Armstrong Park,** which is right across from St. Ann Street on North Rampart Street. Walking into the park, you'll see **Congo Square** immediately to your left, where enslaved people once congregated on Sundays and created music based on the rhythms of their homelands, planting the seeds for what would eventually turn into New Orleans jazz. Veer right to see several statues commemorating jazz musicians (including Louis Armstrong, of course) and Mardi Gras Indians. Head past Satchmo's statue to take a right onto Essence Way, where you'll see the gorgeous soft lines of a statue of

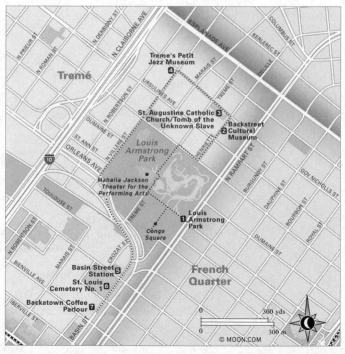

Treme's Petit Jazz Museum

Mahalia Jackson and the front entrance of **Mahalia Jackson Theater for the Performing Arts.**

2 From the statue, head to the right, along the side of the parking lot, then turn right for a block and on your left is the eastern exit onto St. Philip Street. You should be at the intersection of St. Philip and Henriette Delille Streets. Continue onto Henriette Delille for a block and a half to the **Backstreet Cultural Museum,** where you can see Mardi Gras Indian suits and social aid and pleasure club costumes on display and learn about these institutions that are so important to the culture of the Tremé and New Orleans African Americans in general. (Note if that park gate is closed, just turn left when you reach St. Philip and walk three blocks to the corner of St. Philip and North Villere, and back three blocks to Henriette Delille.)

3 Continue up Henriette Delille for half a block to Governor Nicholls Street. Turn left and there's **St. Augustine Catholic Church** right on the corner. Admire the church's soaring tower. If you continue up Governor Nicholls a few feet, you'll see the **Tomb of the Unknown Slave** on your left, right outside the church. This haunting memorial commemorates the thousands of enslaved people whose remains were buried in unmarked graves throughout the city. It consists of a rusting cross made of thick chains with shackles hanging from it.

4 Continue up Governor Nicholls for three blocks to North Villere Street. At that intersection, you'll see **Treme's Petit Jazz Museum** on the left. This tiny, one-room museum is a great place to learn about the history of jazz and New Orleans's role in its creation, from founder and proprietor Mr. Alvin Jackson, who's forgotten more about jazz than most of us will ever know.

5 Leaving the museum, turn right onto North Villere Street and walk for four and a half blocks until the road curves to the left onto

Basin Street. Walk about four blocks to check out **Basin Street Station** on the right. (This area is laid out oddly; you're getting close when you pass Louis Armstrong Park and the entrance to the Lafitte Greenway Trail.) Hit the restrooms, get a bottle of water or cup of coffee, and sit for a moment on one of the benches in the area meant to resemble the old platform waiting area.

outside Basin Street Station

6 Continuing down Basin Street, you'll cross St. Louis Street and you'll be in front of **St. Louis Cemetery No. 1,** arguably the most famous cemetery in New Orleans and definitely the oldest, established in 1789. It's so popular that all visitors can only enter with a registered tour guide. There's a list of registered guides on the website (nolacatholic-cemeteries.org/st-louis-cemetery-1), but there are also guides at the entrance that you can engage without booking in advance. Famous tombs here include that of "Voodoo Queen" Marie Laveau, the one for civil rights activist Homer Plessy, and an as-of-yet-unutilized pyramid-shaped tomb owned by actor Nicholas Cage.

7 A half block down Basin from the cemetery is **Backatown Coffee Parlour.** Grab some coffee and put your feet up!

TREMÉ WALK: WEST OF THE UNDERPASS

TOTAL DISTANCE: 2 miles (3.2 kilometers)
WALKING TIME: 45 minutes-1 hour

This walk winds past the stately houses on Esplanade, to the funky Bayou Road near the fairgrounds, to the area's main thoroughfare, North Broad Street, and down past all the neighborhood restaurants of the Tremé. There's a jump onto the Lafitte Greenway if you're game, and when you're done, you're well placed to head to Mid-City, the French Quarter, or back up the Lafitte Greenway. This is a great late-morning walk. Make an appointment ahead of time to tour Le Musée de f.p.c right when they open (weekdays at 1pm and Saturday at 11am), then plan for a late lunch at Willie Mae's (which is closed on Sundays).

1 Start outside **La Belle Esplanade.** This B&B is the middle of three brightly painted homes on Esplanade Avenue—it's one of the most iconic Creole houses; you'll see photographs of it everywhere. If you plan ahead and call to make an appointment (or if that's where you're

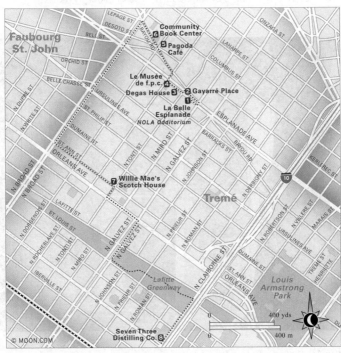

staying), you can meet eccentric owner Matthew King and explore his collection of New Orleans oddities, like voodoo-cursed silverware in the lobby's **NOLA Odditorium.**

2 As you exit, turn your head to the left and you'll see the tiny park **Gayarré Place,** which houses a statue called *Peace, the Genius of History* that depicts the Greek goddess and muse of history, Clio.

3 Walk half a block up Esplanade to the **Degas House,** which will be on your left. There's a nice reproduction of the artist's famous *Little Dancer* statue in front of the stately buildings where a museum and B&B are located. This is an excellent selfie opportunity.

4 Continue up Esplanade for a half block to North Rocheblave Street, where **Le Musée de f.p.c.** sits on the corner. If you've arranged in advance for a tour, go straight in. (It's only about 15-30 minutes from the start of the walk up until this point.) If you want to try your luck as a walk-in, check in with the management, who will be just inside the front door of this gorgeous Creole home.

5 Cross Esplanade and continue on North Rocheblave to Bayou Road. Turn left onto Bayou Road, and walk a block to reach the

Degas House

Pagoda Café, on the right. You can't miss it: It actually looks like an Asian pagoda. Grab a drink or a snack and sit outside on the patio.

6 Cross North Dorgenois and continue for a block up Bayou Road to the **Community Book Center.** Stop in and browse books by Black writers, ranging from local to international. The staff will be happy to help you find whatever you need or talk about the books you're interested in.

Willie Mae's Scotch House

7 Keep heading up Bayou Road for a block, turn left onto North Broad Street and walk eight blocks. It's not the fanciest part of town, but the shops and services are fun to browse and window shop. Turn left onto St. Ann Street and walk three blocks to **Willie Mae's Scotch House.** Get in line and order the fried chicken, the cornbread, and some butter beans and rice once you get seated.

8 Outside of Willie Mae's, turn right onto North Tonti, walk a block, and turn left onto Orleans Avenue. Continue down Orleans Avenue (toward the underpass) for a block and turn right onto North Galvez Street. Walk four short blocks to the Lafitte Greenway, then turn left and walk the greenway to North Claiborne, about four more blocks. Turn right and walk two blocks along North Claiborne to **Seven Three Distilling Co.** Cool down in this beautiful bar space by enjoying a cocktail that uses all house-made ingredients.

Sights

✪ Louis Armstrong Park

This park and cultural touchstone sits just over the border of the French Quarter, welcoming visitors into the historic Tremé neighborhood. The park honors New Orleans's most significant musical influences and is filled with sculptures and plaques. You'll find sculptures of Buddy Bolden, the credited inventor of jazz; Mahalia Jackson, the undisputed Queen of Soul and a Civil Rights activist; and, of course, park namesake Louis "Satchmo" Armstrong, commemorated blowing his iconic trumpet. Newer additions to the park include a statue of Mardi Gras Indian Chief Tootie Montana and a homage to the long-gone French Opera House and the importance of opera in 19th-century New Orleans, done in mosaic tiles.

Just inside the park's front gate is **Congo Square**, the place where New Orleans's slaves once gathered on Sundays to celebrate the music and rhythms of their homelands. Slaves were allowed to sing, drum, and dance one day a week, just at that site. It's where the seeds of American and jazz music took root.

Today, the park provides a vibrant space for musicians, artists, and activists. It's generally quiet, except during weekend festivals and events. It's a perfect place for a lunchtime picnic, or a wander over the lagoon's bridges. It hosts cultural festivals like the Tremé Creole Gumbo Fest and the Louisiana Cajun-Zydeco Festival. It's also the site of free Jazz in the Park concerts every Thursday in the late spring, when local artists and vendors set up along the park paths.
MAP 8: 901 Rampart St., 504-658-3200; 7am-8pm daily; free

sculpture at Louis Armstrong Park by Sheleen Jones-Adenle

Basin Street Station

What was once the office of the New Orleans Terminal Company/Southern Railway Freight has been transformed into an interpretive center covering the history and culture of New Orleans in the early 20th century. Built in 1904 in the neoclassical style, Basin Street Station was for decades the place where visitors to the city would arrive via train. The first level is open to visitors, and it caters to tourists with various exhibits on the city's attractions, a staffed information center, a coffee shop, and a gift shop—it's not a bad place to start your neighborhood wanderings.
MAP 8: 501 Basin St., 504/293-2600, basinststation.com; 9am-5pm daily; free

STORYVILLE

Back during the turn of the 20th century (1897-1917, to be exact), Storyville was New Orleans's red light district. It was proposed by City Alderman Sidney Story, and named after him in a tribute that did not at all please him. Bounded by Iberville, Basin, St. Louis, and North Robinson Streets, Storyville was where the city's brothels and prostitutes were centralized, so that the industry could be regulated (although not technically legalized). Storyville's delights were cataloged in an annually produced guide known as the Blue Book.

The district was critical in the development of jazz music. Most bordellos had music in the lobby to entertain customers, and it was one of the only spots that Black musicians were permitted to play. During the 20 years of Storyville's heyday, the jazz scene evolved, thanks to constant innovation and diverse variations. Most notably, Buddy Bolton (thought to be the earliest practitioner of jazz) and Jelly Roll Morton got their starts in Storyville. A young Louis Armstrong, selling coal to the establishments in the area, was inspired by the new and exciting rhythms and melodies he heard.

Storyville's public profile was raised due to its proximity to the newly built Basin Street train station—and because soldiers heading out to fight in World War I were brawling and carousing there. The Army and Navy ordered the city of New Orleans to shut down Storyville, citing its bad influence on the soldiers. Despite the protests of the city government, Storyville terminated as an official district at midnight on November 12, 1917. The buildings and infrastructure of the area were demolished during the Great Depression to make way for the Iberville public housing projects, leaving nothing behind but its legacy.

Degas House

Constructed in 1852, the expertly restored Degas House is the only former residence of famed French Impressionist Edgar Degas that's open to the public. The artist, whose mother and grandmother were born in New Orleans, lived here from 1872 to 1873 while visiting relatives. During his stay, he painted at least 22 works of art, including *A Cotton Office in New Orleans* (1873), which became the first Impressionist painting ever purchased by a museum. There are no original pieces in the house or museum, but the reproduction of what Degas's bedroom and studio would have looked like is quite engaging. The rest of the museum is decorated with period furniture.

Tours are the only way to visit the museum. Usually conducted by Degas's great-grandnieces, the two-plus-hour tour weaves a tale about Degas's family before and after his stay here, the work he did while in New Orleans, and historical context of the city, which helps to put everything into perspective.

a statue outside the Degas House

You'll enjoy a narrated walk through the house (which is also a well-regarded B&B), view a documentary about the artist's time in New Orleans, and take a guided stroll around the neighborhood, exploring locales mentioned in the artist's letters from New Orleans. For $50 per person, you can opt for the early tour plus a Creole breakfast (9am-10am); reservations are required.

MAP 8: 2306 Esplanade Ave., 504/821-5009, degashouse.com; by guided tour only 10:30am and 1:45pm daily; from $29 adults, $26 seniors and military, $22 students

the Tomb of the Unknown Slave

✪ St. Augustine Catholic Church and the Tomb of the Unknown Slave

Built on a former plantation estate and dedicated in 1842, the St. Augustine Catholic Church is the country's oldest African American Catholic parish. Prior to the American Civil War, the church welcomed both free Black citizens and enslaved individuals as worshippers. One of the church's former parishioners was Homer Plessy, the plaintiff in the landmark U.S. Supreme Court case of *Plessy v. Ferguson*, which confirmed the separate but equal doctrine. In 2008, the church was included on Louisiana's African American Heritage Trail (astorylikenoother.com). It's not generally open to the public, but you can (and should) visit during the Sunday morning Mass (10am), which welcomes believers and nonbelievers alike, for a gospel service. Once inside, you'll see the original pews, the pink Italian marble altar, and French stained-glass windows depicting several saints.

In the shade of the side of the church is the Tomb of the Unknown Slave, a rusting cross made up of thick chains and shackles. The tomb doesn't commemorate an actual grave. Rather, the monument honors the sheer number of people who were victims of slavery, buried in unmarked graves.

MAP 8: 1210 Gov. Nicholls St., 504/525-5934, staugchurch.org; free, donations accepted

TOP EXPERIENCE

St. Louis Cemetery No. 1

Arguably the oldest and most famous of New Orleans's "cities of the dead," St. Louis Cemetery No. 1 was established in 1789, following the Great Fire of 1788, and set outside what was then the city border. Since New Orleans sits below sea level and has a high water table, bodies were buried aboveground.

The cemetery currently contains more than 700 tombs and has interred thousands of people. Most of these aboveground structures are owned by families and designed to hold multiple sets of remains. Though constructed of brick, the elaborate tombs are often covered in concrete or stucco; some of the oldest ones are little more than crumbled ruins and piles of brick dust. Note the segregated Protestant section near the rear of this predominantly Catholic cemetery.

Famous residents here include Homer Plessy (of *Plessy v. Ferguson* fame) and the much-loved voodoo priestess Marie Laveau, whose supposed tomb is a frequent stop on daily tours (please do not mark the grave—preservationists have spent a lot of time and money restoring it to its original condition). Movie star Nicolas Cage has staked his own perpetual claim in this crowded cemetery; just look for the incongruous white pyramid that many locals consider an eyesore.

Visitors unrelated to the deceased may only enter the premises with a licensed tour guide. While several organizations offer guided tours, one of the most well-respected is **Save Our Cemeteries** (504/525-3377, www.saveourcemeteries.org; 10am, 11:30am, and 1pm Mon.-Sat., 10am Sun.; $25 adults, children under 12 free), which leads 90-minute-long excursions through the cemetery. Tours depart from **Backatown Coffee Parlour** (301 Basin St.).

MAP 8: Basin St. between Conti St. and St. Louis St., 504/482-5065; by guided tour only

Restaurants

PRICE KEY

$	Entrées less than $15
$$	Entrées $15-30
$$$	Entrées more than $30

CAJUN AND CREOLE

✪ Gabrielle Restaurant $$$

Greg and Mary Sonnier ran Gabrielle on Esplanade Avenue until Katrina hit; in 2017, they reopened their family restaurant (named for their daughter) on Orleans Avenue. The royal-blue-and-gold exterior is a welcoming sight, and the interior is simple but elegant, with a small bar and local art on the walls. Although they serve a wonderful Friday lunch, the dinner menu is where Chef Sonnier's classic dishes are found—smoked quail gumbo, barbecue shrimp pie, and slow-roasted duck, to name a few. This is an elevated take on old-school New Orleans cuisine, with the focus entirely on flavor. This food won't be as self-consciously Instagrammable as other spots, but honestly, you'll be too busy eating and enjoying to pick up your phone.

Gabrielle Restaurant

MAP 8: 2441 Orleans Ave., 504-603-2344, gabriellerestaurant.com; 5pm-9pm Sun.-Wed., 11am-2pm and 5pm-9pm Thurs.-Sat.

Liuzza's By the Track $

Steps away from the Fairgrounds, Liuzza's is an unofficial headquarters for Jazz Fest, but it's worth checking out any time of year. The gumbo is amazing, but the showstopper is the barbecue shrimp po'boy: all the buttery, rich delight of New Orleans barbecue shrimp already peeled and stuffed into a French bread bun. The Cajun duck dinner and garlic oyster po'boy (a more traditional version) are also great. Many tables are squeezed into the small space, and the bar goes all the way down one side of the restaurant. It's a New Orleans institution, and is definitely not a modern-looking spot, but although well worn, it's clean and always hopping.
MAP 8: 1518 N. Lopez St., 504/218-7888, liuzzasnola.com; 11am-7:30pm Mon.-Sat.

SOUTHERN AND SOUL FOOD

Dooky Chase's Restaurant $$

Established in 1941, Dooky Chase's is one of New Orleans's most famous restaurants. Unassuming on the outside, this classy place, adorned with vibrant Black-created art, is definitely worth a stop. Many locals swear by its Creole and Southern dishes, especially the okra gumbo, fried chicken, and peach cobbler, which are all part of the lunchtime buffet. If you can, try to get a reservation for the greens-filled gumbo *z'herbes*, made only for Holy Thursday (the Thursday before

Easter). Walk-ins and reservations are both welcome.
MAP 8: 2301 Orleans Ave., 504/821-0535, dookychaserestaurant.com; 11am-3pm Tues.-Thurs., 11am-3pm and 5pm-9pm Fri.

Dooky Chase's Restaurant

Lil' Dizzy's Cafe $

This nondescript corner restaurant has long been a favorite among locals. The friendly staff and down-home surroundings make you feel as though you're dining in someone's house, and the homestyle Creole and Southern cuisine is well worth the price. Highlights of the lunch buffet include fried chicken, catfish, and red beans and rice.
MAP 8: 1500 Esplanade Ave., 504/569-8997, lildizzyscafe.com; 10am-3pm Mon.-Sat., 10am-2pm Sun.

Sweet Soulfood $

New Orleans food is not well-known for its vegan-friendly options, especially where hearty soul food classics are concerned. However, Sweet Soulfood has changed that, offering a 100-percent vegan menu that includes dishes like okra gumbo, mushroom ragu with grits, collard greens, barbecue cauliflower, stuffed peppers, and bread pudding. The menu changes each day of the week, but the jambalaya and mac 'n' cheese are available every day. There are lots of gluten-free options, too. This is a place where meat eaters can also leave satisfied. You can see the trays of food as you go down the line, and everything looks delectable and fresh. The service is as sweet as the soul food, so get ready for some friendly conversation. The mint green walls lend a clean feeling, and there's plenty of indoor seating. MAP 8: 1016 N. Broad St., 504/821-2669, sweetvegansoulfood. com; 11am-6pm Mon.-Sat.

Willie Mae's Scotch House $

Between the historic Tremé and Esplanade Ridge neighborhoods, you'll encounter Willie Mae's Scotch House, a legendary, old-school joint primarily known for its unique, almost tempura-like fried chicken, which is both crispy and juicy. The flavorful red beans and rice, cornbread, and lemonade are well regarded, but no matter what you order, you can bet that it won't break the bank. Expect to wait in line during peak lunch hours. MAP 8: 2401 St. Ann St., 504/822-9503; 11am-5pm Mon.-Sat.

FRENCH
Cafe Degas $$

Nestled amid foliage on tree-lined Esplanade Avenue, cozy Cafe Degas serves such superb French cuisine as *les escargots Bourguignons,* salade niçoise, and pan-seared rack of Australian lamb with lamb merguez sausage, ratatouille, and smoked Vidalia onions. There's nothing overly trendy or complicated here,

it's just authentic cooking, reminiscent of true French bistro fare. The ambience is winning, too—it's the ideal spot for a romantic dinner. In warm weather, you can enjoy a meal on the lush garden patio, which is the perfect place to end an afternoon exploring the Fairgrounds area. MAP 8: 3127 Esplanade Ave., 504/945-5635, cafedegas.com; 11am-3pm and 6pm-10pm Wed.-Sat., 10:30am-3pm and 6pm-9:30pm Sun.

MIDDLE EASTERN
1000 Figs $

This is a bright and cozy spot for Mediterranean comfort food. Crisp hot French fries accompanied by creamy, garlicky *toum*, and gorgeous vegetable presentations like roasted beet and feta salad or the winter seasonal radishes all hit the spot alongside grilled meats and crunchy but light falafel. This is a great spot for vegetarians and vegans. Check out their weekday happy hour (3pm-5:30pm Mon.-Fri.), where falafel sandwiches are $4, a falafel platter is $9, house wine is $5, and select beer is $3. MAP 8: 3141 Ponce de Leon St., #1, 504/301-0848, 1000figs.com; 11am-9pm Mon.-Sat.

CARIBBEAN
Coco Hut $

The spices and grilling involved in cooking Jamaican-Caribbean food means keeping the door at Coco Hut open whenever possible, so your nose may just lead you to the right place. Inside the small, brightly colored and occasionally smoky interior, this spot offers jerk chicken and jerk tofu (they have a whole tofu-based vegan menu) but the real prize is whatever fish they're grilling up whole—usually snapper or trout. The menu is on two whiteboards outside, so you can know what you want by the time you walk in. It's a 100-percent halal meat, no-pork kitchen. Drink the special of the house: cane juice with mint and ginger.

MAP 8: 2515 Bayou Rd., 504/945-8788; 11am-7pm Tues.-Sat

COFFEE AND DESSERTS

Backatown Coffee Parlour $

Sweet potato pie! This small, local coffee shop run by husband and wife team and Tremé residents Alonzo and Jessica Knox is built within the footprint of the old Storyville neighborhood, which influenced the elegant design elements. In addition to being a Black-owned business,

Backatown sources their coffee beans from a Black-owned coffee roaster in Mississippi. Backatown provides a number of sweet treats as well as sandwiches, but anything that has sweet potato as an ingredient is sure to be a winner.

MAP 8: 301 Basin St., ste. 1, 504/372-4442, backatownnola.com; 7am-7pm Mon.-Fri., 8am-5pm Sat.-Sun.

Pagoda Café $

This spot near Bayou Road has a pagoda-like rooftop, making it easy to spot. In addition to a full coffee program, the café serves breakfast tacos till 1:30pm, sweet and savory house-made pastries, and a variety of inventive sandwiches and salads. This is one of the only non-Indian restaurants where you can get a mango lassi, which drives home the multi-ethnic international

Backatown Coffee Parlour

vibe. All seating is outdoors—inside is for ordering and cooking only. The menu is vegan- and gluten-free-friendly.

MAP 8: 1430 N. Dorgenois St., 504/644-4178, pagodacafe.net; 7:30am-3pm Mon.-Fri., 8am-3pm Sat.-Sun.

Nightlife

LIVE MUSIC
✪ Candlelight Lounge

Helmed by Tremé-born and -bred Leona "Ms. Chine" Grandison, the Candlelight Lounge will suck you in and make you a part of the experience. It's housed in an unassuming cinderblock building and boasts good music, good food, good people, and good times. There's brass-band music on Wednesday nights, live music every Sunday, and local DJs on Monday nights. Be warned, it's cash only and don't have an ATM on-site. The space is small and a little cramped, but once the band gets going, and everyone in the audience starts dancing (as you will be strongly encouraged to), you'll feel like a member of the community. This is a part of Tremé history, so go support it and have yourself a fine time while doing so.

MAP 8: 925 N. Robertson St., 504/906-5877; 3pm-2am daily; live music cover $5-10, cash only

Kermit's Tremé Mother-in-Law Lounge

Famous local musician Kermit Ruffins has been keeping this historic music club jumping since 2014. The bright murals that cover the building make it easy to spot, but they'll also educate you about the history of the space, with representations of legendary former owners Ernie K-Doe and his wife Antoinette. The name of the lounge is taken from Ernie's 1961 R&B hit "Mother in Law." Inside, the glitzy and over-the-top decor serves as a shrine to Ernie K-Doe's memory. Kermit himself has a standing gig here on Monday and Thursday nights (starting at 6pm, which is pretty early for shows); other local acts like the TBC Brass Band are featured on Sundays. Often, your cover charge will get you free food—everything from red beans to boiled seafood (crawfish, shrimp, crabs), especially if Kermit's playing.

MAP 8: 1500 N. Claiborne Ave, 504/814-1819; 10am-midnight daily; cover $5-20

Kermit's Tremé Mother-in-Law Lounge

the cocktail bar inside Seven Three Distilling Co.

Prime Example Jazz Club

You'll find old-school jazz as well as gospel and international variations within the purple walls of Prime Example. This is one of the few music clubs in the area that has a permanent kitchen serving food every night, including *yakamein*, red beans, po'boys, and other New Orleans specials. You can make a reservations ahead of time for a seat. Past artists include the Delfeayo Marsalis Quartet, Nicholas Payton, and the Sasha Masakowski quartet. The space is very cozy and intimate, so you're right there near the musicians and fellow patrons.

MAP 8: 1909 N. Broad St., 504/701-9007, primeexamplejazz. com; 4pm-midnight Mon., 4pm-3am Tues.-Fri., 7pm-5am; Sat. cover $10-30

BARS AND LOUNGES
Whiskey & Sticks

If sexy, smooth R&B was a place, it'd be Whiskey & Sticks, a high-end but still cozy and welcoming whiskey and cigar bar on Bayou Road. During the week, it's a great place to kick back and enjoy specials like Whiskey Wednesdays (5pm-7pm), with $5 pours of select bourbon and $5 house cocktails. On the weekend, though, it's a party, with cool people, karaoke, dancing, and celebrating. There's a walk-in humidor for choosing and purchasing cigars, which can be smoked on the back courtyard (not inside). It's a true gem and there aren't a lot of spots like it in New Orleans.

MAP 8: 2513 Bayou Rd., 504/444-8454, whiskeyandsticks.com; 4pm-10pm Wed.-Thurs., 4pm-midnight Fri.-Sat., 4pm-9pm Sun.

DISTILLERIES
Seven Three Distilling Co.

There are 73 official neighborhoods in New Orleans, and Seven Three Distilling pays homage to them all with spirits like Gentilly Gin, Irish Channel Whiskey, Black Pearl Rum, and Marigny Moonshine. In addition to the daily tours (which run around 45 minutes), Seven Three has a gorgeous bar area and serves cocktails showcasing all their wares, including bitters and liqueurs they make in-house. Regular cocktails cost $10-12, but their all-day happy hour offers a variety of drinks in the $5-6 range. The distillery also has a spacious retail area where, in addition to Seven Three booze and swag, you can find locally crafted, one-of-a-kind products such as handmade soaps with local ingredients, New Orleans-centric potholders, and cool coasters made from leather or stone.

MAP 8: 301 N. Claiborne Ave., 504/265-8545, seventhreedistilling.com; noon-6pm Fri.-Wed., noon-8pm Thurs.; tour $15

Arts and Culture

MUSEUMS

Backstreet Cultural Museum

New Orleans wouldn't be New Orleans without the Big Easy's vibrant African American culture. Not far from Louis Armstrong Park—the original site of Congo Square, where enslaved African Americans first started creating their own traditions in New Orleans—lies the fascinating Backstreet Cultural Museum. The museum contains the world's most comprehensive collection of costumes, films, and photographs from jazz funerals and pleasure clubs, as well as of Carnival-related groups like the Mardi Gras Indians, the Baby Dolls, and the Skull and Bone Gang. Beyond the permanent exhibits, the museum presents public performances of traditional music and dance. It's small, but densely packed full of costumes, signage, and information.

MAP 8: 1116 Henriette Delille St., 504/522-4806, backstreetmuseum.org; 10am-5pm Tues.-Sat.; $10, cash only

✪ Le Musée de f.p.c.

In New Orleans, the term "free people of color" was used much earlier than in the rest of the pro-slavery southern United States. Due to the relatively less stringent rules of the French colonizers regarding slavery, the Louisiana "Code Noir" required slaves be baptized in the Catholic faith and thus have Sundays off;

costumes at the Backstreet Cultural Museum

249

it also permitted slaves to marry amongst themselves, and prohibited slaveowners from separating families. Importantly, it also provided a process for slaves to buy their freedom. Head up to the beautifully curated Le Musée de f.p.c. for a tour with a knowledgeable docent. This museum relates a side of New Orleans that gets glossed over but is crucial to the city's history. The Greek Revival mansion that houses the museum is full of artifacts and works of art that tell the story of free people of color. The hour-long tours are the only way to access the museum, and are by appointment only.
MAP 8: 2336 Esplanade Ave., 504/323-5074, lemuseedefpc.com; by guided tour only 1pm-4pm Tues.-Fri., 11am-1pm Sat., 1pm-3pm Sun.; $15

Tremé's Petit Jazz Museum

This is a fun way to get a handle on jazz, the music that New Orleans is best known for. This small museum (it really is *petit*) focuses on how Tremé and New Orleans shaped the genre as it came together, influenced by the African rhythms in Congo Square as well as European musical styles. Founder Alvin Jackson is a wealth of knowledge, and he's usually there to put all the seemingly disparate treasures assembled in the room into context. (It's possible, though not nearly as interesting, to browse the museum on your own.) Anyone with a passing or passionate interest in jazz will fall in love with the information and perspective it brings to the subject. And if you're so inclined, the second-floor apartment is available to rent by the night.

Le Musée de f.p.c.

MAP 8: 1500 Governor Nicholls St., 504/715-0332, tremespetitjazzmuseum. com; 11:30am-5pm Mon.-Fri., 10am-5pm Sat.; $10

PERFORMING ARTS

Mahalia Jackson Theater for the Performing Arts

Located within Louis Armstrong Park, the Mahalia Jackson Theater is a popular venue for live concerts, operas, musicals, comedy shows, dance performances, and events. Named for New Orleans-born gospel singer Mahalia Jackson, the large theater (which seats 2,000 people) overlooks Louis Armstrong Park (and the statue of Satchmo himself) and has an illuminated fountain at its front doors. The theater hosts regular performances by the New Orleans Opera Association (504/529-2278 or 504/529-3000, www.neworleansopera.org), the Louisiana Philharmonic Orchestra (504/523-6530, www.lpomusic.com), and the New Orleans Ballet Association (504/522-0996, www.nobadance.com).

MAP 8: 1419 Basin St., 504/287-0350, mahaliajacksontheater.com; hours and ticket prices vary by show

Southern Rep Theatre

This regional theater company has been around since 1986 and in its current location in the converted St. Rose de Lima church since 2018. It's a non-profit organization and produces professional theater as well as smaller readings, shows, and community-focused programs. They also host a monthly circus cabaret and a live, eight-year-long (so far) soap opera about life in New Orleans called *Debauchery!* Originally dedicated to promoting work by Southerners or about the South, Southern Rep now brings new works and regional/world premieres to its stage. In 2019, Southern Rep produced New Orleans native Christina Quintana's *Azul,* and Troi Bechet's *Flowers for Halie.* It's a great spot to get an idea of the state of the dramatic and performing arts in New Orleans.

MAP 8: 2541 Bayou Rd., 504/522-6545, southernrep.com; hours and ticket prices vary by show

The Broad Theater

CINEMA

The Broad Theater

The Broad is a proper movie house, the kind that used to be in every neighborhood back in the early- to mid-20th century. The theater dates back to the 1920s and was fully renovated into a four-screen cinema in 2015. It shows mainstream hits and indie darlings, and always has the time and space for local creators and causes. It's a great movie-watching experience, with craft cocktails and micro-brews available; in addition to the standard popcorn and candy, you can get cheeses, charcuterie, and stromboli.

MAP 8: 636 N. Broad St., 504/218-1008, thebroadtheater.com; 1pm-midnight Mon.-Wed., 11am-midnight Thurs.-Sun.; $10 adults, $8 seniors, military, and children, $8 matinee (before 5:30pm)

Recreation

PARKS AND PLAZAS

Gayarré Place

The focal point of this tiny triangle-shaped park, named after 19th-century Louisiana historian Charles Gayarré, is a neo-classical monument entitled *Peace, the Genius of History.* Made of terra-cotta, it features the Greek muse and goddess of history, Clio. It was originally displayed at the 1884 New Orleans World's Industrial and Cotton Centennial Exposition (now Audubon Park). It's across from the Degas House and sits in the middle of the road, where Esplanade Avenue and Bayou Road diverge.

MAP 8: 2229 Bayou Rd.;
24 hours daily; free

HORSE RACING

Fair Grounds Race Course & Slots

Mid-City's Fair Grounds Race Course & Slots is the third-oldest thoroughbred-racing course in the nation, offering live racing from Thanksgiving through March. An off-track-betting parlor is open year-round, so you can always wager on events elsewhere in the country. Key races at the track include the Louisiana Derby and the Fair Grounds Oaks; it's also the longtime home of the annual New Orleans Jazz & Heritage Festival (www.nojazzfest.com), known more commonly as Jazz Fest. Besides concession stands and two "grab-and-go" eateries, the Fair Grounds has a fancy Clubhouse dining room, which has a strict dress code and is only open on live racing days. In addition to horse races, there are family-friendly events, like "wiener dog" races and exotic animal races (think zebras and ostriches). The crowd here is a friendly one, and everyone loves being able to get up close to the horses before the race. Grab a beer, place a wager, and enjoy the day.

MAP 8: 1751 Gentilly Blvd., 504/944-5515 or 504/948-1111, fairgroundsracecourse.com; 9am-midnight daily; $10 pp for clubhouse, $0-5 pp for grandstand

Shops

GIFTS AND SOUVENIRS
Material Life

This beautifully curated shop has many items you'd want to add to your own material life. With Black-crafted and Black-focused pottery, clothing, art, books, and jewelry, it's hard to classify what kind of shop this is. Owner Carla Williams is happy to talk about any item in the store. Attached to Material Life is the February Gallery, which features photography, historic images, and multimedia art to tell stories of the Black experience.

MAP 8: 2521 Bayou Rd., 504/217-5130, material.life; noon-8pm Mon., 11am-8pm Tues.-Thurs., 11am-9pm Sat.

BOOKS AND MUSIC
✪ Community Book Center

This bookstore and gathering space is the only Black-owned bookstore in New Orleans, and has been in business since the mid-1980s. It's a haven for Black literature and storytelling. Neighborhood kids have picked out their favorite books here for decades, and local writers have been inspired by the feeling of community and solidarity the Community Book Center provides. Bookstore founder Vera Warren-Williams is a wealth of cultural and literary information and seeks to create a haven for all who need it. There's lots of history to learn here.

MAP 8: 2523 Bayou Rd., 504/948-7323; 10am-6pm Mon.-Sat.

Material Life

the Community Book Center

Greater New Orleans   Map 9

There are hidden gems in outlying New Orleans neighborhoods like **Lakeview, Gentilly,** and **New Orleans East.** New Orleans East, or "The East," is an enormous swath of land in the Ninth Ward, north of the Lower Ninth Ward neighborhood. You have to cross the Industrial Canal to get there, so it feels separate from the city. The area is home to a large concentration of African American New Orleanians and, the farther east you go, a significant Vietnamese American population.

   Metairie, in Jefferson Parish, is the city's primary suburb. Jefferson Parish spreads farther west to **Kenner,** and south to **River Ridge** and **Harahan.** Across the Mississippi is the **Westbank,** where you'll find **Algiers, Gretna, Harvey,** and **Marrero.** Both Kenner and the Westbank are full of international culture and authentic cuisine from Latin America to Southeast Asia.

TOP SIGHTS

- Coolest Garden: **Longue Vue House and Gardens** (page 258)

TOP RESTAURANTS

- Best Under-the-Radar Fried Chicken: **Fiorella's Cafe** (page 260)
- Best Seafood and Vietnamese Under One Roof: **TD Seafood Pho House** (page 262)
- Most Unexpected Cuisine: **Mangú** (page 264)

TOP NIGHTLIFE

- Best Spot for Pitching Horseshoes: **Winston's Pub & Patio** (page 267)

TOP RECREATION

- Best Park for Bird-Watching: **Barataria Preserve** (page 268)

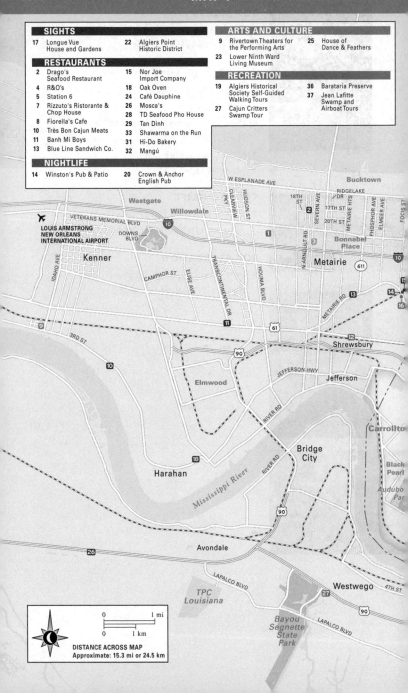

SIGHTS

| 17 | Longue Vue House and Gardens | 22 | Algiers Point Historic District |

RESTAURANTS

2	Drago's Seafood Restaurant	15	Nor Joe Import Company
4	R&O's	18	Oak Oven
5	Station 6	24	Café Dauphine
7	Rizzuto's Ristorante & Chop House	26	Mosca's
8	Fiorella's Cafe	28	TD Seafood Pho House
10	Très Bon Cajun Meats	29	Tan Dinh
11	Banh Mi Boys	33	Shawarma on the Run
13	Blue Line Sandwich Co.	31	Hi-Do Bakery
		32	Mangú

NIGHTLIFE

| 14 | Winston's Pub & Patio | 20 | Crown & Anchor English Pub |

ARTS AND CULTURE

| 9 | Rivertown Theaters for the Performing Arts | 25 | House of Dance & Feathers |
| 23 | Lower Ninth Ward Living Museum | | |

RECREATION

| 19 | Algiers Historical Society Self-Guided Walking Tours | 36 | Barataria Preserve |
| 27 | Cajun Critters Swamp Tour | 37 | Jean Lafitte Swamp and Airboat Tours |

DISTANCE ACROSS MAP
Approximate: 15.3 mi or 24.5 km

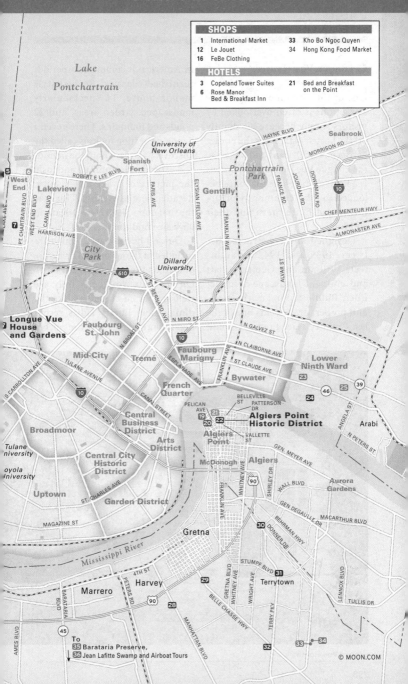

SHOPS	
1 International Market	33 Kho Bo Ngoc Quyen
12 Le Jouet	34 Hong Kong Food Market
16 FeBe Clothing	

HOTELS	
3 Copeland Tower Suites	21 Bed and Breakfast
6 Rose Manor	on the Point
Bed & Breakfast Inn	

Lake Pontchartrain

University of New Orleans

Seabrook

HAYNE BLVD

MORRISON RD

Pontchartrain Park

Spanish Fort

West End

Lakeview

ROBERT E LEE BLVD

CANAL BLVD

WEST END BLVD

PT CHARTRAIN BLVD

LAKE AVE

PARIS AVE

ELYSIAN FIELDS AVE

Gentilly

FRANCE ST

JOURDAN RD

DOWNMAN RD

CHEF MENTEUR HWY

HARRISON AVE

FRANKLIN AVE

ALVAR ST

ALMONASTER AVE

City Park

Dillard University

Longue Vue House and Gardens

Faubourg St. John

Mid-City

Trémé

Faubourg Marigny

N. MIRO ST

N GALVEZ ST

N CLAIBORNE AVE

ST CLAUDE AVE

Lower Ninth Ward

N. BROAD ST

ST BERNARD AVE

TULANE AVENUE

ESPLANADE AVE

FRANKLIN AVE

Bywater

Broadmoor

Central Business District

Arts District

CANAL STREET

French Quarter

PELICAN AVE

BELLEVILLE ST

PATTERSON DR

Algiers Point Historic District

Arabi

Tulane University

Central City Historic District

Algiers Point

VALLETTE ST

McDonogh

Algiers

GEN. MEYER AVE

ANGELA ST

N. PETERS ST

Loyola University

Uptown

ST. CHARLES AVE

Garden District

FRANKLIN AVE

WHITNEY AVE

SHIRLEY DR

WALL BLVD

GEN DEGAULLE DR

Aurora Gardens

MACARTHUR BLVD

MAGAZINE ST

Gretna

BEHRMAN HWY

DONNER DR

Mississippi River

4TH ST

Harvey

PETERS RD

Marrero

BARATARIA BLVD

GRETNA BLVD

WHITNEY AVE

WRIGHT AVE

BELLE CHASSE HWY

MANHATTAN BLVD

STUMPF BLVD

Terrytown

TERRY PKY

LENNOX BLVD

TULLIS DR

AMES BLVD

To Barataria Preserve, Jean Lafitte Swamp and Airboat Tours

© MOON.COM

Sights

✪ Longue Vue House and Gardens

One of the city's most impressive attractions is often overlooked by visitors simply because it's slightly off the beaten path. Near the border between New Orleans and Metairie, the Longue Vue House and Gardens is a lush, exotic estate that once belonged to local community pillars Edgar and Edith Stern and their children.

Designed and constructed between 1939 and 1942 by architects William and Geoffrey Platt and eminent landscape architect Ellen Biddle Shipman, the tranquil property represents one of the last Country Place Era homes built in America. It comprises a period-furnished Classical Revival-style manor house, 14 spectacularly landscaped garden areas, and 22 ponds and fountains. There's even a hands-on section for kids called the Discovery Garden. Both the interior and exterior are stunning and lush, the picture of pre-War elegance, decadence, and wealth. This was the first domicile in New Orleans to have air-conditioning.

Guided house tours, which are included in the admission price, are offered on the hour (4pm last tour). On the tour, you'll not only see well-appointed chambers like the dining room, library, ladies' reception room, and master bedroom, but

Longue Vue House

also modern art exhibits and displays about the creation of Longue Vue. For a lower fee ($7 adults, $4 students and children), you can opt to skip the house tour and simply explore the gardens, but I recommend seeing as much of this place as you can.

MAP 9: 7 Bamboo Rd., 504/488-5488, longuevue.com; 10am-5pm Mon.-Sat., 1pm-5pm Sun.; $12 adults, $10 seniors, $8 students, $5 children 3-10, children under 3 and military free

Algiers Point Historic District

Known as Algiers Point, this residential Westbank neighborhood is filled with a vast cache of notable residences from the early 18th to the mid-20th centuries, including French colonial-style plantation houses, Creole cottages, Haitian shotguns, Greek Revival-style mansions, Victorian structures, and British craftsman-style homes. New Orleans's second-oldest neighborhood, Algiers Point features a handful of pleasant parks, a few B&Bs, several pubs and eateries, and a smattering of shops. Although it's easy to reach, this neighborhood feels distinct from the rest of the city, owing to the mile-wide Mississippi River, which separates it from the French Quarter and the CBD.

From the foot of Canal Street, catch the Algiers Point/Canal Street Ferry (504/376-8180, nolaferries.com or friendsoftheferry.org; 6am-10pm Mon.-Fri., 10:45am-8:15pm Sat., 10:45am-6:15pm Sun.; $2 adults, $1 seniors, children under 3 free), which has been shuttling people across the river since 1827. The trip usually takes about five minutes each way, with the ferry leaving every 30 minutes. The ferry does not transport cars, but you're allowed to bring pets, bikes, and scooters onboard. The final return trips from Algiers Point occur at 9:30pm Monday-Friday, 7:45pm Saturday, and 5:45pm Sunday.

MAP 9: Newton St. and Atlantic Ave. to Mississippi River, Algiers, algierspoint.org

Restaurants

PRICE KEY

$	Entrées less than $15
$$	Entrées $15-30
$$$	Entrées more than $30

CAJUN AND CREOLE

Drago's Seafood Restaurant $$

Drago's is a riotously popular restaurant with limited seating and parking. The emphasis is on seafood, much of it prepared with a Louisiana slant. The charbroiled oysters are their claim to fame and a must-order. The lobster dishes are also noteworthy; try the lobster Marco, a whole lobster stuffed with fresh sautéed shrimp and mushrooms in a light cream sauce, served over angel hair pasta. You can sit at the bar, which affords a clear view of the grill, or dine in one of the noisy, festive dining rooms. With the high volume of business, the waitstaff often seems harried.

MAP 9: 3232 N. Arnoult Rd., Metairie, 504/888-9254, dragosrestaurant.com; 11am-9pm daily

✪ Fiorella's Cafe $

The original Fiorella's Café in Gentilly boasts two years of winning the Best Fried Chicken at the New Orleans Fried Chicken Festival, so it's easy to decide what to get here. Fiorella's also serves Creole Italian favorites like chicken parm and meatballs with spaghetti, along with fried seafood plates and po'boys.

R&O's

The tables are filled during the day with locals and businesspeople from the Gentilly commercial district, making this unassuming family-owned, counter-service restaurant a solid spot in a neighborhood that you might not see otherwise.

MAP 9: 5325 Franklin Ave., New Orleans, 504/309-0352, originalfiorellas. com; 11am-7pm Mon.-Sat.

R&O's $

This Creole-Italian spot in Metairie's Bucktown—a former fishing village on the western side of the 17th Street Canal—is near the shores of Lake Pontchartrain. R&O's offers po'boys, fried and boiled seafood, fantastic muffulettas, and, surprisingly, great pizza. It's family-owned and -operated, and New Orleans-area folks have been coming here for generations. It may not look like much, but the atmosphere is convivial to the point of raucous, with friends and family enjoying the comfort food and each other's company. Try the oyster soup, the R&O special po'boy which is roast beef, ham, and swiss cheese, or one of their homestyle pasta dishes.

MAP 9: 216 Metairie-Hammond Hwy., Metairie, 504/831-1248, r-opizza.com; 11am-3pm Mon.-Tues., 11am-3pm and 5pm-9pm Wed.-Thurs., 11am-10pm Sat., 11am-9pm Sun.

Très Bon Cajun Meats $

Like all the best Cajun places in Louisiana, the nature of Très Bon is blurred. Is it a shop? Is it a restaurant? Très Bon serves dishes made from the ingredients that they stock, so you can eat gumbo, brisket, boudin, and more while you're here, or buy it to make yourself at home.

Happily, this counter service shop is easier to get to than the Boudin Belt out west, so stopping here means you can experience no-frills Cajun fare without going very far. Pulling up to the tiny, almost shack-like building, you can't help but notice (and smell) the smoker in the corner of the parking lot, an auspicious sign for what lies inside. The simple interior has booths and tables, with Cajun-country decor, and is generally filled with locals. Buy a bag of the delicious homemade jerky to take with you, and order some cracklin' for the road. If you have access to a kitchen, you won't regret buying the smoked sausage or *tasso*, found in the refrigerated cases.

MAP 9: 10316 Jefferson Hwy., River Ridge, 504/405-5355, tresbonmeats. com; 9am-8pm Tues.-Sat.

SEAFOOD
Station 6 $$

With a patio overlooking the water, a killer cocktail menu, and seafood so fresh you'd think it was caught mere feet away, Station 6 is a

Très Bon Cajun Meats

down-to-earth, yet high-end, chef-driven restaurant that is one of the area's best kept secrets. Try the red snapper, charbroiled oyster pasta, or crab casserole, and leave room for their signature bread pudding. The happy hour (4pm-6pm Tues.-Thurs.) is cool, too: You'll get six local oysters on the half shell, a local caviar tasting, and a glass of champagne for $15. The service is excellent, both tableside and behind the bar.

MAP 9: 105 Metairie-Hammond Hwy., Metairie, 504/345-2936, station6nola. com; 11am-9pm Tues.-Thurs., 11am-10pm Fri.-Sat., 11am-8pm Sun.

✪ TD Seafood Pho House $

This is the place for Viet-Cajun boiled seafood—crawfish, shrimp, king crab, or whatever's in season, cooked in a Vietnamese-spiced garlic-butter sauce. The pho broth is widely adored, but the *bo bun hue* (a spicy beef and noodle soup with a heartier broth than pho) is rave-worthy. Although located in a strip mall, the interior of the place is clean and modern, with aesthetically pleasing lighting, and a super friendly staff.

MAP 9: 1028 Manhattan Blvd., Harvey, 504/302-1727; 9am-9pm Thurs.-Tues.

VIETNAMESE
Tan Dinh $$

This is the place to get the full-scale Vietnamese experience—not just banh mi and pho, but pretty much every type of Vietnamese dish you can think of. The menu can be a little overwhelming, but there are familiar dishes among the more exotic. They offer a wide range of protein options, like quail, goat, catfish, duck, and frog legs. The clay pot

catfish steak is a must-try. There are more carbohydrate options beyond steamed rice and vermicelli noodles, like *banh bao* steamed buns, crispy sweet rice patties, and pressed vermicelli noodles. Even the beverages can be adventurous, like the Soda *sữa hột gà*, which is soda water with egg yolk and condensed milk. Go beyond your usual Vietnamese restaurant order at this spacious, unpretentious palace of Vietnamese food with warm and helpful service—you'll be glad you did.

MAP 9: 1705 Lafayette St., Gretna, 504/361-8008, tandinhnola.com; 10am-9pm Tues.-Sat., 10am-8pm Sun.

Banh Mi Boys $

This is the place to go with a big appetite. Although they carry a wide selection of traditional Vietnamese banh mi and New Orleans po'boys, it's the specialty sandwiches, smothered fries, and chicken wings that puts the Banh Mi Boys over the top. Favorite sandwiches include the Bang Bang Shrimp banh mi, with fried shrimp tossed in Thai chili sauce, the Japanese-inspired *katsu* chicken banh mi, the Chinese *char siu* rib banh mi, and the *bo kho* banh mi, which is basically a Vietnamese roast beef po'boy, sloppy gravy and all. Don't skip the loaded fries, especially the K-Town fries, with Korean-marinated beef with kimchi, kimchi mayo, and a sunny-side up egg. Most seating is outside on a covered patio, adorned with customized drawings with the restaurant's name and the advice to "Talk Less, Eat More." There's also a handy graphic drawn on the wall inside next to the cash register illustrating the components of a banh mi.

MAP 9: 5001 Airline Dr., Metairie, 504/510-5360, bmbmetairie.com; 11am-8pm Mon.-Sat.

ITALIAN

Rizzuto's Ristorante & Chop House $$$

This Sicilian-Italian restaurant serves awesome steaks, but the other parts of the menu deserve consideration as well. The pastas and Italian meat preparations are great: Try the *tortellacci,* a stuffed house-made pasta with chianti-braised short ribs, marinara, and pecorino Romano. The sleek bar, lush banquettes, and stellar service are what you'd expect to find at any high-end steak house. There's a lovely cocktail and wine list.

MAP 9: 6262 Fleur de Lis Dr., New Orleans, 504/300-1804, rizzutosristorante.com; 5pm-9pm Tues.-Thurs., 11am-3pm and 5pm-10pm Fri., 5pm-10pm Sat., 3:30pm-8pm Sun., bar opens at 4pm Tues.-Sun.

Mosca's $$

If you're looking for an amazing food experience, the trip out to Mosca's will fulfill that desire and then some. Since 1946, Mosca's has been serving traditional Creole-Italian food served in hearty family-style portions. Not much has changed in the intervening years: not the menu, the atmosphere, or the building itself. And that's one of the best things about the place. Be sure to order the Italian salad, oysters Mosca, spaghetti and meatballs, sausage Johnny, or the chicken à la grande. Bring cash; credit cards and checks aren't accepted here.

MAP 9: 4137 US-90, Westwego, 504/436-8950, moscasrestaurant.com; 5:30pm-9:30pm Tues.-Sat.

Oak Oven $$

Celebrating the area's Italian heritage with a fusion of Sicilian, Neapolitan, and New Orleans cuisine, Oak Oven is a neighborhood restaurant that welcomes everyone like regulars. Antipasto choices includes the *frutti di golfo,* a warm shrimp and crab salad with fire-roasted artichokes, and there are some excellent pizza options coming out of their traditional Italian wood oven, like the lamb meatball or the verdure, with cherry tomato, artichokes, spinach, and ricotta. Several of the pastas are made in-house and include gluten-free options. The meat portion of the menu includes traditional preparations like piccata, marsala, and parmigiana. The interior is on the small side and has a rustic vibe; there's also patio seating.

MAP 9: 6625 Jefferson Hwy., Harahan, 504/305-4039, oakovenrestaurant.com; 11am-3pm and 5pm-9pm Mon.-Thurs., 11am-3pm and 5pm-10pm Fri.-Sat.

MEDITERRANEAN

Shawarma on the Run $

Take care of your shawarma, hummus, gyro, and falafel cravings at this tiny, spotless shawarma spot in a strip mall on the Westbank. There are always several spinning cones of meat and the owners are engaging and provide great service. You can also grab a spinach pie or stuffed grape leaf if the urge hits, and the French fries are surprisingly excellent. Oh, and don't forget a beverage—the Lebanese iced tea is killer.

NINE IN THE NINTH

(Contributed by Megan Braden-Perry, a writer born, raised, and still telling her stories in New Orleans. She's an expert in finding under-the-radar spots with amazing food.)

Wards are civic designations, which are different from neighborhood names. Both the Lower Ninth neighborhood and New Orleans East (just north of the Lower Ninth) are in the Ninth Ward of New Orleans. As the biggest of New Orleans's 17 wards, the Ninth Ward is full of amazing authentic New Orleans food.

Messina's at the Terminal

1. BA MIEN

Ba Mien (13235 Chef Menteur Hwy., 504/255-0500, bamien.com) is a Vietnamese restaurant located in Michoud, one of the first New Orleans neighborhoods that Vietnamese immigrants inhabited in the 1970s. The ingredients here are fresh and they pay great attention to detail. I recommend the *bun tom nuong nem nuong* (noodle salad with grilled shrimp and grilled pork paste), *bo tai chanh* (rare beef with onions), and *banh cuon thap cam* (steamed rice roll with minced pork, pork pie, and grilled pork paste). Everything here is truly perfect.

2. BURRITOS GRILL

One of my favorite Mexican restaurants, Burritos Grill (7009 Read Blvd., 504/242-0573) is immaculate and has excellent service. The happy hour margaritas come with a red, white, and green salt rim. My son and I always get the chicken mole enchiladas. A side of *chiles toreados* (blistered chili peppers) and guacamole is always a great idea.

3. CASA HONDURAS

This location of Casa Honduras (5704 Crowder Blvd., 504/244-0005) is just off the freeway at the Crowder exit. The atmosphere is nice and I love sitting at the bar with a shot of *gifiti*, a traditional Garifuna liquor that's served like tequila. A *baleada* (flour tortilla with beans, cheese, and cream) is filling for cheap, but if I'm here

MAP 9: 93 Terry Pkwy., Gretna, 504/373-6669; 11am-9pm Mon.-Sat., noon-8pm Sun.

LATIN AMERICAN
✪ Mangú $

This Dominican restaurant is named for its signature dish, *mangú*, which is creamy, mashed green plantains whipped with butter and served with any number of sauces, meats, and/or vegetables. Some favorite versions include the *chicharrón de pollo* (fried chicken cracklin'), the *chuleta ahumada* (smoked pork chop), and the *longaniza frita* (fried Dominican sausage). It's all comforting and delicious. The cheerfully colored restaurant is the perfect place to try Dominican cuisine for the first time or to revisit if you're already a connoisseur.

for dinner I'll get the *pescado frito* (whole fried fish) and *platano maduro frito* (fried sweet plantains served with beans, cheese, and cream).

4. CASTNET SEAFOOD
Boiled and fried seafood, raw oysters, gumbo, and po'boys await you at Castnet (10826 Hayne Blvd., 504/244-8446). This is my favorite place for seafood po'boys and one of my favorites for gumbo. There's an attached snowball stand that's open seasonally.

5. DAIQUIRI CHEF
New Orleans has so many daiquiri shops, but very few have charm like Daiquiri Chef (3738 Downman Rd., 504/324-6184). I come every Christmas for a gallon of the egg-nog daiquiri, which is the best in town. On a regular day, I love the tropical Hardhead and the green apple-flavored Wine Candy. You can't go wrong here!

6. DEANIE'S ON HAYNE
This location of Deanie's (7350 Hayne Blvd., 504/248-6700) is technically related to the ones in Bucktown, the French Quarter, and Uptown, but it's not the same at all. This one is old-school Creole-Italian, not touristy at all, and it's known for the house-made dressing and sauce. I recommend whatever you see on the marquee outside. That might be trout, eggplant parmigiana, or corn-and-crab bisque. Be sure to get a house salad, so you can try the dressing for yourself.

7. ISLAND FLAVOR BAR AND GRILL
Island Flavor (10711 Chef Menteur Hwy., 504/246-8537) is a restaurant in a strip mall. The service is nice and the drinks at the bar are great. I recommend the jerk chicken, curry chicken, goat, callaloo, and cabbage.

8. MA MOMMA'S HOUSE OF CORNBREAD, CHICKEN AND WAFFLES
Ma Momma's (5741 Crowder Blvd., 504/244-0021, mamommashouse.com) is a restaurant that is as close as you can get to home, outside of eating at someone's actual house. Every meal comes with fleur-de-lis-shaped cornbread and Chef Reero loves to check on customers. I recommend the chicken and waffles, red beans, and fish plate. Check out the all-you-can-eat brunch that happens once a month!

9. MESSINA'S AT THE TERMINAL
So many brunch spots are good just because they've got bottomless cocktails, but Messina's (6001 Stars and Stripes Blvd., 504/241-5300) is splendid for several reasons: the music, the art deco design, the kind chef, and the food, of course! I love the veal and grits, shrimp and grits, and the crab cakes with poached eggs. It's fun watching the planes take off from the airport. Tip: You can switch up your bottomless cocktail and just pay the price of the most expensive bottomless option.

MAP 9: 2112 Belle Chasse Hwy. #7, Gretna, 504/324-9870, letsmangu.com; 11am-8pm Tues.-Thurs., 11am-9pm Fri.-Sat., 11am-5pm Sun.

DELIS AND DINERS
Blue Line Sandwich Co. $
This breakfast and lunch spot in Old Metairie is worth a visit if you're out that way. At the counter, order items like the Duck-Duck-Goose waffle, corned beef and hatch chile hash, or the *cochon de lait* (suckling pig) biscuit. Next, grab a cocktail (investigate the Bloody Mary bar) or beer from the bar and settle into this laid-back, comfy spot for a great meal off the beaten path. It's amid several small businesses on Metairie Road, so parking can be a little tricky.
MAP 9: 2023 Metairie Rd., Metairie, 504/309-3773, bluelinesandwichco. com; 7am-2pm daily

Try Dominican cuisine at Mangú.

Nor Joe Import Company $

Part Italian market, part sandwich shop, Nor Joe's is where you make your cab stop on the way to the airport to pick up a muffuletta to take home in your carry-on luggage. If you'd like to chill on their outdoor patio, you could eat said muffuletta on-site, or try the Italian meatball sub, the Little Joe sandwich with turkey, provolone, and artichoke salad, or a traditional Creole-Italian favorite, the stuffed artichoke. It takes up to 30 minutes to prepare the sandwiches, so order ahead if you're in a rush.

MAP 9: 505 Frisco Ave., Metairie, 504/833-9240, norjoe.com; 9am-7pm Mon.-Sat., 10am-2pm Sun.

COFFEE AND DESSERTS
Hi-Do Bakery $

This is one of the finest New Orleans-Vietnamese bakeries in the entire area. Vietnamese bakeries in the Greater New Orleans region are known for their individual-sized loaves of French bread that fall somewhere between regular French baguettes and New Orleans-style po'boy bread. Hi-Do is particularly known for its carefully designed cakes (shaped like a crawfish or fleur-de-lis), especially during king cake season, when their version is one of the city's favorite's. Their regular pastry program is terrific as well, with flaky croissants (sweet, savory, and stuffed), turnovers, scones, and cinnamon rolls, to name a few. It's cash only.

MAP 9: 439 Terry Pkwy., Terrytown, 504/366-6555; 7am-6pm Mon.-Fri., 8am-6pm Sat.

Hi-Do Bakery

Nightlife

BARS AND LOUNGES

Crown & Anchor English Pub

If you take the ferry to Algiers Point, look around for the bright blue, *Dr. Who*-inspired TARDIS police box: That's the Crown & Anchor. It's a definite English pub vibe they're going for, and really, they nailed it. UK memorabilia hangs on the ceilings and walls, they've got a nice "draught" beer selection, and there are dart tournaments and *Dr. Who* viewings aplenty.

MAP 9: 200 Pelican Ave., New Orleans, 504/227-1007, crownandanchor.pub; 11am-midnight Sun.-Thurs., 11am-3am Fri.-Sat.

✪ Winston's Pub & Patio

The dark wood bar, tables, and sofas all contribute to the authentic pub experience here, which is dark and cozy. For some fresh air, check out the large back patio and landscaped area with a horseshoe pit. With a dozen or so beers on draft (including many local selections) and a great, reasonably priced cocktail menu, this is the perfect place to hang out with friends or a book. There's a basic bar food menu, and they host crawfish boils on the patio during the season.

MAP 9: 531 Metairie Rd., Metairie, 504/831-8705, winstonspubandpatio. com; noon-midnight daily

Arts and Culture

PERFORMING ARTS

Rivertown Theaters for the Performing Arts

This two-stage operation produces 15 shows a year—musicals and children's theater, mostly. It's also community focused, and locals participate in productions that also feature professional actors. Past events include *Spamalot, Mamma Mia, Me and My Girl, Billy Elliot,* and *You're a Good Man, Charlie Brown.* Tickets usually top out at around $40, making this a reasonably priced opportunity for a fun evening out.

MAP 9: 325 Minor St., Kenner, 504/461-9475, rivertowntheaters.com; hours and prices vary by show

Recreation

PARKS AND PLAZAS
✪ Barataria Preserve

The 23,000-acre Barataria Preserve, a unit of Jean Lafitte National Historical Park and Preserve, is a popular bird-watching spot among locals and visitors. Situated on the western bank of the Mississippi River, this enormous preserve contains bayous, swamps, marshes, forests, and roughly nine miles of hiking trails. Don't miss the Bayou Coquille Trail, a half-mile, pavement-and-boardwalk path that's known for sightings of snakes, alligators, nutrias, and some of the more than 300 bird species that dwell here.

At the visitors center (9:30am-4:30pm Wed.-Sun.), check out exhibits that highlight how the Mississippi River created Louisiana's wetlands, the national significance of this region, and the relationship between the land and its people. In the bookstore, you'll find music, field guides, and children's books. Free guided wetlands walks are available Wednesday-Sunday at 10am, and varied ranger talks occur at 2pm on the same days. The park, which is only closed on Mardi Gras Day, is also favored among canoeists, kayakers, boaters, and licensed anglers. No pets, even leashed ones, are allowed at the preserve.

MAP 9: 6588 Barataria Blvd., Marrero, 504/689-3690, nps.gov/jela; 9am-5pm daily; free

SWAMP TOURS
Cajun Critters Swamp Tours

Leaving from Bayou Segnette on the Westbank, these two-hour tours navigate the area's wetlands, swamps, and marshes in an ADA-compliant bayou barge. The pickup/drop-off point is next door to a long-time seafood market called Amy's Seafood, which has freshly caught and harvested fish and shellfish as well as po'boys and smoked sausage to check out before or after the tour. It doesn't get more local than that.

MAP 9: 363 Louisiana St., Westwego, 504/347-0962, cajunswamptour.com; tours at 9:30am and 1:30pm daily (additional tour at 3:30pm spring-fall), $24 adults, $15 children 4-12, children under 4 free

Jean Lafitte Swamp and Airboat Tours

There are a multitude of options for swamp tours in the area surrounding New Orleans, and each is unique in its own way. The Jean Lafitte tours take place in the beautiful Jean Lafitte National Historical Park and Preserve, only a 25-minute drive from downtown New Orleans. You can go on a regular flat-bottomed swamp boat or on a high-speed airboat. A fun option is to go on the 10am swamp tour and then head over to lunch at Restaurant de Familles, a traditional Cajun food restaurant that overlooks the bayou. Hotel pickups are available for an additional fee.

MAP 9: 6601 Leo Kerner Lafitte Pkwy., Marrero, 504/293-2338, jeanlafitteswamptour.com; tours at 10am, noon, and 2pm daily (additional tour at 4pm spring-fall), $29 adults, $15 children 3-12, children under 3 free

WALKING TOURS
Algiers Historical Society Self-Guided Walking Tours

For history, architecture, and music nerds alike, these self-guided walking tours around the least traversed area of New Orleans all start at the Algiers Point ferry dock. The options include an Algiers Point historic tour, an Algiers Point music history tour, and a wider Algiers music tour. It's all done on your own schedule and may lead you to some unexpected places such as the one-time home of Emmett Hardy, whom Louis Armstrong called the king of the cornet, or the site of the burned down Pythian Hall, one of the premier jazz venues in Algiers in the early 20th century.

MAP 9: Starting point: Algiers Point Ferry Terminal, algiershistoricalsociety. org/walking-tours.html; free

great blue heron at Barataria Preserve

Shops

SPECIALTY FOOD AND DRINK

Hong Kong Food Market

It's an Asian food store! It's a fish market! It's a rotisserie and bakery! It's a banh mi shop! It's a bubble tea and shaved-ice parlor! It has a surprising number of excellent whiskeys! Honestly, this place is heaven for food nerds; inspecting every sauce and noodle could take all day. This is where you find that ingredient you've never heard of, especially those called for in Vietnamese, Chinese, and Japanese cuisines. You can also do a surprising amount of cookware shopping here, and often you'll catch New Orleans chefs stalking the aisles. Note: There's a lot of olfactory output happening when you walk in. It's not bad, it's just strong.

MAP 9: 925 Behrman Hwy. #3, Gretna, 504/394-7075, hongkongmarketnola. com; 7:30am-9pm daily

International Market

On the lookout for Indian, Pakistani, and other South Asian treats or ingredients? This is the place to go if you need spices, rice, lentils, cookies/biscuits, chutneys, crunchy chickpeas, and so much more. The cavernous store can feel overwhelming, but it's worth it to stroll up and down each aisle to see what exotic delights await.

MAP 9: 3940 Barron St., Metairie, 504/888-8832; 9am-8pm Mon.-Sat., 11am-6pm Sun.

Hong Kong Food Market

Kho Bo Ngoc Quyen

Jerky and unusual candy make for a surprisingly excellent match at this odd spot that sells a variety of dried and sweet treats. It's in the same shopping center as Hong Kong Market, so that's another reason to hit this area. *Kho bo* is Vietnamese beef jerky—they carry 20 varieties here, with different flavors and levels of salty, spicy, sour, and sweet. You can also find pork floss, which has been dried to the consistency of cotton candy, along with dried and preserved seafood like abalone, cuttlefish, and stingray. The dried fruit selection is equally impressive, with dried sour plum, pickled *makok*, baby mango, and soursop. The candies come in flavors like ginger, tamarind, and coconut.

MAP 9: 925 Behrman Hwy., Gretna, 504/571-5051; 9am-8pm Mon.-Sat., 9am-7pm Sun.

CLOTHING AND ACCESSORIES

FeBe Clothing

Do some fashion seeking at this woman's boutique located along the run of independent shops on Metairie Road. With more than 50 brands of designer clothing and accessories, plus expert service, this is the place to try for a new look or pick up a couple of things to show off. Pro tip: Check out the store's sale loft upstairs.

MAP 9: 474 Metairie Rd., Metairie, 504/835-5250, febeclothing.com; 10am-6pm Tues.-Fri., 10am-5pm Sat. and Mon.

TOY STORES

Le Jouet

This children's toy, book, and bike shop has been in business since 1968. Check out the awesome toy selection (old school, new school, and educational) for all ages, along with play sets and other outdoor stuff like wagons and sandboxes. Gift wrapping is free all year round, and you just can't beat the feeling of joy like you're a kid again while shopping here.

MAP 9: 1700 Airline Dr., Metairie, 504/837-0533, lejouet.com; 9am-6pm Mon.-Sat.

FESTIVALS AND EVENTS

New Orleans is known for its festivals: 130 per year and growing. From the huge ones like Mardi Gras and Jazz Fest, to the new ones just popping up,

like the National Fried Chicken Fest, Top Taco, Fête des Fromages, and the Beignet Festival, there is at least one festival to attend just about any weekend of the year. Yes, even during the dog days of summer.

New Orleans locals and visitors alike love to eat, drink, be merry, parade, and listen to music, which is why the festival culture thrives down here. The city doesn't bat an eye when a new event is proposed. There's always something to celebrate here, no matter how tough life gets.

The festivals happen all over the city, from the French Quarter, to the Riverbend, to Mid-City, and even beyond the city limits. New Orleans's innate hospitality welcomes people from every background to celebrate.

a Mardi Gras Indian in costume

HIGHLIGHTS

⭐ **THE MOST WONDERFUL TIME OF THE YEAR: Mardi Gras** is the world's biggest free party, and it stretches from Three Kings Day to Ash Wednesday. There are many traditions around Mardi Gras, and New Orleans's identity is forever intertwined with it (page 274).

⭐ **THE BIG DADDY OF MUSIC FESTIVALS: Jazz Fest** has been around since 1970 and it's still going strong. There are eight days of music over two weeks, encompassing multiple genres (page 279).

⭐ **BEST SPOT TO SEE THE MARDI GRAS INDIANS:** Head to Central City on **Super Sunday** to celebrate with culture bearers, the Mardi Gras Indians, as they parade and perform (page 284).

⭐ **BEST REASON FOR A FOOD COMA: Hogs for the Cause** serves up meat, beer, a barbecue competition, and live music, raising funds to help families with children with cancer (page 284).

⭐ **BEST SHOWCASE OF A LOCAL INGREDIENT:** An ode to the fruit of summer, the **Creole Tomato Festival** is a simple but lovely celebration (page 287).

⭐ **BEST SPOT TO GET TO TWO-STEPPIN':** At the **Louisiana Cajun/ Zydeco Fest,** you've got a great opportunity to listen to the genre and maybe do some dancing (page 287).

⭐ **BEST MORNING RUN:** With Roller Derby girls wearing horned helmets and carrying inflatable bats, chasing runners in the street, the annual New Orleans **Running of the Bulls** provides some early morning motivation to get moving (page 288).

⭐ **BEST CELEBRATION OF A CULTURAL CULINARY ICON:** You can't go wrong at the **Tremé Creole Gumbo Festival,** where there's dozens of types of gumbo to sample and amazing local brass bands playing (page 294).

Mardi Gras floats are a creative and historic tradition.

✪ Mardi Gras

Few festivals exemplify the joyous spirit of New Orleans more than Mardi Gras (MAHR-dee grah), a French term meaning "Fat Tuesday." If you're a fan of colorful, exciting festivals, there's no better time to visit New Orleans than during Mardi Gras season, which usually falls in February or early March and lasts 2-3 weeks prior to Lent (from Epiphany to Ash Wednesday). Far from the salacious reputation it's garnered from the hordes of Bourbon Street revelers, Mardi Gras is (mostly) family-friendly, especially along the Uptown route.

Festivities include everything from colorful street masks and costumes to gala balls and events. But Mardi Gras's most famous parts are the free public parades sponsored by krewes and featuring colorful floats, marching bands, motorcycle squads, dancers, entertainers, and, sometimes, a royal court (the king, queen, maids, and dukes of a krewe). **Citywide:** mardigrasday.com; hours vary; free

PLANNING TIPS

Know when to go. Carnival season technically begins on January 6 (known as Twelfth Night, or the Feast of the Epiphany), but Mardi Gras Day itself shifts every

Marching bands are an important part of Mardi Gras parades.

season (February 16 in 2021, March 1 in 2022, February 21 in 2023, February 13 in 2024, and March 4 in 2025). Mardi Gras parades usually start about two weeks prior to Fat Tuesday. Although the run up to the big day has lots of great parades, many revelers venture to New Orleans for the weekend preceding the climactic day—from Nyx Wednesday or Muses Thursday through midnight on Mardi Gras.

Book a bed. Make reservations at least three months in advance. Note, too, that many hotels require a minimum stay of three nights (if not more) during Mardi Gras weekend, and costly special-event rates may apply. Although you'll find cheaper hotels in suburbs like Metairie and Kenner (near the airport), staying there will require renting a pricey car and enduring long commutes to reach the main festivities. You'll save time by staying in a more convenient neighborhood, such as in Uptown (the closer to St. Charles Avenue the better), the CBD/Warehouse District, or the French Quarter. If you must use Airbnb, be especially wary about any listings that seem too good to be true.

Strategize your transportation. During Mardi Gras, the French Quarter is closed to non-essential vehicular traffic. (Emergency vehicles and residents with proper ID are still allowed passage.) Hailing a cab can be difficult, so many visitors prefer getting around town via bus, streetcar, or foot. Some even opt to rent a bicycle (or bring their own); just don't forget to wear a helmet. Make sure you know ahead of time which roads will be closed and when. It's entirely possible to be trapped between the parades lining up and the parades starting, in what Uptown residents call "the box." Parking nearby will be a challenge, so plan for that.

Figure out where to set up. You can bring your own chairs, food, beverages, canopies, tarps, and other gear. Do not try to stake a claim ahead of time with those chairs by leaving them unattended, though. It's illegal (and locals think it's tacky). Don't worry too much about bathroom breaks. There are many port-a-potties, businesses, and enterprising entrepreneurs that provide toilets. At the latter two, expect to pay some cash for the privilege.

Use apps and social media. Utilize Facebook, Twitter, and other social networks to find last-minute hotel deals and Mardi Gras-adjacent events and meetups. During the parades, download one of the parade trackers from the local news teams (WWL, WDSU, and WWLTV). They offer updates on parade progress and report on all-too-frequent delays.

PARADES

The vast majority of Mardi Gras parades are on the Uptown route, making St. Charles Avenue the focal point. That's where locals set up in spots they've been using for years, on either the sidewalk or the median (locally known as neutral ground).

The parades consist of several factions. First, the floats, which can number anywhere between 14 and 41, depending on the size of the krewe, or organization, that's sponsoring the parade. Krewe members ride on the extravagantly decorated floats (which are pulled by tractors) centered around a theme.

ALL ON A MARDI GRAS DAY

Although Mardi Gras season is celebrated over a period of several weeks, the pinnacle of the celebration is Fat Tuesday itself. Different parts of the city celebrate in different ways. This itinerary will help you experience a variety of these traditions, starting at sunrise and heading straight through to the end of the party at midnight.

MORNING

If you're on the French Quarter/Tremé side of Canal Street, check out the North Side Skull and Bone Gang as they set off from the Backstreet Cultural Museum at 5am to rouse the neighborhood, going door to door with drums, dancing, and chanting. Then find a spot to watch Zulu roll through on Basin Street or Orleans Avenue.

the famous Krewe of Rex Boeuf Gras float

If you're on the other side of Canal, wake up early to get a good spot to watch both Zulu and Rex, which can be seen at any point on St. Charles Avenue between Jackson Street and Canal Street. Zulu kicks off at 8am and turns onto St. Charles by around 9:30am or so, and Rex will be right after that, kicking off at 10am.

Zulu is an African American krewe, started when Black folks weren't allowed to join other established krewes. The floats have a satirical African theme. Don't be

The second faction includes local high school and college marching bands, which is my favorite part. These kids practice all year long to play in several parades, marching on foot for almost five miles down the parade route, in all sorts of weather. Faction number three is the walking/dancing krewes. This includes local dance school students, and adults who participate in seemingly silly dance routines with punny or naughty names like The Camel Toe Lady Steppers, Disco Amigos, Pussyfooters, Rolling Elvi, 610 Stompers, or the Muff-o-Lottas. Faction number four is the horse riders.

There are several other types of groups that participate, but the most important are the flambeaux carriers, who light the way for the larger night parades. The bearers of these natural-gas-powered torches tend to be African American. The tradition has been ongoing since 1857. Keep a couple of dollar bills or quarters to tip the carriers that pass by, if you like.

There are several interesting parades that take place in or near the French Quarter. The satirical and adults-only Krewe du Vieux is one of the first parades of the season. Chewbacchus is a sci-fi-and-fantasy-themed parade that has dozens of sub-krewes with different themes. Barkus is a dog parade, and 'tit Rex (short for *petit*), which rolls before Chewbacchus, consists of carefully crafted miniature floats, which their makers pull along with strings.

shocked when you realize that everyone in the krewe is wearing blackface. It's a New Orleans Mardi Gras tradition that Zulu leadership are adamant about keeping as part of the krewe's culture. The coveted throw is a decorated coconut. Rex is an old school krewe with the classic "Boeuf Gras" float and the fatted cow as a symbol of the celebration's ancient roots. Rex throws some very pretty ceramic tokens on beads, but they're pretty stingy with them.

AFTERNOON

If you're still up for catching beads, check out the several truck parades. There are four krewes of post-Rex riders, and it's more laid-back than the previous parades. They have decorated floats and fun throws, and it's relatively relaxing. A lot of folks leave after Rex, so there's more room to spread out and more opportunities to catch stuff. It's a perfect activity on a nice day.

Another option is to get on your bike and head to the French Quarter for unrestrained chaos on Bourbon Street. A fun event is the Bourbon Street Awards, a world-famous drag queen contest. If you make it to the other side of the Quarter unscathed, the Marigny is filled with costumed revelers having unofficial mini-parades with homemade floats. It's like the French Quarter, but less chaotic. The St. Anne parade is an annual tradition. Folks in the Marigny participate and get into it. There's a real joy to the festivities.

EVENING

Mardi Gras revelry will last until midnight, officially. That's when the police shut it down, which is part of the tradition, because New Orleans otherwise never stops. There's a genial march of local cops on foot and on horse down Bourbon Street, encouraging revelers to go home. Some folks like to partake in the sacred boeuf gras with a steak dinner, some folks remember other Fat Tuesday traditions, like cooking pancakes, a custom in the United Kingdom. It's a day that starts early, so don't feel like you need to push through till the end.

In Mid-City, Endymion starts at City Park and heads downtown via Carrollton before ending at the Superdome. There are also parades to be found in outlying areas like Metairie, New Orleans East, and Slidell, and on the Westbank.

THROWS

From their floats, krewe members will throw beads, trinkets, toys, and other krewe-branded items. The throws have become more sophisticated and sought-after over the years.

Usually a krewe will have throws that reflect the theme of the parade. These can include doubloons, float-specific beads and medallions, plush toys, LED light-up items, plastic go-cups, and glass beads.

Here are a few fun signature throws: Zulu is the krewe that started the trend of coveted throws, with their decorated coconuts. The Muses ladies elaborately glitter and bedazzle shoes for their signature item, and Nyx does likewise with purses. Not to be outdone, Iris throws sunglasses, Femme Fatale decorates mirror compacts, Tucks decorates both toilet brushes and plungers, and Carrollton throws shrimp boots.

There's a certain etiquette around throws. Don't intercept them if they're meant for kids, and never pick beads up off the ground. Most importantly, it's neither necessary nor acceptable to flash to acquire throws.

KING CAKE

This confection is meant to be enjoyed only from January 6 (Three Kings Day, hence the name) through Mardi Gras. The traditional version is very simple: braided sweet dough, kind of like a cinnamon bun, topped with icing and sugar that's colored purple, gold, and green. Some have fillings, like fruit or cream. There are many variations on the filling (like goat cheese and apple, or chocolate), the dough (brioche or danish), and the decorations (different types of icing, or variations of the colored sugar.) There are also savory king cakes, but they don't really count.

The one thing all king cakes have in common is the baby—a plastic baby, or bean, or pig, or ceramic token—that's hidden in the cake. Whoever gets the piece with the baby is on the hook for bringing a king cake to the next gathering, like the parade route, the office, or a party.

HOW TO ENJOY WITH KIDS

Mardi Gras is easy to enjoy with kids. If you stay away from the adult-themed Krewe du Vieux, you'll be fine. There are some provocative political-satire floats sprinkled throughout the parades, but nothing too uncomfortable for kids. Sometimes, during some of the more popular nighttime parades (like Muses, an all-female krewe), adult parade-goers can get a little aggressive in their quest for coveted throws. Endymion, which rolls in Mid-City through the Tremé to the Central Business District, inspires lots of rowdy behavior; some spots are calmer than others. You can

Mardi Gras Indians are known for their elaborate costumes.

count on all the daytime parades to be more relaxed and kid-friendly.

Despite some of the challenges that nighttime parades pose with potentially inebriated or otherwise rowdy attendees, it would be a shame for kids to miss out on the amazing floats, like the Smokey Mary train or smoke-breathing Leviathan float in Orpheus or the themed floats of all the different krewes.

There's an unwritten rule among Mardi Gras veterans that you don't snatch a throw from a kid, but not everyone follows that. Along the route you'll see the pinnacle of New Orleans engineering, the parade ladder. It's a ladder (usually painted in purple, gold, and green) that has a box on top that families bring for their children to sit in. It gives kids a bit of a height advantage.

Jazz Fest

TOP EXPERIENCE

Established in 1970, this musical extravaganza, which takes place at the Fair Grounds Race Course, has grown to be nearly as popular as Mardi Gras. Held on two long weekends in late April and early May, this event, whose official name is the New Orleans Jazz & Heritage Festival, features music workshops, artisanal and culinary demonstrations, Native American powwow performances, arts-and-crafts vendors, an unbelievable array of food stalls, and numerous stages that buzz with jazz, blues, zydeco, rock, gospel, and folk musicians. Among the top acts who have performed at Jazz Fest are Diana Ross, Willie Nelson, and various members of the Marsalis and Neville clans.

The New Orleans Jazz & Heritage Foundation (1205 N. Rampart St., 504/558-6100 or 888/652-8751, www.jazzandheritage.org), the organization behind this popular festival, also sponsors smaller food-and-music events, all of which are free to attend—though

food and beverage costs always apply. Two of these events occur in the Tremé's Louis Armstrong Park: the Congo Square New World Rhythms Festival (late Mar.) and the Louisiana Cajun-Zydeco Festival (early June). The other two take place in the CBD's Lafayette Square: The Crescent City Blues and BBQ Festival (mid-Oct.) and the Tremé Creole Gumbo Festival (mid-Nov.).

Tremé and Fairgrounds: Fair Grounds Race Course & Slots, 1751 Gentilly Blvd., 504/410-4100, nojazzfest.com; hours vary; $70-85 adults, $5 children 2-10, children under 2 free, food and beverage costs also apply

PLANNING TIPS

Pick a weekend. Unless you can afford a 10-day trip to New Orleans, you'll probably need to choose one of the two festival weekends: the first, which spans the last Thursday-Sunday in April, or the second, which covers the first Thursday-Sunday in May. The complete, eight-day music schedule is usually posted online ahead of time, or you can access the free mobile app. Of course, by the time the detailed schedules are uploaded, it might be too late to book a room, so keep an eye out for information regarding headliners, which is usually leaked to the public well in advance of the finalized schedule.

Consider a pass. If you plan to stay for an entire weekend, consider purchasing one of the limited passes. The **Krewe of Jazz Fest VIP Pass** ($750 first weekend, $1,100 second weekend) enables you to watch all the action at the Acura Stage from an exclusive area, with pedestrian re-entry privileges and access to upscale restroom facilities, a private beverage concession area, and, if available, reserved parking. The **Grand Marshal VIP Pass** ($1,350 first weekend, $2,000 second

Jazz Fest

weekend) offers everything that the Krewe of Jazz pass includes as well as exclusive, upfront access to the other two main stages, the Gentilly Stage and the Congo Square Stage. The **Big Chief VIP Experience** ($1,500 first weekend, $2,000 second weekend) includes everything that the other two passes offer, plus access to a private, air-conditioned VIP Hospitality Lounge and private

a colorful sea of music fans at Jazz Fest

viewing areas near the Jazz and Blues Tents.

Secure your hotel. Advance hotel reservations are highly recommended. You can expect minimum-stay requirements, special-event rates, and last-minute deals, but be aware of potential scams. While concerts and other activities occur throughout New Orleans during Jazz Fest, the main event takes place at the Fair Grounds Race Course, meaning you might prefer staying in Mid-City. Otherwise, you can easily use public transportation from inns and hotels in the Marigny, French Quarter, CBD, Garden District, and other Uptown neighborhoods.

Plan for heat or rain. It's usually hot and humid during Jazz Fest, but rain is always an unpredictable factor (there's almost always at least one day with a torrential downpour). Given the ever-present dirt and hay, the Fair Grounds can quickly become muddy. Pack sunscreen, sunglasses, a hat, a small umbrella, a poncho, a towel, and clothes that you don't mind getting soiled. Some tall mud/rain/shrimp boots would be a boon if it's especially muddy.

Stake your claim. Crowds assemble early each day, especially for perennial favorites and major headliners, who usually play in the late afternoon and early evening. If seeing a certain band matters to you, claim your spot in the morning, preferably before the first musical act begins.

Taste the food. Outside food and beverages are not allowed, so take advantage of the regional cuisine, water, soda, alcohol, strawberry lemonade, and other beverages for sale throughout the festival grounds. Local folks look forward to Jazz Fest culinary offerings all year. You'll encounter a slew of delicious (if pricey) dishes, from meat pies and turkey legs to jambalaya and crawfish bread.

Don't forget souvenirs. Beyond music, exhibits, and demonstrations, Jazz Fest features three separate arts-and-crafts areas—the Congo Square African Marketplace, the Louisiana Marketplace, and Heritage Square (contemporary crafts)—plus various souvenir tents selling commemorative posters, T-shirts, and the like. Bring enough money to purchase a few souvenirs, ranging from colorful hats to glass jewelry to Acadian furniture. While many of these items are relatively affordable, some are far from cheap.

French Quarter Fest

Begun in 1984 to support local musicians, the four-day French Quarter Fest, which typically occurs in early or mid-April, has since evolved into Louisiana's largest free music event. The roughly 20 outdoor stages—from the Old U.S. Mint to Jackson Square to Woldenberg Park—host local and regional jazz, gospel, funk, zydeco, classical, bluegrass, folk, and blues acts, so you likely won't see mega-stars like Sting here (unless he's one of the attendees). Besides live music, you'll also find plenty of food for sale, including jambalaya, boiled crawfish, and snowballs.

French Quarter: Various locations, 504/522-5730 or 800/673-5725, fqfi. org/frenchquarterfest; hours vary; free, though food and beverage costs apply

PLANNING TIPS

Reserve a room. Advance hotel reservations are highly recommended, and you can expect minimum-stay requirements (and higher rates) for most accommodations. Keep an eye out for last-minute deals on social media networks and beware of too-good-to-be-true situations with unlicensed inns and room rentals. While you'll save money by staying in the suburbs, you'll likely lose time trying to commute to the French Quarter (where the entirety of French Quarter Fest takes place), especially since there is usually limited parking. Save time by either staying in the French Quarter or finding a place in the nearby Faubourg Marigny or near the streetcar lines

in the CBD, the Garden District, Uptown, and Mid-City.

Peruse the schedule. The music schedule for the four-day event is usually posted online well in advance of the festival weekend. There's also a free mobile app available, so if you fancy a certain band, you can plan your festival itinerary ahead of time.

Prepare for any weather. Springtime in New Orleans can be blazing hot one day and cool and rainy the next. Anticipate all conditions, and pack sunscreen, a hat and sunglasses, and maybe even a small umbrella. Storms sometimes cancel or delay musical performances, so be prepared for that as well.

Plan your transport. You can easily find a cab at the airport, but once in town, hailing one can be difficult. Unless you're staying in the French Quarter, you may have to rely on buses, streetcars, bikes, or your feet to reach the various stages.

Claim your spot. Crowds assemble early each day, especially for perennial favorites like the Rebirth Brass Band or highly anticipated headliners, who usually play in the late afternoon and early evening. If being close to a particular stage matters to you, stake your claim in the morning, preferably before the first musical act begins. I recommend wandering among the various stages, from one end of the Quarter to the other, listening to a variety of music. You might, after all, discover a new favorite singer or band.

Sample the cuisine. Selling food and beverages through assorted vendors—most of whom represent area bars and restaurants—is one way that the French Quarter Fest has remained a free event. Bringing your own supplies isn't allowed in fenced areas like Jackson Square and the Old U.S. Mint, and you'll get more out of the festival experience if you sample some of the goodies on offer, from po'boys and boiled crawfish to Plum Street snowballs. Be advised, though: Food costs can add up quickly. In general, vendors set up in Jackson Square, near the Old U.S. Mint, and throughout Woldenberg Park.

Other Festivals and Events

JANUARY
Allstate Sugar Bowl

The Mercedes-Benz Superdome is the site of one of the most beloved college football games, the Allstate Sugar Bowl. Typically, it's played in early January between two of the nation's top collegiate teams. In addition to the Sugar Bowl, there's usually the Allstate Fan Fest, which is a free music event that takes place in the parking lot beside Jax Brewery; past performers have included Blues Traveler, the Gin Blossoms, and Trombone Shorty. It's nearly impossible to find a hotel room in New Orleans when this event comes to town, so plan well ahead if you wish to attend.

CBD and Warehouse/Arts District: Mercedes-Benz Superdome, 1500 Sugar Bowl Dr., 504/828-2440, allstatesugarbowl.org; early Jan.; costs vary

MARCH-APRIL
St. Patrick's Day

New Orleans has a large contingent of Irish Americans and St. Patrick's Day is a significant holiday here. Irish establishments throughout the city—including The Kerry Irish Pub in the French Quarter—hold lively parties on St. Paddy's Day (traditionally Mar. 17). Molly's at the Market hosts its own music-filled St. Patrick's Day Parade within a week of the actual holiday, but the city's biggest annual parade by far usually rolls down Magazine Street and St. Charles Avenue, with large Mardi Gras-style floats, oodles of marchers, and plenty of green beads and doubloons. Don't be surprised to see heads of cabbage and other vegetables being thrown to spectators from the floats.

Citywide: Mar. 17, hours vary; free

St. Joseph's Day

Introduced to New Orleans during the 19th century by its many Sicilian immigrants, St. Joseph's Day is still celebrated with great ardor in the city's Italian American community. The observance of this feast on March 19 traces back to the Middle Ages, when Catholics built altars to St. Joseph, who they believed had answered their prayers and delivered them from famine. Modern participants continue to celebrate by constructing elaborate and riotously colorful altars in their homes and churches. Besides a public parade in the French Quarter, smaller celebrations take place in private homes; signs welcome friends and strangers alike to view family altars and enjoy cakes and breads. The Italian holiday has also become significant for the city's Mardi Gras Indians, an African American troupe of Carnival revelers who usually host a vibrant parade on Super Sunday, the Sunday preceding or following St. Joseph's Day.

French Quarter: Various locations, mardigrasneworleans.com/ supersunday.html; Mar. 19, hours vary; free

✪ Super Sunday

The Mardi Gras Indians are an important tradition in the African American community of New Orleans—generations of men and women have hand-stitched elaborate suits and they go out in groups (called tribes) to interact with each other through song and dance. There are three important times for the Mardi Gras Indians: on Mardi Gras Day, usually in the afternoon after the main parades; St. Joseph's Day, on March 19; and Super Sunday, on the third Sunday in March (which usually puts it pretty close to St. Joseph's Day). Super Sunday is the public parade and celebration of this unique group of marchers, who work on their costumes—fitted with enormous headdresses that have intricate beadwork and feathers—all year round. The history of why these different groups

confront each other in the street for a ritualized dance-off is shrouded in mystery, but African American families have passed the tradition down through generations. Other Super Sunday parades occur around town throughout the spring—in the French Quarter, in Bayou St. John near the Tremé, and on the Westbank—but this is the original one that started over 50 years ago and has been hard fought to achieve legitimacy with the city's government and police.

Central City and Broadmoor: A.L. Davis Park, 2600 Lasalle St., noon on the third Sun. of Mar.; free

✪ Hogs for the Cause

Hogs for the Cause, a fundraiser in late March/early April to support children with brain cancer and their families, started small and grew into something enormous. Held at the UNO Lakefront Arena in Gentilly, the pork-centric food festival and barbecue competition is a weekend long event with live music and parties. Ninety teams of pork enthusiasts (with pun-tastic pork names like Aporkalypse Now, Gettin' Piggy With It, Deuce Pigalow Pork Gigolo, and Sweet Swine O Mine) enter the event and competition. The teams are judged on booth design and fundraising success in addition to the actual grilled meat. It makes for an amazing weekend of food, fun, and music, all for a good cause. Everyone's having a great time at Hogs (there are often costumes involved, along with unusual pork preparations), making it one of the best events in New Orleans.

Greater New Orleans: UNO Lakefront Arena, 6801 Franklin Ave., hogsforthecause.org; late Mar./early Apr.; single-day tickets from $30, VIP ticket passes $125-200

Tennessee Williams Literary Festival

Devotees of the city's most famous literary luminary rush to the Big Easy in late March or early April to attend the Tennessee Williams/ New Orleans Literary Festival. For three decades, this event has celebrated the playwright who gave us such iconographic works as *A Streetcar Named Desire* and *The Glass Menagerie.* The five-day gathering is replete with writing classes helmed by experts, celebrity interviews, panel discussions, stagings of Williams's plays, fiction and poetry readings, and the endlessly entertaining Stanley and Stella Shouting Contest. Speakers, instructors, and attendees have included George Plimpton, Dorothy Allison, and Piper Laurie.

French Quarter: Various locations, 504/581-1144 or 800/990-3378, tennesseewilliams.net; late Mar./early Apr.; costs vary

New Orleans Wine and Food Experience (NOWFE)

Local and visiting foodies and wine connoisseurs are in luck every year in mid-April when the New Orleans Wine & Food Experience (NOWFE) comes around. For more than two decades, this mouthwatering event has benefited local nonprofit organizations while showcasing hundreds of national and international wines from more than 100 wineries, along with food from about 75 of the city's top restaurants, including top names like Brennan's and Restaurant R'Evolution. Wine dinners, the Royal Street Stroll (during which a section of the street is closed off and filled with wine and food vendors, along with participating local galleries), and curated experiences round out the multi-day event.

Citywide: 504/934-1474, nowfe.com; mid-Apr.; costs vary

Crescent City Classic

Since 1979, the Crescent City Classic (now known as the Allstate Sugar Bowl Crescent City Classic), one of the nation's largest 10K road races, has been held in New Orleans every March or April, usually on the Saturday of Easter weekend. Roughly 20,000 people from around the globe participate. From its start at the Mercedes-Benz Superdome, the course runs through the French Quarter, then heads up Esplanade Avenue to culminate in City Park. A rollicking post-race festival that's a celebration of local music and cuisine, is free for participants; all other attendees must pay a fee ($15 pp in advance, $20 on-site). The pre-race, two-day health and fitness expo is free for everyone.

Various locations: Mercedes-Benz Superdome to City Park, 504/861-8686, ccc10k.com; Sat. of Easter weekend; costs vary by event

EASTER
Chris Owens Easter Parade

Bourbon Street's reigning matriarch, Chris Owens, has been the Grand Duchess of this high-camp, so-very-NOLA parade for almost 40 years now. The colorful floats throwing beads and Easter trinkets, the marching bands, and the anticipation of seeing what Chris Owens will be wearing makes this a very enjoyable Easter Sunday tradition. It kicks off at the corner of St. Louis and Royal Streets at 1pm.

French Quarter: St. Louis St. and Royal St., frenchquartereasterparade.com; 1pm Easter Sun.; free

City Park Egg Scramble

Prior to Easter Sunday, there are several Easter egg hunts in City Park. The City Park Egg Scramble is a weekend affair, the week before Easter, that provides tens of thousands of eggs for kids to find, along with the opportunity to meet the Easter Bunny and other fun stuff. There's another egg hunt nearby, in the Sydney and Walda Besthoff Sculpture Garden.

Mid-City: City Park, Carousel Gardens Amusement Park and Storyland, 1 Palm Dr., neworleanscitypark.com; 9am-noon Sat.-Sun. before Easter; $10

Easter Sunday Mass at St. Augustine Catholic Church

Obviously, all New Orleans churches will be holding Easter services throughout Holy Week, but if you're interested in a truly joyful and soulful Easter Sunday service, check out the two-hour long Mass that includes one of the best gospel choirs in the city.

Tremé and Fairgrounds: St. Augustine Catholic Church, 1210 Governor Nicholls St., 504/525-5934, staugchurch.org; 10am-noon Easter Sun.; free

Gay Easter Parade

A family-friendly parade for all, the 20-plus-year-old Gay Easter Parade brings the fabulousness of the local LGBTQ community together for the holiday. It starts off at Louis Armstrong Park, at 4:30pm, heads up and down Bourbon and Royal Streets, and ends up near the start, at GrandPre's, a neighborhood gay bar on North Rampart.

French Quarter: Louis Armstrong Park, 901 Rampart St., gayeasterparade. com; 4:30pm Easter Sun.

Historic French Quarter Easter Parade

Easter is a big deal in New Orleans, since it's a high Catholic holiday (Catholicism is the historically dominant religion of the city). Plus, locals like to celebrate just about anything in a splashy fashion. This is the most traditional of all the Easter parades, as well as the first of three that occur on Easter Sunday (they get less formal and more raucous as the day wears on). Leaving from historic Antoine's Restaurant at 9:45am, this parade goes on a short route to get to St. Louis Cathedral in time for 11am Mass. Afterward, the ladies from this parade promenade in Jackson Square, distributing candy before heading back to Antoine's for lunch.

French Quarter: Antoine's Restaurant, 713 St. Louis St.; 9:45am Easter Sun.; free

MAY-JUNE
Bayou Boogaloo

For roughly a decade, the Positive Vibrations Foundation has presented this free, spirited celebration of local culture along the sunny western bank of Bayou St. John, between Dumaine and Lafitte Streets. Typically occurring in mid-May, the three-day event presents a slew of live music, which, in the past, has included local performers like Anders Osborne, Little Freddy King, and Amanda Shaw. As with other Big Easy festivals, you can expect an assortment of arts and crafts for sale, from stained glass to hand-crafted jewelry, as well as a cornucopia of local food vendors, like Blue Oak BBQ, Boucherie, and Clesi's Restaurant & Catering.

Mid-City: 500 N. Jefferson Davis Pkwy., thebayouboogaloo.com; mid-May; $10 requested donation, food and craft costs apply

New Orleans Greek Festival

Alongside Bayou St. John, and within a quick drive of both Lake Pontchartrain and City Park, stands the impressive Holy Trinity Cathedral, which has hosted this lively, well-attended festival every Memorial Day weekend since the mid-1970s. Like any self-respecting Hellenic bash, this one presents live Greek music, Greek-style dancing, and, naturally, traditional Greek cuisine, from souvlaki to baklava. The festival also features a playground, a 5K race, and tours of the cathedral.

Greater New Orleans: Holy Trinity Greek Orthodox Cathedral, 1200 Robert E. Lee Blvd., 504/282-0259, greekfestnola.com; Memorial Day weekend; $8 adults, children under 12 free, food costs also apply

✪ Creole Tomato Festival

The French Market District is home to the Creole Tomato Festival, which has celebrated one of the state's most popular fruits for roughly three decades. During the free, two-day event, which usually takes place during the second weekend of June,

you'll encounter live concerts, cooking demonstrations, culinary discussions, eating contests, tempting food booths, and children's activities. You can also purchase fresh produce, including Creole tomatoes, at the on-site farmers market.

French Quarter: French Market and the Old U.S. Mint, 504/522-2621, frenchmarket.org; 2nd weekend June; free, though food costs apply

Creole Tomato Festival

✪ Louisiana Cajun/ Zydeco Festival

Besides the world-famous Jazz Fest, the New Orleans Jazz & Heritage Foundation also presents the Louisiana Cajun-Zydeco Festival, a free, two-day music event that typically occurs during the first weekend of June. Featuring live music from some of Louisiana's best Cajun and zydeco performers, such as the Lost Bayou Ramblers and Dwayne Dopsie and the Zydeco Hellraisers, this celebration also offers regional cuisine, kid-friendly diversions, and a sizable arts-and-crafts fair.

Tremé and Fairgrounds: Louis Armstrong Park, 901 Rampart St., 504/558-6100, jazzandheritage.org; 1st weekend in June; free, though food costs apply

New Orleans Oyster Festival

This two-day festival held the first weekend of June aims to shatter the myth that oysters should only be eaten in months ending in the letter "r." It also supports coastal restoration and other oyster sustainability initiatives, so get on out there and eat some ersters—you can get 'em raw on the half shell, chargrilled, or dozens of other ways from participating local restaurants. There are plenty of po'boy variations, of course, as well as dishes like oyster linguini bordelaise, oyster tacos, and oyster and artichoke soup. There are also other Gulf seafood favorites to choose from, an oyster shucking competition, local music, and oyster-themed crafts to peruse.

French Quarter: Woldenberg Park, nolaoysterfest.org; first weekend of June; free, though food costs apply

JULY-AUGUST

Essence Fest

In early July, visitors typically descend upon New Orleans for the annual Essence Festival, a four-day celebration of African American music and culture. Besides DJ parties at the Sugar Mill, the main events of this much-anticipated festival consist of concerts and comedy shows at the Mercedes-Benz Superdome and empowerment presentations at the Ernest N. Morial Convention Center. Recent headliners have included Missy Elliot, Mary J. Blige, and Maze featuring Frankie Beverly.

CBD and Warehouse/Arts District: Various locations, essence.com/festival; early July; costs vary

Tales of the Cocktail

Given that the Big Easy is known as a party town, it's only apt that it would be home to the annual Tales of the Cocktail. Started in 2003 and usually occurring in mid- to late July, this five-day event lures a slew of mixologists, authors, bartenders, chefs, and cocktail enthusiasts with its impressive lineup of seminars, dinners, competitions, and tasting rooms. Activities take place in a variety of locations, from the French Quarter's historic Hotel Monteleone to the Harrah's casino in the CBD.

Citywide: 504/948-0511, talesofthecocktail.com; mid-late July; costs vary

✪ Running of the Bulls

Instead of being chased by bulls, participants of the New Orleanian version of the Running of the Bulls flee from plastic bat-wielding, horned helmet-wearing Roller Derby girls. Registered attendees begin to assemble at 6:30am on a sweaty summer morning in mid-July. The short run through the Warehouse District begins at 8am. Afterward, there's a big party with food, drinks, live music, and general merriment. It's a really fun Euro-New Orleans event, combining an

Essence Fest

age-old Spanish tradition with New Orleans-style flavor, including costumes and booze. All proceeds support local non-profits.

CBD and Warehouse/Arts District: The Sugar Mill, 1021 Convention Center Blvd., nolabulls.com; mid-July; $30-95 event participation, free to watch

Hancock Whitney White Linen Night

At this evening block party held at the beginning of August, attendees dress up in white linen and gallery hop in the Arts District along Julia Street. As you stop to admire the art in each gallery (and enjoy the air-conditioning), you can also buy food and drinks from the vendors lining the street. White Linen Night has been the most popular summer event in the city since 1994. If you're still around, hang on to your sweaty outfit for Dirty Linen Night, held the following weekend on Royal Street, at those galleries.

CBD and Warehouse/Arts District: Julia St. between S. Peters and Carondelet, cacwhitelinennight.com; early Aug.; free, though food costs apply

Satchmo SummerFest

New Orleans celebrates the legacy of one of its most famous sons in early August with Satchmo SummerFest, a popular, three-day event that's organized by the same folks behind the equally popular French Quarter Festival. This festival, which mainly takes place on the well-manicured grounds of the Old U.S. Mint, includes live music by brass, swing, and early-jazz bands, plus free dance lessons and an assortment of local cuisine to purchase. At other locations throughout the Quarter, you can experience seminars and exhibits about Louis "Satchmo" Armstrong and his era. During the festival, make time for the special jazz Mass at the St. Augustine Catholic Church, followed by a traditional second-line parade.

French Quarter: The Old U.S. Mint, 400 Esplanade Ave., 504/522-5730 or 800/673-5725, fqfi.org; early Aug.; $5 adults, children under 13 free, food and seminar costs apply

Satchmo SummerFest is a bright spot of fun in the summer heat.

SEPTEMBER

New Orleans Burlesque Festival

In a city known as the birthplace of jazz, where a legal red-light district once thrived, and which once had the largest concentration of burlesque clubs in the country, it's no surprise that burlesque shows are once again popular. In mid-September, an entire four-day event dedicated to this sexy, glamorous, and comedic art descends upon the city. Founded in 2009, the annual New Orleans Burlesque Festival features parties and performances in various locations, plus the main event: a competition in which the world's finest burlesque dancers vie for the Queen of Burlesque title. Indeed, a sight worth seeing.

Various locations: 504/975-7425, neworleansburlesquefest.com; mid-Sept.; costs vary

NOLA On Tap

Since 2009, this beer festival (generally held the third Saturday of September) has evolved into the region's largest beer event. All proceeds from the dog-friendly all-day affair in City Park go to the Louisiana SPCA. There are plenty of puppies to pet and admire while drinking beer from more than 400 local, regional, and national breweries, as well as a robust homebrew section. There's even a certified homebrew competition. The VIP pass ($30) offers early entry and access to a VIP tent with shade and special beers. Bands like The Breton Sound, Flow Tribe, and Johnny Sketch and the Dirty Notes play all day.

Mid-City: City Park Festival Grounds, Friederichs Dr., nolaontap.org; third Sat. of Sept.; $5, plus drink tickets

Southern Decadence

Every Labor Day weekend, the French Quarter and the Faubourg Marigny are flooded with eager participants and onlookers of Southern Decadence, an annual Mardi Gras–like festival that's been celebrating the city's gay lifestyle, music, and culture since 1972. Held at various gay-friendly venues, the six-day event includes dance and pool

Southern Decadence

parties, beefcake contests, singles' mixers, drag shows, and a leather-gear block party. It's one of the wildest and most popular LGTBQ celebrations in the country.

French Quarter and Faubourg Marigny: Various locations, southerndecadence.com; Labor Day weekend; costs vary

OCTOBER
Crescent City Blues & BBQ Festival

The Crescent City Blues and BBQ Festival brings together two of my favorite things: Southern-style soul and blues music and delicious, finger-lickin' barbecue. Head to the CBD's picturesque Lafayette Square for the three-day, mid-October event, where you can savor a pulled-pork sandwich while grooving to the likes of Tab Benoit, Marcia Ball, and Uncle Nephew. This often-crowded festival features two stages, roughly a dozen food vendors, a regional crafts fair, an Abita-sponsored sports bar, and secured bike parking.

CBD and Warehouse/Arts District: Lafayette Square, 540 St. Charles Ave., 504/558-6100, jazzandheritage.org; mid-Oct.; free, though food costs apply

Gretna Heritage Festival

In early October, thousands of revelers cross the Mississippi for Gretna's Heritage Festival, a three-day event presenting live performances by local and international jazz, country, rock, blues, soul, Latino, and Cajun musicians on six different stages. Previous performers have included Cowboy Mouth, the Iguanas, and Amanda Shaw & the Cute Guys. In addition to events at the downtown German Heritage Center, this family-friendly festival features a German beer garden, an Italian village, carnival-style rides and games, and a multiethnic food court. Tickets are usually cheaper online; if you plan to stay the whole weekend, consider purchasing the $60 weekend pass or the $450 VIP Package.

Greater New Orleans: Downtown Gretna, 504/361-7748, gretnafest.com; early Oct.; $25-30 pp, free 12 and under

New Orleans Film Festival

Established in 1989, the nonprofit New Orleans Film Society (NOFS) presents several annual events favored by local cinephiles, and the pinnacle of NOFS programming is the New Orleans Film Festival (NOFF), a popular mid-October event that has honored independent cinema for more than two decades. The weeklong event usually takes place in multiple venues throughout the city, including the Prytania Theatre and the Contemporary Arts Center.

Various locations: 504/309-6633, neworleansfilmsociety.org; mid-Oct.; costs vary

Oktoberfest

Sure, New Orleans loves anything that encourages drinking beer; but there's actually a significant German immigrant population here. Every fall people celebrate this heritage at events all over the city. The big kahuna of Oktoberfest parties is at the Deutsches Haus, home of the New Orleans German heritage appreciation society, along Bayou St. John across from City Park. Members of Deutsches Haus showcase German culture during the most popular German tradition of the year, and they do it right with authentic food, beer, dancing, and music.

Tremé and Fairgrounds: Deutsches Haus, 1500 Moss St., 504/522-8014, oktoberfestnola.com; 1st three weekends in Oct., 4pm-11pm Fri., 1pm-11pm Sat.; $5, though food and drink costs apply, children under 13 free

Tremé Fall Festival

This street festival is held every year in early October to raise funds for maintaining St. Augustine Catholic Church, as well as other community projects. Neighborhood restaurants are represented with local food available for purchase, and a dozen or so arts and craft vendors are always in attendance. There's tons of live music along with kids' drumming circles and appearances by Mardi Gras Indians and other dance groups and social aid and pleasure clubs. It's the perfect way to immerse yourself in this historic New Orleans neighborhood and feel like a part of the community.

Tremé and Fairgrounds: St. Augustine Catholic Church, 1210 Gov. Nicholls St., no phone, hfta.org; early Oct.; free, though food costs apply

HALLOWEEN IN THE CRESCENT CITY

Halloween decorations with a New Orleans spin

New Orleans is a wildly popular place for All Hallows' Eve. People venture here to visit the many voodoo shops and cemeteries, take a haunted walking tour of the French Quarter and mingle with hordes of costumed revelers along Bourbon and Frenchmen Streets.

HAUNTED HOUSES
- Locals and visitors alike flock to attractions like The Mortuary Haunted House (themortuary.net), set inside a former mortuary that's supposedly haunted.

THEMED BALLS AND GALAS
- New Orleans is home to two annual vampire-themed balls: the New Orleans Vampire Ball, sponsored by Anne Rice's Vampire Lestat Fan Club (arvlfc.com), and the Endless Night Vampire Ball (endlessnight.com).

Voodoo Music + Arts Experience

Halloween weekend is usually a busy time of year in New Orleans. Besides vampire balls and impromptu parades, the city has long been host to the three-day Voodoo Music + Arts Experience, a boisterous City Park event that features art installations as well as live musical performances. Past performers have ranged dramatically from Soundgarden and Marilyn Manson to Janelle Monae and Dr. John. Tickets are offered as general admission or Loa VIP, the latter of which includes express entrance onto the festival grounds, free massages and hot shaves, food and drink specials, full bar services, and exclusive access to reserved viewing areas, among other amenities. Though tickets might be available on-site, be prepared for sold-out crowds. For ticketing questions, contact Elevate (877/569-7767). Mid-City: City Park, 1 Palm Dr., worshipthemusic.com; Halloween weekend; from $125 pp for weekend, children under 10 free

NOVEMBER
Boudin, Bourbon & Beer
These three comestibles make life worth living. The Emeril Lagasse

- For less bloodthirsty revelry, purchase a ticket to the New Orleans Witches' Ball, hosted by the New Orleans Black Hat Society (nobhs.org),

SPOOKY TOURS

- Vampire tours are available through Haunted History Tours (hauntedhistory-tours.com) and Bloody Mary's New Orleans Tours (bloodymarystours.com).
- Take a walking ghost tour through Historic New Orleans Tours (tournewor-leans.com) or Spirit Tours New Orleans (neworleanstours.net).

LGBTQ-FRIENDLY EVENTS

- Simply known as Halloween in New Orleans (gayhalloween.com), this weekend-long bash has evolved into one of the biggest LGBTQ parties in the country. If you're looking for well-dressed drag queens, this is the time to visit the Big Easy.

FAMILY-FRIENDLY EVENTS

- New Orleans hosts family-friendly events like Audubon Zoo's Boo at the Zoo (auduboninstitute.org/boo-zoo), which usually occurs during the last two weekends of October and features trick-or-treat fun, a ghost train, and a haunted house.
- On Halloween itself, Molly's at the Market presents Jim Monaghan's Halloween Parade (mollysatthemarket.net/halloween), a spirited procession through the French Quarter.
- The Krewe of Boo! (kreweofboo.com) is the city's official Halloween parade, typically entailing a downtown procession of colorful, mildly scary floats created by Kern Studios.

RELATED HOLIDAYS

- New Orleans is predominantly Catholic, which means that All Saints' Day (Nov. 1) and All Souls' Day (Nov. 2) are fairly important holidays—a time when many residents make a point of visiting their loved ones at cemeteries.
- Lots of locals celebrate the Mexican holiday of Día de los Muertos by dressing in black, painting skulls on their faces, and congregating in front of the St. Louis Cathedral—truly a sight to behold.

Foundation has been putting on this stellar lineup of sausage, booze, and music since 2011; it's a favorite of chefs, foodies, and bourbon aficionados. The early November event challenges New Orleans chefs to create and execute a creative boudin dish, like boudin and collard green tamales or duck boudin rangoon. Although boudin is the name of the game, it's not just boudin that's served—sweets and vegetarian dishes are also available, along with bourbon cocktails and Abita beers. Bands like the Honey Island Swamp Band and Sweet Crude play through the night. The 610 Stompers all-male

dance club also usually strut their stuff at some point.

CBD and Warehouse/Arts District: Champion Square, Lasalle St., boudinbourbonandbeer.com; early Nov.; tickets $135-150

Oak Street Po-Boy Festival

Though relatively new on the Big Easy's foodie scene, the Oak Street Po-Boy Festival has quickly become a much-anticipated event every fall. For one day in late November, residents and out-of-towners converge at the intersection of Oak Street and South Carrollton Avenue in Uptown's Riverbend area for the mouthwatering event. Besides listening to a ton of live music, attendees can peruse arts and crafts, learn about the history of the po'boy, and, of course, sample a variety of local cuisine from more than 30 restaurants. You'll have the chance to taste an assortment of po'boys, including variations (both traditional and creative) on BBQ shrimp, roast beef, sausage, and many others.

Oak Street Po-Boy Festival

Uptown: Oak St. and S. Carrollton Ave., poboyfest.com; late Nov.; free, though food costs apply

✪ Tremé Creole Gumbo Festival

Combining gumbo and brass-band music, this free mid-November festival in Louis Armstrong Park is one of the best events in the city. The array of gumbo includes dark roux chicken and sausage, Creole filé, and seafood, along with vegan and gluten-free versions of the iconic dish. Other comfort Creole dishes like red beans, *yakamein,* and fried fish plates ensure there's something for everyone (every booth has at least one vegetarian/vegan option). Enjoy music from brass bands like Hot 8, Rebirth, and the Tremé Brass Band, and check out the gumbo cooking demos from local experts.

Tremé and Fairgrounds: Louis Armstrong Park, 901 Rampart St., 504/558-6100, tremegumbofest.com; mid-Nov.; free, though food costs apply

THANKSGIVING
Bayou Classic Weekend

Thanksgiving weekend is the Bayou Classic, a college football game between two HBCU (historically black college/university) rival teams from Louisiana: Southern University and Grambling State. The Friday before the game is the Greek Show, where sororities and fraternities show off their moves with a dance and chant competition, and the Battle of the Bands, where the marching bands from each school try to outperform each other. On Saturday, before the 4pm kickoff, the Bayou Classic Parade rolls starting at 9am from Elysian Fields Avenue down North Peters Street to Canal Street, wending its way through the CBD to City Hall. Great marching-band music is guaranteed, along with float riders tossing commemorative beads. And then there's the game at the Superdome, with a spot for fans to watch for free in the adjoining Champions Square.

CBD and Warehouse/Arts District: Mercedes-Benz Superdome, 1500 Sugar Bowl Dr., 504/827-1892, mybayouclassic. com; Thanksgiving weekend; costs vary by event

Fair Grounds Race Course Opening Day

Behold the lesser-known event of the Fair Grounds Race Course. The opening day of racing, which coincides with Thanksgiving Day, is a great celebration of equestrian shenanigans, booze, gambling, haberdashery, and gigantic hats.

CHRISTMAS NEW ORLEANS STYLE

Christmas season decorations

Christmastime is simply huge in New Orleans, observed with great fanfare as befits a city that loves to have fun and clings dearly to long-held traditions. Known as "Christmas New Orleans Style," the celebration entails a variety of events and activities throughout the month of December. Besides City Park's dazzling Celebration in the Oaks, there are jazz, gospel, and choral concerts held at St. Louis Cathedral and a variety of clubs, including Preservation Hall. In the period leading up to Christmas Day, New Orleans celebrates in typical style with a holiday parade hosted by the Krewe of Jingle. On Christmas Eve, more than 150 bonfires light up at precisely 7pm to guide Papa Noel through the St. John the Baptist and St. James parishes of Cajun Country. It's a centuries-old tradition.

Jackson Square plays host to public Christmas caroling, usually a free event that occurs on the Sunday prior to Christmas. Historic buildings throughout the French Quarter and Garden District are gussied up with Christmas lights and decorations. Revelers can enjoy a variety of seasonal walking tours, including the Candlelight Tour of Historic Homes and Landmarks, held in mid-December and often including such attractions as the Beauregard-Keyes House, the Old Ursuline Convent, the 1850 House, the Gallier Historic House, and The Historic New Orleans Collection.

Beyond the moderate weather, Hanukkah celebrations, and New Year's Eve fireworks extravaganza, December is also an excellent time for foodies. After all, this is the season of Réveillon, an ancient Creole and Catholic celebratory feast dating to the 1830s. Although it was originally held on Christmas Eve and New Year's Eve, Réveillon now happens throughout the month of December and is celebrated by everyone, regardless of religious affiliation.

Still, for many people, the most special Réveillon dinners are held on Christmas Eve or New Year's Eve. The Christmas meal, typically the more restrained of the two eves, was traditionally held after midnight Mass at St. Louis Cathedral. Families would return home and spend time together sharing a fairly austere meal of egg dishes, sweetbreads, and a rum cake. The New Year's Eve feast consists of elaborate desserts, plenty of whiskey and wine, and lots of laughing, singing, and dancing.

Dozens of restaurants in New Orleans offer special Réveillon menus in December. These are prix-fixe menus, usually four or five courses, and many establishments offer Réveillon on Christmas Eve, Christmas Day, New Year's Eve, and New Year's Day, although you should reserve well ahead for these dates.

This is an uber-local thing to do on Thanksgiving, and there's a "see and be seen" New Orleans society vibe surrounding the event. There are several Thanksgiving buffets scattered around the building, if you want to chow down.

Tremé and Fairgrounds: 1751 Gentilly Blvd., 504/944-5515, fairgroundsracecourse.com; 9am doors open, 11am Thanksgiving Day first race; general admission free, $10 clubhouse admission, food costs extra

DECEMBER
Celebration in the Oaks
From late November through early January, City Park comes alive for Celebration in the Oaks, a fabulous holiday light show that draws more than 165,000 visitors annually. Sights include a lighted tableau inspired by the beloved children's tale *Cajun Night Before Christmas,* a 20-foot-tall poinsettia Christmas tree in the botanical garden, and the fancifully illumined Storyland and Carousel Gardens. You can drive through the park, walk the two-mile route, or see it via a quaint train ride ($5 pp). This magical trip through the largest live-oak forest in the world is not to be missed during the holidays. Be sure to take advantage of the live music and inexpensive refreshments as well.

Tremé and Mid-City: City Park, 5 Victory Ave., neworleanscitypark.com; late Nov.-early Jan. $10 pp, children under 3 free

NOLA Christmas Fest
A kid-friendly event held in the convention center that starts the week before Christmas and ends on December 31, NOLA Christmas Fest provides sledding, skating, and a snowball fight area that New Orleans wouldn't otherwise see, along with visits with Santa, a Christmas tree showcase, and amusement rides like the Kringle Carousel and Winter Whirl. This is like a Norman Rockwell Christmas for the new millennium. For maximum deliciousness, check out the cookie-making workshop, breakfast with Santa, and a gingerbread house exhibit that will wow folks of all ages.

CBD and Warehouse/Arts District: New Orleans Ernest N. Morial Convention Center, 900 Convention Center Blvd., 504/582-3000, nolachristmasfest.com; mid-late Dec.; $20 Mon.-Fri., $25 Sat.-Sun.

WHERE TO STAY

New Orleans's lodging scene has been expanding to fit the ever-growing number of travelers heading this way, be it for conferences, major events like Jazz Fest or Saints games, bachelor and bachelorette parties, or getaways to experience the history, food culture, and romance of the city.

Le Richelieu

Hotel construction has reached a fevered pitch to meet the demands. Even chain hotels are realizing that visitors want a unique experience; a growing number of boutique brands are popping up with special bar and restaurant offerings. Some of the best new restaurants in the city are in hotel lobbies.

One factor in choosing where to stay is whether you have a car or not. Fortunately, staying in the main neighborhoods of the French Quarter, the Faubourg Marigny, the CBD, the Garden District, Uptown, and Mid-City will ensure convenient access to the streetcar lines. Neighborhoods beyond that area are accessible by bus or app-based ride-hailing services.

Accommodations in New Orleans are smoke-free. Most of privately owned inns have minimum stay requirements, particularly during the peak winter and spring seasons. At such times, you'll need to book well ahead of time; expect higher rates. (This is especially true for events like New Year's Eve, the Sugar Bowl, Mardi Gras, French Quarter Fest, and Jazz Fest.) Even in the slower summer season, certain annual events—such as the Essence Festival and Southern Decadence—might necessitate a hotel reservation.

Given the sheer number of motels, hotels, inns, and cottages available in the Big Easy, choosing an accommodation can be daunting. Luckily, there are many websites and organizations willing to help. If

HIGHLIGHTS

✪ **MOST THOUGHT-PROVOKING YET IRREVERENT HOTEL:**
The Saint Hotel leans into its theme. The extremes of heaven and hell await you in every nook and corner (page 302).

✪ **MOST RELAXING ROOFTOP BAR:** The rooftop terrace at **Catahoula Hotel** is a cozy oasis with a pergola, tropical plants, and comfortable seating (page 303).

✪ **MOST LITERARY:** Named for the nation's first female newspaper owner, Eliza Jane Nicholson, **The Eliza Jane** tips its hat to the newspaper era (page 303).

✪ **BEST SMELLING B&B:** The courtyard of **Auld Sweet Olive Bed & Breakfast** is surrounded by ever-blooming sweet olive trees, which smell as nice as they sound. It's a perfect olfactory oasis in the city (page 306).

✪ **COOLEST RENOVATION:** The **Hotel Peter and Paul** was once a convent, but today it offers a modern luxe experience (page 307).

✪ **BEST FOR ANTIQUES BUFFS:** The owners of the **Park View Historic Hotel** are avid antiques collectors and sellers, so every corner of every room is furnished with gorgeous pieces (page 309).

✪ **BEST FOR DESIGN NERDS:** The **Alder Hotel** is a renovated nurses' dormitory from the 1960s. Every part of the space pays homage to the golden age of mid-century modern design (page 310).

✪ **BEST HOTEL PARTY: The Drifter Hotel** is a jumping, jiving joint with live music, DJs, and an active pool scene (page 311).

✪ **BEST PLACE TO COMMUNE WITH THE SPIRIT OF TENNESSEE WILLIAMS:** The famous writer was once a long-term guest of the glamorous **Pontchartrain Hotel** (page 312).

✪ **BEST PLACE TO WATCH MARDI GRAS PARADES: Hotel Indigo** has the best location along the St. Charles Avenue parade route. The hotel also sets up several spots for guests to watch the festivities (page 313).

✪ **BEST SPOT TO COMBINE BUNK BEDS AND A BAR: The Quisby,** a sleek spot on St. Charles, provides a comfy shared space for weary travelers to lay their heads after one hell of a happy hour (page 314).

✪ **BEST B&B WITH ITS OWN MUSEUM:** The gorgeous **La Belle Esplanade** houses the Odditorium, which displays New Orleans-related miscellany, including glass eyes and voodoo-cursed silverware (page 314).

✪ **BEST VIEW OF THE FRENCH QUARTER:** The **Bed and Breakfast on the Point,** located right across the Mississippi from the French Quarter, offers the best views of New Orleans's famed neighborhood (page 316).

PRICE KEY

$	Less than $150 per night
$ $	$150-300 per night
$ $ $	More than $300 per night

you're looking for a bed-and-breakfast, consult the Professional Innkeepers Association of New Orleans (PIANO, bbnola.com) or the Louisiana Bed & Breakfast Association (LBBA, louisianabandb.com). For more specific accommodations, consider Historic Hotels of America (800/678-8946, historichotels.org).

If you want to save a little money, consider visiting during the summer or fall. You also might want to take advantage of the special packages that many hotels and inns offer; depending on the deal, these can appeal to families, gourmands, romance-minded couples, and those in town for special events. Finally, most accommodations listed in this guide include standard amenities like air-conditioning.

CHOOSING WHERE TO STAY

FRENCH QUARTER

The density of hotels in the French Quarter is high. Even if you're a few blocks from Bourbon Street, late night revelry will be loud. Several of the accommodations listed in this guide are either further afield from the party scene or have interior rooms that will block out all street noise.

CBD AND WAREHOUSE/ ARTS DISTRICT

If you're here for a convention or have hotel points, this is your spot. The CBD is more than just business, though, since there's lots of art and restaurants in this area as well. In addition to independent hotels, boutique imprints of major hotel groups are popping up here. For example, the Eliza Jane is part of the Unbound Collection by Hyatt, and it's far from a cookie cutter-type of place.

FAUBOURG MARIGNY AND THE BYWATER

This area has great B&B options, and is perfect for enjoying the inclusive vibe of corner bars, local restaurants, and adorable Creole cottages and shotgun houses. A larger hotel here is the Hotel Peter and Paul, which means there are more options to easily enjoy the eclectic Marigny and Bywater.

GARDEN DISTRICT AND IRISH CHANNEL

Heading away from the hustle and bustle of the central downtown neighborhoods, you'll find a more peaceful environment with B&Bs and small hotels alike. The proximity to some of the city's best restaurants and shopping makes this a great spot. The accommodation options range from historic inns and hotels along St. Charles Avenue to funky affordable spots in the quieter Lower Garden District, which has lots of great bars, coffee shops, restaurants, and shops.

UPTOWN AND RIVERBEND

Most lodging options in this neck of the woods are going to be smaller B&Bs. The Alder Hotel breaks that mold, providing a reasonable hotel option a bit removed from St. Charles Avenue and Magazine Street, but is close to up-and-coming areas like Freret Street and Maple Street. This area is great for parents visiting students of Tulane or Loyola.

WHICH NEIGHBORHOOD?

Depending on how you plan to spend your time, some neighborhoods will be better home bases than others.

IF YOU ONLY HAVE A WEEKEND...
...stay in the CBD or Warehouse/Arts District, close to the energy of the French Quarter and the history of the Garden District, with galleries, museums, and restaurants galore.

IF WANT TO SUPPORT BLACK-OWNED BUSINESSES...
...book a room in the Tremé, a historically Black neighborhood that is in the midst of a resurgence.

IF YOU WANT TO PARTY...
...the French Quarter is the place for you. You'll find a party on every block, not just Bourbon Street.

IF YOU'RE TRAVELING ON A BUDGET...
...check out the hostels and inns in the Garden District and Irish Channel.

IF YOU WANT TO BE SURROUNDED BY LIVE MUSIC...
...stay in the Faubourg Marigny or the Bywater for proximity to nightly live music on Frenchmen Street and St. Claude Avenue.

IF YOU AREN'T REALLY A CITY PERSON...
...head Uptown. As long as it isn't Mardi Gras season, many of the area's offerings are in quiet neighborhoods surrounded by beautiful live oaks.

IF A MORNING JOG IS PART OF YOUR ROUTINE...
...stay in Mid-City and enjoy the proximity to the many trails snaking through City Park.

IF YOU'RE A SERIOUS FOODIE...
...you're in luck. There are great eats in every neighborhood in New Orleans.

MID-CITY

Mid-City accommodations get booked up fast for Jazz Fest, but the neighborhood has plenty of charm on its own, with City Park and great neighborhood dining. Parking here is a lot easier (and cheaper) than the downtown area. The biking trails in City Park and the Canal streetcar provide other transportation options.

TREMÉ AND FAIRGROUNDS

Like Mid-City, this neighborhood is popular during Jazz Fest. The Tremé and Fairgrounds are perfect for people that want to experience the beauty and history of the city in a peaceful setting. It's still close and central to the city's other neighborhoods and attractions.

ALTERNATIVE LODGING OPTIONS

There are more hostels popping up throughout the city that provide a variety of sleeping options. You can even get a private room at several hostels. Greater New Orleans has a few options that are away from the main city area. If you need to stay near the airport, there are several decent chain options like the Holiday Inn, Comfort Suites and Radisson, which all offer free shuttles to the airport and free parking. Although it's a haul to get to New Orleans proper, any money spent getting in and out of the city is more than offset by the cheap rates. New Orleans traffic can be surprisingly awful depending on the time of day, so staying close to the airport could save you some stress on your departure day.

If RV-ing is your thing, there are a couple great RV parks. The **French Quarter RV Resort** (504/586-3000, fqrv.com) is right on the edge of the Quarter, plus it has a courtyard with a pool and bar. The **Pontchartrain Landing Marina and RV Park** (504/286-8157, pontchartrainlanding.com) is right on Lake Pontchartrain and offers a free shuttle to the French Quarter, plus an on-site pool and restaurant/bar. There are also a couple bare bones (but much cheaper) options in New Orleans East.

French Quarter Map 1

Soniat House Hotel $$$

This is a "hidden" French Quarter hotel that takes up three former residences on Burgundy Street. Two of the buildings have been merged; the third is on the other side of the street. The larger facility has a verdant first floor courtyard surrounded by rooms, as well as rooms on the second and third floors, accessed through the interior. (The elevator goes to the third floor only.) The building across the way, over the Sonnier Antique Shop, has 10 suites. All rooms are furnished with antiques that create an old-school, upper-class vibe. There's a large communal balcony for relaxing and watching the French Quarter go by.
MAP 1: 129 Burgundy St., 504/571-9854, soniathouse.com

Bienville House Hotel $$

In the very heart of the French Quarter, the Bienville House was originally built in 1835. Converted to a hotel in the 1960s, the historic look and feel has been maintained, but with the bonus of upgraded amenities. Several rooms have balconies surrounding the hotel's courtyard and salt-water pool; others have their own small outdoor patio. Some rooms are deep in the interior of the hotel and actually have no windows—which can be a blessing for light sleepers who want to stay in the often-raucous Quarter. The bathrooms all have walk-in showers with marble floors and tiles, and the deluxe and superior rooms have mahogany four-poster beds. A hot breakfast and an afternoon snack are included.
MAP 1: 320 Decatur St., 504529-2345, bienvillehouse.com

Soniat House Hotel

Le Richelieu $$

One of the Quarter's most popular mid-priced hotels, Le Richelieu books up quickly. Contained within two historic buildings, the 69 guest rooms are clean and simple, but with reproduction antiques, varying color schemes, and, in some cases, pleasant views. There are also 17 suites with spacious sitting areas. This European-style property lies along a quiet stretch in the Lower Quarter, not far from the French Market and the Marigny. An on-site café serves breakfast all day, and there's also a lounge, an unheated swimming pool, and 24-hour concierge services. The hotel offers satellite TV, laundry and babysitting services, and secured self-parking ($25/day).
MAP 1: 1234 Chartres St., 504/529-2492 or 800/535-9653, lerichelieuhotel.com

✪ The Saint Hotel $$

Figure out if you want to be naughty or nice during your stay at The Saint Hotel. While the bar downstairs is a red velvet, goth-inspired, burlesque-show-hosting den of sin, the rooms are crisp and white with lots of natural light, embodying their motto, "Play Naughty. Sleep Saintly." The one exception is the Lucifer Suite, which is a huge two-bedroom suite decorated in red and black, with risqué art and a stripper pole/disco ball combination stage. The rooms all feature modern bathroom amenities; each of the five suites have free-standing oversized soaking tubs. The lobby is filled with marble

The Saint Hotel

cherub statues, decadent art, oversized furniture, and a pool table.
MAP 1: 931 Canal St., 504/522-5400, sainthotels.com

City House Hostel $

City House is clean and fun, with helpful staff and walls decorated by artists that have passed through the hostel's halls. Set on the second floor of a building practically overlooking Canal Street, the hostel offers one bathroom for every eight guests, which means there are 11 private, lockable bathrooms, each with a toilet and a bathtub/shower combo. Rooms range from two to six sets of bunk beds, sleeping 4-12 comfortably. The common areas include a huge open kitchen, several seating areas, and a nightly beer pong game. Between 9pm and 10pm, guests can have a free beer. Quiet hours kick in at 10pm and last till 10am the next morning.
MAP 1: 129 Burgundy St., 504/571-9854, cityhousehostels.com

SUPPORT LOCAL LODGINGS

Look, I get it. Hotels are expensive, and Airbnb seems like a reasonable alternative that also allows visitors to experience the neighborhoods and all that New Orleans culture firsthand. The problem is, when property owners rent whole buildings to out-of-towners, it takes that space away from people who live and work here, driving up rents, and forcing a good majority of the city's everyday culture-bearers and service industry out of Orleans Parish altogether. There are neighborhood businesses that can't attract locals, because the locals aren't there—just people visiting on the weekends.

In this guide, I've included inns, B&Bs, and hostels in every corner of the city, and I urge you to stay at one of these lovely places. Licensed businesses are accountable to their guests and adhere to strict city and state regulations. People open up these lodgings because they love hosting people from other places, meaning you get an invaluable local resource out of the deal.

Unfortunately, it wasn't possible to include every indie accommodation in the guide. For more listings, check out BBNOLA.com, run by the Professional Innkeepers Association of New Orleans (PIANO). The listings include all price ranges throughout many neighborhoods.

Central Business District and Warehouse/Arts District Map 2

✪ Catahoula Hotel $$

With only 35 rooms, the Catahoula Hotel, a converted townhouse in the CBD, provides a personalized experience in a cozy and relaxed setting.

artwork in the courtyard of the Catahoula Hotel

Rooms feature Casper mattresses, rainfall shower heads, and furnishings made with Louisiana cypress wood. The rooms are set up so that the sink and shower seem to be part of the main space, as opposed to a separate bathroom. (There is a private toilet, of course.) Piscobar, just off the lobby, focuses on cocktails made with the Peruvian grape-based spirit pisco. On sunny days, head to the rooftop bar to experience a city oasis (and view) you can't find anywhere else.

MAP 2: 914 Union St., 504/603-2442, catahoulahotel.com

✪ The Eliza Jane $$

The Eliza Jane might be part of the Hyatt organization but it's steeped in local lore and history. The hotel's namesake, Eliza Jane Nicholson, was the country's first woman newspaper publisher, back in 1876, for the *Daily Picayune,* which was housed in the building the hotel occupies today. The 196 rooms and suites at The Eliza Jane feature exposed brick, floor-to-ceiling windows, beautifully outfitted bathrooms, and plush mattresses and bedding. The public spaces are equally stunning, with an atrium and courtyard filled with New Orleans-inspired decor and art. Couvant, one of the city's hottest French restaurants, is just off the lobby.

MAP 2: 315 Magazine St., 504/882-1234, hyatt.com

International House Hotel $$

This stunning hotel occupies a 1906 Beaux-Arts building that once served as a bank and is now one of the coolest addresses in town. The 117 rooms, suites, and penthouses are decorated in stylish, muted tones with stereo systems, down comforters, and Aveda bath products. A 24-hour concierge and pricey valet parking are available. There's no pool, but you can work out in the fitness center and relax in the top-notch spa afterward. Given the fashionable clientele it courts, it's no surprise that the hotel's Loa cocktail bar is a favorite spot for the well-heeled to rub elbows. Several times each year, the ornate lobby is decorated to celebrate a particular festival or holiday that's dear to New Orleanians, from All Saints' Day in early November to St. Joseph's Day in March.

MAP 2: 221 Camp St., 504/553-9550 or 800/633-5770, ihhotel.com

The NOPSI Hotel $$

The NOPSI used to be the New Orleans Public Service Inc. headquarters building, which once provided electricity and gas to homes in New Orleans and operated the streetcars and buses. Original features include vaulted ceilings, grand columns, and terrazzo floors. The guest rooms of this 1920-era building are bright, with plenty of sunlight and cream-colored walls and floors with blue accents. The rooftop pool area is studded with luxury cabanas and boasts Above the Grid, a bar serving drinks and snacks. In the lobby, enjoy a libation from the gin-focused bar, or wander into the hotel's restaurant, Public Service, for creative cuisine from Chef Neal Swidler and swanky cocktails with an emphasis on bourbon.

MAP 2: 317 Baronne St., 844/439-1463, nopsihotel.com

Old No. 77 Hotel & Chandlery $$

The Old. No 77 Hotel & Chandlery beckons you with a hip, vintage

The NOPSI Hotel

vibe and the acclaimed **Compere Lapin** restaurant and bar. The 167 guest rooms pay homage to the former warehouse by incorporating industrial design elements, and there are three Artist's Suites that feature the art and design aesthetic of local artists. In-room amenities include a fancy Tivoli Bluetooth clock radio, local food and drink in the honor bar, and pet-friendly options.

MAP 2: 535 Tchoupitoulas St., 504/527-5271, old77hotel.com

St. James Hotel

St. James Hotel $$

This boutique hotel doesn't feel like a hotel when you walk in—off to the right is a lovely parlor, and the check-in desk is an actual desk, where you sit down and chat with the person checking you in. The 84 rooms, which all have hardwood floors and rustic wood headboards, with furniture to match, are spread out over two buildings, with secret courtyards to discover en route. Every morning, a complimentary croissant and coffee/tea on a silver tray is delivered to your room; it's a nice touch of old-world luxury.

MAP 2: 330 Magazine St., 504/304-4000, saintjameshotel.com

Lafayette Hotel $

This centrally located spot next to Lafayette Square and the inbound streetcar line has been a hotel since its construction in 1916. Although periodic renovations keep the space up-to-date, the early-20th-century charm endures, for a very reasonable price. The rooms are nicely but not overly appointed, with simple and comfortable furniture. Several rooms have balconies that overlook St. Charles Avenue. The Petite Rooms are some of the best values in town. Pet-friendly rooms are available as well.

MAP 2: 600 St. Charles Ave., 888/626-5457, lafayettehotelneworleans.com

Faubourg Marigny and the Bywater

Map 3

✪ Auld Sweet Olive Bed & Breakfast $$

A Creole mansion built in the 1850s, this cheerful B&B went through several iterations before being acquired by scenic artist Stuart Auld in the 1990s, which explains the gorgeous art painted on the walls throughout the home. The architecture and design of the common areas are stunning, and each of the seven rooms are one of a kind gems. Sweet olive trees encircle the courtyard, blooming throughout the year and perfuming the air.

MAP 3: 2460 N. Rampart St., 504/947-4332, sweetolive.com

B&W Courtyards $$

This B&B looks unassuming and almost invisible from the street. Walk in, though, and you'll discover hidden courtyards and Creole cottages. There are five guest rooms across three buildings, all connected by small, intimate courtyards. The rooms have brightly painted walls that go well with the antique features of the interior architecture. A full breakfast is served every morning, but if your goal is total privacy, it's easy to accomplish: All rooms have a private entrance and are spaced well apart from each other.

Auld Sweet Olive Bed & Breakfast

MAP 3: 2425 Chartres St.,
800/585-5731, bandwcourtyards.com

Hotel Peter and Paul

✪ Hotel Peter and Paul $$

This converted Catholic school, church, rectory, and convent takes up an entire block of Burgundy Street and is the largest and only full-service hotel in the neighborhood. The Henry Howard-designed building has been restored to jaw-dropping and awe-inspiring glory. No two of the hotel's 71 rooms are alike: They range from clean lines and classic design to sumptuous luxury. In the former rectory is the Elysian Bar (504/356-6769, theelysianbar.com; 7am-midnight daily), a unique, funky bar and restaurant that locals enjoy as much as guests.
MAP 3: 2317 Burgundy St.,
504/356-5200, hotelpeterandpaul.com

Royal Street Courtyard $$

This rambling old mansion has a classic antebellum feel, accented with high ceilings, floor-to-ceiling windows, and restored hardwood floors throughout. There are a few tricks to get a room in a place like this for a bargain: First, check out the two "loft economy" rooms in the back if you're traveling alone, or investigate the two rooms upstairs that have private bathrooms located down the hall from the bedrooms. The beautiful location, lush back courtyard, and expansive porch out front round out the experience.
MAP 3: 2438 Royal St., 504/943-6818,
royalstreetcourtyard.com

Royal Street Inn and R Bar $$

This "bed and beverage" offers five unique and beautifully furnished suites above the popular R Bar, just off Frenchmen Street. Although there's no breakfast included, guests do get a couple of free drinks downstairs. The luxe, mid-century modern rooms have shared access to a balcony overlooking the street (only the Royal Suite has private access).
MAP 3: 1431 Royal St., 504/948-7499,
royalstreetinn.com

Madame Isabelle's House in New Orleans $

This low-budget hotel/hostel welcomes backpackers looking for a cheap bed but also accommodates budget travelers looking for privacy. There are three dorm-style bedrooms (one male, one female, and one mixed), a private room that sleeps three with a shared bathroom, and three private rooms with en-suite bathrooms. The owner hails from South Korea and has put together a boho-Asian-rococo design aesthetic that includes a lush, gorgeous courtyard and several other outdoor spaces. A couple of cats knock about, one of them, called Missy Izzy, is allegedly the spirit of former resident Madame Isabelle. A free breakfast is provided, and the garden also has a hot tub.
MAP 3: 1021 Kerlerec St.,
504/509-4422, isabellenola.com

Garden District and Irish Channel

Map 4

Henry Howard Hotel $$$

Low key luxury is the name of the game at the Henry Howard Hotel. Located a block behind St. Charles Avenue, this stately mansion has been completely transformed into an elegant, urban paradise. Step into a grand lounge with 12-foot ceilings and a chandelier, which also features a bar that's open 24 hours a day. Eighteen high-ceilinged rooms have locally crafted bed frames, mattresses that are so comfortable that people actually buy them from the hotel, and fun portraits of the family who now own the hotel. Valet parking is available.

MAP 4: 2041 Prytania St., 504/313-1577, henryhowardhotel.com

Creole Gardens Guesthouse & Inn $$

This colorful 19th-century antebellum mansion, located a block away from the St. Charles Avenue streetcar, is comprised of three houses set around a central courtyard. The rooms in each house are individually themed, with choices that include the more traditional Mansion Rooms, with clawfoot tubs; the funky, vibrant Bordello Room, an homage to the famous madams of the old Storyville brothels; and the Cottage Rooms, which are fun, bright, and good for families. A hot breakfast is included, using only humanely sourced proteins.

MAP 4: 1415 Prytania St., 504/569-8700, creolegardens.com

The Green House Inn $$

Constructed in 1840, this Greek Revival-style townhouse-turned-B&B may have traditional antiques and paintings throughout, but it also has a contemporary edge. The saltwater swimming pool and hot tub tucked in the verdant and cozy courtyard is clothing optional. The nine flower-named rooms all offer king-size beds, deluxe sheets and towels, and all-natural bath products. Go for the Hibiscus Room, the only one with its own tub. The inn is completely pet-friendly, with no breed or size restrictions. Additionally, the inn offers breakfast, gated off-street parking, and easy access to area attractions, like Coliseum Square and The National WWII Museum.

MAP 4: 1212 Magazine St., 504/525-1333, thegreenhouseinn.com

The Atlas House $

In the heart of the Lower Garden District, this family-run hostel is comprised of two large, converted Victorian-style houses as well as a detached house in the back. The space is old, beautiful, and quirky, and the prices are the lowest in the area. There are dormitory rooms that sleep six people in addition to several private rooms (though most share a bath). Communal areas include a kitchen, porch, lounge, and central courtyard with a barbecue and hot tub. The hostel regularly arranges activities, such as movie nights, pub crawls, and group kayaking. The hot breakfast is complimentary, there are bikes to rent, and laundry is available for a fee.

MAP 4: 1354 Magazine St., 504/400-4851, theatlashouse.com

Uptown and Riverbend   Map 5

Chimes Bed and Breakfast $$

A longtime favorite in the Uptown area, this delightful inn has just five lovingly furnished rooms facing a lush courtyard. Each has an elegant queen-size bed, fine linens, French doors, high ceilings, and hardwood or slate floors; two rooms have fireplaces, and two others have daybeds that can accommodate an additional guest. An expansive continental breakfast, a stocked refrigerator, and laundry room access are included. This is a great base for exploring Uptown.

MAP 5: 1146 Constantinople St., 504/453-2183, chimesneworleans.com

Park View Historic Hotel

The Columns Hotel $$

The Columns is well known to visitors as a great spot to sit overlooking St. Charles Avenue while sipping delightful beverages, but its lodgings are more under-the-radar. There are 20 guest rooms on the second and third floors of this dark wood-accented hotel, along with a sitting parlor, a ballroom, a bar, a lounge, and a tea room where an included breakfast is served to guests and other light meal items are on hand during the day. The hotel used to be a private home but has been a full-service hotel since 1980. All the rooms are different sizes and have different layouts, as befitting this historic and unique property. One room is an homage to the movie *Pretty Baby,* which was filmed at the hotel.

MAP 5: 3811 St. Charles Ave., 504/899-9308, thecolumns.com

✪ Park View Historic Hotel $$

Situated just beside Audubon Park, the aptly named Park View Guest House is ideal for travelers planning to explore Audubon Zoo, the nearby campuses of Tulane and Loyola, and the rest of Uptown. The convenient St. Charles streetcar line is just a stroll away. Erected in 1884, this magnificent, recently restored inn lures guests with its antique furnishings, luxurious beds, complimentary breakfasts and afternoon refreshments, and amicable staff. Relax on the inviting porch or, if you're lucky, on the upper balconies, which afford pleasant views of the oak-filled park.

MAP 5: 7004 St. Charles Ave., 504/861-7564, parkviewguesthouse.com

Southern Comfort Bed & Breakfast $$

A couple of blocks north of the St. Charles streetcar line, this gorgeous B&B offers convenient access to the city's major attractions yet has all the ambience of an intimate hideaway. Built in 1910, the delightful cottage has three unique guest rooms, each tastefully decorated and furnished with antique pieces as well as period reproductions. Every room features an honor bar and Sonoma bath products. Guests can take advantage of the full gourmet breakfasts, concierge services, communal refrigerator, and free parking.

MAP 5: 1739 Marengo St.,
504/895-3680,
southerncomfort-bnb.com

✪ Alder Hotel $

This midcentury-modern, 90-room hotel on the Ochsner medical campus (the property was the nurse dormitory in the 1960s) is a great home base for travelers. Free parking is

Alder Hotel

included in a private lot, it's less than a mile to the St. Charles streetcar line, and it's merely steps away from some of the finest eats in all of Uptown, on Freret Street. The hotel, which is locally owned, pays homage to the building's past with historic photographs of the neighborhood from decades ago, and provides a free continental breakfast. There are two types of rooms: with a single king bed or two queens. All rooms have a kitchenette and a sleeper sofa.

MAP 5: 4545 Magnolia St.,
504/207-4600, alderhotel.com

Mid-City   Map 6

1896 O'Malley House $$

Not far from the busy intersection of Canal Street and North Carrollton Avenue, the O'Malley House is one of the more hidden, less-touristy inns in the city. It's named for one of New Orleans's most prominent Irish citizens of the late 19th century, newspaper publisher Dominick O'Malley. This gracious, Colonial Revival-style mansion features original cypress-wood mantels, pocket doors, and other artful details. The eight sumptuous suites

are filled with exceptional antiques, handsome Oriental rugs, plush four-poster beds, and elegant tables. Most rooms have whirlpool tubs. Run by exceedingly hospitable hosts, the house lies within walking distance of several restaurants and just steps from the Canal streetcar line, which links City Park to the French Quarter. An especially bounteous continental breakfast is included.

MAP 6: 120 S. Pierce St., 504/488-5896,
1896omalleyhouse.com

Canal Street Inn $$

This gorgeous Canal Street mansion is steps away from the nearest streetcar stop and is perfectly situated to explore any direction of New Orleans your plans take you. Antique furniture and bed frames elevate the experience of staying in such a lovely house, as does the "relaxation room," where massage appointments are available. The daily breakfast can be taken with other guests in the formal dining room, or if you're just not up to small talk first thing in the morning, you can eat privately on the screened-in back porch. The outdoor space is lovely, too, with a pergola, water feature, and hot tub. Off-street parking is also available, including a special spot for electric car charging.

MAP 6: 3620 Canal St., 504/483-3033, canalstreetinn.com

✪ The Drifter Hotel $

This mid-century modern motel has been gorgeously restored and is one of the city's most aesthetically well-designed places. They also host bawdy summertime pool parties. The gatherings are inclusive and welcoming, with a good mix of locals and visitors whooping it up with live music or a DJ. Plus, there's

The Drifter Hotel

poolside yoga on the weekends. The hotel bar, called No Vacancy, faces both into the lobby (filled with a combination of mid-century-mod comfy and workspace-appropriate furniture) and outward, to the pool. It's open all day to guests and other visitors (they also serve Cherry Coffee espresso drinks and cold brew). The rooms are all the same size, with either a king or two queen beds that have custom-made Casper mattresses, Aesop toiletries, and no television—the motel's mission is to create a space where you meet new people and exchange ideas—and swim topless, drink, and dance. Before booking here, be aware that the pool area, which all the rooms surround, is party central till all hours of the night. It *will* be loud and rowdy.

MAP 6: 3522 Tulane Ave., 504/605-4644, thedrifterhotel.com

NOLA Jazz House $

Viewed from the street, the NOLA Jazz House hostel is nondescript but inside, it opens onto a space with brightly painted jazzy scenes on the walls. There are no-frills but clean private rooms that sleep 1-6 people, as well as a mixed dorm room. (Everyone shares the bathrooms.) Included is a free breakfast, spots to relax both inside and out, and a killer location right in front of a streetcar stop.

MAP 6: 3416 Canal St., 504/975-1311, nolajazzhouse.com

Oakview Bed and Breakfast $

The unassuming exterior gives way to a beautiful home furnished with antiques, well located near the intersection of City Park Avenue and North Carrollton Avenue. The rooms on the first floor all have deep jetted tubs and roomy walk-in showers, with an original claw foot tub in the upstairs room. Most rooms have their own sitting area separate from the bedroom. With a full breakfast every day, this might be one of the best deals in town.

MAP 6: 1172 City Park Ave., 504/495-7405, oakviewbnb.com

Site 61 Hostel $

Site 61's sci-fi-inspired decor makes this completely renovated 100-plus-year-old house a fun place to hang out without being too precious or hardcore. (There's a *Firefly*-themed common room, and if you know what that means, then you need to check this place out.) The old-fashioned and the futuristic come together in a somewhat steampunk manner, making this hostel very comfortable to kick around in. It's also one of the only hostels in New Orleans that doesn't impose an age limit on guests. The seven rooms on the top floor (with specific themes like *Doctor Who, The Matrix,* or *Star Wars*) are all dorm-style, sleeping either two, four, or six people in sturdy custom-built bunk beds. Also upstairs are six full bathrooms, a couple of which can be reserved for exclusive use. Downstairs has two en-suite rooms, but they're mostly for staff.

MAP 6: 3701 Tulane Ave., 504/304-9974, site61nola.com

Central City and Broadmoor

Map 7

✪ Pontchartrain Hotel $$$

The Pontchartrain has a glamourous history. It was initially built as a luxury apartment building in 1927 and converted into a hotel in the 1940s. A 2017 renovation managed to retain the charm and style of its past while adding all of the comforts and amenities suited to the present—including a fitness center and library. The rooms are spacious and homey, yet elegant. There's a picture of former long-term guest Tennessee Williams in every room. Breakfast and lunch can be found at the Whistle Stop café, and dinner at the Jack Rose. Don't miss the stunning views from the rooftop bar, Hot Tin.

MAP 7: 2031 St. Charles Ave., 504/941-9000, thepontchartrainhotel.com

Grand Victorian Bed & Breakfast $$

This majestic home on the corner of Washington and St. Charles Avenues is perfectly located in front of a streetcar stop, with easy access to uptown and downtown. The six spacious rooms and two suites retain the woodwork and other architectural details of the home's original design and construction. Although the rooms have a vintage look, the amenities are modern, including TVs, luxury mattresses, and whirlpool tubs. Some rooms are also ADA-compliant. A continental breakfast is served in the sunny dining room or on the porch. There are also concierge services and free parking.

MAP 7: 2727 St. Charles Ave., 504/895-1104, gvbb.com

✪ Hotel Indigo $$

This contemporary space provides both squeaky-clean comfort and a subtle charm that reflects the images and history of the neighborhood. The rooms and bathrooms are spacious, with hardwood floors and colorful murals above the bed. The hotel's location is perfect for Mardi Gras parades—especially with its private outdoor terrace overlooking St. Charles Avenue—as long as you don't mind things being a little crazy. The cocktail bar and bistro provides snacks and drinks, and the business center and gym are great for folks who aren't in full-blown vacation mode.

MAP 7: 2203 St. Charles Ave., 504/522-3650, neworleansindie.com

Auberge NOLA Hostel $

This well-run, traditional hostel is set in a converted New Orleans Victorian. The Auberge has a community kitchen, a great courtyard and outdoor space, a couple of private rooms, and fantastic social opportunities, both with fellow hostellers and with the city of New Orleans itself. Every night there's a different activity, from a cookout

lobby of the Pontchartrain Hotel

or party in the courtyard, to a bar crawl down Magazine Street or St. Charles Avenue, to outings to see the Soul Rebels on Thursday nights or Rebirth Brass Band on Tuesday nights. Aside from the few private rooms with en-suite bathrooms, the bathrooms are communal.

MAP 7: 1628 Carondelet St., 504/524-5980, aubergehostels.com

the lobby at The Quisby

✪ The Quisby $

To envision The Quisby, think modern Scandinavian design, a historic building, and incredible location, then throw in a badass lobby bar. All the beds are bunk style (locally constructed and topped with memory foam mattresses), and everything is super clean, sleek, and streamlined. The rooms sleep 2-6 people and all have an en-suite bathroom. There are 120 beds and twice as many USB ports. Complimentary coffee, pastries, and fruit are available for breakfast, and the bar's happy hour is 7pm-8pm every day.

MAP 7: 1225 St. Charles Ave., 504/208-4881, thequisby.com

Tremé and Fairgrounds   Map 8

Ashton's Bed & Breakfast $$

One of the city's most elegant inns sits in a laid-back neighborhood, far from touristy hot spots. Built in 1861, this Greek Revival-style, antebellum mansion features an inviting veranda, lush gardens, a shady rear yard, and, within the main house and patio wing, eight spacious, uniquely decorated, and impeccably furnished rooms. Each room is named after events, landmarks, or other iconic images unique to New Orleans, such as Bourbon Street, Mardi Gras, and the Creole Queen. All have tall ceilings, luxurious linens, and individual thermostats. Secured parking and a full gourmet breakfast are included.

MAP 8: 2023 Esplanade Ave., 504/942-7048, ashtonsbb.com

✪ La Belle Esplanade $$

This is a B&B run on personality, as the infinitely quotable innkeeper Matthew King says. He insists that his main purpose isn't selling beds (or breakfast), but rather a unique New Orleans experience. Every morning at the fun and funky La Belle Esplanade sees a breakfast with locally sourced products like Bellegarde bread, cheese from St. James Cheese Co., donuts from Blue Dot, or Terranova sausage. Each of the five rooms has a clawfoot tub, a private balcony, vintage furniture, and a unique personality. On the inn's first floor is the Odditorium, a mini museum that contains voodoo-cursed cutlery and other assorted New Orleans ephemera befitting the name.

MAP 8: 2216 Esplanade Ave., 504/301-1424, labelleesplanade.com

La Belle Esplanade

Monrose Row Bed & Breakfast $$

The Greek Revival-style building that now houses the intimate Monrose Row Bed & Breakfast was originally constructed in 1839 for local baker Charles Monrose. Today, the carefully restored inn offers three individually decorated two-room suites with antique furnishings. Two of the rooms overlook the charming courtyard, while the third occupies the entire third floor of the main house. A continental breakfast is included.

MAP 8: 1303 Governor Nicholls St., 504/616-6377, monroserow.com

New Orleans Guest House $

With its lush, peaceful courtyard (with resident cats that may approach for some attention), the New Orleans Guesthouse serves as a popular yet intimate hideaway for budget travelers. The 14 guest rooms have high ceilings, antique furnishings, and, in many cases, vibrant color schemes. It's right across the street from the French Quarter, so you can leave your car in the small but secured on-site lot.

MAP 8: 1118 Ursulines Ave., 800/562-1177, neworleansguest.house

✪ Bed and Breakfast on the Point $$

Take the ferry across the Mississippi to stay in Algiers Point—this bed & breakfast is only three blocks from the ferry station, making it very convenient to get to the French Quarter and beyond while staying in a more subdued environment. The historic Greek Revival home, originally built in 1849, houses four suites (the Delaronde Suite shares a bath). This spot doesn't take credit cards but does require a deposit for all stays. They prefer a mailed check, but will grudgingly accept PayPal.
MAP 9: 405 Delaronde St., New Orleans, 504/723-4717, bedandbreakfastonthepoint.com

Copeland Tower Suites $

Sometimes you need to stay outside of the city, perhaps to be closer to the airport, or to visit family, or because Metairie is just the best home base for you. The Copeland Tower Suites was built as an office building for local restaurant powerhouse Al Copeland, who started the Popeye's fried chicken franchise. Today it's an all-suites property, with modern amenities, a full kitchen, and a separate bedroom. It's about halfway between the French Quarter and the airport, and it's near plenty of shopping.

MAP 9: 2601 Severn Ave., Metairie, 504/888-9500, choicehotels.com

Rose Manor Bed & Breakfast Inn

Rose Manor Bed & Breakfast Inn $

This nine-room inn is located in the upscale Lakeview neighborhood, which is away from the hustle and bustle of the rest of the city, but still close to City Park and the lakefront. The common areas and guest rooms are furnished with antiques and reproductions, resulting in an old-fashioned feel with the benefit of modern conveniences. A continental breakfast is included in the cost of the room. There's a two-night minimum, except during special events when the minimum is four nights.
MAP 9: 7214 Pontchartrain Blvd., New Orleans, 504/282-8200, rosemanor.com

DAY TRIPS

New Orleans is a unique city with centuries of culture, and the same applies to all of southern Louisiana. To get the full Louisiana experience, you'll need to leave New Orleans and experience for yourself how the rest of the state differs from the Crescent City. You have to cross parish lines to find the different Cajun cultural communities that have settled throughout the region; each is a little different from the next. Ditto for environmental diversity: Go beyond the city to explore swamps, islands, bayous, and other singular Louisiana cities that have added as much to the cultural dialogue as New Orleans has.

For the best bang for your buck, there are three different areas close to New Orleans that are well worth a day's or weekend's sojourn. The Lake Area covers the vicinity around Lake Maurepas, as well as a brief foray into the River Plantation historic district. Avery Island is a complete surprise in the middle of the South Louisiana bayous off of Vermilion Bay—supporting not only a nature preserve but also a

statue at the Whitney
Plantation Museum

thriving manufacturing farm and the Tabasco hot sauce factory. And no trip to Louisiana is complete without enjoying the food, music, and people of Lafayette, the epicenter of Acadiana. All three of these trips give insight to local history you wouldn't find if you stayed in New Orleans.

Expand your focus beyond the city to find just a few of the other treasures that Louisiana has in store. And make sure to buy some boudin, cracklin', or jerky on the way.

HIGHLIGHTS

⭐ **MOST IMPORTANT PLANTATION TOUR:** Practically a required stop for understanding the realities of slavery, the **Whitney Plantation Museum** is dedicated to educating visitors without white-washing history (page 319).

⭐ **SMOKIEST ANDOUILLE:** There are as many ways to prepare andouille as there are places to find it, but **Jacob's World-Famous Andouille & Sausage,** in Laplace, makes the smokiest version (page 324).

⭐ **BEST CULTURAL BREWERY:** Enjoy a beer, a tour, some live music, and the opportunity to hang out with some friendly Cajun folks at **Bayou Teche Brewing** (page 326).

⭐ **BEST LIVING HISTORY MUSEUM:** A village set back in time, the fascinating **Vermilionville** recounts the Cajun experience through historic buildings, music and dance performances, and regional cuisine (page 327).

⭐ **MOST AUTHENTIC CAJUN EXPERIENCE:** Tap your toes to Zydeco and Cajun bands at **La Poussiere,** an old-fashioned Cajun dance hall (page 329).

⭐ **WHERE TO SUPPORT LOCAL ARTISTS AND CAJUN TRADITIONS:** At **NUNU Arts and Creative Culture Collective,** visual arts, music, and storytelling are all used to capture the history of this unique region (page 330).

⭐ **BIGGEST FRANCOPHILE MUSIC FESTIVAL:** Experience the **Festival International de Louisiane,** a massive five-day party that showcases all kinds of Francophone fun (page 331).

⭐ **BEST NATURE WALK:** At Avery Island's **Jungle Gardens and Bird City,** you can choose to drive or walk through a fascinating natural habitat that houses birds, turtles, and gators (page 335).

⭐ **ODDEST FESTIVAL:** In Abbeville, witness the creation of an omelet made with more than 5,000 eggs, then partake of the results at the **Giant Omelette Celebration** (page 336).

⭐ **BEST B&B FOR CATCHING YOUR OWN DINNER:** The owner of **Crawfish Haven/Mrs. Rose's Bed & Breakfast** allows you to catch crawfish and boil them yourself (page 338).

PLANNING YOUR TIME

The Lake Area is a leisurely day trip. You'll be back in time to make your dinner reservations. A trip to Avery Island offers several possibilities. On its own, it's an overnight trip. Abbeville and New Iberia are the best spots to eat and stay after visiting Avery Island, but they're also worth a wander on their own. You can also link Avery Island with a Lafayette trip, meaning it could be a nice 3- to 4-day getaway.

Lafayette is about an hour north of Avery Island. The Lafayette area has so much going on, it could be anywhere between an overnight or a week-long getaway, depending on what you want to do and see. Lafayette, Breaux Bridge, Arnaudville, and Scott are all within 40 miles of each other. There's lots to eat and some good B&Bs to check out in that area.

To do these trips in a loop, visit the Lake Area on your first day, then stay near Avery Island that night. Next, head to Lafayette for 1-2 days. This route means you won't spend too much time on I-10; the secondary roads are more fun and interesting to drive anyway.

It's worth checking the dates of when the various festivals are, either to make sure and catch them, or to avoid the crowds. The biggest one is Festival International de Louisiane, which takes over downtown Lafayette and closes tons of streets during the last weekend in April. Other events to be aware of include the Boudin Festival, in Scott, which happens in early/mid-April; the Giant Omelette Celebration in Abbeville in November; and New Iberia's Delcambre Shrimp Festival in mid-August and its Sugarcane Festival in late September. Keep in mind, most places have their own Mardi Gras traditions as well.

The Lake Area

This quick trip from New Orleans includes a visit to LaPlace, the andouille capital of the world; a swamp tour that covers the quiet tributaries of Lake Maurepas; a classic Louisiana seafood shack; and the only plantation tour that's worthy of your time, money, and attention. These destinations are all west of New Orleans, off of I-10.

These attractions can be easily reached by car; it's possible to loop around and take in all three areas in one trip. Start with a visit to the Whitney Plantation, then proceed to LaPlace for andouille and Lake Maurepas for a swamp tour. You'll head north from there to visit Middendorf's, then return to New Orleans.

EDGARD
✪ WHITNEY PLANTATION MUSEUM

The Whitney Plantation Museum (5099 LA-18, Edgard, 225/265-3300, whitneyplantation.com; 9:30am-4:30pm Wed.-Mon., last tour at

Day Trips

61

49

St. Francisville

61

Mississippi River

71

10

190

Baton Rouge

Eunice

190

Port Barre

Opelousas

★ BAYOU TECHE BREWING

★ NUNU ARTS AND CREATIVE CULTURE COLLECTIVE

49

Arnaudville

★ LA POUSSIERE

10

10

Breaux Bridge

Achafalaya River

Crowley

35

Lafayette

Bayou Teche

White Castle

1

13

★ CRAWFISH HAVEN/ MRS. ROSE'S BED & BREAKFAST

★ VERMILIONVILLE

★ FESTIVAL INTERNATIONAL DE LOUISIANE

Donaldsonville

167

31

New Iberia

Abbeville

14

Avery Island

Lake Verret

★ GIANT OMELETTE CELEBRATION

★ JUNGLE GARDENS AND BIRD CITY

90

Lake Palourde

White Lake

Vermilion Bay

West Cote Blanche Bay

Morgan City

Marsh Island State Wildlife Refuge

Atchafalaya Bay

Gulf of Mexico

0   20 mi

0   20 km

© MOON.COM

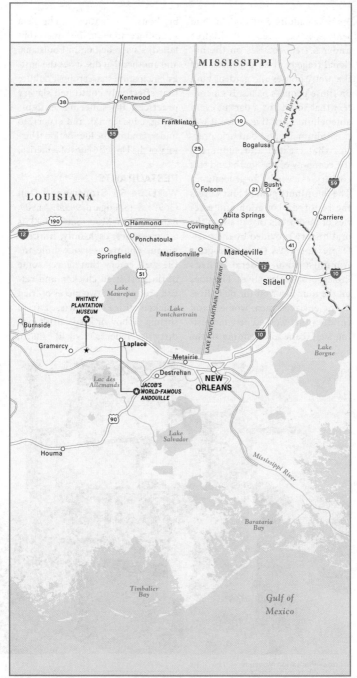

MISSISSIPPI

Pearl River

38

Kentwood

Franklinton

10

55

25

Bogalusa

59

Folsom

21

Bush

Carriere

LOUISIANA

Abita Springs

190

Hammond

Covington

12

Ponchatoula

Springfield

Madisonville

41

Mandeville

10

51

12

Slidell

Lake
Maurepas

Lake
Pontchartrain

10

WHITNEY
PLANTATION
MUSEUM

Lake
Borgne

Burnside

Laplace

Metairie

Gramercy

Destrehan

NEW
ORLEANS

Lac des
Allemands

JACOB'S
WORLD-FAMOUS
ANDOUILLE

90

Lake
Salvador

Mississippi River

Houma

Barataria
Bay

Timbalier
Bay

Gulf of
Mexico

LAKE PONTCHARTRAIN CAUSEWAY

3pm; $23 adults, $20 students and seniors, $10 children 6-18, children under 6 free) focuses on the national tragedy of slavery instead of the pretty houses and gardens built on those people's backs. It's a context that should be a part of every antebellum narrative, since it was this inhumane and barbaric practice that created and supported the economy of the South (and this country, as a whole) for generations. The 90-minute guided tour covers the restored plantation and a series of memorials that draw on the oral history provided by the post-Depression WPA (Works Progress Administration) Federal Writer's Project of slave narratives. The stops on the tour focus on the daily lives of the enslaved men, women, and children that worked here harvesting sugarcane and tending to the big house for centuries. There's a stunning exhibit on the largest (but failed) slave rebellion in Louisiana, and another that discusses the post-Emancipation sharecropper culture that effectively continued slavery practices. It's sobering, enlightening, educational, and crucial to understanding the foundational history of the United States of America.

RESTAURANTS

Westside 66 Grocery and Deli (3691 LA-18, Edgard, 985/497-6909, 8am-3:30pm Mon.-Sat., $3-8) is a bare-bones, cash-only, limited-menu, counter-service hole-in-the-wall eatery that serves some of the best fried chicken and catfish around. Get two pieces of fried chicken with French fries, a fried shrimp po'boy, or fried catfish over dirty rice. It doesn't look like much,

Whitney Plantation Museum

but it's perfect for a quick bite after a tour at the Whitney Plantation. Everything's fried fresh to order.

GETTING THERE

From New Orleans, it's 50 miles to Whitney Plantation via I-10 West, I-310 South, LA-3127, and US-18. The drive takes about an hour.

LAKE MAUREPAS AND THE MANCHAC SWAMP

Lake Maurepas is the second largest lake in Louisiana—right after nearby Lake Pontchartrain. The two lakes are separated by a narrow area that contains both the Manchac Swamp and I-55, which runs north-south and crosses I-10 at LaPlace.

TOP EXPERIENCE

SWAMP TOURS

Taking a boat tour of this area, rather than trying to explore it independently, is your best bet for having a good experience. Tour guides here tend to be funny and folksy, and they know all the best spots to take you. You can find tours all over the place: Honey Island Swamp near Slidell, Cajun Pride Swamp off of the Maurepas Swamp Wildlife Area, the Barataria Swamps and Wetlands, Bayou Segnette, Jean Lafitte National Historical Park and Preserve, Bayou Black/Gibson, and other spots. A lot of these places can be driven to in less than a half hour, either under your own steam or by arranging transportation with the tour company.

Part of the fun of a swamp tour is spotting gators. If there's a swamp, there's likely a gator nearby. If it's wintertime and chilly out, you may not have much luck spotting them, however. They're cold blooded animals and tend to hibernate by burying themselves in mud at the bottom of the swamp. Once it warms up, though, there'll be gators a-plenty, swimming and sunning themselves on logs.

Cajun Pride Swamp Tours (110 Frenier Rd., LaPlace, 504/467-0758, cajunprideswamptours.com; tour times 9:30am, noon, 2:25pm, 4:15pm; $27 adults, $16 children 4-12) operates in a privately owned wildlife refuge in the Manchac Swamp, so you'll feel like you're far away from civilization for an hour or two. The swamp boat captains are old-school South Louisiana characters who know the waterways and inhabitants (both human and animal) of the area like the back of their hands. You'll share the large flat-bottomed boat with about 25-30 other folks, though more intimate tours are available for a fee. (The boats are covered in case of rain.) If there are gators around, your captain will throw them marshmallows to draw them close to the boat so you can snap photos. The tour also includes a history of the Manchac Swamp, and Frenier, the tiny Cajun town that sits within it. It's a fascinating look at the area's wildlife and plant life, and the people who exist alongside them. You can get your tickets at a discount if you order in advance online. Transportation from New Orleans is available for an additional cost.

RESTAURANTS

Middendorf's (30160 US-51, Akers, 985/386-6666,

middendorfsrestaurant.com; 10:30am-9pm Wed.-Sun.; $5-25) makes the platonic ideal of fried catfish, along with everything else that comes from the Gulf. The swamps are also represented, with fried alligator bites, turtle soup, and broiled frog legs. There are many dishes for every taste: barbequed oysters on the half shell, boiled local crab, and a stuffed and broiled whole flounder. Middendorf's sits on a tributary between Lake Maurepas and Lake Pontchartrain and is a fantastic spot to catch the sunset. Attached to the restaurant is a dock, which allows locals to boat in. There's also an extensive, covered waterfront dining area. It's a great casual place filled with history and the flavor of an old-school fishing village.

GETTING THERE

To get to the Lake Maurepas and Manchac Swamp area, take I-10 west from New Orleans, then I-55 or LA-51 north, depending on your destination. Accounting for traffic, it will take 45-60 minutes to drive 25-40 miles.

LAPLACE

Andouille is a Cajun smoked pork sausage, which gets its flavor from the spice and smoke in the meat. It's usually coarsely ground and is used as a base for many traditional local recipes like gumbo, red beans, and jambalaya.

Although LaPlace is certainly not the only Louisiana town making andouille, there's a definite local style. Here, the sausage has a large diameter and is made with paper-thin casings. Some say it's because of the German population that settled in this area, since the local andouille

Cajun Pride Swamp Tours

is reminiscent of the thick smoked sausage native to Germany.

FESTIVALS AND EVENTS

It's not a huge surprise that LaPlace, the Andouille Capital of the World, holds an annual Andouille Festival (2900 Hwy 51, LaPlace, 985/652-9569, andouillefestival.com; $3 adults, $1 children 3-12, does not include carnival rides) celebrating all things smoked sausage. It takes place in mid-October, so it's a nice time of year to get to 'festing. While the focus of the food is certainly on andouille, there are other dishes to try, and there's music, a second line, a kids' tent, and carnival rides. It's a fun little regional fair.

SHOPS

✪ Jacob's World-Famous Andouille & Sausage

You might think you'd have to drive all the way to Cajun Country to get authentic Cajun smoked meat, but Jacob's World-Famous Andouille & Sausage (505 W. Airline Hwy., LaPlace, 985/652-9080, cajunsausage.com; 8am-6pm Mon.-Sat.) is only about 40 minutes from New Orleans, and worth the drive. The Jacobs family was one of the first groups of German settlers in the

SIDE TRIP TO ABITA BREWING

Abita beer

Abita Beer is entrenched in Louisiana life and is also very popular elsewhere. Started in 1986, Abita is the oldest continually operating brewery in the state. It started in Abita Springs because of the great chemical composition and taste of the water and they still use water pumped directly from the aquifers, without treatment of any sort. They produce at least a dozen different kinds of beer every year, from their year-round flagship beers to their seasonal beers. They also brew limited releases. Their Harvest series celebrates Louisiana crops; their special Bourbon Street series features imperial stout and Baltic porter aged in bourbon barrels.

The Abita Visitor Center and Tap Room (166 Barbee Rd., Covington, 985/893-3143, abita.com; 10am-7pm Sun.-Thurs., 10am-8pm Fri.-Sat.) is a fun jaunt from New Orleans. At the tap room you can sample and purchase dozens of experimental beers along with Abita's flagship and seasonal brews. The guided brewery tour (every half hour, 2pm-3pm Wed.-Thurs., 1pm-3pm Fri. and Sun., 10:30am-3pm Sat.) lasts about a half hour, is family-friendly, and includes four sample pours of Abita beer. The tour costs $5 (free for guests under 21). Self-guided tours (10am-4pm Mon.-Tues., 10am-1pm Wed.-Thurs. and Sun., 10am-noon Fri.) are free, but don't include any samples.

Abita Springs is about 45 minutes away from New Orleans; a trip here involves crossing 24 miles of the longest bridge over water in the world, the Causeway Bridge. If you don't want to drive, you can join the NOLA Brew Bus (nolabrewbus.com) to check out Abita on Thursdays and Sundays at 12:30pm.

If you're interested in checking out other breweries in the area, Chafunkta Brewing Company (69123 Skybrook Rd., Mandeville, 985/869-0716, chafunkta-brew.com; 5pm-9pm Wed.-Fri., noon-9pm Sat., noon-6pm Sun.) and Old Rail Brewing Company (639 Girod St., Mandeville, 985/612-1828, oldrailbrewing.com; 11am-9pm Sun. and Tues.-Thurs., 11am-10:30pm Fri.-Sat.) are close by via car or by bike on the Tammany Trace bike path.

area. This butcher shop and smokehouse has been selling the family's andouille since 1928. The andouille here looks nothing like what you might find in the grocery store: It's dark and wizened from the smoking and curing process, and it tastes amazing! You can also find other meat specialties like *tasso*, hogshead cheese, and smoked turkey and chicken. Nearby is **Wayne Jacob's Smokehouse** (769 W. 5th St., 985/652-9990), which is unrelated to this place, but if you like your andouille less smoked and spicier, or just want to explore the different meats, check it out.

GETTING THERE

To get to LaPlace from New Orleans, head west on I-10; it's right off of the interstate. The drive is only 30 miles and it takes 35-45 minutes to get there, depending on traffic.

Acadiana

The area known as Acadiana (also referred to as Cajun Country) encapsulates the towns of **Lafayette, Scott, Breaux Bridge,** and **Arnaudville.** The area is diverse in its population and attractions. "Cajun" is the modern derivative of Acadian, which is what the original French-speaking settlers of this area were known as. Acadians came to the area in the mid-18th century after being expelled from Canada by the British. In addition to the folks who live and work in the small city of Lafayette, there are college kids attending University of Louisiana-Lafayette. Lots of small towns surrounding Lafayette, populated with people who farm and fish for a living. East of Lafayette are Breaux Bridge and Arnaudville, small towns with a quiet charm and local feel. Scott, west of the city, is a good place to get some boudin—there are several very popular boudin and Cajun meat spots clustered together here, just off the highway.

SIGHTS

✪ BAYOU TECHE BREWING

The founders—the three Knott brothers—of **Bayou Teche Brewing** (1094 Bushville Hwy., Arnaudville,

337/754-5122, bayoutechebrewing. com; 11am-5pm Mon.-Wed., 11am-9pm Thurs.-Sat., noon-5pm Sun.) built this rapidly growing brewery as a "cultural brewery," which means they incorporate the sounds, tastes, language, arts, and history of Acadiana into everything they do. The beers that Bayou Teche brews are designed to complement the food of Louisiana—spicy stews and soups, smoked meats, fresh seafood—which creates endless opportunities to partner with local restaurants. With a wide variety of beers—from their hoppy Swamp Thing IPA, to the blonde ales and lagers that go down well in the Louisiana heat, to even a traditional *biere de garde*—there's something for everyone. There are brewery tours (free) every Saturday at 12:30pm, 3:30pm, and 5pm. Saturdays and Sundays are Cajun jam fests, with Cajun-influenced pizza and performances by local musicians. This brewery is more than just a place to drink beer. It's truly representative of its community.

ACADIAN CULTURE CENTER

The National Park Service's **Acadian Cultural Center** (501

decor at Bayou Teche Brewing

Fisher Rd., Lafayette, 337/232-0789, nps.gov/jela/new-acadian-cultural-center.htm; 8am-5pm daily; free) offers an excellent overview of Cajun history and culture. Housed within a contemporary building designed to resemble a Cajun cottage, the museum space contains well-labeled, often large-scale exhibits, artifacts, and photos. You can easily spend an hour in here absorbing the lore of Cajun music, family life, cooking, language, and fishing, and exploring the serpentine route that the Acadians took from Nova Scotia to reach Southern Louisiana. Through exhibits as well as varied films, you'll have a gut-wrenching but inspirational look at the plight of the Cajuns and their astonishing resolve, balanced with the love of celebration and tradition that has kept them a distinct cultural group to this day. Check the calendar online for interpretive programs and performances, which are scheduled regularly through the year.

✪ VERMILIONVILLE

Vermilionville (300 Fisher Rd., Lafayette, 337/233-4077, vermilionville.org; 10am-4pm Tues.-Sun.; $10 adults, $8 seniors, $6 students, children under 5 free) is a must-visit for understanding Cajun culture. This 23-acre, living history compound comprises five restored historic houses, 12 reproduction period buildings, and exhibits about the area's indigenous people, wetlands, and Cajun and zydeco music (which is performed live here regularly). You can attend cooking demonstrations, eat at the casual La Cuisine de Maman restaurant, and walk along a nature trail identifying Louisiana plant life. Vermilionville is near the Lafayette airport and several modern warehouses, but once you enter the recreated village, it feels quite authentic; there's even a lazy bayou running through the property. The buildings here include a chapel and presbytère, where a clergyman would have lived; an Acadian barn where volunteers engage in boat-building and net- and trap-making; and several residences, the oldest dating from 1790. Every element of Vermilionville sheds light onto the culture of the area's original Cajuns, from homestyle cooking to live music and dance programs. As a bonus, the staff members are knowledgeable and enthusiastic.

an exhibit in Vermilionville

RESTAURANTS

There is so much good food in the area, from greasy spoons to traditional fancy places to cafes to low-key meat markets, you can't go wrong. This is by no means an exhaustive list, it's just a few places that showcase the range of cuisine in the Lafayette area.

Although pizza and other Italian dishes are the main attraction at Bread and Circus Provisions (258 Bendel Rd., Lafayette, 337/408-3930, bandcprovisions.com; 11am-5pm Tues., 11am-3pm 4pm-10pm Wed.-Fri., 11am-2:30pm and 4pm-10pm Sat.; $7-20), there are some Cajun-influenced delights on the lunch and brunch menus, like five-day-cured pork cracklin' and boudin-stuffed beignets. The modern, funky vibe and a killer cocktail menu makes this a fun place for a meal or just to hang out.

The historic building that houses Café Vermilionville (1304 W. Pinhook Rd., Lafayette, 337/237-0100, cafev.com; 11am-2pm and 5:30pm-9pm Mon.-Fri., 5:30pm-9pm Sat.; $10-40) has been around since the early 19th century, and has been home to the white-tablecloth restaurant for two generations of the Veron family. The historic interior has been designed to provide an elegant atmosphere, and the outdoor courtyard hosts weekly live local music in the spring and fall, in addition to providing the backdrop for romantic al fresco dining. The food is excellent, with lots of seasonal specials and some traditional favorites like gumbo (both meat and seafood), pan-seared Gulf fish topped with crabmeat, and white-chocolate bread pudding.

Smoked meat, sausages, and boudin are the order of business at Johnson's Boucaniere (1111 St. John St., Lafayette, 337/269-8878, johnsonsboucaniere.com; 7am-3pm Tues.-Fri., 7am-5:30pm Sat.; $4-10), where the heartiest of breakfasts awaits you. They also serve sandwiches and plate lunches. Try the stuffed grilled cheese—on a biscuit if it's the morning or on a bun for lunch—which is essentially smoked meat wrapped with cheese and then pressed on the grill. It's life changing. With seating out on the front porch and friendly service, what more could you need? Save room for the bread pudding for dessert.

Another place for hearty Acadian breakfasts (served till 11am weekdays, noon on weekends) is Tante Marie (107 N. Main St., Breaux Bridge, 337/442-6354, jamsandbiscuits.com; 6am-8pm Mon.-Thurs., 6am-10pm Fri.-Sat., 8am-2pm Sun.; $5-15), which hosts local musicians on Friday and Saturday nights, and Saturday and Sunday mornings. You'll be able to dance off dishes like the boudin breakfast burrito or Chicken Bayou Teche, which is chicken stuffed with sausage, topped with a bacon-cream-cheese sauce, and served with Cajun rice. They also do plate lunch specials during the week for $9, from red beans and sausage on Mondays to fried catfish on Fridays.

You've got to check out the Zydeco Breakfast on Saturdays at Buck & Johnny's (100 Berard St., Breaux Bridge, 337/442-6630, buckandjohnnys.com; 11am-2pm Sun.-Mon., 11am-9pm Tues.-Thurs., 11am-10pm Fri., 8am-10pm Sat.; $6-25) to start your weekend off right.

Buck & Johnny's makes Cajun-style dishes, with a focus on Cajun-inspired pizzas and pastas, and hosts live music Thursday, Friday, and Saturday nights as well as Saturday mornings.

NIGHTLIFE

In this part of the world, restaurants that don't have live music are the exception. You can catch Cajun and zydeco bands at a number of places throughout the area, but Lafayette and the neighboring towns support any and all genres of music. Popular Blue Moon Saloon & Guesthouse (215 E. Convent St., Lafayette, 337/234-2422 or 877/766-2583, bluemoonpresents.com; show times vary) has a large outdoor deck where musicians of all types perform Wednesday through Sunday to an all-ages crowd. This place, which also offers affordable overnight accommodations, is usually packed with locals and visitors alike.

The funky exterior of Artmosphere (902 Johnson St., Lafayette, 337/233-3331, artmosphere.vpweb.com; 11:30am-2am daily) is a draw for anyone passing by, and the arty atmosphere (see what they did there?) continues inside, where there's a bar, a stage for musicians to play Wednesday through Sunday, and tables for eating, drinking, and watching. The menu is pretty good, with pizzas, sandwiches, burgers, and the like, and it's served late. Artmosphere attracts nationally recognized acts like the Pine Leaf Boys and Michael Juan Nunez, as well as local bands with a wide variety of musical styles.

For an opportunity to step into another era, check out the pre-Prohibition vibe and decor of The Grouse Room (1919 Kaliste Saloom Rd., suite 303, Lafayette, 337/806-9098, thegrouseroom. com; 7pm-midnight Wed., 8pm-2am Thurs.-Sat.), a cocktail bar, live music venue, and overall cool place. There's no cover for the dueling pianos on Thursday nights; bigger acts take the stage Fridays and Saturdays, but the intimate setting makes for a sophisticated and enjoyable atmosphere.

✪ LA POUSSIERE

On the weekends, check out the last old-fashioned Cajun dance hall, La Poussiere (1301 Grand Point Ave., Breax Bridge, 337/332-1721, lapoussiere.com; show times vary Thurs.-Sun.; cover $5-10). Here you'll find an authentic Cajun country experience. The tradition has been going on since 1955 and they've hosted hundreds of legendary Cajun musicians and thousands of enthusiastic dancers in that time. Newcomers are welcome: You'll be a part of the community by the time the music ends. You can dance, or just watch the band and the dancing around you—some of these folks are tremendous! It's a one-of-a-kind cultural adventure.

ARTS AND CULTURE

In Lafayette, the Acadiana Center for the Arts (101 W. Vermilion St., Lafayette, 337/233-7060, acadianacenterforthearts.org; galleries 10am-5pm daily, free; performance times and ticket prices vary) showcases both the visual and performing arts—including but not limited to films, theater, opera, concerts, and small participatory festivals.

All artists are local to Acadiana, and the ever-changing gallery exhibits have included paintings in the Baroque style, art influenced by Haitian culture, and textile arts by the local quilting guild. The large, modern building houses a performance space, galleries, and smaller event spaces. It's right in downtown Lafayette.

✪ NUNU ARTS AND CREATIVE CULTURE COLLECTIVE

There are a number of opportunities to view, purchase, and participate in local art and culture in this region. NUNU Arts and Creative Culture Collective (1510 Hwy Courtableau, LA-93 E., Arnaudville, 337/754-5990, nunucollective.homesteadcloud.com; 11am-4pm Thurs.-Sun.), in the rural and picturesque town of Arnaudville (which has held onto its Cajun French dialect longer than the rest of Acadiana) supports the community, its artists, and its culture bearers. This cultural center provides classes, gallery space, and a general gathering place for locals, and the opportunity to bring local art to visitors from around the world through its gallery marketplace. From the outside, the building seems ramshackle, but inside is a treasure trove of information on modern Cajun culture. The neighboring barn is where live music events, dances, and general revelry happens. Three resident galleries are permanent fixtures in the main building, all of which offer authentic local crafts, art, and vintage items. Other rotating vendors include literary galleries, textile displays and shops, and a gift shop with all sorts of locally made pottery, jewelry, and other crafts. Events happen at NUNU frequently; on any given Saturday, you might find a farmers market, a Francophone cultural immersion experience, or local poetry readings.

FESTIVALS AND EVENTS

Outside New Orleans, no part of the state enjoys a good festival more than Acadiana. Scores of engaging events are held in towns throughout the region, practically year-round. Courir de Mardi Gras, also known as Cajun Mardi Gras, happens on and around Fat Tuesday in small towns and villages throughout South Louisiana. There are larger celebrations and parades in Lafayette and Vermillionville. These celebrations stem directly from European rural traditions involving specific costumes (think masked rag dolls), French musical performances, and, of course, dancing and parading. Courir is French for "run," so every celebration will have a race as the focal point of the festivities. For a great online resource, check out lafayettetravel.com for listings of the many events leading up to Mardi Gras proper.

Early in April, the region's famous sausage, boudin, gets its own festival in the town of Scott. Boudin is the ultimate Cajun food: It's made with pork shoulder, rice, and occasionally pork liver. Scott has no less than five excellent purveyors of boudin. The Scott Boudin Festival (Lions Club Rd., Scott, 337/233-1130, scottboudinfestival.com; $5 on Fri.-Sat, free on Sun. and for kids under 6) is where you'll find multiple mouthwatering preparations of this spiced pork and rice sausage, along with local Zydeco music and Cajun variants. Don't miss the boudin eating contest and the Cajun and Zydeco dance competitions.

In early May, fans of mudbugs (crayfish) gather at the Breaux Bridge Crawfish Festival (Breaux Bridge, 337/332-6655) to sample various iterations of the star of the festival and listen to live Cajun and zydeco music. In mid-October, just as the hot weather is beginning to break, Lafayette holds its rollicking Festivals Acadiens et Creoles (Girard Park, Lafayette, festivalsacadiens.com), a chance for visitors to learn about Cajun culture through its rich musical traditions. You can learn the Cajun waltz or two-step, and find out how accordions and fiddles figure into the

sounds of Cajun song and dance. Outside Mardi Gras, this is one of the region's most popular, well-attended festivals, comprising several smaller events, including the Festival de Musique, the Bayou Food Festival, the Louisiana Craft Fair, and Louisiana Folk Roots.

✪ FESTIVAL INTERNATIONAL DE LOUISIANE

Lafayette hosts the annual Festival International de Louisiane (downtown Lafayette, 337/232-8086, festivalinternational.org; free), a massive five-day music festival and street fair in late April that showcases all kinds of local and French/French-speaking countries' music, French-language plays, and other Francophone fun, plus more local food than you can shake a stick at. Check out dishes like sweet potato

festival goers in Lafayette

GAS STATION GOURMET

You might not expect it, but Louisiana gas-station convenience stores, especially in small towns, offer excellent home-cooked, traditional Cajun food.

Billy's Mini-Mart (24467 US-190, Krotz Springs, 337/566-2318, billysboudin. com; 4am-10pm Sun.-Wed., 4am-11pm Thurs.-Sat.) is my favorite stop for local Cajun meat. The gas pumps don't work anymore, but the convenience store inside is like what you'd see at any gas station. The boudin is outstanding (they make it themselves). You'll see pretty much every customer parked, leaning on their vehicle, and eating some boudin before heading back on the road. Another former gas station-turned-market is Billeaud's (111 E. Main St., Broussard, 337/837-6825, billeauds.com; 6:30am-7:30pm Mon.-Sat., 8am-3:30pm Sun.), which has a pretty slick website for such a humble operation. Their boudin and cracklin' are amazing.

From the gas station exterior of College Junction Mudbugs (101 Veterans Dr., Eunice, 337/457-4252; 5am-9pm Mon.-Fri., 6am-9pm Sat.), you'd never guess the high quality of the food they serve—everything from crawfish and grilled fish to boudin, country fried steak, and barbecue pork.

This is not just an experience for road trippers, luckily. There's plenty of gas station food in New Orleans that's also worth your time. At the Magazine Street Jetgo, Shawarma On the Go (3720 Magazine St., 504/269-6427, shawarmaonthego.com; 11am-9pm Mon.-Sat., 11am-8pm Sun.) provides gyros, falafel, and Persian iced tea. New Orleans's top gas-station food, however, is fried chicken. Some of the best versions can be found at the Magnolia Discount (3415 S. Carrollton Ave., 504/482-8823; 24 hours daily), Key's Fuel Mart (1139 N. Rampart St., 504/301-4598; 24 hours daily), and at the Louisiana Super Saver (1641 Louisiana Ave., 504/891-6670; 7am-9pm daily).

---

beignets, Cajun egg rolls, and praline chicken. It's a local favorite due to the music performances and that Lafayette laissez-faire.

RECREATION

The Bayou Teche Experience (317 E. Bridge St., Breaux Bridge, 337/366-0337; 7am-7pm daily) is a small tour operator that provides a close-up bayou exploration experience with kayak and canoe tours through the Lake Martin swamp and Bayou Teche, a 125-mile waterway that runs through Breaux Bridge, Arnaudville, and New Iberia. The two-hour guided tours are brimming with information about the history and culture of the area, as well as about the wildlife you might come across. The tours are tailored to individual interests, be

they Natural History and Wildlife, Cajun Heritage, or Eco-Tourism.

SHOPS

In downtown Lafayette, art lovers should stop by the Sans Souci Fine Crafts Gallery (219 E. Vermilion St., Lafayette, 337/266-7999, louisianacrafts.org; 11am-5pm Tues.-Fri., 10am-4pm Sat.) featuring the traditional and contemporary works of members of the Louisiana Crafts Guild. Housed within a 19th-century structure, this well-regarded gallery features textiles, jewelry, pottery, glass, and wood.

In Scott, there are tons of Cajun meat shops as soon as you get off the highway. Locals have their preferences, because each shop's version of boudin is slightly different in flavor and texture. My two favorites are Billy's Boudin & Cracklin (523 Apollo Rd., Scott, 337/232-1114, billysboudin.com; 6:30am-7pm Mon.-Fri., 7am-7pm Sat.-Sun.) and Don's Specialty Meats (730 I-10S Frontage Rd., Scott, 337/234-2528, donsspecialtymeats.com; 6am-7pm Mon.-Thurs., 6am-8pm Fri.-Sat., 7am-8pm Sun.). Billy's boudin is tender, but meaty. They'll cut up the links for you when you order them hot, which makes it easy to eat on the go. They also have a drive-through window. Don's boudin has a slight spiciness that never crosses the line to too hot. The cracklin' at both places is great, also.

Breaux Bridge has a surprising number of vintage and antiques shops to check out. There are half a dozen of them in a two- to three-block radius on Bridge Street. The best place to start is at Lagniappe Antique Mall (124 W. Bridge St., Breaux Bridge, 337/507-2036, breauxbridgeantiques.com; 10am-6pm Tues.-Sat., noon-5pm Sun.). It's a large (air-conditioned!) antiques mall with more than 30 sellers and individual antiques dealers. There are also coffee shops, bistros, and restaurants in the neighboring blocks, so it's a lovely way to spend a lazy afternoon. From books to vintage clothing, to furniture to original art to fancy chandeliers, you can find a lot of Louisiana and Cajun Country history if you dig deep enough.

WHERE TO STAY

With rates lower than most of the nearby cookie-cutter motels, the Bayou Cabins Bed & Breakfast (100 W. Mills Ave., Breaux Bridge, 337/332-6158, bayoucabins.com; $60-135) is a fun and funky alternative. There are 13 cozy cabins right by the Bayou Teche, close to downtown Breaux Bridge. The cabins are rustic but endearingly furnished: one has old newspaper for wallpaper, and one is decked out in 1950s-style furnishing. There's also a home-style café on the premises serving boudin, cracklin', and beignets. A full breakfast is included Wednesday through Sunday.

For a getaway right on the water, check out Cajun Country Cottages (1138 Lawless Tauzin Rd., Breaux Bridge, 337/332-3093, cajuncottages.com; $160-195), which provides five peaceful cottages surrounding a private lake (it's stocked with fish if you're inclined to cast a line off your porch). The Acadian-style structures are furnished in a rustic and comfortable design, with fully equipped kitchens. A full breakfast is delivered to your door every morning in a basket. The use of boats and canoes is included for all guests.

The nine rooms at T'Frere's House Bed & Breakfast (1905 Verot School Rd., Lafayette, 337/984-9347, tfrereshouse.com; $110-155) range in style from crisp and modern to Mardi Gras themed to old-fashioned four-poster beds and antiques. Enjoy a welcome cocktail on the front porch or the glass-enclosed patio overlooking the gardens. The common areas have country-style antiques and the rooms are bright and welcoming. The management and staff are full of southern hospitality. Don't sleep through breakfast—it's well worth getting up for.

TRANSPORTATION

Lafayette is about 135 miles from New Orleans, a shade over two hours' drive on I-10. Between New Orleans and Baton Rouge, there's often a lot of traffic. West of Baton Rouge, there's a separate, elevated four-lane highway that passes through swampland and the Atchafalaya Basin that can get backed up pretty fast if there's an accident.

Avery Island and Vicinity

Avery Island is a strange mix of nature, industry, and tourism. And it's not, in fact, an island. Rather it's a salt dome, which rises gently above the surrounding wetlands and has been a source of commercial salt since the 1860s. On top of the dome is the Tabasco plant, a family business that's been operating here since 1868. Avery Island also has a curated scenic route called the Jungle Gardens that can be driven or walked, with all sorts of birds, swamp creatures, and plants. It's a world of its own. Not too far away are New Iberia and Abbeville, a couple of towns that present an authentic Cajun way of life. It's about two hours away from New Orleans, making it a long day of driving for a day trip, so I suggest staying overnight and relaxing.

SIGHTS
TABASCO FACTORY

Avery Island's claim to fame is its multi-generational Tabasco sauce production facility, which Edward McIlhenny first bottled here in 1868. The family-friendly tour of the McIlhenny Company's Tabasco factory (337/365-8173 or 800/634-9599, tabasco.com; 9am-4pm daily; $5.50 general, children under 4 free) is a self-guided experience that starts in the museum, which traces not only the history of the company, but also of the island and its salt mine. From there, clearly marked signs guide visitors to see a small greenhouse filled with peppers, then learn about the barreling process (with a rather pungent walk by a barrel-aging facility with fermenting pepper sauce), and see a bottling line in action (if you're there during the week). Then it's off to check out various Tabasco memorabilia, the gift shop, and the on-site cafeteria-style restaurant, which serves dishes that are prepared with Tabasco's various hot sauces.

a stop on the Tabasco factory tour

Jungle Gardens on Avery Island

✪ JUNGLE GARDENS AND BIRD CITY

Jungle Gardens and Bird City (337/369-6243, junglegardens.org; 9am-5pm daily, $8 adults, $5 children under 13) is a garden complex bisected by a narrow four-mile country lane. You can tour the attraction in less than an hour by car, or in a few hours on foot. There are several spots to park along the drive, so you can get a closer look at the area. Thousands of subtropical plants and trees, including massive moss-draped live oaks, grow throughout these wild gardens, which are home to deer, turtles,

Bird City

nutria, rabbits, black bears, and alligators. The gardens also include the most complete collection of camellias in the world and a Buddhist temple containing a Buddha statue that is thought to date back to the 12th century. Although the gardens are open year-round, they're less thrilling in winter (Nov.-Feb.), when much of the plant life is dormant and the alligators hibernate.

Take a few moments to observe Bird City, a massive nesting ground for graceful great white egrets. Long stilted platforms rise out of a marshy pond, and the egrets build nests here. The egrets are most prolific from December through July, when you may see hundreds gathering branches, mating, courting, and putting on a spectacular show. A three-story observation deck sits opposite the nesting platforms, close enough for a true Instagram moment. The attraction is owned by the McIlhenny family, who also run the Tabasco factory. Discounted combination tickets to both the factory and Jungle Gardens are available.

RESTAURANTS

The entire southern coastal area of Louisiana is well-known for its oysters. Abbeville has a number of excellent oyster houses, but Shucks! (701 W. Port St., Abbeville, 337/898-3311, shucksrestaurant. com; Mon.-Thurs. 11am-9pm, Fri.-Sat. 11am-10pm; $9-25) is one of the most highly regarded, with half a dozen different oyster preparations. They also serve Cajun standards like crawfish étouffée, and specialties like seafood pasta with grilled oysters, shrimp, and crawfish tails. Prices are very reasonable, the

335

service is great, and the ambience is relaxed and family friendly.

Suire's Grocery & Restaurant (13923 LA-35, Kaplan, 337/643-8911, suires.yolasite.com; 5:30am-6:30pm Mon.-Sat., 6:30am-1:30pm Sun.; $5-$15) is one of those places that doesn't look like much from the outside, but once you smell what's cooking and taste the food, it's a revelation. Kaplan is about a 50-minute drive west of Avery Island. If you're interested in trying the Cajun classic turtle sauce piquant, this is where to do it. You won't find it made with such love and care anywhere else. No matter if you get the plate lunch special of the day, fried oysters, or gumbo, save room for dessert, or at least take one of the homemade treats—like fig cake, pecan pie, or strawberry tarts—to go.

The gumbo and beloved over-stuffed po'boys feature fresh local seafood at the lunch counter of **Bon Creole** (1409 E. St. Peter St., New Iberia, 337/367-6181, bon-creole.com; 11am-9pm Mon.-Sat., 11am-2pm Sun.; $4-13) but their burgers are also well regarded. It's very casual, with mismatched tables and chairs and lots of memorabilia as decoration. The quick turnaround makes it very popular with locals for lunch. Bon Creole fans are known to drive an hour or two just to get their hands on a shrimp po'boy.

ARTS AND CULTURE

The **Bayou Teche Museum** (131 E. Main St., New Iberia, 337/606-5977, bayoutechemuseum.org; 10am-4pm Thurs.-Sat.; $5 adults, $3 seniors, military, and students, children under 5 free) celebrates and passes along the history of this small hamlet founded by Spain in 1779. There's a lot of information about local Mardi Gras customs, the local steam-ship industry, and shipwreck lore. And then there's the studio of late local artist George Rodrigue; it was dismantled from the artist's home in California and reassembled here, in his hometown.

FESTIVALS AND EVENTS

New Iberia's **Louisiana Sugar Cane Festival** coincides with the harvesting of sugarcane in late September and is one of the oldest celebrations in the state, first held in 1937. Sugarcane continues to be an economic factor in this part of Louisiana, and the festival celebrating it is serious business. It's got a coronation ball to crown Queen Sugar and King Sucrose, a contest to judge the best cook of sugary treats, and a *fais do do,* which is a Cajun dance party with live zydeco music.

✪ GIANT OMELETTE CELEBRATION

Festivals in this part of Louisiana are smaller and community focused; take the **Giant Omelette Celebration** (giantomelette.org) in Abbeville, held the first weekend of November. The signature event is the creation of a 5,000-egg omelet made in a 12-foot skillet, followed by the attendees eating the omelet. The festival is based on a legend that involves Napoleon, who loved omelets so much that when he and his army were traveling through southern France, he ordered the townspeople to gather all the eggs and make a huge omelet. The cooking of the omelet occurs on the afternoon of day two; leading up to it there's music and dancing and kids' activities.

SHOPS

On the way to Avery Island, be sure to stop by **Black Kettle Cajun Meats & Market** (825 US-90, Patterson, 985/412-6073; 7am-5pm Tues.-Sun., 7am-3pm Sat.) for what they call a Cajun Breakfast—hot boudin and cracklin'. There's lots here you can buy to take with you, including hot jambalaya egg rolls, crawfish boudin, and pepper-jack boudin balls. There's nowhere to sit and eat, so if you're hungry, hop up on your car hood to enjoy the goodness.

New Iberia is one of the region's best towns for shopping, as it's home to several boutiques and antiques shops. Check out **Books Along the Teche** (106 E. Main St., New Iberia, 337/367-7621 or 877/754-0849, booksalongtheteche.com; 9:30am-5:30pm Mon.-Fri., 9:30am-5pm Sat.), a small, first-rate independent bookstore that offers both new and used books. It specializes in regional books and music, and has signed copies of all of the books by long-time New Iberia resident James Lee Burke, author of the popular Dave Robicheaux detective novels.

The locally owned women's clothing and accessory boutique **Alex Malay** (206A E. Main St., New Iberia, 10am-6pm Mon.-Sat.) focuses on empowering the women who shop here. The clothing is unique, fun, and sophisticated—and there's even an in-house Alex Malay makeup line and a super cute collection of purses and shoes. Prices are surprisingly reasonable for the quality of the items and service.

Cane River Pecan Company (254 W. Main St., New Iberia, 800/692-3109, caneriverpecan.com; 10am-6pm Mon.-Sat.) is the perfect place to get edible gifts. They sell their locally harvested pecans in tins and bags of all different sizes and flavors, including chocolate-covered, honey-glazed, praline, and salted/roasted.

WHERE TO STAY

You have to drive a bit (anywhere between 25-60 minutes) to get to a place to stay if you're on Avery Island, but the local inns are so unique and steeped in local culture that it's worth it. For example, **Rip Van Winkle Bed & Breakfast** (5505 Rip Van Winkle Rd., New Iberia, 337/359-8525, ripvanwinklegardens.com; $135-$170) is located on the grounds of the Rip Van Winkle Gardens, a gorgeous stretch of moss-draped oak trees, peacocks, and semi-tropical plants and flowers. The gardens and the mansion are available to tour (10am-7pm daily; $12 adults, $10 seniors, $6 children 6-17) but is free for those staying in the two guest cottages. It's the closest place to stay from Avery Island, about a 25-minute drive.

In Abbeville, the **Ducote Williams House** (401 North St. Charles St., Abbeville, 337/898-0048, ducotewilliams.com; $95-125) has a couple of rooms and provides a huge dose of southern hospitality along with a bed and full Cajun breakfast. It's right between Abbeville's adorable downtown and its residential historic district, so it's great for walks.

The Gouguenheim (101 W. Main St., New Iberia, 337/364-3949, gouguenheim.com; $225-325) offers four luxury suites right on the banks of the Bayou Teche, on New Iberia's downtown Main Street. It was converted from a ballroom that was constructed in 1894, and has a large veranda that wraps around the second floor. Hardwood floors, detailed woodwork, exposed brick, and elegant furnishings give the suites the feel of a small boutique hotel. Bonus for James Lee Burke fans: The included breakfast is at the neighboring Victor's Café, a staple background spot in Burke's Dave Robicheaux series.

✪ CRAWFISH HAVEN/ MRS. ROSE'S BED AND BREAKFAST

A truly excellent adventure awaits you at Crawfish Haven/Mrs. Rose's Bed and Breakfast (6807 Hwy. 35, Kaplan, 337/652-8870, crawfishhaven.net; $125-150), about an hour's drive from Avery Island. At this inn, you can go on crawfish excursions ($50 pp), which include boiling and eating your catch. You can also try your

Rip Van Winkle Bed & Breakfast

hand at catching some with a net on the banks of the pond behind the building for free. The owner is an excellent Cajun cook, and in addition to the breakfast included with the stay, you can arrange for him to cook (or teach you to cook) a Cajun dinner.

TRANSPORTATION

Avery Island is southwest of New Orleans, heading west on I-10, south on I-310, and west on Route 90, a 141-mile drive. The entire drive is about 2 hours and 15 minutes. The final stretch, taking LA-329 till it ends at the entrance of the island is only about 15 minutes.

BACKGROUND

The Landscape

GEOGRAPHY

Southern Louisiana has a unique geography, shaped by rivers, deltas, and its low elevation (averaging 100 feet above sea level). New Orleans's usefulness in trade and travel due to its location between the Gulf of Mexico, Bayou St. John, and Lake Pontchartrain is what attracted indigenous people to the area, and later, those who would colonize it.

RIVERS AND WETLANDS

The Mississippi River plays a vital role in the appearance, development, and economy of New Orleans. The river forms the border between Mississippi and Louisiana, cutting directly through Baton Rouge and New Orleans before emptying into the Gulf of Mexico. At its

the Mississippi River

end, the mighty river and its many tributaries form a fan-shaped delta. The Mississippi River is the definitive drain for about 40 percent of the United States.

The Mississippi River Delta, which extends across the southern Louisiana shoreline, took about 6,000 years to form. Its largest tributary, the Atchafalaya River, flows into the western end of the delta, southeast of Lafayette. The Atchafalaya's delta will eventually fill in much of northern Atchafalaya Bay, and will come to resemble the fully formed Mississippi River Delta.

339

Louisiana's jagged shoreline comprises 3 million wetland acres, roughly 40 percent of the entire nation's marsh ecosystem. Unlike the considerably more stable Gulf shorelines, Louisiana's coast is continuously shifting, the result of the evolving play between the Gulf currents and the flow of the Mississippi and other tributaries. Climate change and other human influence such as fracking in the Gulf have resulted in the loss of 2,000 square miles of Louisiana coast, and it continues to disappear at the rate of one football field every 100 minutes.

These wetlands have historically been natural hurricane barriers; however, they've shrunk due to coastal erosion from oil and gas canals and other phenomena. Now, the hurricanes batter them, combining fresh and salt water to create a brackish water environment that is slowly killing the indigenous plant and wildlife in these natural sanctuaries.

BAYOUS

Rivers aren't the only major waterways found in southern Louisiana. Bayous are also an important part of the regional culture. The word "bayou" derives from the Choctaw term for a river, *bayuk*. These sluggish bodies of water are large enough here that they'd be called rivers elsewhere in the country. Some of the larger bayous include Teche (which flows through St. Martinville and Breaux Bridge), Vermilion (which flows through Lafayette), LaFourche (which runs through Houma), and Boeuf (which passes near Opelousas in St. Landry Parish).

LAKES AND LAGOONS

In the southern part of the state, many "lakes" are really salt- or brackish-water lagoons that were once bays or inlets of the Gulf but became sealed off by the formation of barrier beaches or delta ridges. The largest and most famous of these is Lake Pontchartrain, which is traversed by one of the longest bridges in the world, the 24-mile Lake Pontchartrain Causeway Bridge (known colloquially as the Causeway). Other examples include Barataria Bay, south of New Orleans; Lake Maurepas, west of Lake Pontchartrain and connected to it by Bayou Manchac; and Lake Salvador, just southwest of New Orleans and fringed by Jean Lafitte National Historical Park and Preserve.

CLIMATE

Southern Louisiana is jokingly called the northernmost coast of Central America, and not just because of its banana-republic politics—it also has a climate that's more similar to Costa Rica's than to that of most of the United States. It is considered a semi-humid, subtropical zone, and it almost never receives snow; in New Orleans, when the temperature occasionally dips to freezing on the coldest winter evenings, locals bundle up as though they're about to run the Iditarod. New Orleans's average rainfall is about 64 inches of rain annually. It's rainy all year, with the highest totals in the summer and the lowest in October, but there are no bone-dry months here.

With a low atmospheric ceiling and high humidity, nighttime-to-daytime low and high temperatures

SUMMERTIME IN NEW ORLEANS

Summer in New Orleans is steamy, sticky, and so much cheaper than the rest of the year. If you're willing to adjust to heat indexes in the 90s every day and downpours every afternoon, you can pretend you're a character in turmoil in a Tennessee Williams play and support New Orleans's economy during the slowest time of the year.

"Slow" is the watchword here. Get a hat, put on sunscreen, arm yourself with water, walk slowly, and stick to the shade. Make frequent stops for cold drinks, snacks, shopping, and perusing galleries, and enjoy the sweet air-conditioning inside. Check the hours of places you want to visit, because a lot of businesses have reduced summer hours, and some spots take a week or two off in July or August.

Airfare should be reasonable, and there will be lots of hotel deals, so it's a great time to try something on the fancy side. Local restaurants offer summer prix fixe menus for low prices—some even attach it to the temperature the day before, so if you show up for lunch the day after a 93-degree day, a two-course lunch will be $9.30. There are a few times during summer when the quiet environment and low pricing doesn't apply, like during Essence Fest and Tales of the Cocktail, so double-check your dates if it doesn't seem like you're getting much of a deal.

don't usually span a great range. The mean temperature for the year is about 71°F, but New Orleans usually feels warmer; there's less breeze and the concrete roads and buildings tend to absorb and retain heat. Average high temperatures in New Orleans in summer (mid-May through September) are about 90°F, with nighttime lows averaging a still warm 73°F. In winter (December, January, and February), highs average a pleasant 65°F, with lows a manageable 45°F. Winter is a wonderful time to visit. Summer can be simply unbearable on the most humid days, even with air-conditioning. The touristy French Quarter, which can be littered with garbage along Bourbon Street and outside bars on weekend mornings, can feel and smell positively foul on a summer day. Spring and fall are fairly genial times to visit. Temperatures can easily reach into the 90s during warm spells, but

more typically average in the upper 70s in October and November and in March and April.

New Orleans itself averages 110 days a year with completely sunny skies, and about the same number of days with rain. Otherwise, it's partly sunny or partly cloudy, depending on whether you're an optimist or a pessimist.

HURRICANE SEASON

The weather has been a hot topic in southern Louisiana for as long as people have lived here—long before Hurricanes Katrina and Rita barreled through the state in 2005. Hurricane season begins in June each year and lasts through November. Hurricanes have always been a threat to the Louisiana shoreline, and given the increasing numbers and magnitude of these storms in recent years, it is likely Louisiana will have plenty of brushes with violent storms in the future.

History

PRE-COLONIZATION

The Lower Mississippi Valley was once home to almost 40 nations of indigenous peoples, in the area the Chocktaw called Bulbancha, meaning "place of many tongues," which bordered the Malbancha— "river of many tongues"—the pre-colonial term for the Mississippi River. These 40 nations were politically, culturally, and linguistically diverse. While at the trade markets (on the site where the French Market and Café Du Monde sit today), the multilingual nations spoke the agreed-upon Mobilian Trade Language. Trade was seasonal due to the annual rise and fall of the river.

For political and defense purposes, many of these nations formed alliances with each other and relocated near the river, building fortified settlements for protection. Controlling territory along the gulf coast waterways was conducive to successful trade activity. Alliances also formed to protect the indigenous people from enslavement by the earliest visitors to North America. The nations brokered alliances with French settlers for mutual benefit. As European colonization grew, however, the effects on the local tribes were devastating due to forced relocation, disease, enslavement, and massacre. Some Native Americans managed to thrive in Louisiana, many of their members intermarrying with African Americans. Today, Chitimacha, Houma, Tunica-Biloxi, Coushatta, and Choctaw

settlements are officially recognized by the state, but there are dozens more that still inhabit the area. Many geographical names in New Orleans and Louisiana have indigenous origins, among them Chef Menteur (Chief Liar), Tchoupitoulas ("village of the Choupic people"), Tangipahoa ("corncob eating people"), Bogalusa (which means "black water"), Opelousas ("black leg"), and Ponchatoula ("hanging hair"). *Note:* Thanks to Alaina Rene for sharing her knowledge of pre-colonial First Nations history.

FOUNDING OF NEW ORLEANS

Louisiana's period of French rule was barely more than three generations—France would cede the territory to the Spanish in 1762 before occupying it again for a short period preceding the Louisiana Purchase. Neither the first nor second period of French rule proved to be profitable for France, and from a colonial perspective, one could say that the entire episode was a failure. On the flip side, the French occupation planted the seeds for the emergence of New Orleans as one of young America's most fascinating cities.

New Orleans was not the first French settlement in Louisiana, although explorer Pierre Le Moyne, Sieur d'Iberville, did establish a toehold near the city on March 3, 1699. That same year, the French built a permanent fort about 90 miles east in Biloxi (now Mississippi) and, three years later, another, 60 miles east in Mobile (now Alabama). The first permanent French settlement to go up in what is now Louisiana, in 1714, was Natchitoches, a still-charming small city in northwestern Louisiana, about 300 miles northwest of New Orleans. By the late 1710s, however, France had already failed to invest substantially in its new settlement, and unable to fund a full-fledged colony, the monarchy transferred control of Louisiana to Antoine Crozat, a French financier of considerable acclaim.

Crozat was able to make little headway with Louisiana, and just five years later, control of Louisiana was shifted to Compagnie d'Occident, led by a wealthy Scotsman named John Law. It became quickly apparent to Law and other authorities, however, that the southern Mississippi was vulnerable to plays for control by the two key competing European powers in colonial America, Great Britain, and Spain. To protect their interests, the French built a new fort in 1718, along the lower Mississippi, christening the settlement La Nouvelle-Orléans, after Philippe, Duc d'Orléans. A handful of settlements were added along the Mississippi River to the north, and in 1722, France named young New Orleans the territorial capital of Louisiana.

The beginnings of Nouvelle Orléans were almost pathetically modest. The site, at a sharp bend of the Mississippi River more than five feet *below* sea level, was little more than bug- and alligator-infested swampland, which the city's earliest residents shored up with landfill and dams. Part of the settlement covered one of the few bumps of higher ground along the river's banks. The site was chosen in part because a bayou (now known as Bayou St. John) connected the Mississippi River at this point to Lake Pontchartrain, which itself emptied into the Gulf. For eons, the area's Native Americans had used the bayou as a shortcut for getting from the river to the Gulf without having to paddle all the way south, nearly another 100 miles, to where the Mississippi entered the Gulf.

Today's French Quarter, also known as the Vieux Carré (literally, Old Square), encompassed all of New Orleans for the first several decades. It was anchored by the Place d'Armes, which would later be renamed Jackson Square. The river's course in relation to the city has changed slightly since the city's founding; in the early days, Jackson Square faced the riverfront directly, whereas today a significant strip of land and levee acts as a barrier between it and the river.

John Law can be credited with making the earliest effort to attract European settlers to Louisiana. His first successful campaign brought not Frenchmen but Germans to the new territory. Law would convince Germans to move to Louisiana as indentured workers, meaning they were bound to work for an established period, and once their service commitment was complete, they were granted freedom. Law's Occidental Company used all the usual trickery and false advertising common throughout Europe in those days to attract immigrants and investors: It promised vast riches, huge mining reserves, and easy agricultural opportunities, virtually none of which was accurate.

During Law's first few years of controlling Louisiana, his company managed to convince about 7,000 mostly German and French residents to migrate to Louisiana. A significant percentage of these migrants died from disease or starvation, as the colonial authorities were in no position at all to feed, clothe, and house the arrivals. In all likelihood, if you stayed in Louisiana during these early days, you did so only because you hadn't the means to return to Europe. Word of the false promise of Louisiana spread quickly back to France, but authorities allowed Law and his company to administer the territory until 1731, when the French monarchy finally stepped in to resume control.

Law was the first person responsible for importing West African slaves to Louisiana. His Compagnie d'Occident also owned the French Compagnie du Senegal, which controlled all French slave trade. During a roughly 10-year period, about 3,000 slaves, mostly Senegalese, were taken from their homeland to Louisiana. Slaves worked on the handful of early plantations and also on the countless smaller subsistence farms that developed around southern Louisiana, most engaged in the production and export of indigo and tobacco.

Back in control of the colony from 1731 through 1762, France failed to turn Louisiana into a profitable venture. Furthermore, its strategic importance diminished sharply as England developed an upper hand during the French and Indian War, which had begun in 1754, toward

controlling Canada. In 1762, France hatched a diplomatic scheme to help impel Spain to join it and rout the British: It secretly handed over the Louisiana Territory to Spain in the Treaty of Fontainebleau. In fact, the territory stayed in the family, as France's King Louis XV simply transferred the land to his own cousin, Spain's King Charles III.

The move ended badly for both France and Spain. France lost the war with Britain in 1763 and lost control of Canada. And Spain ended up with a lemon. One might argue that France really didn't lose a colony so much as rid itself of what had become an enormous and depressing financial burden. Furthermore, as part of the peace treaty between the joint powers of Spain and France with their victor, Great Britain was awarded all of Louisiana east of the Mississippi River, which became known as West Florida. Spain kept a much larger tract, which included all of Louisiana west of the river, along with a critical little area along the lower Mississippi River called Île d'Orléans, which included the city of New Orleans. France was free of any part of Louisiana.

SPANISH RULE

The actual physical transfer of Louisiana, and especially New Orleans, to Spain was an unmitigated disaster fraught with rebellion, virtual martial law, and ugly acts of violence. It didn't help that the residents of New Orleans had no idea that they had become subjects of Spain until 1766, when the first Spanish governor, Antonio de Ulloa, arrived that March and, like a wicked stepmother, immediately instituted strict rule upon the city's inhabitants.

Almost as immediately, there were insurgencies, and in 1768, the situation became particularly dire when locals actually drove Ulloa and his cronies clear out of town. Spain hired a tyrannical military man, General Alejandro O'Reilly, to beat down the rebellion, which he did in August 1769. He managed to get Spain in firm control of New Orleans, a rule that would last until the United States orchestrated the Louisiana Purchase in 1803, for although France technically owned Louisiana at that time, Spaniards continued to govern the city's day-to-day affairs right through to the end.

The Spanish, like the French, made every possible effort to boost the colony's population, sending plenty of Spaniards to Louisiana. From a cultural standpoint, Louisiana remained squarely French, as the colonists from France far outnumbered any newcomers. The only reason the appearance of the French Quarter today more closely resembles Spanish colonial than French colonial architecture is that two huge fires burned much of the city during the Spanish occupation, and many of the new buildings that went up were constructed by Spanish authorities. It's Spain's influence that resulted in the wrought-iron balconies, shaded courtyards, and other features that typify French Quarter architecture.

Ironically, the majority of the newcomers to Louisiana during the Spanish period were actually French, or French-speaking, refugees. The most famous were the Acadians, who had been cruelly expelled from the Maritime provinces of Canada after the British victory. The French immigrants living in Acadian Canada were typically rounded up and forced onto ships—some were sent back to France, and others were reluctantly taken in by certain British colonies in what is now the United States. Many died during passage or of poverty that they encountered where they landed. Spain, looking to boost the population of the Louisiana colony, enthusiastically welcomed the Acadians, who arrived in two major waves, the first in 1764 and then in an even larger one in 1785. Most of them settled in the marshes and swamplands of south-central and southwestern Louisiana. In Louisiana, the name Acadian gradually morphed into Cajun, as we all know it today, and Lafayette, Louisiana, became the hub of Cajun settlements.

Louisiana's makeup changed a bit during the American Revolution, as Spain worked in concert with the American colonists to undermine their rivals, the British. They sent supplies and munitions to the colonists, and in 1779, after formally declaring war on Britain, their Louisiana militia captured all of the British settlements of West Florida. This included all of the Gulf Coast region between the Mississippi River and the Perdido River, which today forms the east-west state border between Alabama and Florida. Per the terms of the Treaty of Paris in 1783, Spain's assistance was, at the war's conclusion, rewarded with a chunk of land that included all of both East Florida (today's Florida) and West Florida (which today

CREOLE SOCIETY

For a time, New Orleans deviated from rural Louisiana in its relative tolerance of racial diversity. The *gens de couleur libres* (free people of color) were, in many cases, well-educated and quite able to forge livings as builders, designers, artisans, and chefs. These early Creole immigrants were in a large way responsible for the intricate and fanciful Creole cottages and other buildings still found throughout the city and southern Louisiana, and these same immigrants helped to develop New Orleans's inimitable Creole cuisine, which blended the traditions of France, Spain, the Caribbean, Africa, and even the American frontier and Native Americans.

Intermingling was considerable in this early New Orleans society, as wealthy Europeans and Creoles commonly had mistresses, some who were *gens de couleur libres,* quadroons (one-fourth black), octoroons (one-eighth black), or some other mix of Anglo, Latin, African, and Native American descent. It's largely for this reason that the term Creole, when used for people, is rather confusing. The name was first applied to upper-crust French settlers born in Louisiana but descended from mostly wealthy European families, as the very word derives from the Spanish *criollo,* a term that described people born in the colonies rather than born in Europe or, for that matter, Africa. These days, just about any New Orleanian or Louisianian who can claim some direct combination of French, Spanish, Caribbean, and African blood can justly consider him- or herself a Creole, the exception being the descendants of the original French-Canadian refugees from Acadia, known as Cajuns.

In 1790, about 10,000 new refugees from Saint-Domingue moved into New Orleans, doubling the population. In many respects, it was this final wave of French-speaking people from Haiti—white colonists of French descent and free people of color *(gens de couleur libres)*—that ultimately established the French-Caribbean character that exists to this day in New Orleans.

includes Alabama, Mississippi, and the nine Louisiana parishes east and north of the Mississippi River, now sometimes referred to as the Florida parishes).

LOUISIANA PURCHASE

With the young United States now in control of all the land east of the Mississippi River (except for East and West Florida), New Orleans and the entire Louisiana Territory grew dramatically in strategic importance. New Orleans became the seaport serving America's interior, as important rivers throughout Ohio, Kentucky, and Tennessee all fed into the Mississippi.

In yet another secret treaty, however, Spain in 1800 decided to transfer all of the Louisiana Territory, including New Orleans, back to France. The actual residents of New Orleans never even knew they were residents of a French colony for the three years they were back under the country's rule. In 1803, the United States bought Louisiana from France for a mere $15 million. Even by the standards of that day, $15 million was a paltry sum for such an enormous parcel of land—approximately one-third of the land that now makes up the present-day continental United States. Because Spain still possessed East and West Florida, the nine Louisiana parishes east and north of the Mississippi River remained in Spanish hands until 1810, when the American residents of West Florida declared their independence and asked to be annexed by the United States.

Upon buying Louisiana from France, the United States immediately split the territory in two at the 33rd parallel, which today forms the northern border of Louisiana. All land south of that point became known as the Territory of Orleans, and, confusingly, all land to the north became known as the Territory of Louisiana.

The United States accepted the Territory of Orleans as the state of Louisiana on April 30, 1812. It thereby became the 18th state of the union. The political system, with William C. C. Claiborne as governor and New Orleans the capital, continued largely as it had from the time of the Louisiana Purchase.

America wasted no time in exploiting its new purchase, as thousands of entrepreneurial-minded settlers flocked to the busy port city during the first decade after the Louisiana Purchase. They were not welcomed in the French Quarter at all, and in fact, the original Creoles would have nothing to do with American settlers for many decades. Some of these upstarts immediately began amassing great riches in shipping and trade enterprises, building lavish homes in the American Sector, which is now the Central Business District (CBD). Canal Street divided the two enclaves, and the median down this street came to be considered New Orleans's "neutral ground." Today, the city's residents refer to any street median as a neutral ground.

By the early 1800s, a century's worth of immigrants from all walks of life had contributed to one of the most racially, culturally, and economically diverse populations in the nation. Freed prisoners from France, Haitian refugees, slaves, European indentured servants, American frontiersmen, Spanish Canary Islanders, nuns, military men, and others now formed New Orleans's population.

SLAVERY AND PLANTATIONS

For decades, New Orleans's largest import was enslaved people, who were brought to the city through the Middle Passage in chains, under horrendous conditions. The Atlantic slave trade was banned in 1807, but the focus quickly turned to domestic slave trading. Wherever there was commerce, there were slave traders. Slavery was the backbone of the economy.

There's a misperception that slaves had it easier in New Orleans as opposed to the rest of the South. This is due to the Code Noir, a French law that mandated that slaves take Sundays off (which led to musical gatherings in Congo Square and the opportunity to take paid side jobs) and that they could buy themselves and their family out of slavery. This created a culture of free people of color, who established the Tremé, the first free African American neighborhood in the United States. While this was admittedly different from the rest of the country (and indeed ceased once the United States took possession of Louisiana), it was still slavery.

The River Road plantations just outside the city have glamourized this portion of history, giving the minimum of attention to the slaves whose labor led to the property's success. I do not recommend visiting these places. The only plantation worth visiting is the Whitney Plantation Museum, which focuses on the lives of the people who were bought and sold like chattel.

CIVIL WAR AND RECONSTRUCTION

When South Carolina seceded from the Union in December 1860 after the election of Republican Abraham Lincoln, who sought to curb the spread of slavery, it set off a flurry of similar withdrawals among other southern states, with Louisiana seceding on January 26, 1861, the sixth state to do so. It then joined in the effort toward war in becoming a member of the Confederate States of America.

Although much of the fighting took place in the coastal and mid-Atlantic states, New Orleans and Louisiana were vulnerable to Union attack. If the Union army could capture and control the Mississippi River, it could cut off supply lines between the Confederacy and any states west of the river, and it could enjoy a continuous supply line to the interior Midwest. Anticipating just such an attack, the Confederates built fortifications along the river south of New Orleans.

In April 1862, Captain David G. Farragut led a flotilla of Union Navy ships to the mouth of the Mississippi, where it proceeded north toward New Orleans. He made it with little trouble, shelling and ultimately disabling the Confederate fortification and sailing rather easily to capture the South's largest city. Immediately, New Orleans was named the Union capital of all the territory held by the Federal army

in Louisiana. The Confederate state government moved west about 60 miles to Opelousas and then scrambled nearly another 200 miles northwest to Shreveport, where it remained until the war's end.

The period immediately after the Civil War, known as Reconstruction, was a grim one, and its policies, which attempted to create an integrated society of whites and free blacks, backfired. President Lincoln signed the Proclamation of Amnesty and Reconstruction into law in December 1863, and so, even before the war had ended, a civil government was established in those parts of Louisiana held by Union troops. When the war ended, this civil government assumed control of the state. Early on, it seemed as though little had changed for blacks, even though slavery had been formally abolished by this civil government. A number of the former Confederate leaders of prewar Louisiana held office in this new civil government, which immediately passed the infamous Black Codes. These edicts placed enormous restrictions on the rights and freedoms of the state's African Americans, who were also denied the right to vote.

These conditions led to an extreme seesaw of power between the Republican and (largely ex-Confederate) Democratic sides of the government, which would bitterly divide Louisianians and precipitate tragic violence for the rest of the 19th century and well into the 20th. Blacks struck back against the government in New Orleans, first by rioting violently in 1866 until finally the federal government stepped in to impose order.

These same issues, revolts, and riots flared up in other Southern states, and Congress responded by drafting the Reconstruction Acts in 1867 and 1868, which President Andrew Johnson vetoed, but which passed with a two-thirds' majority nonetheless. And so, formally, began the period of Reconstruction in the American South.

Reconstruction dictated that the 10 ex-Confederate states that had been returned to the Union would lose their rights to self-govern, and the federal military would instead step in to govern until these states rewrote their constitutions with laws and language that Congress deemed acceptable. In effect, Louisiana was no longer a state until it submitted to the wishes of the federal government. The federally controlled state government then drafted a new constitution in March 1868, which wholly deferred to the sentiments of Congress: Adult males of all races were granted the right to vote—excepting fully declared ex-Confederates, who actually had their voting rights revoked—and blacks were assured full civil rights. Interestingly, when the new constitution was presented to Louisiana citizens, voters approved it overwhelmingly. The majority of those who registered to vote that year were black; whites, discouraged and disgusted by the process, largely stayed away from the polls.

Pro-Union white Southerners (called "scalawags" by their detractors), opportunity-seeking whites from the North (called "carpetbaggers" by their detractors), and former slaves held the clear majority of political seats in Louisiana (and many other Southern states) during the eight years of Reconstruction. Among these Republican officeholders were Louisiana's first elected black governor, P. B. S. Pinchback, and the first black U.S. senator, Blanche K. Bruce, as well as black members of the U.S. Congress and black holders of just about every state political post.

In the meantime, the most ardent opponents of Reconstruction, including quite a few prominent ex-Confederate leaders, went to extreme lengths to sabotage, tear down, and otherwise render ineffective the state's Republican leadership. From this effort came the development of such anti-black groups as the Ku Klux Klan (in northern Louisiana), the Knights of the White Camellia (in southern Louisiana), and the especially terror-driven White League. These and other groups, sometimes systematically and sometimes randomly, intimidated, beat, and often lynched blacks and white sympathizers. The White League took credit for the assassination of several Republican-elected officials. About 3,500 members of the White League attempted to overthrow the state government during what came to be known as the Battle of Liberty Place in New Orleans in 1874. During a fierce riot, they took over the city hall, statehouse, and state arsenal until federal troops arrived to restore order. For the next four years, the troops remained in New Orleans, overseeing the city's—and the state's—order.

During the course of Reconstruction, the voting situation in Louisiana grew increasingly volatile, as whites intimidated or threatened blacks to keep them from voting and rallied voter support among anti-Republican whites. More and more officials and congressmen sympathetic to the South gained office, and they, in turn, pardoned and restored voting rights to many of the ex-Confederates.

White Democrats were swift in removing from blacks any rights they had gained during Reconstruction, and then some. In 1898, the state constitution was rewritten. Without expressly denying suffrage to blacks, it required poll taxes, literacy, and property ownership in order to vote, which disqualified most of the state's black voters.

While Reconstruction had a profoundly negative effect on the plight of blacks, a few strides were made during the 19th century. Many blacks ended up returning to work at a subsistence level on the farms where they had once been slaves, but some headway was made in education and social relief. The federal government established the Freedmen's Bureau, which helped to fund public schools for blacks throughout the South and issued other forms of assistance and economic relief.

The economy of the rural South faltered greatly after the Civil War, and various depressions, labor problems, and episodes of social unrest conspired to put many large and small farm owners out of business. For much of the 19th century, a large proportion of southern farms were run by sharecroppers, whereby the owners of the land—many of them northerners who had bought failed farms—gave tenants equipment and materials to farm the land and live on a fairly basic level. The workers were also entitled to a small cut of the crop yield. Farm production in Louisiana began to increase under this system, but it was still far lower than before the Civil War, and even with bounteous crops, many farmers could not make ends meet.

New Orleans, whose economy had been devastated by the war, gradually staged an economic comeback during the course of the next half century. The renewed growth in cotton and sugarcane trafficking helped to jump-start the city's shipping and trade economy, and the mouth of the Mississippi River was deepened and made accessible to much larger ships, many of which sailed from ports much farther away than in earlier times. Railroads were built across much of Louisiana, and in 1914, the opening of the Panama Canal brought new trade to New Orleans by way of Latin America. The city's population stood at 290,000 by 1900, with the state population up to about 1.4 million.

20TH CENTURY

Louisiana's economy began to diversify throughout the early 20th century, much more so than in most other agrarian southern states. Significant sources of oil were discovered in the northwestern part of the state, and natural gas sources were developed all over Louisiana. In 1938, huge oil deposits were discovered off the coast, and a massive oil-drilling industry grew up in southern Louisiana, especially in the towns southeast of Lafayette and southwest of Houma. Salt and sulfur mining also became a big contributor to the economy, chiefly in the southern belt extending from Lake Charles to southeast of Lafayette.

The farming economy continued to suffer through the early 1900s, and a severe recession took hold throughout the 1920s. The growing anguish and desperation among rural farmers helped to promote the ascendancy of one of the most notorious and controversial political figures in American history, Huey P. Long, a colorful, no-nonsense straight talker whose fervently populist manner played well with poor farmers and laborers. Long declared war on big corporations, especially Standard Oil, and took up the cause of small businesses and the common people. His actions early in his political career squarely favored those he claimed to want to help. Long was elected governor in 1928 and then U.S. senator in 1930, although he kept the governor's seat until 1932, when a handpicked successor took office. Still, he pretty much called the shots in state politics right up until his death. Long was assassinated in 1935 by Dr. Carl Weiss, the son-in-law of one of his political archenemies.

Long was instrumental in developing state public assistance and public works programs across Louisiana during the Great Depression, but he was also infamous for his nepotism and corruption, routinely buying off colleagues and tampering with the political process. The "Kingfish" ran the state like a fiefdom, and he actually ended up preventing federal funds from reaching the state during his last few years in office as a U.S. senator. Long may have died in 1935,

but his brother, Earl K. Long, succeeded him as governor, as did his son, Russell Long. Until the early 1960s, anti- and pro-Long factions continued to dominate Democratic party politics and therefore, because Democrats controlled just about everything in Louisiana, state politics.

World War II boosted the Louisiana economy with its need for mineral and oil resources. It was during this period that Louisiana developed the massive refineries and chemical plants still found along much of the Mississippi River and all through the lower third of the state (especially Lake Charles and Baton Rouge), and it was also during the 1940s that the state's population demographic changed so that more Louisianians lived in cities than in rural areas.

At the same time, many rural citizens, especially blacks fed up with the state's segregation and racial mistreatment, left the South to seek factory jobs in Chicago, Oakland, and other northern and western cities. Other Louisianians moved to southeastern Texas, where jobs at refineries, factories, and shipyards in Beaumont, Orange, and Port Arthur abounded.

SEGREGATION

In a post-Reconstruction New Orleans, a shoemaker named Homer Plessy boarded a whites-only railroad car and kicked off the lawsuit of *Homer v. Plessy,* which brought about the "separate but equal" doctrine. (There's a historical marker in a pocket park at the corner of Press and Royal Streets to commemorate the spot of Plessy's arrest.) This led to the city and state segregating everything under the sun.

Attorney A. P. Tureaud, a high-ranking member of the National Association for the Advancement of Colored People (NAACP) filed a lawsuit (*Joseph P. McKelpin v. Orleans Parish School Board,* 1940) to ensure pay equity for teachers among all public schools, regardless of the race of the teacher or the school. Segregation continued in New Orleans until 1958, in the wake of the *Brown v. Board of Education of Topeka Kansas* ruling, which made segregation unconstitutional. The segregation laws known as the Jim Crow laws were later further dismantled by the signing of the Civil Rights Act in 1964 by President Lyndon B. Johnson.

Legalized segregation has left an indelible mark on the African American community in New Orleans that is still being felt today.

HURRICANE KATRINA

The infamous hurricane's center just missed the city on August 29, 2005. It came ashore in Louisiana as a Category 1, the lowest hurricane level. However, the storm had been barreling toward the city at a Category 5 (the highest level), so mandatory evacuations were called for. The post-hurricane storm surge caused many of the levees and floodwalls maintained by the U.S. Army Corps of Engineers to fail—letting in a devastating wave of water—specifically the 17th Street Canal right near the lake, the Industrial Canal levee in the Lower Ninth Ward, and the London Avenue Canal floodwall that flooded Broadmoor and Mid-City. Close to 1,500 people lost their lives and many more lost their homes in this avoidable tragedy. Recovery from the storm and flooding was slow. It took weeks for residents to be allowed back into the area to take stock of the damage. Almost half of the city's African American population never came home again.

Local Culture

The strongest influence on New Orleans may arguably be French, but no one nationality represents a decisive majority here. The city's distinctive cuisine and music, the pervasive infatuation with things carnal and pleasurable, the Gothic literary traditions, and the longstanding practice of voodoo-tinged Catholicism are legacies contributed not only by the French and Spanish settlers, but by the vast numbers of Acadian refugees ("Cajuns"), enslaved people brought from West Africa, American frontier settlers and traders, German farmers, Irish and Italian laborers, Slavs, Creole refugees from Haiti, and Vietnamese. These people haven't just left their mark on a particular neighborhood during a specific period; they've migrated to New Orleans in significant enough numbers to have a pervasive and lasting influence. The cultural gumbo has resulted in some rather odd traditions that last to this day.

Many street and neighborhood names are pronounced differently in New Orleans than anywhere else in the world, from Conti (KON-tie) and Cadiz (KAY-diz) Streets to the Michoud (MEE-shoh) neighborhood. Sometimes, French and Spanish names are pronounced roughly as the French and Spanish would pronounce them; sometimes, they're pronounced as virtually nobody else on the planet would say them.

Given the ethnic diversity of southern Louisiana, it's no surprise that residents tend to practice a variety of religions, or none at all. New Orleans was founded by Catholics, as evidenced by historic landmarks like the St. Louis Cathedral, and influenced by cultural traditions such as Mardi Gras. Nevertheless, you'll spot a wide array of religious institutions here, from Touro Synagogue to the First Unitarian Universalist Church of New Orleans.

The cuisine unique to New Orleans also borrows widely from myriad cultures with ingredients and dishes like filé (a powder of dried sassafras leaves popularized by the Choctaw), jambalaya (a rice casserole very similar to Spanish paella), okra (a podlike vegetable introduced by enslaved Africans), and crawfish (a small freshwater crustacean that's prevalent in local waters).

AFRICAN AMERICAN CULTURE
MARDI GRAS INDIANS
The Mardi Gras Indians are comprised of 40 or so "tribes," groups of black New Orleans residents who pay homage to the area's indigenous culture with their hand-sewn,

intricately decorated suits and head-dresses. Although the history of how the Mardi Gras Indians came into existence isn't fully known, there's evidence to support that some enslaved Africans escaped into the bayous where indigenous peoples lived, and that they were protected by them. It's thought that the first Mardi Gras Indian tribes and encounters began in the mid-19th century.

Mardi Gras Indian tribes can be found facing off against each other during Mardi Gras and on St. Joseph's Day (March 19). Additionally, all of the tribes in the Mardi Gras Indian Nation come together every year on Super Sunday, the Sunday closest to St. Joseph's Day, to parade in Central City.

There is an order to the procession: First up are the Spy Boys, who have slightly less ornate suits and will occasionally run ahead of the group. The First Flag carries the tribe's flag, followed by the tribe's Wildman, the enforcer. Then comes the Big Chief, the leader. When they meet each other, the opposing Big Chiefs posture about the excellence of their suits and the winner is dubbed "the prettiest."

SECOND LINES
Sunday second line parades run from September to May. They're based on the brass band funerals that New Orleans social aid and pleasure clubs (communities of black residents) once provided for all their members. The first, or main, line is where the band played, accompanied by club members and mourners. The second line was made up of people who just followed

the music. Nowadays, second line parades aren't connected to funerals. The first line of musicians and costumed club members dance, and everyone else comes out to join them in the second line. The entire parade is now known as a second line.

SOUTHERN ETIQUETTE

New Orleans has always been a big city with small-town sensibilities, and many New Orleanians adhere to the same temperament and traditions of other Southern states; you'll often hear "please," "thank you," "yes, ma'am," and "no, sir" while visiting New Orleans. It's also common for restaurant staff to call patrons "sweetie" or "darling." Residents appreciate qualities like modesty, chivalry, patience, and friendliness, and while having a good time is encouraged in the Big Easy, being loud and disrespectful is rarely tolerated. Although some old-fashioned manners have gone by the wayside in modern-day New Orleans, others are still common: always open doors for others, smile at and make eye contact with strangers, use proper table manners, apologize when you're at fault, and say "excuse me" when having to walk in front of someone.

By the same token, it's easy to misinterpret the friendliness that you'll surely encounter. When walking through the French Quarter, many a tourist has been stopped by a seemingly friendly local with a scam up his or her sleeve. One such scam entails what seems like a harmless wager: A man might approach you and say, "I bet I can guess where you got those shoes," and if you choose

to accept his challenge, he'll inevitably win with a simple reply, "On your feet." So, as in any major U.S. city, it pays to be both courteous and cautious.

Because of the region's multiethnic history and reliance on tourism, foreigners and tourists are generally welcome here. Overall, the residents are helpful, hospitable, and gregarious, so while in New Orleans, do as the natives do. Be kind and considerate, ask for help when you need it, thank others for their time, and, as a courtesy, seek permission before taking a photo.

PRONOUNCIATIONS

Many visitors often wonder how to pronounce "New Orleans." Though it's sometimes heard as "N'AW-luhns" in movies and TV commercials, native New Orleanians definitely don't pronounce it this way. The more conventional incorrect pronunciation is "NOO or-LEENS." Say it this way, and you'll be marked as an outsider (probably a Northerner), but at least, you won't be accused of being disrespectful. Locals pronounce the city's name in a handful of relatively similar ways, the simplest and most common being "noo OHR-lins." You don't have to say it with a big, silly drawl or with delicious emphasis, as if you're in a Tennessee Williams play. Just say it quickly and casually, though you might hear some locals, especially those with aristocratic tendencies, pronounce it "noo OHR-lee-ahns."

As for the name of the state, that is a bit more straightforward. Here, you have two options: "LOO-zee-ann-ah" or "le-WEE-zee-ann-ah."

Both pronunciations are common and considered acceptable.

Pronouncing the rest of the rivers, lakes, towns, and streets of New Orleans and Louisiana can be extremely tricky for outsiders. "Correct" pronunciation isn't really the point here.

If you'd rather not sound like an outsider, do your best to learn the major place-name pronunciations. Granted, locals won't generally torment you for mispronouncing words, especially since, depending on one's regional accent, there are often two or more commonly accepted (though hotly debated) ways to pronounce the same word.

THE ARTS

While New Orleans is known for its fine art galleries and historical architecture, and has inspired countless writers, artists, actors, and filmmakers over the decades, its biggest artistic claim to fame is indeed its music. This city is one of the world's most dynamic live-music scenes. Jazz was invented here, a conglomeration of mostly African-American traditions that has rural counterparts elsewhere in southern Louisiana in the form of zydeco and Cajun music.

There are only a handful of large-scale venues for formal concerts; in fact, many big-name musicians favor comparatively smaller stages when in town. New Orleanians are loyal, knowledgeable, and excited about music, and performers appreciate the enthusiasm, relishing the chance to play a club that's small enough to encourage a close connection between the musicians and the fans. It takes almost no planning and very

little effort to find a place to catch a jamming live show in New Orleans, even on a Monday or Tuesday night. Just check the listings in the *Gambit* or *The Times-Picayune,* or simply stroll through the French Quarter or Faubourg Marigny. Dozens of clubs bellow music from their doors every night of the week, and many of these places seldom charge a cover, though they will typically have a one- or two-drink minimum.

JAZZ

Jazz wasn't invented in one definitive instant—it evolved over 20 or 30 years during the early part of the 20th century and in several parts of New Orleans's African American community. The state has produced several jazz luminaries, among them Jelly Roll Morton, Sidney Bechet, and crooner Harry Connick Jr.

Jazz music typically uses both individual and collective improvisation, syncopation, and distinctive vocal effects, and it has its origins in European, African, and Caribbean traditional music. Commonly, you'll hear blues vocalizing sung to jazz instrumental accompaniment. Many people trace jazz to a popular cornet player named Buddy Bolden, who performed regularly in New Orleans from the mid-1890s until about 1910. Through the 1910s and '20s, ragtime-style jazz and other music forms, with a spontaneous, upbeat tempo, began to attract a following, albeit an underground one, in New Orleans.

This thoroughly modern and iconoclastic style of music was not, initially, well received by the mainstream. In fact, it was shunned by organizers of Mardi

Gras parades for years. During the early years, many people considered this musical style to be scandalous and impudent—they criticized it at least as harshly as early critics of rock-and-roll denounced that music. Jazz was seen as a crude bastardization of more acceptable musical styles. But through time, jazz would win the hearts of even the harshest naysayers, and today, there's really no style of music for which the city is better regarded.

ESSENTIALS

Transportation

GETTING THERE

New Orleans's airport is well served by most major airlines and has direct flights to many of the nation's largest cities. In late 2019, the new MSY airport opened, boasting an improved architectural aesthetic and more local food and beverage options. It's conveniently located in a nearby suburb and is pleasant to fly into and out of. The city also has direct Amtrak train service and Greyhound bus service from many big cities, but these modes of transport are often quite time-consuming and, especially in the case of trains, not always less expensive than flying. Some travelers arrive here via cruise ship and many come by car—the major east-west I-10 runs directly through New Orleans, less than a half mile from the French Quarter.

Daiquiris are a well-known drink in New Orleans.

AIR

Louis Armstrong New Orleans International Airport (MSY, 1 Terminal Dr., Kenner, 504/303-7500, flymsy.com), 15 miles west of downtown New Orleans via I-10, is a massive facility that accommodates the entire Gulf South with service on several airlines. It's easy to find direct flights from most major U.S. cities. It's also possible to fly direct from London, Frankfurt, Latin America, and the Caribbean.

Commercial air service is also available to Baton Rouge, Lafayette, and Lake Charles. Generally, it's more expensive to fly to one of the smaller regional airports than to New Orleans, especially when factoring in the cost of renting a car. Situated roughly eight miles north of downtown Baton Rouge via I-110, **Baton Rouge Metropolitan Airport** (9430 Jackie Cochran Dr., 225/355-0333, flybtr.com) is served by American Airlines, Continental Airlines, Delta Air Lines, and US Airways, with frequent direct flights to and from Atlanta, Dallas, Houston, and Memphis. **Lafayette Regional Airport** (200 Terminal Dr., 337/266-4400, lftairport.com) is three miles southeast of downtown Lafayette via US-90. It's served by American Eagle, the Delta Connection, and Continental Express, with direct flights to and from Atlanta, Dallas, Houston, and Memphis. **Lake Charles Regional Airport** (500 Airport Blvd., 337/477-6051, flylakecharles.com) is nine miles south of downtown Lake Charles via LA-385. You can take direct flights to and from Houston, courtesy of Continental Airlines, and Dallas, courtesy of American Airlines. If you choose to fly into one of these three regional airports, you'll have to rent a car to reach New Orleans; Avis, Budget, Hertz, National, and Enterprise serve all three locales.

Airport Transportation

Depending on traffic, the 15-mile trip from the airport to the French Quarter can take 25-35 minutes by car. A **taxi** from the airport to the Central Business District (CBD) has a set rate of $36 for one or two passengers and $15 per person for three or more passengers. Pickup occurs at the arrival curb outside of the baggage claim on Level 1. All cabs are legally required to accept credit cards. Extra baggage might incur an additional charge.

Lyft, Uber, and other ride-hailing services pick up outside of the baggage claim on Level 1, between doors 9 and 11. Depending on location and timing, the fare will range $30-35 (subject to surge pricing).

To save a little money, opt for the **Airport Shuttle** (504/522-3500 or 866/596-2699, airportshuttleneworleans.com; $24 adult one-way, $44 adults round-trip, children under 6 free), which offers shared-ride service to hotels in the French Quarter, the CBD, and Uptown as well as the Ernest N. Morial Convention Center. Purchase tickets at the Airport Shuttle ticket booth, at the Level 1 baggage claim between doors 3 and 4.

Public buses are available from the curb outside of the ticket lobby on Level 3. The Regional Transit Authority (RTA, 504/248-3900, norta.com) provides the **Airport Express 202 bus** ($1.50) with service between MSY and New Orleans. Pick up locations in New Orleans include two separate downtown locations. Stops include Elk Place at Canal, or Loyola at Howard, near Union Station. You can also hop aboard the **Veterans/ E1 bus** (504/818-1077 or 504/364-3450, jeffersontransit.org; $2), which provides service from MSY to downtown, with a travel time of approximately (50) minutes.

To get to the MSY Rental Car Center, you'll need to take the **rental car shuttle.** It departs from in front of the long-term parking garage every five minutes.

TRAIN

Amtrak (800/872-7245, amtrak.com) operates three rail routes across southern Louisiana, all of which include stops at the New Orleans Amtrak Station (1001 Loyola Ave.; 5am-10pm daily). Amtrak offers a number of promotions and special rail passes (which allow you to overnight in U.S. cities served by Amtrak), making this a practical way to visit several places on one pass. The USA Rail Passes are available in three travel durations: 15 days/8 rail segments ($460 adults, $230 children 2-12), 30 days/12 rail segments ($670 adults, $345 children 2-12), and 45 days/18 rail segments ($900 adults, $450 children 2-12). All passes allow you to hop between routes during your trip. Even with a pass, you'll still need to reserve a ticket for each train you plan to board. There are rental car agencies at Amtrak stations in most big cities.

These rail routes serve New Orleans:

- City of New Orleans runs daily from Chicago to New Orleans, with major stops in Memphis, Jackson, and Hammond (19 hours).
- Crescent runs daily between New York City and New Orleans, with major stops in Philadelphia, Baltimore, Washington DC, Charlotte, Atlanta, Birmingham, and Slidell (30 hours).
- Sunset Limited, an east-west train, runs from Los Angeles to New Orleans three times weekly, with major stops in Tucson, El Paso, San Antonio, Houston, Lake Charles, and Lafayette (48 hours).

BUS

Greyhound (800/231-2222, greyhound.com) is the definitive bus provider for New Orleans, with frequent and flexible service throughout the country. Buses depart daily from the New Orleans Greyhound Station (1001 Loyola Ave., 504/525-6075, 5:15am-10:30am, 11:30am-1pm, and 2:30pm-9:30pm daily) with multiple stops throughout Louisiana to many neighboring states. Travel times can be significantly longer than by train (although not always), but fares are generally much cheaper.

If you're planning a lengthy trip, consider Greyhound's Discovery Pass, which you can buy in increments of 7-60 days, allowing unlimited stopovers throughout the duration of the pass. Different types and prices of passes are available to U.S., Canadian, and international travelers. As with Amtrak's USA Rail Passes, a ticket is required for each bus trip taken with the Discovery Pass.

CAR

The New Orleans metro area is about 20 miles from west to east and 10 miles from north to south. The I-10 runs directly through New Orleans and provides the closest access to the French Quarter. West of the Quarter, the I-10 connects with the Pontchartrain Expressway (US-90) in the CBD. The Pontchartrain Expressway splits west through Uptown; south alongside the Garden District, crossing the Mississippi River; and north to Mid-City and

I-610. Though traffic can be difficult in this city, you can usually get from one end of New Orleans to the other in about 30-40 minutes.

If you plan to stay in New Orleans the entire time you're visiting this region, then you won't need a car. If, however, you're planning one or two days outside the city, rent a car downtown for a short term. A car may also be handier than public transportation for exploring Uptown and Mid-City. Consult the Louisiana Department of Transportation & Development (225/379-1100, dotd.la.gov) for maps, publications, and extensive information about public transportation, highway safety, traveler resources, road conditions, and upcoming projects.

Car Rental

Just about all the major car rental agencies are represented at MSY: Advantage (800/777-5500, advantage.com), Alamo (800/462-5266, alamo.com), Avis (800/331-1212, avis.com), Budget (800/527-0700, budget.com), Dollar (800/800-4000, dollar.com), Enterprise (800/736-8222, enterprise.com), Hertz (800/654-3131, hertz.com), National (800/227-7368, nationalcar.com), and Thrifty (800/847-4389, thrifty.com). In New Orleans, rates for car rentals typically start at $30 daily for economy cars but can easily rise at busy times, such as during Mardi Gras or when conventions are in town. Weekly rates begin at $180 for an economy car and $200 for a midsize car. While most car-rental agencies will only rent to properly licensed drivers who are at least 25 years old, some will rent to customers between the ages of 21 and 24, as long as they have a valid credit card and driver's license and are willing to pay a daily surcharge of $27.

GETTING AROUND

New Orleanians rarely refer to compass directions when discussing how to navigate the city. The city is bound on one side by the highly irregular Mississippi River, which forms the western, southern, or eastern border; main roads tend to run parallel or perpendicular to the river. Since the river's direction changes, this means that New Orleans's street grid also changes its axis in different places. As a result, most residents employ the terms "lakeside" (meaning north toward Lake Pontchartrain) and "riverside" (meaning south toward the Mississippi) when referring to streets perpendicular to the river. The terms "upriver" or "uptown" refer to westerly directions; the terms "downriver" or "downtown" are used for easterly directions. For example, Canal Street, which tourists generally consider a north-south thoroughfare, actually runs in a southeasterly direction toward the river. If you're still confused, be sure to have a city map with you at all times, as this is one place where it is absolutely indispensable—whether you're walking, driving, taking public transportation, or even using cabs. New Orleans is very much a collection of neighborhoods, and residents refer to neighborhood names almost as much as specific streets.

PUBLIC TRANSPORTATION

New Orleans is served by a network of buses and streetcars, operated by the New Orleans Regional Transit Authority (RTA, 504/248-3900, norta.com). The standard fare is $1.25 per person ($0.40 seniors, children under 3 free) plus $0.25 per transfer; express buses cost $1.50 per person. You must pay with exact change by depositing coins or inserting $1 bills into the fare box at the front of the bus or streetcar. Food, beverages, smoking, and stereos are not permitted on buses and streetcars.

The handy Jazzy Pass, a magnetized card presented upon boarding the bus or streetcar, allows unlimited rides during the active period; it's available in 1-day ($3), 3-day ($9), or 31-day ($55) increments. The 1-day pass can be purchased on the bus or streetcar, though only cash is accepted. Other passes are available from various hotels, banks, and retailers, such as Walgreens. Check out RTA's website to purchase passes online that can be mailed in advance. There's also a smartphone app that allows you to purchase and use tickets and passes. The app and website also show where the various transportation options are in real time.

Taking an Uber, Lyft, or taxi at night is highly recommended over public transportation, especially when traveling solo. Have the ride-hailing apps set up on your phone ahead of time or note the name and number of a couple of cab companies.

Bus

Bus service is available throughout the city, and all RTA buses can accommodate people with disabilities. The one-way fare is $1.25 (plus $0.25 per transfer) and passengers must pay with either exact change (coins or $1 bills) or the Jazzy Pass.

Tourists often utilize the Magazine line (11), which runs from Canal Street in the CBD through the Garden District and Uptown, along a six-mile stretch of galleries, shops, and restaurants, before ending at Audubon Park. Another important route is the Jackson-Esplanade line (91), which runs from Rousseau Street in the Garden District, through the CBD, along the north edge of the French Quarter, up Esplanade Avenue, and past City Park, ending at the Greenwood Cemetery. For a complete map of all bus lines, plus individual maps and schedules, visit the RTA website (norta.com).

Streetcar

The RTA also operates New Orleans's iconic streetcars. The one-way fare is $1.25 per person (plus $0.25 per transfer), and passengers must pay with either exact change (coins or $1 bills) or the Jazzy Pass.

The famous St. Charles streetcar line, which operates 24 hours daily, runs along St. Charles and South Carrollton Avenues, from Canal Street to Claiborne Avenue; a one-way trip lasts about 45 minutes. Given their historic status, the St. Charles streetcars are exempt from ADA (the Americans with Disabilities Act) compliance, so unfortunately passengers with disabilities may have trouble boarding them. The St. Charles line has been in operation since 1835, when it began as the main railroad line connecting the city of New Orleans with the resort community of Carrollton, now part of the city; the olive-green cars date to the 1920s, when they were built by the Perley Thomas Company. Today, the line is a wonderful, scenic, and atmospheric way to travel between the CBD and Uptown.

The Canal Street streetcar line (24 hours daily) extends from Canal Street to Mid-City before splitting into two branches. The "Cemeteries" branch runs from the foot of Canal Street, not far from the ferry terminal for Algiers Point, all the way up to the historic cemeteries along City Park Avenue. The "City Park/Museum" branch takes North Carrollton Avenue to Esplanade Avenue, right beside City Park and the New Orleans Museum of Art. A one-way trip along either branch lasts about 30 minutes.

The Riverfront streetcar line (7am-10:30pm daily) uses newer streetcars and runs a short but scenic 1.8-mile route along the Mississippi River, from the French Quarter to the CBD. These modern red streetcars were built by New Orleans metal- and woodworkers; a one-way ride lasts about 15 minutes.

The relatively short Loyola-UPT line (6am-midnight daily) travels between the downtown Amtrak station, the intersection of Canal and Rampart Streets, and Harrah's New Orleans before linking with the Riverfront route.

The Rampart-St. Claude line (6am-11:30pm daily) runs from Canal Street to Elysian Fields on North Rampart Street, which turns into St. Claude Avenue, providing streetcar access across the back of the French Quarter into the Marigny. For maps and schedules of all five streetcar lines, visit the RTA website (norta.com).

Ferry

The Algiers Point/Canal Street ferry (504/309-9789, nolaferries. com or friendsoftheferry.org; 6am-9:45pm Mon.-Fri., 10:45am-8pm Sat., 10:45am-6pm Sun.; $2 adults, $1 seniors, children under 3 free) provides ferry service across the Mississippi River, from the foot of Canal Street in the CBD to Algiers Point. The five-minute service no longer transports vehicles; the boat departs every 30 minutes on either shore. The Lower Algiers/Chalmette ferry (6am-8:45pm daily; $2 adults, $1 seniors, children under 3 free) offers hourly service between Lower Algiers and the East Bank community of Chalmette; the trip usually lasts 15-20 minutes. Contact the Crescent City Connection Police (504/376-8180) for up-to-the-minute information regarding breakdowns.

TAXI, PEDICAB, AND RIDE-HAILING SERVICES

Taxi rates within the city typically start at $3.50 per ride, plus $2 per mile thereafter; there's also a charge of $1 for each additional passenger. You will often find taxis waiting at major intersections near Bourbon Street and other nighttime hot spots in the Quarter. Be sure to use taxis operated by licensed and established cab companies, such as Checker Yellow Cabs (504/943-2411), New Orleans Carriage Cab (504/207-7777, neworleans-carriagecab.com), United Cabs (504/522-9771 or 504/524-9606, unitedcabs.com), and White Fleet Cab and Elk's Elite Taxi (504/822-3800). Taxi rates are often higher during peak times, such as Mardi Gras and Jazz Fest; expect to pay $5 per person or the meter rate, whichever is greater.

As an alternative to taxis, hop aboard one of the pedicabs often seen trolling the streets of the French Quarter. Operated by knowledgeable guides and equipped with safety belts, headlights, and flashing taillights, these eco-friendly, person-powered vehicles can accommodate up to three or four passengers, making them ideal for getting you and a couple friends back to your home or hotel after a long night of partying in the Quarter. There are two pedicab companies in the city: Bike Taxi Unlimited (504/891-3441, neworleansbiketaxi.com), which serves the French Quarter, the Faubourg Marigny, the CBD, the Arts District, and Uptown; and NOLA Pedicabs (504/274-1300, nolapedicabs.com), which mainly serves the Quarter, the CBD, and the Arts District. Standard fares are $5 per passenger for the first six blocks, after which each passenger will be charged $1 per city block. During special events, such as Mardi Gras, expect to pay $50 per half hour and $100 hourly.

Ride-hailing services like Lyft and Uber are generally quicker, more reliable, and cheaper than cabs.

DRIVING

When driving in New Orleans, be forewarned that many streets are one-way and riddled with pot-holes, street parking in the French Quarter, CBD, and Warehouse District is scarce, and garage and hotel parking is expensive. Given the city's compact size, many travelers rely on motorcycles and bikes, which are often much easier to park on the street. If you do bring or rent a car to explore the Greater New Orleans area, note that most city roads have speed limits of 25-35 mph; two-lane state and U.S. highways generally have speed limits of 55 mph along narrow rural stretches and 70 mph in wider spots. Roads in rural areas are sometimes very heavily patrolled by police. They are also highly unsafe to speed on—they're bumpy and narrow, with virtually no shoulders. As in other parts of the country, it's illegal to drive without a seatbelt or while intoxicated.

Parking

Finding street parking in the French Quarter is especially tough because most blocks are restricted for residents with permits. In such cases, you can usually park for no more than two hours during the restricted time period (or you'll pay a $75 fine). Many hotel properties in the Quarter have no dedicated parking facilities. You'll find parking meters throughout the French Quarter and CBD—both the old-fashioned, coin-operated meters as well as ones that accept dollar bills and credit cards and offer a printed receipt to place on your dashboard. The Parkmobile app helps keep track of time left on the meter, and lets you pay electronically. Meters are typically enforced Monday-Saturday 8am-6pm; while they're not usually enforced on Sundays or holidays, always read the meters before parking. If you're staying beyond the downtown area, it might be better to park in the Uptown or Mid-City neighborhoods and use public transportation to visit the French Quarter and CBD.

If you do decide to park on the street, be sure to read the parking signs carefully; the rules can differ from neighborhood to neighborhood and some violations can be extremely costly—from $30 for an expired meter to $200 for parking on a French Quarter sidewalk.

Avoid parking vehicles longer than 22 feet overnight in the French Quarter and CBD, and having three or more unpaid parking violations. If your car is towed, contact the Claiborne Auto Pound (504/565-7450 or 504/565-7451). For general questions about parking in New Orleans, consult the city's Parking Division (504/658-8200).

Travel Tips

FOREIGN TRAVELERS

International travelers are required to show a valid passport upon entering the United States. The U.S. government's Visa Waiver Program (VWP) allows tourists from many countries to visit without a visa for up to 90 days. To check if your country is on the list, go to http://travel.state.gov. To qualify, you must apply online with the Electronic System for Travel Authorization (ESTA, cbp.gov) and hold a return travel ticket to your country of origin dated less than 90 days from your date of entry. All other temporary international travelers are required to secure a nonimmigrant visa before entering Louisiana.

Upon entering Louisiana, international travelers must declare any dollar amount over $10,000 as well as the value of any articles that will remain in the country, including gifts. A duty will be assessed for all imported goods, though visitors are usually granted a $100 exemption. Illegal drugs, Cuban cigars, obscene items, toxic substances, and prescription drugs (without a prescription) are generally prohibited. In order to protect American agriculture, customs officials will also confiscate certain produce, plants, seeds, nuts, meat, and other potentially dangerous biological products. For more information, consult the U.S. Customs and Border Protection (703/526-4200, cbp.gov).

TRAVELING WITH CHILDREN

Although New Orleans tends to be geared more toward adults than children, there are nevertheless some outstanding attractions for kids, such as the Audubon Aquarium of the Americas, the Audubon Butterfly Garden and Insectarium, Blaine Kern's Mardi Gras World, the Audubon Zoo, Storyland at City Park, and the Louisiana Children's Museum, right in the CBD. Many of the excursions offered throughout the city, such as swamp tours, riverboat rides, and haunted strolls, are a big hit with kids, especially teenagers. For more ideas, consult neworleanskids.com, which offers a slew of tips regarding family-friendly hotels, restaurants, attractions, and activities.

While plenty of inns and hotels welcome children—such as the Quarter's Ritz-Carlton New Orleans and the CBD's Loews New Orleans Hotel, both of which offer babysitting services—some lodging options are adults-only establishments.

SENIOR TRAVELERS

Although the wild nightlife scene around the French Quarter can be off-putting to some, New Orleans is overall quite appealing to senior travelers, particularly those who appreciate historical architecture and one-of-a-kind attractions, such as The National WWII Museum. Any of the neighborhood B&Bs I've listed in Uptown, the Marigny and Bywater, or the Garden District would be perfect for a relaxed, full-service experience.

Even better, seniors often qualify for age-related discounts at restaurants, attractions, and other establishments throughout New Orleans. The American Association of Retired Persons (AARP, 888/687-2277, aarp.org) offers members a myriad of travel discounts as well as a newsletter that often touches on travel issues. Road Scholar (800/454-5768, roadscholar.org) also organizes a wide variety of educationally oriented tours and vacations that are geared toward seniors; some even highlight the distinct cultures of New Orleans and Lafayette.

In general, New Orleans and southeastern Louisiana are exceptionally helpful places, so senior travelers should have little trouble finding assistance here.

LGBTQ TRAVELERS

New Orleans is a bastion of gay-friendliness, with gay newspapers, numerous gay and lesbian organizations and gay-owned businesses, and several gay-dominated bars and nightclubs, many of which are in the midst of the nightlife district in the French Quarter. Locals tend to be rather blasé about the sight of two women or two men walking hand in hand in the Big Easy, especially in the Quarter, the Faubourg Marigny, and Uptown, which tend to have the highest lesbian and gay populations. Some tourists, however, come from less tolerant places, and sadly, drunken disagreements occasionally occur along Bourbon Street, where the city's straight and gay nightclub rows collide.

Three annual events—Mardi Gras in the late winter, the Southern Decadence celebration over Labor Day weekend, and Halloween in the fall—draw the greatest numbers of gay and lesbian visitors to New Orleans, but the city is always popular with gay and lesbian travelers. Many inns and B&Bs, especially in the Faubourg Marigny, are gay-owned.

For more information about gay and lesbian activities, consult the free bimonthly *Ambush Mag* (ambushmag.com). The same publication also has a website just for gay goings-on during Mardi Gras (gaymardigras.com). Another helpful website is gayneworleans.com.

RESOURCES FOR TRAVELERS OF COLOR

New Orleans's Black population has molded most of the history and traditions that make the city what it is. I've written about Black-owned businesses in this guide whenever possible, but of course I couldn't get to them all.

Two exuberant occasions for Black folks to visit and party in New Orleans are the Essence Festival in July and the HBCU Southern-Grambling college football game and associated activities, which occurs over Thanksgiving weekend in November.

Here are some resources to start your immersion in the strong cultural identity of Black New Orleans:

- The Where Black NOLA Eats Facebook Group was started to provide a safe place to discuss Black chefs and businesses. There are lots of great local recommendations, plus access to a constantly updating map of Black-owned restaurants and eateries in the city.
- All Bout Dat Tours (504/457-9439, allboutdat.com) runs a daily tour that focuses on significant Black historic sites, and frames them through an African American lens. They also do custom tours depending on your interest.
- Le Musée de f.p.c. (page 249) and the McKenna Museum of African American Art (page 226) are run by the same

foundation and are excellent springboards to explore Black life and culture here. Le Musée de f.p.c is an excellent resource to learn about the historic African, Creole, and African American experience in New Orleans, Louisiana, and the wider South, with an informative tour and antiques on display. The McKenna Museum focuses on minority art and artists and is beautifully and thoughtfully curated with another tour through the facility putting all these people and artworks into context.

- The Tremé (page 230), the first free person of color neighborhood in the country, is key to understanding Black culture in New Orleans. Although gentrification has hit the area, you can still find important spots like the New Orleans African American Museum (1417-1418 Governor Nicholls St., 504/218-8254, noaam.org), the Backstreet Cultural Museum, St. Augustine Catholic Church, and the Tomb of the Unknown Slave. The neighborhood is home to many amazing Black-owned businesses and restaurants.
- Ronald Lewis's House of Dance and Feathers (page 105) is in the Lower Ninth Ward. Not only does he have an amazing collection of Mardi Gras Indian costumes, but Mr. Lewis himself is an incredible resource for talking about the predominantly Black Lower Ninth Ward.
- Visiting the Whitney Plantation Museum (page 319) is a hard day, but it's worthwhile to understand Black history in the South using Black voices to tell the tale.

TRAVELERS WITH DISABILITIES

Within new hotels, some large restaurants, and most major attractions, you can expect to find wheelchair-accessible restrooms, entrance ramps, and other helpful fixtures; RTA buses are wheelchair-accessible. However, New Orleans has many hole-in-the-wall cafés, tiny B&Bs, historic house-museums with narrow staircases or uneven thresholds, and other buildings that are not easily accessible to people using wheelchairs. Unfortunately, the city's historic streetcars are also not wheelchair-accessible. If you're traveling with a guide animal, be sure to contact every hotel or restaurant in question to confirm access and accommodation. A useful resource is the Society for Accessible Travel & Hospitality (212/447-7284, sath.org).

TRAVELING WITH PETS

Although pets aren't allowed within many of New Orleans's hotels, restaurants, and stores, several places do welcome them, including state park campgrounds and some downtown hotels. Typically, guests will be asked to keep pets on a leash at all times, walk animals in designated areas, control their behavior so as not to disturb or endanger others, and always pick up their droppings. Barking or aggressive dogs are usually forbidden everywhere. When in doubt, call ahead to verify the pet policies of a particular hotel, park, attraction, or establishment.

BUSINESS HOURS

Standard business hours for banks tend to be 9am-4pm Monday-Friday, with limited hours on Saturday. Many bars stay open 24 hours daily; otherwise, bars close between 2am and 4am.

Smaller attractions are frequently staffed by volunteers and tend to have limited hours; call ahead to ensure that the place you want to go will be open, or to set up an appointment to visit. In many cases, hours for popular attractions are reduced on Sunday and may fluctuate during the summer months. Given New Orleans's laid-back vibe, posted hours and other policies aren't always observed, especially in the case of small or privately owned businesses.

COSTS AND TIPPING

As a town that relies heavily on tourism, New Orleans has its share of pricey hotels, restaurants, boutiques, and parking lots. Luckily, it's easy to find deals here. Staying outside the Quarter and CBD can often save you quite a bit of money, especially since public transportation is very inexpensive. There are also plenty of affordable eateries, vintage shops, and close-to-free attractions throughout the city; at many attractions, children, college students, senior citizens, military personnel, and holders of AAA cards will receive substantial discounts. However, most retail items and services cost more than their listed price due to sales taxes. The state sales tax is 4 percent, while the sales tax for Orleans Parish is 5 percent; this means that in New Orleans, most goods and services will incur a rather high sales tax of 9 percent. In Metairie, Kenner, and other cities in Jefferson Parish, goods and services will incur an 8.75 percent sales tax. The hotel tax in New Orleans is a whopping 13 percent.

Given the city's reliance on tourism, tipping is critical here. Although the amount of a gratuity depends on the level of service received, there are general tipping guidelines. Restaurant servers should receive 15-20 percent of the entire bill, while pizza delivery drivers should receive at least 10 percent. Taxi and limousine drivers should receive at least 15 percent of the entire fare, while valets, porters, and skycaps will expect around $2 per vehicle or piece of luggage. The housekeeping staff of your inn or hotel also deserves a tip; a generally accepted amount is $2-5 per night.

Tour guides, fishing guides, and other excursion operators should be tipped as well. No matter how much such experiences cost, the gratuity is never included in the quoted price. How much you choose to tip is entirely up to you. While the exact amount of a tip will depend on the cost, length, and nature of the trip in question—not to mention your satisfaction—it's generally accepted to tip 10-20 percent of the overall cost. If a guide or operator makes an exceptional effort, then it's highly recommended to increase the size of the tip accordingly.

PUBLIC RESTROOMS

In the French Quarter, you'll find public restrooms at the Shops at Canal Place, the Shops at Jax Brewery, and the French Market. Plenty of bars and restaurants also have reliable facilities, which you're welcome to use as long as you're willing to purchase something. Public urination is a frequent occurrence in New Orleans (usually in the French Quarter and on Bourbon Street) and can result in being ticketed or getting arrested.

Health and Safety

HOSPITALS

There are several well-regarded hospitals and clinics in New Orleans and its environs, including the Tulane Medical Center (1415 Tulane Ave., 504/988-5263, tulanehealthcare.com), the closest general hospital to the French Quarter and the CBD; University Medical Center (2000 Canal St., 504/702-3000, umcno.org), in Mid City; and the Ochsner Baptist Medical Center (2700 Napoleon Ave., 504/899-9311, ochsner.org), an Uptown hospital with a 24-hour emergency room.

There are several conveniently located Urgent Care facilities around the city; the Ochsner Health System has several in the city, the most central being the French Quarter location (201 Decatur St., 504/609-3833, ochsner.org; 9am-5:30pm Mon.-Sat.).

If you're in need of emergency dental care, consider the Louisiana

Dental Center (2121 Magazine St., 504/218-8370, ladentalcenter.com; 8:30am-4:30pm Mon.-Thurs., 8:30am-3:30pm Fri., 8:30am-1:30pm Sat.), which offers several locations in southeastern Louisiana, from Metairie to Gonzales. Most medical and dental facilities will require insurance or a partial payment before admitting patients for treatment or dispensing medication.

PHARMACIES

Some pharmacies in New Orleans and southeastern Louisiana include Walgreens (619 Decatur St., 504/525-7263 or 800/925-4733, walgreens.com; 8am-10pm daily) in the French Quarter; CVS (4901 Prytania St., 504/891-6307 or 800/746-7287, cvs.com; 24 hours daily) in the Uptown area; and Rite Aid (760 Harrison Ave., 504/483-2383 or 800/748-3243, riteaid.com; 7am-9pm Mon.-Sat., 8am-8pm Sun.) in Lakeview. In all cases, the in-house pharmacy has shorter hours than the rest of the store, so be sure to call ahead.

EMERGENCY SERVICES

All of Louisiana is tied into the 911 emergency system. Dial 911 free from any telephone (including pay phones) to reach an operator who can quickly dispatch local police, fire, or ambulance services. While this service also works from cell phones, you may find it difficult to make calls from rural areas or offshore waters, where reliable cellular service isn't always guaranteed. For non-emergencies, contact the Louisiana State Police (504/471-2775, lsp.org) or the New

Orleans Police Department (nola.gov/government/nopd)—including the First District (501 N. Rampart St., 504/658-6010) in the Tremé, the Second District (4317 Magazine St., 504/658-6020) in Uptown, the Fifth District (4015 Burgundy St., 504/658-6050) in the Bywater, and the Eighth District (334 Royal St., 504/658-6080) in the French Quarter. In the event of a hurricane or other natural disaster, contact the New Orleans Office of Homeland Security and Emergency Preparedness (504/658-8700) for instructions and evacuation assistance.

CRIME AND HARASSMENT

New Orleans has a reputation for crime—partially deserved, partially exaggerated. Crimes such as muggings and carjackings can occur anywhere in the city, including in or near tourist areas. Pay attention to your surroundings at all times and be smart.

The most frequent targets of crime in New Orleans are inebriated tourists, and these, unfortunately, are easy to find in the French Quarter late at night. The simplest way to keep safe is to avoid drinking yourself into a stupor. If anticipating a night of revelry, keep the name and address of your hotel written down someplace safe—but never write your hotel room number down somewhere that a thief or pickpocket could get it. Carry the name and number of at least one or two cab companies and keep your cell phone handy.

If you require assistance while in downtown New Orleans, contact

SafeWalk (504/415-1730; 10am-10pm daily), a free service provided in the CBD and Arts District. With at least 20 minutes' advance notice, Public Safety Rangers will escort residents and visitors to their cars or other areas within the designated zone. If you do find yourself in trouble, whether in the CBD or another area of New Orleans, don't hesitate to find a phone and dial 911. Remember that the time it takes police and emergency vehicles to reach you will depend upon your location.

If you witness a crime of any kind while in New Orleans, contact the Greater New Orleans Crimestoppers (504/822-1111, crimestoppersgno.org) to offer an anonymous tip. Likewise, you can consult the Orleans Parish Sheriff's Office (504/822-8000 or 504/826-7045, opcso.org).

HEATSTROKE

Hot, sunny days are common in southeastern Louisiana, and it's crucial to prepare for them. Apply sunscreen frequently and liberally. Prolonged sun exposure, high temperatures, and little water consumption can cause dehydration, which can lead to heat exhaustion—a harmful condition whereby your internal cooling system begins to shut down. Symptoms may include clammy skin, weakness, vomiting, and abnormal body temperature. In such instances, you must lie down in the shade, remove restrictive clothing, and drink water.

If you do not treat heat exhaustion promptly, your condition can worsen quickly, leading to heatstroke (or sunstroke), a dangerous condition whereby your internal body temperature starts to rise to a potentially fatal level. Symptoms can include dizziness, vomiting, diarrhea, abnormal breathing and blood pressure, cessation of sweating, headache, and confusion. If any of these occur, head to a hospital as soon as possible.

HURRICANE PREPARATION

The Atlantic hurricane season generally runs June-November, but the truth is that hurricanes are infrequent in this region. Nevertheless, it's always a good idea to be prepared for the worst.

If you do plan to visit New Orleans during hurricane season, the best advice is to get appropriate travel insurance to cover the costs of your trip and evacuation, pay attention to the National Weather Service (62300 Airport Rd., Slidell, 504/522-7330 or 985/649-0357, srh.noaa.gov), National Oceanic and Atmospheric Administration website (NOAA, noaa.gov), and local media/social media. Make sure you have cash and rain gear, keep your cell phone charged, and keep valuables and identification with you at all times if there's a chance something will develop.

INSURANCE

Insurance is highly recommended while traveling in southeastern Louisiana. Whether you're a U.S. citizen driving your own car or an international traveler in a rented RV, you should invest in medical, travel, and automotive insurance before embarking upon your trip in order to protect yourself as well as your assets. Research your insurance options and choose the policies that best suit your needs and budget. For travel insurance (which should include medical coverage), consider a company like Travel Guard (800/826-4919, travelguard.com).

WATER SAFETY

Given New Orleans's location at the southern end of the Mississippi River, it's not surprising that some people would question the safety of its water supply. In general, the tap water here is relatively safe. It's tested daily by the Sewerage & Water Board of New Orleans (swbno. org) for microbial, organic, chemical, and metallic contaminants.

While visiting New Orleans, you might venture into the countryside, bayous, and lakes beyond the city. If so, you'll encounter a lot of brackish water, which you should never drink. In various places, you may also find fresh water, and while the water may look inviting, don't take a chance. Many of Louisiana's inland bodies of water may be tainted with *Giardia lamblia,* a nasty little parasite that is most commonly transmitted through mammal feces. The resulting illness, giardiasis, can result in severe stomach cramps, vomiting, and diarrhea. While Halizone tablets, bleach, and other chemical purifiers may be effective against such organisms, your best bet is to use an adequate water filter (which filters down to 0.4 micron or less) or boil the water for at least five minutes.

SMOKING

All restaurants in New Orleans are nonsmoking, and, as of April 2015, a citywide ban has made smoking illegal inside taverns, lounges, concert halls, hotels, and other establishments throughout New Orleans. You can, however, still smoke outside, such as on balconies and in courtyards, depending on the place in question.

WILDLIFE

With its humid, subtropical climate and prevalence of marshes, southeastern Louisiana is home to a wide array of insects, from harmless dragonflies to more bothersome critters. Perhaps the biggest concern is mosquitoes, whose stings can cause itchy red welts or worse. Mosquitoes are typically more prevalent June-September, when the humidity is at its worst. To protect against these relentless creatures, use a combination of defenses, including light-colored clothing, long-sleeved shirts, long pants, closed shoes, scent-free deodorant, and insect repellents containing DEET. Avoid grassy areas and shady places and instead seek open, breezy locales (especially out on the water) and avoid peak hours for mosquito activity, namely sunrise and sunset. Try to open and close your car doors quickly and keep your car windows rolled up, as there's little worse than being stuck in a vehicle with a roving mosquito.

If you're stung you should be fine, unless you have an unforeseen allergy or the mosquito is a carrier of a disease like the West Nile virus. Beyond cleaning the affected area and treating it with calamine lotion, hydrocortisone cream, or aloe vera gel, all you can do is take some anti-inflammatory or antihistamine medication for the pain and swelling and wait for the skin to heal.

In the spring, all the lovely oaks become home to buck moth caterpillars that have little spikes on their backs filled with toxin. Don't pick any up that have fallen from the trees, because those microscopic spikes will embed themselves under your skin, and the toxin hurts. If stung, wash the area with soap and water, but air dry or use a hair dryer so as not to drive the stingers in farther. Find some duct tape or scotch tape to rip the spikes out as soon as possible.

If you sit or step on an ant hill, prepare for the very real possibility that you've annoyed a hive of fire ants and they will bite you mercilessly.

Swarming termites don't bite or sting, but the sheer number of them can be overwhelming for some people. If you come across a swarm, generally in the spring, cover all orifices and expect to see some under your clothes later. Swarming termites hit hard and fast, and then leave.

Insects aren't the only perils in the wild. While hiking amid southeastern Louisiana's forests, marshes, and beaches, be careful where you step; it's easier than you think to trip on a root or other obstruction. Refrain from digesting any tempting berries, flowers, and plants without first consulting local residents or expert field guides.

Since much of southeastern Louisiana comprises undeveloped marshes and forests, not to mention surrounding waters, you're bound to encounter wild animals. While many of these, such as lizards and shorebirds, are fairly harmless, more dangerous creatures, such as alligators, live here, too. To avoid perilous encounters with such animals, don't venture into places like Barataria Preserve or the Atchafalaya Basin by yourself, and try to observe all wildlife from a distance. Although it should go without saying, never taunt, disturb, or feed any of the wildlife.

Information and Services

MAPS AND TOURIST INFORMATION

For general information about traveling in southeastern Louisiana, your best source is the state-run Louisiana Office of Tourism (800/994-8626, louisianatravel. com), which offers a tour guidebook, interactive maps, travel tips, and oodles of information about the state's accommodations, restaurants, attractions, events, live entertainment, and outdoor activities, plus live operators willing to assist with your tourism needs. Visitors to the Big Easy should also consult the city's convention and visitors bureau, New Orleans & Company (2020 St. Charles Ave., 800/672-6124, neworleans.com; 8:30am-5pm Mon.-Fri.) or the New Orleans Tourism Marketing Corporation (2020 St. Charles Ave., 504/524-4784, neworleans.com; 9am-5pm), both of which provide a slew of information about the city's myriad lodging, dining, and activity options. The New Orleans Welcome Center (529 St. Ann St., 504/568-5661, crt.state.la.us; 8:30am-5pm daily) also provides maps and brochures and arranges tours. For information about the Greater New Orleans area, consult the Jefferson Convention & Visitors Bureau (1221 Elmwood Park Blvd., Ste. 411, 504/731-7083 or 877/572-7474, visitjeffersonparish.com). The Northshore, Tangipahoa Parish, Baton Rouge, Houma, Lafayette, and Lake Charles all have helpful CVBs as well.

In a state known for its tourism industry, you'll find no shortage of helpful maps, including those produced by AAA (800/564-6222, aaa.com), which offers both a *Louisiana/Mississippi* state map ($5 nonmember, free for members) as well as a *New Orleans* map ($5 nonmember, free for members) that features smaller maps of the city's airport and streetcar system. Rand McNally (800/333-0136, randmcnally.com) publishes several helpful maps, including an easy-to-fold *Louisiana* map ($8), a folded *New Orleans, Hammond, Ponchatoula, Slidell* map ($6), a folded *Baton Rouge, Shreveport, Bossier City* map ($6), a laminated *Streetwise New Orleans* map ($7), and a comprehensive *New Orleans Street Guide* ($20). If exploring the backcountry, you may also want to order an official topographical (topo) map produced by the U.S. Geological Survey (888/275-8747, usgs.gov).

MONEY

Bank debit cards and major credit cards (like Visa and MasterCard) are accepted throughout southeastern Louisiana, especially in major cities like New Orleans and Baton Rouge. Automated teller machines (ATMs) are prevalent, and most banks—such as Chase (800/935-9935, chase.com), Regions (800/734-4667, regions.com), Iberia Bank (800/682-3231, iberiabank.com), First NBC Bank (866/441-5552, firstnbcbank.com), First Bank and Trust (888/287-9621, fbtonline.com), and Bank of Louisiana (800/288-9811, bankoflouisiana.com)—provide access to ATMs inside and/or outside their branches. (Be prepared to pay $2-3 per ATM transaction if the machine isn't operated by your bank.)

Many bars, eateries, stores, and tour operators will accept only cash or travelers checks, so you should never rely exclusively on plastic. Foreign currency can be exchanged at the Whitney Bank branch (900 Airline Dr., Kenner, 504/838-6491 or 800/844-4450, whitneybank.com; 8:30am-4pm Mon.-Fri.) in the ticket lobby of the Louis Armstrong New Orleans International Airport; cash advances and travelers checks are also available here. For up-to-date exchange rates, consult xe.com.

COMMUNICATIONS AND MEDIA
WI-FI AND CELL PHONE COVERAGE

There's no city-wide Wi-Fi access, but you can find it in fast food spots, almost any coffee shop or brewery, some restaurants, and the airport. During large events like Jazz Fest or along the Mardi Gras parade routes, cell service slows considerably.

NEWSPAPERS AND PERIODICALS

The major newspaper for New Orleans is *The New Orleans Advocate* (nola.com), which provides up-to-date information about restaurants, sporting events, and live entertainment. For nightlife and live music listings, pick up a copy of the monthly *OffBeat Magazine* (offbeat.com); the website includes a monthly electronic newsletter, for which you can sign up online, and a free smartphone app keeps club listings in your pocket. The monthly *Where Y'at* magazine (whereyat.com) also offers information about the city's dining and nightlife scenes. The city's alternative paper is *Antigravity* (antigravitymagazine.com), which is published monthly.

Where Traveler (wheretraveler.com/new-orleans) is a useful, well-produced monthly, with excellent dining, shopping, arts, and events coverage. Other helpful publications include *The Louisiana Weekly* (louisianaweekly.com), *Louisiana Kitchen & Culture* (louisiana.kitchenandculture.com), and *Louisiana Cookin'* (louisianacookin.com).

For regional publications, check out *64 Parishes,* published by the Louisiana Endowment for the Humanities, which analyzes historic and current events and trends throughout all 64 of Louisiana's parishes. For a publication focused on Gulf Coast stories, including a lot of New Orleans coverage, *Country Roads Magazine* (countryroadsmagazine.com) is great.

RADIO AND TELEVISION

Local radio and TV stations can be useful sources of information for everything from upcoming concerts and festivals to weather updates during hurricane season. For excellent local music, tune your radio to WWOZ (90.7 FM, wwoz.org), which typically plays jazz, blues, and R&B, plus healthy doses of swing, Cajun and zydeco, country and bluegrass, and gospel. Other popular radio stations in the Big Easy include WWNO (89.9 FM, wwno.org), which is broadcast from the University of New Orleans and offers classical music, cultural programming, and NPR news; WTUL (91.5 FM, wtulneworleans.com), Tulane University's progressive radio station; and WRNO (99.5 FM, wrno.com), which offers an all-news format featuring the likes of Rush Limbaugh, Glenn Beck, and other conservative personalities. The city's four main TV stations include WWL-TV (wwltv.com), the CBS affiliate; WDSU (wdsu.com), the NBC affiliate; WGNO (abc26.com), the ABC affiliate; and FOX8 (fox8live.com).

RESOURCES

Glossary

andouille: (an-DOO-ee) a spicy, smoked pork sausage prepared with garlic and Cajun seasonings and used in dishes like red beans and rice, gumbo, and jambalaya

bananas Foster: a rich dessert consisting of bananas, butter, brown sugar, cinnamon, and rum, served over vanilla ice cream, invented at Brennan's in the French Quarter

bayou: (BAHY-oo) a sluggish body of water within a marsh, prevalent throughout southern Louisiana

beignet: (ben-YAY) a squarish, fried pastry made from doughnut batter and sprinkled with powdered sugar

blackened: a Cajun preparation that involves coating fish or meat with a spicy seasoning blend and flash-frying it in a hot, cast-iron pan

boil: a quintessential, often seasonal Cajun seafood dish in which shrimp, crabs, or crawfish are boiled in a spicy broth; also refers to the communal experience of preparation and eating together

boudin: (boo-DAN) a hot, spicy pork sausage typically mixed with onions, herbs, cayenne pepper, and cooked rice

café au lait: (KAFF-ay oh LAY) a hot drink made equally of coffee (usually coffee with chicory) and steamed milk

Cajun: a term referring to the French Acadians that relocated from Canada to southern Louisiana

cochon de lait: (koh-SHON duh LAY) a French term that literally means "pig in milk" and regionally refers to a Cajun pig roast

Coke: a term used locally to describe any soda; also known as a "soft drink"

court bouillon: (KOO-boo-YAWN) a Creole-style, tomato-based bouillabaisse, or seafood stew, the most popular version being redfish court bouillon

cracklin': the crispy residue that remains after rendering pork fat

Creole: a term referring to the descendants of French, Spanish, and Caribbean slaves and natives

Crescent City: a nickname for New Orleans, referring to how the Mississippi River curves around the city

Crescent City Connection: (CCC) the twin cantilever bridges that span the Mississippi River and connect the East Bank of New Orleans with the West Bank; formerly known as the Greater New Orleans Bridge (GNO)

dressed: an expression used when ordering a sandwich, meant to indicate that everything (e.g., lettuce, tomato, and mayonnaise) be included

étouffée: (ay-too-FAY) a dark roux of seasoned vegetables, usually poured over rice and served with shrimp or crawfish

fais do-do: (FAY doh-doh) a Cajun dance party

filé: (FEE-lay) ground sassafras leaves used to season gumbo and other dishes

gallery: a second-floor balcony that covers the sidewalk, especially common in the French Quarter

gris-gris: (GREE-gree) a voodoo good-luck charm

gumbo: a thick filé soup made from a roux and filled with ingredients like chicken, andouille, okra, shrimp, and crab meat, served with rice

hoodoo: the ancient West African practice of "folk magic," which, in New Orleans, incorporates European and Native American influences and involves the use of herbs, incense, candles, talismans, and Biblical psalms

jambalaya: (juhm-buh-LAHY-uh) a Cajun or Creole rice dish containing celery, onions, tomatoes, spices, and meats like chicken, sausage, and seafood

lagniappe: (LAN-yap) a French expression meant to indicate a bonus

laissez les bons temps rouler: (lay-ZAY lay BAWN tawn ROO-lay) a French expression meaning "let the good times roll"

mirliton: (MER-li-tawn) a pear-shaped squash commonly stuffed with seasoned meat or seafood; also called "chayote"

mudbug: a slang expression for crawfish, the freshwater shellfish that other states refer to as "crayfish"

muffuletta: (muff-uh-LET-uh) a round, oversized sandwich made from Italian bread, ham, salami, mortadella, provolone, and olive salad; also spelled "muffaletta"

neutral ground: the grassy part between the paved areas of a boulevard; known elsewhere as a median

nutria: a large, beaver-like rodent commonly seen in the canals and swamps of southern Louisiana, often considered a nuisance due to its destructive tendencies

parish: the official term for a county in Louisiana

pirogue: (PEE-rohg) a small, flat-bottomed canoe, prevalent throughout southern Louisiana

po'boy: the quintessential New Orleans sandwich, made on French bread, with fillings like roast beef or fried shrimp; also spelled "po-boy," "po boy," or "poor boy"

praline: (prah-LEEN or PRAY-leen) a sweet confection made from pecans, cream, butter, and caramelized brown sugar

red beans and rice: a traditional New Orleans dish consisting of kidney beans and a spicy gravy, often served with ham hocks, *tasso,* or andouille

rémoulade: (rey-moo-LAHD) a spicy, mustard-based sauce, typically served with boiled shrimp

Romeo spikes: 19th-century, cast-iron protrusions at the top of ground-floor gallery polls in the French Quarter, meant to deter male suitors from shimmying upward for unauthorized, nighttime visits to young women

roux: (roo) a slowly cooked mixture of butter (or water) and flour used to thicken gumbo, sauces, and soups

Sazerac: a popular cocktail made with bitters, Pernod, sugar, lemon oil, and rye whiskey or bourbon

shotgun: a one-level architectural style whereby all rooms are positioned consecutively, interconnected by doors in lieu of a hallway

snowball: a cup of shaved ice served with flavored syrups; usually called a "snow cone" in other states

Spanish moss: a specific epiphyte that resembles a grayish, lacy cluster and typically hangs from live oak trees

tasso: smoked beef or pork sausage, specially seasoned and often used in regional stews and pastas

Twinspan: the two parallel bridges that cross Lake Pontchartrain, from New Orleans to the Northshore

Vieux Carré: (VOO kah-RAY) a reference

to the French Quarter, meaning "old square" in French

voodoo: an ancient West African religious faith that, in New Orleans, blends African, Haitian, Native American, European, and Catholic traditions; also known as the "dancing religion"

where y'at?: a local expression used in place of "Where are you?"

Who dat?: a local idiom meaning "who is that?" that was originally used in poetry, minstrel shows, and movies and now serves as a chant of team support for the New Orleans Saints, fans of which are known as "Who Dats"

Yat: an English dialect spoken throughout the Greater New Orleans area, heavily influenced by European, Southern American, and Louisiana French accents; also referring to a native New Orleanian who speaks with this Brooklyn-style accent, commonly heard in communities like Chalmette

zydeco: (ZAHY-di-koh) a blues-influenced, Cajun-style type of dance music popular in southern Louisiana and typically featuring the sounds of guitars, violins, and accordions

Suggested Reading

CUISINE

Braden-Perry, Megan. *Crescent City Snow: The Ultimate Guide to New Orleans Snowball Stands,* Lafayette, LA: University of Louisiana, 2017. This is part guidebook, part diary, and part biography of 50 snowball stands and their customers in the greater New Orleans area.

Gaudin, Lorin. *New Orleans Chef's Table: Extraordinary Recipes from the Crescent City,* Guilford, CT: Lyons Press, 2019. A look at New Orleans food through the eyes of its chefs, with reviews of restaurants, mouthwatering recipes, and beautiful food photography.

Link, Donald, and Paula Disbrowe. *Real Cajun: Rustic Home Cooking from Donald Link's Louisiana.* New York, NY: Clarkson Potter/Publishers, 2009. A culinary expedition through Cajun Country, the childhood home of Chef Donald Link, the

co-owner of New Orleans-based restaurants Cochon, Herbsaint, Pêche, Butcher, and Gianna.

Pearce, Elizabeth. *Drink Dat New Orleans,* Woodstock, VT: Countryman Press, 2017. Pearce, a New Orleans-based drinks historian, leans into the culture of the cocktail here, weaving history and information about great places to get your booze on.

Rohen, Sara. *Gumbo Tales: Finding My Place at the New Orleans Table,* New York, NY: W.W. Norton & Company, 2008. Food writer and New Orleans transplant Rohen finds her way through the culinary traditions of the city before and after Katrina.

Williams, Elizabeth M. *New Orleans: A Food Biography,* Lanham, MD: Rowman & Littlefield, 2013. Williams, former executive director of the Southern Food and Beverage

Museum, located in New Orleans, has a deep understanding of the culinary history and traditions of the Crescent City and is excited to share them in this book.

lesser-known bars and events, and a slew of obscure activities favored by the author, his friends, and other locals—as described in this unconventional guide.

RECREATION AND TRAVEL

Bronston, Barri. *Walking New Orleans: 30 Tours Exploring Historic Neighborhoods, Waterfront Districts, Culinary and Music Corridors, and Recreational Wonderlands*. Birmingham, AL: Wilderness Press, 2015. Written by a lifelong resident of New Orleans, this guide offers a wide array of self-guided tours, each of which includes dining and recreational tips.

Douglas, Lake, and Jeannette Hardy. *Gardens of New Orleans: Exquisite Excess*. San Francisco, CA: Chronicle Books LLC, 2001. This sumptuous tome, filled with photographs by Richard Sexton, takes readers into the many secret and sensuous gardens of the Big Easy.

Fry, Macon, and Julie Posner. *Cajun Country Guide*. Gretna, LA: Pelican Publishing Company, Inc., 1999. Originally published in 1992, this in-depth tour guide of Cajun Country offers extensive anecdotes and histories on just about every town in the region, large or small.

Welch, Michael Patrick. *New Orleans: The Underground Guide*. Baton Rouge, LA: Louisiana State University Press, 2014. Beyond the traditional jazz, dishes, and carriage rides that visitors expect, New Orleans is home to Bohemian locals, genre-defying music, transnational cuisine,

MUSIC AND CULTURE

Alvarado, Denise. *The Voodoo Hoodoo Spellbook*. San Francisco, CA: Red Wheel/Weiser, LLC, 2011. Written by a New Orleans-born native Creole who has spent a lifetime studying indigenous healing traditions, this folk-magic compilation offers serious practitioners a slew of authentic prayers, spells, rituals, and instructions.

Armstrong, Louis. *Satchmo: My Life in New Orleans*. Cambridge, MA: Da Capo Press, Inc., 1986. Originally published in 1954, this is the definitive autobiography by the definitive New Orleans jazz icon.

Berry, Jason, Jonathan Foose, and Tad Jones. *Up from the Cradle of Jazz: New Orleans Music Since World War II*. Lafayette, LA: University of Louisiana at Lafayette Press, 2009. A terrific survey tracing the history of music in the Big Easy, from the 1940s to the post-Katrina era.

Florence, Robert. *New Orleans Cemeteries: Life in the Cities of the Dead*. New Orleans, LA: Batture Press, Inc., 1997. An insider's history and tour of the city's famous aboveground cemeteries.

Gessler, Diana Hollingsworth. *Very New Orleans: A Celebration of History, Culture, and Cajun Country Charm*. Chapel Hill, NC: Algonquin Books of Chapel Hill, 2006. Filled with the author's detailed sketches and watercolors, this charming book celebrates all that makes southern Louisiana unique, from Jackson Square and the Garden District to Creole cuisine and Cajun music.

Huber, Leonard V. *Mardi Gras: A Pictorial History of Carnival in New Orleans.* Gretna, LA: Pelican Publishing Company, Inc., 2003. A decent overview of the city's most famous celebration, originally published in 1977.

Lomax, Alan. *Mister Jelly Roll: The Fortunes of Jelly Roll Morton, New Orleans Creole and "Inventor of Jazz."* Los Angeles, CA: University of California Press, 2001. Originally published in 1950, this fascinating examination of a New Orleans jazz luminary also explores the development of the city's music scene.

Ondaatje, Michael. *Coming Through Slaughter.* New York, NY: Vintage Books, 1996. Penned by the author of *The English Patient* and originally published in 1976, this colorful tale illustrates the life of Buddy Bolden, one of the earliest New Orleans jazz greats.

Piazza, Tom. *Why New Orleans Matters.* New York, NY: Harper Perennial, 2005. A look at the music, people, and culture of New Orleans and the city's cultural significance.

Tallant, Robert. *Voodoo in New Orleans.* Gretna, LA: Pelican Publishing Company, Inc., 2003. Written by the author of *The Voodoo Queen* and originally published in 1946, this classic compendium covers one

of New Orleans's most fascinating topics.

HISTORY AND GEOGRAPHY

Asbury, Herbert. *The French Quarter: An Informal History of the New Orleans Underworld.* New York, NY: Thunder's Mouth Press, 2003. In an unconventional look at the city's seedy side, Asbury's colorful account, originally published in 1936, surveys the city's infamous red-light districts, illegal gaming, and other not-so-legitimate activities.

Baum, Dan. *Nine Lives: Mystery, Magic, Death, and Life in New Orleans,* New York, NY: Spiegel & Grau, 2010. This gripping book brings multiple points of view to growing up in New Orleans at different times, under different skins, and what happened to everyone after Katrina hit.

Brinkley, Douglas. *The Great Deluge: Hurricane Katrina, New Orleans, and the Mississippi Gulf Coast.* New York, NY: William Morrow & Company, Inc., 2006. This is one of the most comprehensive and insightful accounts of Hurricane Katrina, written by a noted historian and Tulane professor who experienced the storm's devastating aftermath firsthand.

Campanella, Richard. *Bienville's Dilemma: A Historical Geography of New Orleans,* Lafayette, LA: University of Louisiana, 2008. Richard Campanella is a national treasure and we in New Orleans are lucky to have him writing books and articles about the city. *Bienville's Dilemma* takes the reader from its geological origins through to post-Katrina analysis. Another good one to check out is *Bourbon Street: A History* (2014), which explores the cultural history of this infamous and polarizing street.

Chase, John Churchill. *Frenchmen, Desire, Good Children...and Other Streets of New Orleans!* Gretna, LA: Pelican Publishing Company, Inc., 2001. Originally published in 1949, this humorous book reveals the origin of the Big Easy's fascinating, often hard-to-pronounce street names.

Duncan, Jeff. *From Bags to Riches: How the New Orleans Saints and the People of Their Hometown Rose from the Depths Together.* Lafayette, LA: Acadian House Publishing, 2010. Focusing on the 2009-2010 football season that culminated in the New Orleans Saints's first Super Bowl win, a sports columnist for *The Times-Picayune* demonstrates how the struggling NFL team and the people of New Orleans and the Gulf Coast bolstered one another in the years following Hurricane Katrina.

Garvey, Joan B., and Mary Lou Widmer. *Beautiful Crescent: A History of New Orleans.* Gretna, LA: Pelican Publishing Company, Inc., 2013. Originally published in 1982, though recently updated by Kathy Chappetta Spiess and Karen Chappetta, this is considered a definitive text for tourists, historians, and tour guides alike. It's a concise history offering details about the city's founding, changing European rule, African American community, jazz heritage, and notable figures and events.

Krist, Gary. *Empire of Sin: A Story of Sex, Jazz, Murder, and the Battle for Modern New Orleans.* New York, NY: Broadway Books, 2014. This deeply researched book about the crime before and during the era of Storyville paints a picture of a city just on the verge of losing control.

Johnson, Walter. *Soul by Soul: Life Inside the Antebellum Slave Market.* Cambridge, MA: Harvard University Press, 1999. Using narratives, court records, bills of sale, and other documents to trace the harrowing legacy of slavery, this book offers a gripping and raw account of North America's largest and most notorious slave market, which was centered in New Orleans.

Piazza, Tom. *Why New Orleans Matters.* New York, NY: HarperCollins Publishers, 2005. This heartfelt, firsthand celebration of the Big Easy after Hurricane Katrina makes a case for why it's so important that the city rebuild and flourish.

Solnit, Rebecca and Rebecca Snediker. *Unfathomable City: A New Orleans Atlas.* Berkeley, CA: University of California Press, 2013. This beautiful book combines cartography, geography, and history perfectly, befitting an atlas of New Orleans.

Sublette, Ned. *The World That Made New Orleans: From Spanish Silver to Congo Square.* Chicago, IL: Lawrence Hill Books, 2008. A well-researched study of the Crescent City's economic and cultural roots prior to the 20th century.

Williams, T. Harry. *Huey Long.* New York, NY: Vintage Books, 1981. Originally published in 1969, this gripping biography explores the infamous "Kingfish," the man who shaped Louisiana politics for many years after his death.

FICTION AND PROSE

Brite, Poppy Z. *Liquor: A Novel,* New York, NY: Three Rivers Press, 2004. This pre-Katrina-set novel features two chefs and childhood friends in love and trying to find success as restaurateurs as they navigate New Orleans's culinary underworld and, even worse, the city government. There's a prequel, *Second Line* (2009), that includes the novellas *The Value of X* (2003) and *D*U*C*K* (2007), as well as two sequels: *Prime* (2005) and *Soul Kitchen* (2006).

Burke, James Lee. *The Tin Roof Blowdown.* New York, NY: Simon & Schuster, 2007. Set in the wake of Hurricane Katrina, this gripping mystery is one of 20-plus novels in a popular crime series featuring Dave Robicheaux, a homicide detective living in southern Louisiana. Other titles include *The Neon Rain* (1987), *Purple Cane Road* (2000), and *Creole Belle* (2012).

Cable, George Washington. *Old Creole Days: A Story of Creole Life.* Gretna, LA: Pelican Publishing Company, Inc., 1991. In this reprint of his 1879 story collection, Victorian novelist and essayist Cable, who wrote many popular books about the city, captures life in old Creole New Orleans during the 19th century.

Chopin, Kate. *The Awakening and Selected Stories.* New York, NY: Penguin Putnam, Inc., 2002. One of the great literary classics of the South, Chopin's 1899 novella focuses on a woman who flouts New Orleans Creole society by leaving her husband and children.

Clark, Joshua, ed. *French Quarter Fiction: The Newest Stories of America's Oldest Bohemia.* New Orleans, LA: Light of New Orleans Publishing, LLC, 2003. This riveting anthology explores "America's oldest Bohemia" through the eyes of local writers like John Biguenet, Andrei Codrescu, and Tennessee Williams.

Hambly, Barbara. *Free Man of Color,* New York, NY: Bantam Books, 1997. The Benjamin January series spans 12 books focused on a free Creole black man in pre-Civil War New Orleans who solves crimes using his medical expertise while trying to avoid derision, imprisonment, or worse due to his race. *Free Man of Color,* the introductory book of the series, focuses closely on the plaçage traditions in Creole society.

Keyes, Frances Parkinson. *Dinner at Antoine's.* New Orleans, LA: Second Line Press, 2013. Originally published in 1948, this classic New Orleans novel revolves around the apparent suicide of a young woman and the subsequent efforts to prove that she was murdered.

Long, Judy, ed. *Literary New Orleans.* Athens, GA: Hill Street Press, 1999.

A delightful anthology of fiction, poetry, memoirs, and essays by some of the city's most notable authors, including James Lee Burke, William Faulkner, and Tennessee Williams.

Percy, Walker. *The Moviegoer.* New York, NY: Vintage Books, 1998. Percy was one of Louisiana's most talented writers, and this existential story about a New Orleans stockbroker, originally published in 1961, is one of his finest.

Rice, Anne. *Interview with the Vampire.* New York, NY: Alfred A. Knopf, Inc., 1976. Perhaps the Garden District's most famous former resident, Anne Rice has set several vampire and witchcraft tales, including the first of her acclaimed *Vampire Chronicles* series, throughout the New Orleans area.

Saxon, Lyle, and Robert Tallant. *Gumbo Ya-Ya: Folk Tales of Louisiana.* Gretna, LA: Pelican Publishing Company, Inc., 1987. This reprint offers an enthralling look at the state's legends and practices.

Smith, Julie. *New Orleans Mourning.* New York, NY: St. Martin's Press, 1990. An award-winning entry in the series of popular mystery books revolving around New Orleans policeman Skip Langdon.

Toole, John Kennedy. *A Confederacy of Dunces.* Baton Rouge, LA: Louisiana State University Press, 1980. A critically acclaimed tragicomic novel, this peculiar tale presents a bizarre yet entertaining cast of New Orleans characters.

Warren, Robert Penn. *All the King's Men.* Orlando, FL: Harcourt Brace & Company, 1990. A thinly veiled fictional look at the life of Governor Huey Long, Warren's Pulitzer Prize-winning work is a gripping and compelling study of one of 20th-century America's most controversial figures.

Williams, Tennessee. *A Streetcar Named Desire.* New York, NY: New Directions Publishing Corporation, 2004. Originally published in 1947, this is Williams's seminal play, set in New Orleans. Less famous but more directly about life in the French Quarter is *Vieux Carré,* which was inspired by journals that Williams kept while living in New Orleans.

Suggested Viewing

The lush landscape, lively music clubs, and well-preserved historic districts of southern Louisiana have long been favored by filmmakers and television producers. The classic, Oscar-winning films *Jezebel* and *A Streetcar Named Desire* were both partially shot in this region, and more recent productions have included the television spin-off *NCIS: New Orleans* and HBO's much-acclaimed series *Treme,* which authentically chronicles the lives of various Big Easy residents and musicians in the wake of Hurricane Katrina.

Angel Heart (1987). Written and directed by Alan Parker, starring Mickey Rourke, Robert De Niro, and Lisa Bonet. In this sultry thriller, based on a novel by William Hjortsberg and partially shot in New Orleans, New York-based gumshoe Harry Angel follows a voodoo trail to the Big Easy in search of a missing singer.

The Big Uneasy (2010). A documentary produced by actor and New Orleans resident Harry Shearer, this film investigates the true reason the city flooded in the aftermath of Katrina—shoddy construction and poor maintenance of levee walls and the city's pumping system—by following two teams of investigating scientists and a whistleblowing engineer.

Girls Trip (2017). This bawdy, rowdy comedy follows four friends as they kick back in New Orleans during the Essence Festival. It stars Regina Hall, Queen Latifah, Jada Pinkett Smith, and Tiffany Haddish.

Interview with the Vampire: The Vampire Chronicles (1994). Written by Anne Rice, directed by Neil Jordan, and starring Tom Cruise, Brad Pitt, Antonio Banderas, Kirsten Dunst, and Christian Slater. In this award-winning adaptation of Anne Rice's acclaimed novel, a brooding vampire records his epic history, beginning with a life-altering encounter with the flamboyant vampire Lestat in 18th-century New Orleans. Partially filmed in Louisiana, the movie showcases famous landmarks like Lafayette Cemetery No. 1.

Pretty Baby (1978). Written by Polly Platt, directed by Louis Malle, and starring Brooke Shields, Susan Sarandon, and Keith Carradine. In this sobering, Oscar-nominated drama, a young girl grows up in a brothel in Storyville in 1917 New Orleans. Much of the brothel filming took place in The Columns Hotel on St. Charles Avenue.

The Princess and the Frog (2009). Written by Ron Clements, John Musker, and Rob Edwards, directed by Ron Clements and John Musker, and featuring the voices of Anika Noni Rose, Bruno Campos, Keith David, Jennifer Cody, Jenifer Lewis, Oprah Winfrey, Terrence Howard, and John Goodman. Inspired by the classic story "The Frog Prince," this animated, Oscar-nominated fantasy tells the story of a New Orleans waitress who embarks on a journey to turn a cursed frog back into a human prince. This family-friendly musical incorporates many local attributes, including jazz, voodoo, streetcars, swamps, and landmarks like Jackson Square.

Runaway Jury (2003). Written by Brian Koppelman, David Levien, Rick Cleveland, and Matthew Chapman, directed by Gary Fleder, and starring John Cusack, Rachel Weisz, Gene Hackman, and Dustin Hoffman. Based on a John Grisham novel and featuring iconic New Orleans settings like Café Du Monde and St. Charles Avenue, this riveting thriller pits a juror and his girlfriend against a man who manipulates court trials.

12 Years a Slave (2013). This horrifying story of a free black man sold into slavery was based on the real-life story of Solomon Northup, who wrote the book on which this Steve McQueen-directed film is based. It's an unflinching look at slavery and was shot in New Orleans, with scenes set here. There's a plaque commemorating the location of the slave pen that Northup was held in on the corner of Esplanade Avenue and Chartres Street.

When the Levees Broke: A Requiem in Four Acts (2006). Directed by Spike Lee. Originally televised as an HBO mini-series, this Emmy-winning documentary examines the disastrous effects of Hurricane Katrina on New Orleans, including the government incompetence that led to the tragic flooding and the subsequent abandonment of the city's more underprivileged citizens.

Digital and Internet Resources

SMARTPHONE APPS

Happy Hour (Drinker's Edition)
This app will let you know of any happy hours happening near you at that very moment or in the near future.

National Park Service Tours (New Orleans Jazz)
This is a comprehensive 16-stop self-guided walking tour that covers the stops of the official Jazz Walk of Fame along with other significant stops, with audio background and appropriate musical cues.

NOLA Slave Trail
This is a great resource to find your way around the commemorative markers that the city put up for its tricentennial celebration. It offers an overview of the history of the slave trade in New Orleans.

NOLA Twitter
This can be hard to pinpoint, but search on #nola or #neworleans to get your bearings. Some good folks to start following are: @skooks, @KevinAllman, @YesICandice,

@MySpiltMilk, @DavidMora, @NOLArain, @NOLAheat, and @animatedGeoff. This isn't official New Orleans; it's the real deal.

Parade trackers (WWL and WDSU)

Get one of these on your phone if you're planning on checking out any Mardi Gras parades. It has real-time updated route maps along with info on delays.

TRAVEL

GayNewOrleans.com

www.gayneworleans.com

Here, gay and lesbian travelers will find advice about tours, attractions, bars, restaurants, and accommodations, plus gay-friendly organizations and events, such as PFLAG and Southern Decadence.

GoNOLA

www.gonola.com

Frequently updated, with timely articles by local writers about food, drink, events, and culture. It's a great place to get ideas.

LouisianaTravel.com

www.louisianatravel.com

The state's official online travel source provides a variety of links related to events, attractions, hotels, restaurants, and entertainment options throughout Louisiana.

New Orleans & Company/New Orleans Tourism and Marketing Official Guide

www.neworleans.com

This comprehensive website offers a ton of resources for travelers to the Big Easy, including maps, current temperatures, and information about the city's music, dining, shopping, lodging, nightlife, tours, festivals, attractions, and outdoor recreation. In addition, find comprehensive information about area accommodations, attractions, and activities, plus maps, itineraries, coupons, and a neighborhood guide.

GENERAL INFORMATION

City of New Orleans

www.nola.gov

The city's official website allows you to pay for parking tickets, receive up-to-date emergency information, and find resources for area attractions, shopping locations, sporting events, and transportation facilities.

State of Louisiana

http://louisiana.gov

The official state website comes in handy when you're looking for detailed information about regional demographics, state and local politics, the state library system, various state departments, weather and road conditions, and fishing licenses.

U.S. Department of State/Bureau of Consular Affairs

www.travel.state.gov

International travelers will find guidelines for flying into and out of southern Louisiana.

HISTORY

The Historic New Orleans Collection

www.hnoc.org

Get a look at what The Historic New Orleans Collection has on display. The actual museum is always free.

MEDIA

Big Easy Magazine
www.bigeasymagazine.com

A progressive voice bringing news, events, and information online.

The Lens
www.thelensnola.org

An investigative, non-profit online publication that serves the public interest, with well-researched long-form stories and a focus on transparency.

Neutral Ground News
Neutralgroundnews.com

On the city's satire website, you can read about what's annoying or amusing New Orleans today.

The New Orleans Advocate
www.nola.com

Produced by the state's most widely read newspaper, this website ranks among the most informative online resources related to New Orleans.

WWOZ
www.wwwoz.org

The "Guardians of the Groove," WWOZ's website is the place for all things music related—news, listings calendar, and you can even listen to the live broadcast, which will come in handy once you're back home and missing the beat of the city.

Index

Restaurants Index

Nightlife Index

Shops Index

Hotels Index

Acknowledgments

This book is the culmination of over a year of researching, interviewing, networking, photographing, and writing. I wanted to create a resource that was different than other guidebooks—that focused on the city's neighborhood cultures rather than the well known (and admittedly impressive) historic institutions. Things are changing so rapidly in New Orleans, especially the food and drink scene.

I couldn't have done this without the support of my team at Avalon Travel—Leah Gordon, Ravina Schneider, and Albert Angulo. Their knowledge, professionalism, and senses of humor got me through some stressful times. Thank you to the talented Megan Braden-Perry, who contributed a native (like, back through generations) perspective, and is a pre-eminent Black and truly local New Orleans voice and writer. Hire her for everything, y'all. Thank you to Alaina Rene, who helped guide me to the usually glossed-over Native American history of the area, which was a thriving port city, community, and cultural center for centuries before the French joined the party.

It took a village, so to speak, to create the content for his book, and for that I'm grateful to the local folks who provided their wisdom, opinions, and recommendations (even if they didn't realize it!): Lorin Gaudin (my dining partner in crime), Amanda Westbrooks, Amy Sins, Mark Schettler, Kim Ranjibar, Polly Watts, Travis Clark, Scott Gold, Susan Ford, Todd Price, and just so many more. Thank you to Brandon "B-Mike" Odom for permitting me the use of a photo of one of his murals, and thank you also to New Orleans & Company, the Audubon Institute, The Historic New Orleans Collection, Jeremy Smith with the French Market Corporation, and Charlie Whinhem with the Louisiana Office of Tourism for allowing me access to their photo libraries.

And, of course, thanks to my husband Tom, whose support of me and this (sometimes overwhelming and wearying) project was sometimes the only thing that got me through just one more round of edits or retracing a neighborhood walk for the nth time. I love you, and thank you for being my biggest fan.

Photo Credits

All photos © Nora McGunnigle except: Title page photo: Audubon Institute; page 2 © Paul Broussard and New Orleans & Company; Audubon Institute; Gourmet Reise and New Orleans & Company; page 4 © (top left) Audubon Institute; (left middle)Todd Coleman and New Orleans & Company; (bottom) Todd Coleman and New Orleans & Company; page 5 © Cafebeanz Company, Dreamstime.com; page 6 © King Ho Yim, Dreamstime.com; page 8 © (top) Paul Broussard and New Orleans & Company; (bottom) Paul Broussard and New Orleans & Company; page 9 © Paul Broussard and New Orleans & Company; page 10 © (top) The Roosevelt New Orleans; (bottom) Reciprocity Images, Alamy Stock Photo; page 11 © Paul Broussard and New Orleans & Company; page 12 © (top) Todd Coleman and New Orleans & Company; (bottom) Joe Ferrer, Dreamstime. com; page 13 © Peek Creative Collective, Dreamstime.com; page 15 © (bottom) Legacy1995, Dreamstime.com; page 16 © (top) Ray Zacek, Dreamstime.com; page 18 © (bottom) Historic New Orleans Collection; page 20 © Maksym Fesenko, Dreamstime. com; page 21 © (bottom) Wellesenterprises, Dreamstime.com; page 23 © Paul Broussard and New Orleans & Company; Cia Pix, Dreamstime.com; page 28 © (bottom) Cheryl Gerber and New Orleans & Company; page 29 © (top) Zack Smith and New Orleans & Company; page 31 © Zack Smith and New Orleans & Company; page 33 © (top) Valentin Armianu, Dreamstime.com; Historic New Orleans Collection; Paul Broussard and New Orleans & Company; page 40 © Historic New Orleans Collection; page 41 © Susan Poag, Audubon Institute; page 42 © (top) Wilsilver77, Dreamstime.com; page 47 © Zack Smith and New Orleans & Company; page 51 © Zack Smith and New Orleans & Company; page 54 © Zack Smith and New Orleans & Company; page 55 © (top) Paul Broussard and New Orleans & Company; page 56 © (bottom) Paul Broussard and New Orleans & Company; page 59 © Dark Roux Photography and New Orleans & Company; page 60 © (top) Audubon Institute; page 72 © (top) Paul Broussard and New Orleans & Company; page 76 © (bottom) Paul Broussard and New Orleans & Company; page 83 © (top) The Roosevelt New Orleans; page 88 © Paul Broussard and New Orleans & Company; page 100 © Paul Broussard and New Orleans & Company; page 101 © Zimmytws, Dreamstime.com; (top) Paul Broussard and New Orleans & Company; page 102 © (top) Zack Smith and New Orleans & Company; page 109 © (bottom) Paul Broussard and New Orleans & Company; page 111 © (bottom) Zack Smith and New Orleans & Company; page 114 © Zack Smith and New Orleans & Company; page 115 © Louisiana Office of Tourism; page 117 (top) Paul Broussard and New Orleans & Company; page 119 © Traveling Newlyweds and New Orleans & Company; page 125 © Paul Broussard and New Orleans & Company; page 133 © Gourmet Reise and New Orleans & Company; page 136 © (bottom) Paul Broussard and New Orleans & Company; page 155 © Audubon Institute; Audubon Institute; Lorin Gaudin; page 161 © (top) Audubon Institute; page 162 © (top) Audubon Institute; page 164 © (bottom) F11photo, Dreamstime.com; page 165 © (top) Emilysfolio, Dreamstime.com; page 173 © (top) Paul Broussard and New Orleans & Company; page 174 © (bottom) Zack Smith and New Orleans & Company; page 178 © Zack Smith and New Orleans & Company; page 179 © (bottom) Paul Broussard and New Orleans & Company; page 183 © (bottom) Audubon Institute; Paul Broussard and New Orleans & Company; Zack Smith and New Orleans & Company; page 196 © (bottom) Zack Smith and New Orleans & Company; page 198 © (top) Zack Smith and New Orleans & Company; page 210 © (top) Zack Smith and New Orleans & Company; Paul Broussard and New Orleans & Company; page 219 © Paul Broussard and New Orleans & Company; page 220 © (bottom) Paul Broussard and New Orleans & Company; page 231 © Louisiana Office of Tourism; La Belle Esplanade; page 239 © Ehw258, Dreamstime.com; page 240 © Paul Broussard and New Orleans & Company; page 255 © Ehw258, Dreamstime. com; National Park Service; page 259 © Scott Simon and New Orleans & Company;

More from Moon east of the Mississippi

Road Trip Guides

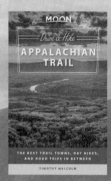

MOON
Drive & Hike
APPALACHIAN TRAIL

THE BEST TRAIL TOWNS, DAY HIKES,
AND ROAD TRIPS IN BETWEEN

TIMOTHY MALCOLM

MOON
BLUE RIDGE PARKWAY
Road Trip

INCLUDING SHENANDOAH & GREAT SMOKY
MOUNTAINS NATIONAL PARKS

JASON FRYE

MOON
NASHVILLE TO NEW ORLEANS
Road Trip

NATCHEZ TRACE PARKWAY · MEMPHIS ·
TUPELO · MISSISSIPPI BLUES TRAIL

MARGARET LITTMAN

City Guides

MOON
ASHEVILLE
& THE GREAT
SMOKY MOUNTAINS

MOON
BOSTON

CAMERON SPERANCE

MOON
CLEVELAND

DOUGLAS TRATTNER

MOON
NASHVILLE

MARGARET LITTMAN

MOON
NEW ORLEANS

NORA McGUNNIGLE

MOON
NEW YORK CITY

CHRISTOPHER KOMPANEK

MOON ROAD TRIP GUIDES

Drive & Hike
APPALACHIAN TRAIL

THE BEST TRAIL TOWNS, DAY HIKES, AND ROAD TRIPS IN BETWEEN

TIMOTHY MALCOLM

BLUE RIDGE PARKWAY
Road Trip

INCLUDING SHENANDOAH & GREAT SMOKY MOUNTAINS NATIONAL PARKS

JASON FRYE

CALIFORNIA
Road Trip

SAN FRANCISCO, YOSEMITE, LAS VEGAS, GRAND CANYON, LOS ANGELES, & THE PACIFIC COAST HIGHWAY

STUART THORNTON

NASHVILLE TO NEW ORLEANS
Road Trip

NATCHEZ TRACE PARKWAY • MEMPHIS • TUPELO • MISSISSIPPI BLUES TRAIL

MARGARET LITTMAN

NEW ENGLAND
Road Trip

BOSTON, ACADIA NATIONAL PARK, WHITE MOUNTAINS, BERKSHIRES, NEWPORT, AND CAPE COD

JEN ROSE SMITH

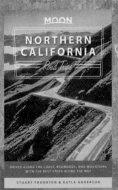

NORTHERN CALIFORNIA
Road Trip

DRIVES ALONG THE COAST, REDWOODS, AND MOUNTAINS WITH THE BEST STOPS ALONG THE WAY

STUART THORNTON & KAYLA ANDERSON

OREGON TRAIL
Road Trip

HISTORIC SITES, SMALL TOWNS, AND SCENIC LANDSCAPES ALONG THE LEGENDARY WESTWARD ROUTE

KATRINA EMERY

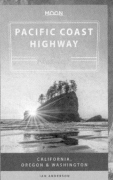

PACIFIC COAST HIGHWAY

CALIFORNIA, OREGON & WASHINGTON

IAN ANDERSON

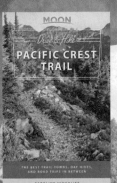

Drive & Hike
PACIFIC CREST TRAIL

THE BEST TRAIL TOWNS, DAY HIKES, AND ROAD TRIPS IN BETWEEN

CAROLINE HINCHLIFF

Advice on where to sleep, eat, and explore

Detailed driving directions including mileage and drive times

Itineraries for a range of timelines

MOON

PACIFIC NORTHWEST
Road Trip

SEATTLE, VANCOUVER, VICTORIA, THE OLYMPIC PENINSULA, PORTLAND, THE OREGON COAST & MOUNT RAINIER

ALLISON WILLIAMS

MOON

ROUTE 66
Road Trip

JESSICA DUNHAM

MOON

SOUTH FLORIDA & THE KEYS
Road Trip

WITH MIAMI, WALT DISNEY WORLD, TAMPA & THE EVERGLADES

JASON FERGUSON

MOON

SOUTHWEST
Road Trip

LAS VEGAS, ZION & BRYCE, MONUMENT VALLEY, SANTA FE & TAOS, AND THE GRAND CANYON

TIM HULL

MOON

VANCOUVER & CANADIAN ROCKIES
Road Trip

VICTORIA, BANFF, JASPER, CALGARY, THE OKANAGAN, WHISTLER & THE SEA-TO-SKY HIGHWAY

CAROLYN B. HELLER

MOON

YELLOWSTONE TO GLACIER NATIONAL PARK
Road Trip

JACKSON HOLE, CODY, THE GRAND TETONS & THE ROCKY MOUNTAIN FRONT

CARTER G. WALKER

Sights Around the World

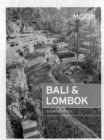

BALI & LOMBOK
CHANTAE REDEN

CANADIAN ROCKIES
WITH BANFF & JASPER NATIONAL PARKS
HIKE·CAMP
SEE WILDLIFE
ANDREW HEMPSTEAD

ECUADOR
& THE GALÁPAGOS ISLANDS

FIJI

ICELAND

JAPAN
JONATHAN DEHART
PLAN YOUR TRIP, AVOID THE CROWDS,
AND EXPERIENCE THE REAL JAPAN

MOROCCO

PRAGUE, VIENNA & BUDAPEST

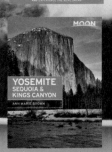

YOSEMITE
SEQUOIA & KINGS CANYON
ANN MARIE BROWN

Outdoor Adventure

Drive & Hike
APPALACHIAN TRAIL
THE BEST TRAIL TOWNS, DAY HIKES,
AND ROAD TRIPS IN BETWEEN
TIMOTHY MALCOLM

Drive & Hike
PACIFIC CREST TRAIL
THE BEST TRAIL TOWNS, DAY HIKES,
AND ROAD TRIPS IN BETWEEN
CAROLINE HINCHLIFF

YELLOWSTONE TO GLACIER NATIONAL PARK
Road Trip
JACKSON HOLE, CODY, THE GRAND TETONS
& THE ROCKY MOUNTAIN FRONT
CARTER G. WALKER

MAP SYMBOLS

═══ Major Hwy	▨ Pedestrian Friendly	------ Trail	········ Ferry
─── Road/Hwy	▨ Tunnel	▥▥▥ Stairs	━•━•━ Railroad

▪ **Sights**	⊛ City/Town	▲ Mountain
▪ **Restaurants**	◉ State Capital	✦ Unique Feature
▪ **Nightlife**	○ National Capital	🗑 Waterfall
▪ Arts and Culture	✪ Highlight	⚑ Park
▪ Recreation	★ Point of Interest	▲ Archaeological Site
▪ Shops	● Accommodation	▼ Restaurant/Bar	TH Trailhead
▪ Hotels	■ Other Location	P Parking Area

CONVERSION TABLES

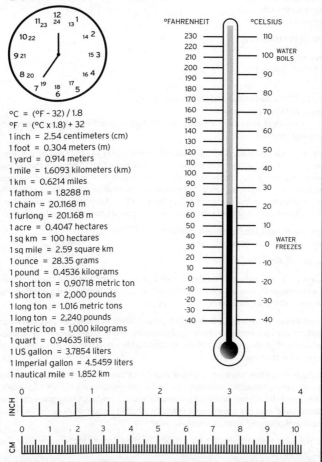

°C = (°F - 32) / 1.8
°F = (°C x 1.8) + 32
1 inch = 2.54 centimeters (cm)
1 foot = 0.304 meters (m)
1 yard = 0.914 meters
1 mile = 1.6093 kilometers (km)
1 km = 0.6214 miles
1 fathom = 1.8288 m
1 chain = 20.1168 m
1 furlong = 201.168 m
1 acre = 0.4047 hectares
1 sq km = 100 hectares
1 sq mile = 2.59 square km
1 ounce = 28.35 grams
1 pound = 0.4536 kilograms
1 short ton = 0.90718 metric ton
1 short ton = 2,000 pounds
1 long ton = 1.016 metric tons
1 long ton = 2,240 pounds
1 metric ton = 1,000 kilograms
1 quart = 0.94635 liters
1 US gallon = 3.7854 liters
1 Imperial gallon = 4.5459 liters
1 nautical mile = 1.852 km

MOON NEW ORLEANS
Avalon Travel
Hachette Book Group
1700 Fourth Street
Berkeley, CA 94710, USA
www.moon.com

Editor: Leah Gordon
Editorial Assistance: Rachael Sablik
Acquiring Editor: Nikki Ioakimedes
Series Manager: Leah Gordon
Copy Editor: Caroline Trefler
Graphics Coordinator: Scott Kimball
Production Coordinator: Scott Kimball
Cover Design: Faceout Studios, Charles Brock
Interior Design: Megan Jones Design
Moon Logo: Tim McGrath
Map Editor: Albert Angulo
Cartographer: John Culp
Indexer: Rachel Kuhn

ISBN-13: 9781640491434

Printing History
1st Edition — May 2020
5 4 3 2 1

Front cover photo: Tim Bieber, Getty Images
Back cover photo: Audubon Institute

Printed in China by RR Donnelley